DISENGAGEMENT

Eugène Hinterhoff

DISENGAGEMENT

WITH A FOREWORD BY

Sir John Slessor

Atlantic Books

STEVENS & SONS LIMITED

1959

First published in 1959
by Stevens & Sons, Limited,
of 11 New Fetter Lane
in the City of London
and printed in Great Britain
by Wembley Press, Limited,
of Perivale, Middlesex

Contents

PART ONE

THE STATUS QUO

PART TWO

IN SEARCH OF A SOLUTION

PART THREE

THE CRUX OF THE MATTER

APPENDICES

Foreword

Captain Hinterhoff's book is a valuable contribution to constructive thought on the vital subject of how to end the present dangerous deadlock in Europe. It contains in Parts I and II a valuable summary of the innumerable proposals and counter-proposals, official and unofficial, submitted during the past decade, which more than justifies Mr. Van Zeeland's view that a regrettable feature of NATO policy has been "a disappointing, obstinate and even dangerous immobilism."

One need not agree with everything the author says, such as that "the strategy of deterrence leaves to the West the very limited choice between an atomic holocaust or capitulation"; the real strategy of deterrence—as exemplified in the strategic concept governing Saceur's plans—which so many people seem to misunderstand, does no such thing. But the author is perfectly right in suggesting that adherence to the *status quo* (which anyway is constantly changing), talk about German reunification in freedom, liberation of captive peoples, peaceful co-existence, relaxation of tension and so on are no substitute for a practical, constructive, long-term master-plan for a political solution.

Captain Hinterhoff is an advocate of what is so misleadingly described as Disengagement and in his final pages submits what he calls a blue-print, drawing upon previous proposals by various authorities which he summarises in earlier pages.

It is really no good referring contemptuously to "Disengagement" as a Socialist pipe-dream. Actually the first reasonably concrete plan involving a policy of ultimate withdrawal of foreign troops from Europe was submitted not by a Socialist politician but by a Conservative soldier. It contains risks—of course it does. What policy involves no risks? Certainly not the so-called policy of the West over

vii

the past decade, which the author rightly describes as a tale of lost opportunities. The simple fact is that the object of military strength is not to preserve any *status quo* but to provide time for a political solution. The statesman cannot abdicate his responsibility by hiding behind the soldier. The Great Deterrent is not a maginot line behind which we can afford to sit and do nothing. It is up to the statesmen to arrive at a common working consensus on the broad outline of the political situation they want to create, and then to set about patiently and persistently creating it. They must recognise from the beginning that it must be a cautious, step by step process that will take a decade or more to bring to fruition. And they must not be inhibited by the belief (which the author's summary of past events reminds us need by no means be taken for granted) that the Kremlin will never agree. The paramount need is to regain the initiative and present the peoples either side of the Iron Curtain with a dynamic alternative to the present dreary impasse, of which they are becoming increasingly sick.

JOHN SLESSOR.

Preface

It may be true that political and military power in the second half of the twentieth century has largely passed to the great states of U.S.A. and U.S.S.R., but Europe retains her historical importance, not so much as a contender for world power but, sadly enough, as a contemporary battle-field, one of the areas on which the spheres of influence (to adopt a suddenly relevant nineteenth-century term) of the great powers converge and touch.

Across a divided Germany, NATO and the Soviet *bloc* watch and wait. The raising of a flagpole becomes a matter of international concern and " incidents " are an everyday commonplace.

The search for a solution to the inflamed condition of world affairs has led to two opposed concepts, " containment " and " disengagement." The charting of contemporary history is notoriously fraught with dangers, but I believe that the evidence is now strong enough to suggest that the policy of containment has failed and that a true solution must be sought in a determined attempt to relieve tension. Call this attempt " a policy of withdrawal," " a zone of controlled armaments," " a belt of neutrality " or, finally, " disengagement ": it matters little. What is now important is that the attempt should be made, and if this present effort to document and analyse the course of disengagement since the war is of some value for the future, I shall be content.

E. H.

Acknowledgments

I AM grateful to the authors and publishers of the following works for their kind permission to reproduce extracts in this book:

ARON, R.
   On War, Atomic Weapons and Global Diplomacy (Secker & Warburg, 1958).

BYRNES, F.
   Speaking Frankly (Harper, 1947).

CHURCHILL, SIR W.
   "Triumph and Tragedy": Second World War, Vol. VI (Cassells, 1954).

DALLIN, D.
   Russia and Post-War Europe (Yale U.P., 1943).

GARTHOFF, R.
   Soviet Strategy in the Nuclear Age (Stevens, 1958).

HEALEY, D.
   A Neutral Belt in Europe (Fabian Society, 1958).

KENNAN, G.
   Russia, the Atom and the West (Oxford U.P., 1958).

KISSINGER, H. S.
   Nuclear Weapons and Foreign Policy (Oxford U.P., 1957).

MONTGOMERY, FIELD-MARSHAL LORD
   Memoirs (Collins, 1958).

NOEL-BAKER, P.
   The Arms Race (Stevens, 1958).

SIEGLER, H.
   The Reunification and Security of Germany (Verlag Für Zeitarchive, 1957).

WARBURG, J.
   Germany, Key to Peace (Deutsch, 1954).

I am also grateful to the publishers of Foreign Affairs, W.E.U. Assembly Documents, The New Leader, The Observer and The Sunday Times for permission to reproduce extracts from their publications.

PART ONE
THE STATUS QUO

1

Containment

Fundamental Western Policy

THE essence of Western political strategy in the protracted global conflict between the Soviet *bloc*, including Red China, and the United States and its allies consists, in a simplified and geopolitical sense, in containing along the 20,000 miles of the Soviet *bloc* the pressure of the centrifugal forces of that vast Eurasian land-mass.

The method of containing this pressure has gradually crystallised itself during the last decade into a more or less loosely knit system of military alliances, such as NATO, the Baghdad Pact, SEATO, ANZUS, backed, above all, by the chain of American air bases.

The purpose of this political strategy, formulated as long ago as 1947 in the United States, is to maintain the state of affairs created by the secret agreements with Russia in Teheran in 1943 and in Yalta in 1945. This state of affairs is known as the *status quo*.

This "New Order" for the world was based upon Roosevelt's belief in a solidarity of Four Great Powers—the United States, Great Britain, the Soviet Union and China (which, a few years after the war, had shrunk to a small Nationalist bastion in Formosa).

In point of fact, this solidarity never existed—except the Anglo-American one—and was simply the result of wishful thinking, stemming from a lack of understanding of Russian policy and of Communist doctrine.

From the start, the membership of China in this Four Powers "Club," which was supposed to rule and police the post-war world, divided into spheres of influence, was a mistake and only added to the subsequent confusion.

As a result of the agreements in Teheran and Yalta, which arbitrarily carved the whole world, like a baron of beef, into spheres of influence, several countries, which, before the last war, enjoyed full sovereignty and independence, became engulfed into the Soviet colonial Empire. The list of all those countries which have been absorbed into the Soviet *bloc* is very impressive and perhaps worth while recalling: the three Baltic States, Poland, Czechoslovakia, Hungary, Bulgaria, Roumania, Albania, part of Austria, Mongolia, Sinkiang, the Kurile Islands and North Korea.

Yet few observers in the West seemed to be particularly worried at the end of the war about the political, strategic and moral implications of current developments. Undoubtedly, if Russia had been content with her war booty and had concentrated on rebuilding her devastated economy and integrating the territories which she had overrun into the Soviet *bloc*, the capitals of the West would have been content.

When one thinks now, in the short perspective of the fourteen years which divide us from V-Day, of the various speeches, lectures, debates and articles by prominent politicians and writers, especially during 1943–1945, extolling the Big Three, one can realise to what extent public opinion in the West was then befogged by the massive propaganda poured out during the war from official institutions like the Ministry of Information in Britain or the Office of War Information in the United States.

In this context one sentence from Professor Edward Hallett Carr's book, *Conditions of Peace*, which greatly influenced political thinking and planning in this country, illustrates the state of mind prevailing in the West during the war. In the last chapter, "The New Europe," the author took a critical look at the independence secured in Europe by several small countries as a result of the collapse of three Empires, and advocated the setting up of a high Authority:

. . . Great Britain and the United States, together with Russia, should place their overwhelming power . . . behind the Authority and make it effective over the area in which it operates. . . .

Stalin mistakenly tried to achieve too much in his life-time and, consequently, his actions, culminating in the Communist *coup* in Czechoslovakia, not only destroyed the enormous capital of goodwill for Russia created during the war, but also tore to shreds the illusions of peaceful co-existence with Russia.

The disappointment of Western leaders has been acute: even now complaints can be heard levelled at the dual character of Soviet policy. The West often remarks how frequently Soviet declarations of willingness to co-operate with the West and take part in international conferences, whose aim is the reduction of international tension, have been in contradiction to Soviet actions in various parts of the world, which have led only to greater tension.

In trying to explain this phenomenon, voices with some authority have suggested that there is no such thing as a Soviet master-plan, but that Soviet policy is rather the result of frictions among the inner circle of the Soviet oligarchy over the conduct of foreign policy.

Even such a profound expert on Russia as Mr. George Kennan, in his recent testimony before the Senate Foreign Relations Committee on February 4, 1959, said:

I believe that the Russian policy is the product not of any single mind but of many; that these are not always in agreement and that the Soviet policy often represents a compromise between them; that the Soviet intentions change as the world situation develops; and that our own actions and attitudes are an important determinant of these.[1]

And yet the Soviets have been able to overcome, without too much difficulty, the internal convulsions after Stalin's death, to suppress the uprisings in Eastern Germany in

[1] *New Leader*, February 13, 1959.

1953 and in Hungary in 1956 and to get the situation in Poland under control; at the same time, they have conducted without any interruption their flexible policy of political, ideological and economic expansion, crowned with many successes in several parts of the world.

One cannot resist asking how all this would have been possible if Soviet policy had not been conducted in accordance with some long-term plans, flexible enough to be adapted to the changing situations in the world?

As the result of Soviet policy, the West has suffered during the last decade a series of defeats, increasing with an alarming crescendo by the end of 1956.

Field-Marshal Lord Montgomery, in a lecture, " The Present State of the Game in the Contest between East and West," delivered at the Royal United Service Institution on October 24, 1958, produced two maps as evidence of the cold war balance sheet; one showed the situation in the world in 1945, and the other one showed how things stood in 1958. The contrast between these two maps, illustrating the progress of Soviet expansion and encroachment on the free world, was simply terrifying. And yet if Field-Marshal Montgomery had cared to produce one more map, namely, that of 1939, the impact on the audience would perhaps have been even stronger.

Those two maps were the best proof that the political strategy of the West, as formulated in 1947, and aimed at the maintenance of the *status quo*, has failed lamentably. At the same time, they also showed that the term *status quo* not only does not correspond to reality but has become, in fact, a misleading fiction.

Soviet Policy

We began this survey by stating that the fundamental aim of the political strategy of the West is the maintenance of the *status quo*.

It would seem, in fact, that one of the main reasons for the present international tension, called the cold war, is a profound difference in the meaning of the words *status quo* for the West and for the Soviet Union.

When, during the last war, President Roosevelt spoke with Stalin about the merits of democracy, each of them understood it in his own way: equally, the mysterious words *status quo* with all their implications, mean something completely different for the Soviet leaders and for Western statesmen and politicians. Quotation from Walter Lippmann's conversation in Moscow with Mr. Khrushchev, reported in the *New York Herald Tribune* in October, 1958, is most enlightening, because it can be considered as a key to the Soviet policy:

> . . . I must set down what is the more important part of his conception of the *status quo*. In his mind, the social and economic revolution now in progress in Russia, China, and elsewhere in Asia and Africa *is* the *status quo*, and he wants us to recognise it as such. In his mind, opposition to this revolution is an attempt to change the *status quo*. Whereas we think of the *status quo* as the situation as it exists at the moment, he thinks of it as the process of revolutionary change which is in progress. He wants us to recognise the revolution not only as it is but as it is going to be.[2]

One of the main reasons for the failure of the Western policy of containment is the fact that, whereas the Western Alliance, headed by the United States, consists of Powers and States which could be called static, the Soviet Union is, above all, a revolutionary Power. In this confrontation of static Powers with a dynamic, revolutionary Power all the advantages must lie naturally in favour of the latter. How could one otherwise explain this phenomenon: that a country which only a few decades ago faced a hostile world and was so weak that all the so-called Soviet experts predicted its imminent collapse, has emerged as the most powerful State in Europe and as a threat to the world.

[2] *The Communist World and Ours*, p. 13.

In this context it is useful to quote Henry Kissinger:

> Part of the answer is to be found in the tendency of the Powers, which represent the *status quo*, to confront the revolutionary Power with methods they learned in a more serene environment. . . . The Powers that represent the *status quo* are at a profound psychological disadvantage *vis-à-vis* a revolutionary Power. . . . A revolutionary Power confronts the legitimate order with a fearful challenge. . . .[3]

The West hoped at the end of the last war that by giving to Russia so many concessions, especially in Eastern Europe, claimed by Russia for her security, she would be willing to continue her wartime co-operation with the West. But the Soviet refusal to sign the Bretton Woods agreement in December, 1945, the fraudulent elections and the imposition by Soviet bayonets of Communist puppet régimes in Eastern Europe, slowly deprived the West of its sweet illusion of the possibility of a *modus vivendi* with Russia. The final blow was the Soviet *coup* in Czechoslovakia, which, in fact, gave the stimulus to the Brussels Treaty and, later on, to NATO.

These defensive pacts in the West were the result of a slow realisation that the *coup* in Prague could, *mutatis mutandis*, be repeated in any other part of Europe. Equally, it was the outbreak of war in Korea which galvanised the West and transformed NATO from a paper pact into a reality.

As Kissinger rightly remarked:

> . . . after the death of Stalin there took place a new outburst of speculation that the "basic" change had occurred in Soviet thinking.[4] "The Soviet leaders," said John Foster Dulles in 1956, "are scrapping thirty years of policy based on violence and intolerance."

Further quotation from Kissinger's book is equally enlightening:

> The situation is doubly paradoxical because of the exasperation with which the Soviet leaders regularly have repudiated the

3 *Nuclear Weapons and Foreign Policy*, p. 317.   4 *Ibid.*, pp. 322–323.

notion that a change of tactics on their part implies an abandonment of their basic doctrines. " . . . if anyone thinks," Khrushchev said at the height of the peace offensive, " that we shall forget about Marx, Engels and Lenin, he is mistaken. This will happen when shrimps learn to whistle " (in Russian—" kogda rak swistniet ").

In spite of Mr. Khrushchev's very clear statement, Western leaders have a tendency to take any Soviet lip-service at its face value: during a recent conversation between Mr. Adlai Stevenson and Mr. Khrushchev in Moscow in October 1958, the Soviet leader declared that Soviet policy has never been an aggressive one, that on the contrary it has always been a defensive one. At the same time, according to Mr. Khrushchev, it is the policy of the West which has always been an aggressive one, in spite of all assurances of the Western leaders to the contrary.

Furthermore, according to Mr. Khrushchev, the intervention of Soviet troops in Hungary had nothing to do with aggression and had a purely defensive character aimed at the suppression of a counter-revolution and at the prevention of Hungary's defection from the Warsaw Pact. At the same time, British and American landings in Jordan and Lebanon were nothing less than naked acts of aggression, in spite of the fact that these actions were taken at the request of the legitimate governments of those countries.

These utterances of Mr. Khrushchev, like the definition of *status quo* which he gave to Mr. W. Lippmann, could be regarded as another key to the Soviet policy. For him— as for all his predecessors—only the Soviets have the right to expand by all conceivable means, all of which are justified if they can be of advantage to Russia. Something similar was said by Adolf Hitler many years ago: " Everything that suits Germany is right " (Alles ist recht was dem Deutschen Volke nutzt "). Consequently, for Mr. Khrushchev, *status quo* does not mean the perpetuity of the existing state of affairs, but, on the contrary, a process of solidifying Soviet gains or of improving the Soviet position before the next move in the right direction, in other words only a transitory period in the implementation of a long-term plan.

This flexibility of the Soviet criteria could be also illustrated by the Soviet approach to the last war: during its first stage, when Russia was Germany's ally, Stalin described it as a war between the capitalist States: however, when Hitler attacked Russia, the same war became immediately a just war, waged in defence of Russia. It was extremely interesting and enlightening to talk during the last war with the White Russians, coming from various walks of life: all of them felt immensely proud of the achievements of the Red Army, and not one of them had any excuses to offer over the territorial expansion of the Soviet Union and, in particular, over the enslavement of Eastern Europe. In their eyes Stalin was merely pursuing the traditional policy of old Tsarist Russia, the only difference being that he succeeded where the Tsars had failed.

These views of the White Russians, heard all over the free world, only confirm that present Soviet foreign policy is merely an improved and much streamlined *cliché* of the policy of old Imperial Russia. A reading of the books on the secret negotiations which took place during the first half of the First World War between Tsarist Russia and her Western allies suggests that, if there had been no Revolution and if after the First World War Russia had remained a partner of the victorious *Entente Cordiale*, her ambitions of territorial expansion would have been as dangerous for the peace of the world as the present ambitions of the Soviet Union.

In fact, if after the Allied victory Russia had remained in the Allied camp and there had been no revolution, the whole of Eastern and Central Europe east of the line Stettin-Trieste would have been either completely within Russian control or within the sphere of Russian influence. The Slav countries in the Balkans would have formed a natural continuation of the newly annexed Russian territory at Adrianople. Little Greece, Russia's new neighbour, would have felt her influence. Little Hungary, situated as it would have been between Russia in the East and Yugoslavia in the South, would have been as dependent on the St. Petersburg Government as Slovakia and Bohemia. In the Baltic Sea, as in the Black Sea, the Russian Navy would have enjoyed unlimited supremacy. Finally, the Russian islands in the Aegean would have become the bases for Russian influence in the Eastern Mediterranean, in Egypt and in the Middle East.

It is not hard to realise that in these circumstances the old Anglo-Russian antagonism would have arisen again almost automatically. Only this time the antagonism would have had a more violent outcome: Russia, as the principal victor in the World War, could not have failed to become Britain's chief rival not only throughout Europe, but also in the Middle East.

As early as 1915 Thomas Masaryk, the founder of independent Czechoslovakia, summed up London's attitude to Russia's expansionist demands: "The next war will probably be England and Germany against Russia."

Unfortunately for the West, Soviet Russia, intent also on territorial expansion, has turned out in the long run to be a much more formidable and dangerous opponent than the old Tsarist Russia.

In the struggle after the last war between the Soviet Union, aggressively led by Stalin, and the West, whose leaders were looking forward to peaceful co-existence with Russia, the initiative was always in the Soviet hands. In addition, in a struggle which has slowly embraced the whole world, the Soviets have been able either to make use of the local Communist Parties, which obey their orders from Moscow and act as a huge Fifth Column, or to ride on the crest of the wave of post-war anti-Western feeling in Africa, the Middle East and Asia.

As Robert Strausz-Hupé wrote:

> The Russian Communists saturated with a dynamic philosophy of history and astride a formidable territorial base of

operations, saw what the West did not: that "the august, unchallenged and tranquil glories of the Victorian age " tarnished by the First World War, were to depart forever amidst the rising commotion of Asia and Africa.[5]

The history of Soviet penetration during the last few years into that great arc of territory that runs from China's northern frontiers through South-East Asia and the Middle East and Africa, can best illustrate the dynamic nature of Soviet policy. Apart from Red China, which is a problem in itself, all these Soviet successes show that Russia has been able in several sectors either to breach or leapfrog the perimeter of Western system of alliances. In an offensive conducted by ideological and economic penetration, the Communists always assumed the role of liberators of the peoples of that area from former imperialists. The West, on the other hand, as we shall see in the next chapter, has jettisoned the policy of liberation, clutching desperately to the policy of containment, hoping that Russia will do likewise.

In addition to a political and ideological offensive the Soviet Union, especially after Stalin's death, embarked upon an economic offensive which eventually has become even more difficult to counter than her political and ideological penetration.

These Soviet efforts to expand economic relations with several countries of the so-called non-committed area, spreading also in the direction of Latin America, involve not only trade and trade missions and fairs but also credit, technical assistance, technical exchanges, and, of course, propaganda. The centralised character of Soviet operations, subordinated to a political master plan, makes them extremely efficient and difficult to combat with similar weapons.

This economic offensive is part of a major operation, aimed at weakening the West by depriving it of essential

---

[5] *Study in Protracted Conflict*, p. 9.

raw materials. As Field-Marshal Lord Montgomery said in the lecture referred to earlier: " Russia will now plan to bring about the collapse of the economic system of the free world so that she can point to her system as the right one to adopt." The following case—one of many—is an excellent illustration of the thesis that Soviet economic offensive is one of the weapons of her political policy: Russia, during the last few years, has been devoting more and more attention to the Yemen, a small, poor country with only some four million inhabitants and without any natural resources, for one reason only, namely, that the Yemen lies at the entrance to the Red Sea and has great strategic importance. Consequently, during these last few years, Russia has given the Yemen some eighty million dollars in credits and another twenty will be given soon: in addition a large mission of technical advisers is training Yemenite armed forces in the use of arms of Soviet origin.

The sum total of these methods of Soviet offensive in many parts of the world constitutes for the West a global challenge. But, in spite of all her aggressiveness, Russia probably does not intend to use force to implement her policy.

Stalin, who was perhaps more ruthless than Khrushchev, was careful enough during the Berlin blockade to avoid using the term " blockade " and used only the term " technical difficulties " which could be lifted at an hour's notice.

Equally, the first shipment of arms to Egypt in the autumn of 1955 was of Czechoslovak origin to avoid involving the Soviet Union in any embarrassing situation should the West react vigorously.

This suggests that brinkmanship is something foreign to Soviet policy and that Russia has no intention of launching an offensive war. Mr. George Kennan, in his fifth Reith lecture, delivered in December 1957, said:

> Of all the countries of this great area [South-East Asia and Middle East] only certain ones in the Middle East have a

common border with Russia; and even here, I have not seen the evidence of a Soviet intention to launch any overt military aggression.[6]

On the strength of these arguments, one could conclude that Russia—so long as it suits her policy and intentions—is always ready to negotiate—and to keep—a settlement, as, for instance, has happened in Austria and Vietnam. A similar view has been expressed by Mr. Walter Lippmann in his summing up of his talk with Mr. Khrushchev:

> I feel sure that the Soviet domination of Eastern Germany, of Poland, Czechoslovakia and Hungary is precarious and impermanent. Moreover, I think that the rulers of Russia know this and that, if they could think, which they have not, of any safe way to disengage, they would eventually accept some such settlement.[7]

The Failure of Containment

The policy of the West towards the Soviet Union, as pointed out in the previous sections, consists in containing along the perimeter of the Soviet Union the pressure of the centrifugal forces of that vast Eurasian land mass.

This policy was formulated in 1947 by Mr. George Kennan, then chief of a " Policy planning staff " in the Department of State. It was given systematic formulation by him first of all in his article, " The Sources of Soviet Conduct," published originally under the pseudonym " X " in the July issue of *Foreign Affairs*, and later on expounded in various articles and in his book *American Diplomacy in 1905–1950*.

According to Mr. Kennan, " . . . the main element of any United States policy towards the Soviet Union must be that of a long-term, patient but firm and vigilant containment of Russian expansive tendencies." [8] Further on he pointed out: " . . . it will be clearly seen that the Soviet

6 *Russia, the Atom, and the West*, p. 74.
7 *The Communist World and Ours*, p. 53.
8 *American Diplomacy in 1905–1950*, p. 119.

pressure against the free institutions of the Western world is something that could be contained by an adroit and vigilant application of counter-force at a series of constantly shifting geographical and political points, corresponding to the shifts and manoeuvres of Soviet policy. . . ." [9] As Mr. James Burnham remarks in his book, *Containment or Liberation*, which severely criticised the policy of containment: " The policy of containment was in accord with the liberal sentiment that has been prevalent in official American circles. At the time of its formulation in 1947, it was a natural enough response to the given world situation." [10] Indeed, at that time public opinion was only slowly recovering from the hangover of the war-time honeymoon with Russia, when rosy prospects of peaceful co-existence with Russia were the order of the day.

In the United States the fate of a number of prominent people such as James Forrestal, General D. MacArthur, Major-General Orville Anderson, Stuart Symington, and a few others who had the courage to oppose the purely defensive policy of containment, and clamoured for a more resolute foreign policy towards Russia, pointed to the increasing popularity of the new policy of containment.

As Mr. James Burnham writes:

> As a temporary expedient, there was something to be said for containment. In 1946–47 the United States and its friends were not politically, morally or intellectually prepared to undertake a positive strategy against Soviet .power. Some of them were in virtual collapse from the blows of the war, and the rest were in the middle of a headlong mobilisation. A defensive manoeuvre that while covering a shift in the cycle could perhaps slow the opponent's advance was in order, and about all that could be hoped for. The trouble is that the State Department has insisted in transforming a temporary expedient into a principle. [11]

The policy of containment has developed in two principal stages. In the first, which lasted from the beginning

[9] *Ibid.*, p. 120.
[10] p. 29.

[11] *Supra cit.*, p. 35.

until the latter part of 1951, the emphasis was on economic rehabilitation. The sums spent on foreign economic aid at first exceeded heavily those spent for military aid. In the second phase, which started largely due to the psychological impact of war in Korea and the hysterical fear of Soviet aggression which swept across Western Europe, the ratio was reversed and the emphasis increasingly put on military assistance, which culminated in the setting up of various military alliances along the Soviet perimeter, especially NATO.

Enormous effort and sacrifice of all kinds has been made by the West during the last ten years or so to implement this political doctrine, which became also the basis of Western military strategy—aimed at the maintenance of the *status quo*; and for this very reason priceless opportunities in various parts of the world have been irretrievably lost.

Thus if, for instance, the first cargo of Czech arms for Egypt had been confiscated by the West—in spite of vociferous protestations from the Soviet delegate at the United Nations—there might have been no Soviet penetration into the Middle East for some time—and none of the chain reaction of subsequent events. Equally, if immediate action had been taken after Nasser had nationalised the Suez Canal, when public opinion all over the West was unanimous in condemning him, the situation in the Middle East might have been restored and Soviet penetration halted. However, instead of restoring the *status quo* by direct action, the West looked for an excuse to do so: the Israeli offensive provided the West with the hypocritical formula of a police action, and when Israel accepted the French-British ultimatum the ground opened under Sir Anthony Eden's feet.

Similarly, if immediate action had been taken by the British and American troops, which happened at that time to be in Jordan and Lebanon, after the coup in Iraq, or if at least Turkey had not been prevented by pressure from

Washington from intervention, again, the situation in that country might have been partly restored to normal; and at least the Soviet penetration would have been halted.

In these cases—and the list is far from complete—the West never had the courage to restore the *status quo* by taking calculated risks: an exaggerated caution became an alibi for cowardice. If we look, in the perspective of all the post-war years, at the balance sheet of the policy of the containment, we must now admit that it is largely in the red.

From the military point of view this policy has not prevented Russia from outflanking the NATO southern flank; or from exposing the Baghdad Pact to very serious strains and stresses: in point of fact, after the recent withdrawal of Iraq the name " Baghdad Pact " has become as anachronistic as the term *status quo*.

The advocates of the policy of containment would say that, after all, NATO as a product of that policy has dispelled the danger of Soviet aggression in Europe and stabilised the whole situation in the West: on the other hand, although fully admitting the very great value of the Atlantic Alliance for the overall cohesion of Western Europe and the feeling of security engendered by the deterrent " umbrella " and " shield," it can be argued that the Russians have never seriously intended overt overland aggression in Europe.

After all, Russia could have attacked, and with the greatest ease, soon after the war when the West overhastily disbanded its overwhelming military power, and when Europe, still in chaos and infested with Communist Parties, lay open to Soviet aggression. In this context it is pertinent to recall General Eisenhower's First Annual Report to the Military Standing Committee in Washington after he took up his post as Supreme Commander in Europe in February 1951; he then wrote that the forces under his command, in case of Soviet aggression: " . . . could have offered no more than a token resistance. . . ."

If the Russians did not invade Western Europe, which they could easily have done, during those years when there was no NATO and when a Russian advance towards Calais or Paris would have been a walk-over, it was not because they were deterred by the few A-bombs which were then in the American hands, but because Stalin realised that a war in Europe would have meant an explosion of accumulated hatred in Eastern Europe against the Communist régimes, an explosion which could have overwhelmed the Soviet armed forces in that vast area, ruling out any operations against Western Europe.

It must be pointed out that, whereas for the peoples of the West the idea of a new war was abhorrent, for the millions behind the Iron Curtain it meant their liberation: it was something they were waiting for, hoping for and praying for, and the feelings of those millions of people, well known in the Kremlin, were the best deterrent against any aggression in Europe.

This point brings us to another aspect of the policy of containment, namely its rigid approach towards the sanctity of the territory within the Soviet perimeter.

Whereas Russia is free to operate and to conduct her cold war with all the methods at her disposal, the West, with the exception of efforts to penetrate the Iron Curtain on the radio waves, carefully avoids interfering in the affairs of the vast territory inside the Soviet perimeter.

As Mr. Strausz-Hupé has written:

> . . . the Soviets have been immune from outside intervention because American policy-makers have stuck to the mystique of the containment doctrine which established—semi-officially so to speak—the boundaries of the Communist untouchable " zone of peace." [12]

It was in this spirit that, during the Hungarian uprising, both President Eisenhower and John Foster Dulles promptly made statements that the United States was " not seeking

[12] *Study on Protracted Conflict*, p. 22.

allies in Eastern Europe. . . ." And it is probably with the same intention, as a result of Dulles' initiative, that the NATO Council at its meeting in Bonn in May 1957, passed a resolution which has been made public that, in the case of an uprising in Eastern Germany, the West would give any assistance short of military intervention.

The year before the Hungarian uprising, President Eisenhower at the Geneva Summit Conference in July 1955, startled the whole world by assuring the Soviet leaders that the United States would never use force, except in strict defence, thus releasing the Soviets from any fear of attack. As Mr. Edgar Mowrer, in his article " Power and World Order," writes:

> Such a one-sided restraint would lead the United States to almost certain defeat. . . . using our national power only to meet aggression and territorial expansion by force seems bound to result in slow retreat and the attrition of the West's power.[13]

Unfortunately, a similar statement by President Eisenhower at his Press conference on March 10, 1959, that the United States would not use their ground forces for the defence of Berlin, could only increase Soviet aggressiveness and make future negotiations with the Russians more difficult.

The recent events in Tibet have been a painfully typical example of this state of affairs.

Since 1949, when the Chinese invaded Tibet, and feeble protests were made by Mr. Nehru and Britain, no action has been taken or even contemplated: it has been tacitly admitted that Tibet is, so to speak, in China's sphere of influence, and a curtain of silence has descended.

Subsequent events in Tibet developed strictly in accordance with the usual Russian pattern: as the result of a Sino-Tibetan agreement in 1951, the Chinese secured the right to set up military bases throughout the whole country, while guaranteeing national autonomy; at the same time, in

[13] *The New Leader*, February 23, 1959.

order to speed up the process of absorption, they practically cut Tibet off from the outer world.

The recent revolt by the Tibetans proves that for them, as a few years ago for the Hungarians and the East Germans, freedom has a meaning and is worth fighting for. Obviously, Tibetan resistance, which is anxiously watched all over South-East Asia, exposed, as that area is, to imminent threat from Chinese expansion, has an enormous moral and political significance: such resistance could be sustained only by supply of arms from Formosa and from the West. Even prolonged hostilities in Tibet would not bring nearer the danger of a major war; the conflict would remain a typical local war, increasingly embarrassing for China from all points of view.

On the other hand, if China is finally allowed to swallow Tibet, it will be not only another proof of the failure of the policy of containment but a symbol and a warning to all other small States bordering China, Laos, Thailand, Cambodia, Burma and, perhaps, Hongkong, that in due course their time will come as well, in accordance with the Chinese time-table—with the West helplessly watching from afar.

We have already pointed out that one of the principles of the policy of containment is non-interference within the " untouchable " sphere of influence of the Soviet *bloc*. On the other hand, the recognition by China of the Algerian rebel government in Cairo ought to have excused the West from such a high-minded approach to the Tibetan rising.

As far as Mr. Nehru's attitude in this matter is concerned, he could find in the annals of history a rather striking analogy between Dr. Benes and himself. By closing his eyes upon Tibet's struggle against China, Mr. Nehru is slowly preparing for his country the same fate that Dr. Benes prepared for Czechoslovakia.

If, however, he had the courage to take the initiative into his hands and try to restore Tibet's independence, internationally guaranteed, he would establish on his northern frontier a powerful buffer State, providing for India real security against the danger of aggression from China.

Equally, initiative from the West and, above all, from the SEATO Powers, which belong after all to a world-wide system of alliances, even if based only on the principles of containment, would at least restore the *status quo* and prevent further dangerous erosion.

It would, however, be unfair to accuse the political leaders of the West of being unable to produce anything except the purely defensive policy of containment. On the contrary, especially in the early days of NATO when the ambitious plan for raising some 100 divisions was discussed at the Lisbon Conference in 1952, and Western atomic superiority seemed, according to some Western scientists, indisputable for at least one decade, political leaders such as President Truman and later on Mr. Dulles, publicly expressed the hope that, in view of the growing military potential of the West, Russia would " one day roll back. . . ."

This exhilarating vision of Soviet troops reeling Eastwards, based purely on wishful thinking and complete ignorance of Soviet efforts in the technological field, was also one of the predominant arguments in Dr. Adenauer's oratory at the time when he was again putting his countrymen into military uniforms.

However, nothing was done by the West in those days to take advantage of its supremacy in the field of atomic arms, and as M. Raymond Aron has written:

> It was during the years 1945–49 when the United States enjoyed an atomic monopoly that the Soviets won their greatest successes (the consolidation of the Communist régimes in Eastern Europe, the conquest of China by the Communist Party). It was also during those years that the diplomacy of Moscow was most aggressive—in Czechoslovakia, in Berlin, at international conferences and in its propaganda. . . .[14]

[14] *On War, Atomic Weapons and Global Diplomacy*, p. 9.

In spite of Soviet weakness in many fields, which ought to have been well known to the Western governments, the West stuck to the policy of containment, believing that the *status quo*—although already dented in several places—could be maintained by the military stalemate in Europe, based upon the formula: Western nuclear power against Soviet supremacy in conventional forces.

The discovery by Russia of the secrets of H-bomb production, which swept away all Western supremacy in the field of atomic armaments, was a profound shock for the West. A prominent German political writer, Dr. W. Schütz, has put it in this way:

> The discovery that it no longer was possible to achieve a sufficient technological and military superiority to alter the balance of power between East and West decisively was bound to be shocking. . . . In addition, this fact made all the planning and expectations in the West—however unrealistic they might have been—completely anachronistic.[15]

The answer to the discovery by the Soviets of the secrets of H-bomb production has been the intensification of the arms race, as the only method of maintaining the elusive *status quo*.

Before closing this section, which has dealt with the policy of containment, it would be apposite to quote Mr. Henry Kissinger's remarkable book, *Nuclear Weapons and Foreign Policy*:

> In the process of defining our strategic interests we cannot avoid facing another fact of the nuclear age little in accord with our predilections: the difficulty, if not impossibility of holding a perimeter of twenty thousand miles while always remaining on the defensive politically, militarily and spiritually. . . . A policy impelled primarily by a desire to prevent an expansion of the Soviet sphere ensures that militarily we will be forced always to fight at the point of our greatest weakness; that diplomatically we will always contest issues of maximum embarrassment to us; that spiritually we will convey an impression

---

15 "New Initiatives for a New Age: A German View," *Foreign Affairs*, April 1958, p. 466.

of uncertainty. . . . in any conflict the side which is animated by faith in victory has a decided advantage over an opponent who wishes above all to preserve the *status quo.* . . .[16]

Furthermore, and this ought to be discouraging to the Western policy-makers, the Soviet leaders utterly distrust the Western policy of containment. Mr. Lippmann writes of his first talk with Mr. Khrushchev:

> Our policy of military containment with its forward positions on their own borders is in their minds conclusive proof that Lenin was right. They suspect us profoundly, and that is why they are stubbornly reluctant to negotiate any concession which would give us even a slight tactical, much less strategic, advantage in case of war.[17]

In spite of all the efforts of Western diplomacy, which accepted the policy of containment, primarily designed as an expedient, as the basic principle and foundation of the policy of the West, " to "—as M. Aron has put it—" slow history," it has been impossible to protect its product, namely, the *status quo*, from various forms of erosion.

In addition, it has turned out that the *status quo*, apart from being an elusive *fata morgana*, contains also the seeds of other dangers, the revival of German militarism and the rising might of Red China, to which we shall return in subsequent chapters.

[16] p. 429.
[17] *The Communist World and Ours*, p. 38.

2

The Erosion of the Status Quo

As stated in the closing sentences of the previous chapter, the efforts of Western policy during the last decade to maintain the *status quo* have failed.

The *status quo*, which to Western eyes represents something static but to the eyes of the Soviet leaders represents only a part or a stage in a process, has been subject during these years to severe strains and stresses. Further, it is also subject to a continual process of erosion, which in this chapter we shall try to analyse.

The Soviet Offensive

In the protracted conflict between the Soviet Union and the West, Russia has, unfortunately, enjoyed the advantage of always being in a position to take the initiative. She has been able to apply her pressure at whatever point of the globe best suited her and the various ways and means used to achieve her purpose have been applied with great flexibility.

In addition, the reaction of the West, always on the defensive, has been, as Senator John K. Kennedy has put it, " exaggeratedly military." [1]

A similar view has been expressed by Kennan in his fifth Reith lecture :

> To me, one of the most puzzling phenomena of this post-war era has been the unshakable conviction of so many people that the obvious answer to the threat of a growth of Communist influence is a military alliance or a military gesture. . . . [2]

---

[1] " A Democrat Looks at Foreign Policy," *Foreign Affairs*, October 1957.
[2] *Russia, the Atom and the West*, pp. 74–75.

How extensive has been this policy of the United States in building military alliances along Russia's perimeter, can be best expressed by quoting Mr. Foster Dulles:

> Since 1945 we have entered into collective security treaties with 42 other nations and we have less formal arrangements with several more.[3]

In spite of this mobilisation of the greater part of the free world under the leadership of the United States and in spite of the tremendous military power at its command, the West has seldom had the courage to take a firm, determined and resolute stand in the defence of the *status quo*. In this context it is interesting to quote again Senator Kennedy:

> . . . hardly had we announced the intention to " liberate " the satellite states of Europe before the Berlin riots occurred. After we found ourselves unable to turn this uprising to more than slight propaganda advantage, we tended to switch to the view that the states of Eastern Europe were closed cells. The Administration saw little hope that new generations could wrench themselves from the Communist spell; yet it was precisely university youth and labour unionists, both peculiarly exposed to Soviet indoctrination, who led the rebellions against domination from Moscow. Once again the United States was able to offer little assistance during the ordeal.[4]

At the same time there are a few examples of how a little determination and courage, such as the Western action in Greece in 1947, the landings in Jordan and Lebanon, the stand over Quemoy or over Persia, have achieved the desired results.

It may well be said by those who do not agree with the author's criticism of the policy of containment that he is advocating a policy of liberation which, in a nuclear age, should be ruled out as tending towards war. The purpose of this study, however, is to show that the dynamic Soviet challenge makes it imperative to consider fresh methods

---

[3] " Challenge and Response in United States Policy," *Foreign Affairs*, October 1957, p. 30.
[4] *Op. cit.*, p. 47.

whereby a foreign policy can be formulated and applied, which may successfully either stay the erosion of the *status quo* or lead to some constructive alternative.

The Precarious Nature of the Military Stalemate

The present *status quo* in the world, and particularly in Western Europe along the demarcation line dividing the Atlantic alliance from the Soviet *bloc*, is based upon a military stalemate. The essence of this stalemate is that, owing to the existence of new weapons of mass destruction, war has become much too dangerous to be regarded simply as the means of implementing a policy, and has ceased to be so regarded.

As Mr. G. Kennan, in his fourth Reith lecture, has put it:

> . . . the weapon of mass destruction is a sterile and hopeless weapon which may for a time serve as an answer of sorts to itself as an uncertain sort of a shield against utter cataclysm, but which cannot in any way serve the purposes of a constructive and hopeful foreign policy.[5]

It is an accepted view in the West that the realisation by both sides that, in case of war, either could inflict on its opponent the most terrifying injuries will serve to deter any attempt to unleash a nuclear war.

This view has taken many years to mature into a military doctrine and, consequently, to be accepted into political thought. An anonymous military writer, writing in *The Observer* under the pseudonym " Nucleus," has put it thus:

> . . . although the phenomenon of balance of power is military in origin its results can become effective only through emanations from the minds of politicians, and their minds are battlefields of large numbers of conflicting factors. . . .[6]

[5] *Russia, the Atom and the West*, p. 56.
[6] " Dwindling Deterrent," *The Observer*, December 7, 1958.

The origin of this military and political strategy based upon deterrence can be traced in Field-Marshal Montgomery's lecture, which has already been mentioned [7]:

> . . . before the advent of the nuclear weapons we had been building up conventional forces with which to defeat attack. It gradually became clear that if we relied only on such forces, then we could never match the conventional strength which could be deployed against us by the Communist *bloc*. The only alternative was to state publicly that if we were subjected to a major attack we would use the nuclear deterrent as a weapon to help in our defences—even if nuclear weapons were not used against us in the first instance. And that is how we stand today.[8]

In other words, the gradual refashioning of Western strategy and its increased reliance on weapons of mass destruction were the results of the inability of the West to produce enough divisions to ensure a *balanced system of defence*.

Mr. Irving Krystol wrote in 1958:

> . . . England and other countries of Western Europe . . . could exert themselves to see that the defence of Western Europe is conceived and conducted in terms of conventional armaments rather than atomic ones—that if and when a crisis arises it would not *necessarily* degenerate into a holocaust. This, oddly enough, was the original idea behind NATO. But the idea lapsed when the European nations failed to produce the necessary soldiers, as a consequence of which American troops in the European theatre were supplied with atomic weapons.[9]

The original idea behind NATO to which Mr. Krystol referred in his article appeared in the resolutions of the NATO Council meeting at Lisbon in 1952 to raise in Europe ninety-six divisions within the next few years.

However, raising conventional forces would have meant some financial sacrifices and an increased period of conscription, which would have been very unpopular with the

---

[7] *Supra*, p. 6.
[8] "The Present State of the Game in the Contest between East and West," R.U.S.I., October 24, 1958.
[9] "Thoughts on the Bomb," *The New Leader*, June 30, 1958.

electorates in the various Western democracies; consequently, the Western Governments embarked on something which they considered to be cheaper, namely, a policy of building up deterrent weapons, partly as a substitute for soldiers and partly in the hope that they would deter aggression. The Western military planners were slow to realise that the Russians, at a cost of one American division with its enormous administrative tail, were able to raise two or three of equal fighting power: equally, if appropriate economy measures had been taken to reduce drastically the " grossly overstaffed NATO "—as Field-Marshal Montgomery put it—and various other agencies, like WEU, which very much duplicate NATO work, it would have allowed, perhaps, for at least a few more divisions to be put into the front line.

Unfortunately this strong belief, so deeply rooted in the West, that the possession of nuclear weapons will make any major war improbable is not at all shared in the Soviet Union. One of the most prominent American experts on Soviet strategy, Mr. Raymond Garthoff, writes:

> What is the Soviet image of future war? . . . The initial strategic strikes by modern jet bombers, intercontinental and ballistic missiles, and submarine-launched missiles, will wreak devastation upon both the United States and the Soviet Union and upon their chief allies. But does mutual devastation spell mutual defeat? The Soviet answer: NO . . . this enormous mutual destruction will probably consume the major portion of the respective long-range air and missile forces. This is a crucial phase of the war, which a weak or ill-prepared power could lose. But it is *not* the decisive stage of war . . . the heart of such capability is the ground forces—trained for nuclear war, armed with nuclear weapons—and here the war would begin with a serious imbalance: a preponderance of the Soviet forces.[10]

This Soviet self-assurance stems probably from underestimation of the horrors of thermo-nuclear warfare, which, according to all leading military writers in the West, would amount to total destruction.

[10] *Soviet Strategy in the Nuclear Age*, p. 13.

In the conditions of broken-back warfare, with all supply depots and pipelines and, above all, oilfields, completely devastated, and with communications systems in havoc, the picture of any organised operation by larger units amidst the smouldering and radioactive ruins would appear to be an illusion.

In this context it would be useful to quote Captain B. H. Liddell Hart:

> Old concepts and definitions of strategy have become not only *obsolete* but *nonsensical* with the development of nuclear weapons. . . . To aim at " winning a war," to take " victory " as your object, is no more than a state of lunacy. For a total war with nuclear weapons would be fatal to both sides.[11]

Compared with the picture of a diversified, flexible and well-balanced Soviet strategy, it is obvious that Western strategy, owing to its excessive reliance on deterrence, has become one-sided, unbalanced and consequently unsound. As the prominent French General L. Chassin has written:

> . . . our future armed forces must be able to face simultaneously two completely different types of war. . . .

Again, Liddell Hart, a writer much more recognised abroad than in his own country, has made the point clear:

> . . . the insanity of planning a defence that is bound to be suicidal, has become so obvious except to the planners themselves. . . .[12]

This excessive reliance on weapons of mass destruction, primarily as a deterrent, and the subsequent neglect of conventional forces which have been gradually reduced to the completely secondary role of a trip-wire or " plate glass window," cannot but revive painful memories of experience in Korea. Before the war broke out in Korea, it had become almost a generally accepted view in the United States that a strong air force would be completely sufficient

---

[11] " Basic Problems of European Defence," *Marine Corps Gazette*, September 1958.
[12] *Marine Corps Gazette, op. cit.*

to assure success in any future military operations, and, in particular, in Korea. Unfortunately, even complete mastery in the air could not save American troops, in the initial stages of war, from disaster on the battlefield, and only the army, supported, of course, by the tanks and air force, *almost* won that war. If at that time the American Administration had had the courage to take the calculated risk " of launching Chiang Kai-shek " without getting involved in a land campaign in the vast plains of Manchuria, the course of events in the Far East, and consequently the whole balance of power, would have been radically different.

Let us state at this juncture, quite candidly, that all talk about the frightening disparity between the Soviet *bloc* forces and the ground forces of the West, under the command of SHAPE, stems to a great extent from lack of understanding of the experience of the last war and from ignorance of the facts and figures and of Soviet strategy.

It is relevant at this point to quote the authoritative views of a German general, Major-General W. F. von Mellenthin:

> Is the Red Army invincible? . . . even in the critical years of 1944–1945, our soldiers never had the feeling of being inferior to the Russians—but the weak German forces were like the rocks in the ocean, surrounded by endless waves of men and tanks . . . it would be wrong to regard them [the Russians] as invincible as long as the strength ratio is not fantastically unequal. . . . Experience gathered in the war shows that the Germans fought successful actions with a strength ratio of 1:5. . . . Success was sometimes achieved at an even more unfavourable strength ratio. . . .[13]

Let us now examine, in the light of official documents, the situation in Europe in the event of a hypothetical direct Soviet overland attack: according to the Report " The Present State of European Security," which was based upon figures supplied by SHAPE, the Soviet and satellite armed

[13] *Panzer Battles*, p. 290.

forces on the Central European front are estimated as follows [14]:

> In Eastern Germany, six Soviet armies, totalling twenty divisions; in Poland, two Soviet divisions; in Hungary, six–seven Soviet divisions; in Western Russia, three airborne divisions, plus a further ten divisions of various types; in addition, the satellite armies make the following contribution: Eastern Germany, seven divisions; Poland, eight divisions; Czechoslovakia, six divisions; and some 10,000 men in national service in Hungary. . . . The Central front is therefore open to attack without any period of mobilisation by a force of fifty–sixty divisions, although the twenty satellite divisions must be considered of varying reliability to the Soviets.[15]

In other words, at best this would mean that if there were no revolt in Eastern Europe the Russians could muster for a war against Western Europe not more than some fifty to sixty divisions, although they would be wise to keep their satellite forces, amounting to one-third of that figure, far from the front line. A situation may, however, arise where the Russians will be able to rely on their satellite armed forces, that is, if West German troops, in the course of operations find themselves on Polish or Czechoslovak territory. Mr. James Burnham makes quite clear what the consequences would be:

> . . . if German troops appear as the principal forward elements of the North Atlantic armies the political result will be to convince the East European units that they confront only a disguise for the World War all over again. Their anti-germanism will tend to cancel their anti-communism and to consolidate them behind Moscow.[16]

Clearly, the use of the units of the Bundeswehr under such circumstances would amount to an error of the first magnitude: it would display utter disregard of elementary rules of psychological warfare.

[14] This Report was submitted on behalf of the Committee on Defence Questions and Armaments to the Assembly of WEU on July 2, 1958, by Mr. Fens, Rapporteur.
[15] " The Present State of European Security," *supra*, p. 9.
[16] *Containment or Liberation*, p. 91.

A recent official publication, *The Handbook on Arms Control and Related Problems in Europe*, which appeared in May 1959 under the auspices of the American Senate Foreign Relations Sub-Committee on Disarmament, gives even more reassuring estimates, based upon figures supplied by the Director of U.S. Central Intelligence: " It seems, however, that the numbers are roughly comparable and that neither side in Germany proper seriously overbalances the other in terms of mere numbers." [17]   It certainly states that: " The disparity is much greater, however, in regard to the organised military forces which each side has in reserve in the European area outside Germany proper "; but it continues:

> 136 Red Army divisions, out of a national total of about 175, are said to be deployed in European Russia; that is, that portion of the Soviet Union, west of the Ural Mountains. . . . Out of the overall total of 175 Soviet divisions under arms, twenty are normally believed to be in southern border districts, twenty-five in the Caucasus [under Marshal Rokossovsky, deployed against Turkey] and seven in the southern satellites. . . .[18]

In all this amounts to 52 divisions: if we subtract these 52 divisions, stretching from the northern tip of Norway to the Balkans, from the 136 in all European Russia, there remain only 84 divisions from which the Soviet High Command could draw. These estimates, based on a sober appraisal by SHAPE and the U.S. Central Intelligence, must be compared with figures mentioned for instance by Lord Home, in the course of a debate in the House of Lords on December 18, 1958. Objecting to the idea of setting up a neutral zone in Europe, he said: " . . . it would produce a situation in which Russia's 210 divisions and the 70 satellite divisions would have a great advantage because they have much the greater freedom of deployment, naturally in Europe." [19]   Quite how the Soviet High Command would

[17] p. 6.
[18] p. 12.
[19] *Hansard*, p. 546.

conjure up such astronomical figures like a rabbit top hat, was not specified.

Moreover, there is a further gross error in Lord Ho. arithmetic: the establishment of a neutral zone wo.... entail the withdrawal of Western Germany from NATO and of the countries of Eastern Europe from the Warsaw Pact. The term " satellite" would belong entirely to history; in case of Soviet aggression against Western Europe, Soviet troops would first have to cross the territory of Eastern Europe, former Soviet " satellites," now defended by their own national armed forces.

Against this overrated Soviet steam-roller or wall of steel and flesh, reputedly to bulldoze the weak NATO shield, but which consists only, in fact, of some twenty to thirty Soviet divisions, the Supreme Commander in Europe will be able to put in the front line some twenty divisions (although his target is thirty divisions) and therefore the ratio of force will not exceed the figure of 1:2, or perhaps even less. General Norstad has himself said:

> One must also bear in mind that in a thermonuclear war—and if it comes to a war in Europe, it will most likely be such a war—only the troops which are on the spot and deployed for action when the balloon goes up, really matter.

It is again pertinent to quote Liddell Hart, who writes:

> The ratio of space to force is apt to be the crux of the matter . . . even in such a very wide front like in Russia it became evident that a well-conducted mobile defence could be maintained *indefinitely* unless the attacking side had an overall superiority exceeding 3 to 1.[20]

He continues elsewhere:

> Even though the Russians benefited from the exceptionally wide space of the Eastern Front, the defence repelled attacks delivered with a superiority of seven to one or even more. Moreover, the German Panzer divisions, by virtue of their mechanised mobility, often succeeded in covering and defending frontages up to twenty miles against very heavy odds.[21]

[20] *Marine Corps Gazette, op. cit.*
[21] " Defence Against the Odds," *The Manchester Guardian*, June 16–17, 1959.

Therefore, talk about the frightening disparity between the Soviet hordes and Western conventional forces seems, in the light of the above authentic official figures, to be something close to nonsense.

However, the tragedy of this kind of talk in the West is that it reinforces belief in the necessity of building up Western strategy around the deterrent.

It is interesting at this point to recall the stern warning issued by General M. Ridgway, former NATO Supreme Commander, who, in his position of Army Chief of Staff, conducted a losing battle against the " New Look " that was based upon an increasing belief in the decisive role of nuclear weapons at the expense of conventional forces. General Ridgway had to retire in June 1955, and in three articles in *The Saturday Evening Post* he wrote:

> To me the lessons of that conflict [in Korea] were clear— that hope of peace rests solidly on strength for war. It also shattered, I hoped forever, the dreamy-eyed delusions which possessed the minds of many then—that the threat of the nuclear weapon alone could keep the peace: and of that corollary phantasy, the nebulous faith that war, even a little war, could be won by air and naval power alone. . . . We are falling again into the error which cost us so much blood and agony in Korea —the delusion that the foot soldier is obsolete and that naval power and air power alone can insure a peaceful world.

He continued with much bitterness:

> I felt I was being called upon rather to destroy than to build a fighting force, upon which rested the world's best hope for peace. . . . Yet, present forces cannot support American diplomacy fully, for, if military power is to be an instrument of diplomacy, it must be real and apparent to all concerned.[22]

In view of the latest reappraisal of American strategy, especially the decreasing probability of the use of the deterrent and the greater importance of conventional forces, General Ridgway's words deserve much attention.

This mental process and the strategy resulting from it

[22] January–February 1956.

makes it only too difficult, if not impossible, to reverse the present trend which is leading us towards continuation of an arms race, unchecked by anything more lasting than the balance of power which the balance of mutual terror provides.

At this juncture it would be useful to get rid of another myth based—like that of the perpetuity of the *status quo*—upon the military stalemate, namely, the myth of the stalemate itself. A few quotations from a very enlightening article by Mr. A. Wohlstetter, a member of the Rand Corporation, will illustrate the argument:

> Deterrence . . . is not automatic. . . . Matching weapons misconstrues the nature of the technological race. . . . Perhaps the first step in dispelling the nearly universal optimism about the stability of deterrence would be to recognise the difficulties in analysing the uncertainties and interactions between our own wide range of choices and the moves open to the Soviets. . . . As a result strategic deterrence, while feasible, will be extremely difficult to achieve, and at critical junctures in the 1960s we may not have the power to deter attack.[23]

A similar view has been expressed by Mr. K. Knorr:

> It cannot be taken for granted that this parity of deterrent power will necessarily endure . . . there is no assurance that such an upset in the balance of effective terror will not occur. . . .[24]

In an article, " Russia versus U.S.—New Look at the Balance of Power," the following view was expressed:

> Within the last three years, two changes have occurred that affect the balance the military power: (1) The Soviets have acquired intercontinental missiles and they have the means of attacking the United States direct; (2) The Soviets, too, have greatly increased their submarine fleet giving them the capability of hitting the United States with medium- or short-range missiles. The West does not know how many intercontinental missiles Soviet Russia does have or whether Russia does hold a real superiority over the United States in that weapon. The

---

[23] " The Delicate Balance of Terror," *Foreign Affairs*, January 1959, pp. 212, 215, 217.

[24] *The Crisis in U.S. Defence*, p. 10.

weight of evidence is, however, that Russia holds a definite lead. It is known that Russian submarines are constantly lurking in waters off the United States.[25]

In the unrelenting arms race, there is always the danger that, if the Russian scientists should discover an offensive weapon which they considered would give the Soviet an absolute and indisputable superiority over the West, or, alternatively, a defensive weapon which would make Russia immune from any form of Western retaliation, the discovery would radically upset the balance of power and the present *status quo*.

Unfortunately, if such a weapon should be discovered by the Western scientists, there is little probability—as experience has already shown—that the West will make proper use of it or take the appropriate opportunity to fortify its own negotiating position: the Russians will be able to catch up and restore the uneasy balance of mutual terror.

Consequently, the situation will remain, at best, as General Norstad put it in his speech before the American Council for NATO in January 1958:

> . . . an endurance test of an unknown duration: or the West can be faced one day with a technological breakthrough, with consequences difficult to assess. . . .

The Shrinking of American Bases

Basically, Western strategy is based upon a system of alliances, backed by the ring of American bases along the Soviet perimeter.

In implementing this policy, Strategic Air Command has established bases in Great Britain, Iceland, Greenland, Turkey, several countries of the Middle East, North Africa and the Far East. In all these bases, large American bombers, B-47s and B-52s, loaded with thermo-nuclear bombs, are, twenty-four hours a day, kept in readiness to

[25] *U.S. News and World Report*, June 22, 1959, p. 75

strike at an instant's notice at Russia's most vulnerable targets, selected in accordance with an elaborate plan.

The views of Mr. P. Nitze, former Director of Policy Planning Staff in the State Department and Vice-Chairman of United States Strategic Bombing Survey, are worth quoting:

> The United States is vulnerable to direct attack only from bases on the Eurasian land mass and from submarines. The U.S.S.R. is vulnerable to attack not only from North American bases but also from bases closer in on the periphery of the Eurasian land mass itself and from seas controlled by the navies of the West. Given anything approaching equality in numbers and quality of planes, missiles and the other elements of modern delivery systems, the geographic factor should give the West the possibility of a continuing and decisive margin of superiority. . . .
>
> The land bases ringing the U.S.S.R., close in, are subject to the sovereign control not of the United States but of the countries on whose territory they are located. A military policy which contributes to neutralism in those countries may rob the West of that geographic advantage which is potentially its greatest strength. . . .
>
> If the bases from which a Western strike can be mounted are thirty in number, the enemy will have a far easier task in establishing air control than if those bases are 300 or 3,000 in number and if they are geographically well dispersed and varied in character.[26]

Extensive quotation from Mr. Nitze's article is interesting because he shows the great importance to the West of the air bases, also because many events which have taken place since his article was published, particularly in North Africa and the Middle East, have seriously affected the whole situation as far as those bases are concerned.

During the last few years the Suez fiasco, which could easily have been avoided, has shattered British prestige and influence in the Middle East, and the Eisenhower Doctrine, which was intended to replace it, has proved unable to halt the Soviet advance into that important area. As a result,

[26] "Atoms, Strategy and Policy," *Foreign Affairs*, January 1956, pp. 192, 193.

anti-Western feeling in those countries has become much stronger, making precarious the situation of various Western bases.

Nor has the situation in Morocco and Tunis developed very favourably for the West, because the independence secured by these two countries has also made the Western position rather uncertain. As a result, the United States will have to lose within the next three to five years the biggest of all her overseas bases, the group in Morocco. This group of bases, which cost about one billion dollars, consists of four S.A.C. bases, a large naval base, hundreds of miles of jet-fuel pipelines and a huge supply depot, which supplies American and Allied air units all over Southern Europe. The importance of these bases is shown by the fact that about a quarter of the present number of S.A.C. bombers, including the long-range B-52s, can operate from them.

When it comes to withdrawal of these bases in Morocco, S.A.C. will have to operate from its greatly inferior and incomplete bases in Spain. Further, and this is much worse, if Morocco should fall under the spell of Soviet charm, as has happened to Egypt, Syria and especially to Iraq, there will be always the possibility that the American bases, developed with such care, could be used by the Soviets. In any case, Morocco has already given Russia permission to establish a legation in Rabat.

Another result of the growing anti-Western feeling in the Middle East is that the fate of another big American base, at Dharan in Saudi Arabia, is uncertain.

The Americans are not the only ones under increasing pressure to quit. The fate of the large and important French naval base at Bizerta is in balance. President Bourguiba is determined to get the French out of Bizerta; the open support given by the Tunisian Government to the Algerian rebels will not make negotiations with the French any easier.

At the same time, Iraq's withdrawal from the Baghdad Pact—which was the natural sequence of the *coup* and the chain reactions of the Anglo-French fiasco at Suez—means the winding up of a powerful British base at Habbaniya. Apart from the very great inconvenience to Britain of being deprived of her right to fly over Iraq territory *en route* for the Commonwealth, this base could accommodate bombers large enough to take part in hypothetical operations, together with S.A.C., against Russia's " soft under-belly."

Obviously, all these factors must, in the long run, affect the potential of the deterrent, and consequently the balance of power which forms the basis of the *status quo*.

This process of erosion on the number of American air bases has not been limited to the Middle East and North Africa: during the last few years, as a result of increasing Communist influence in Iceland, the position of American combined air and naval bases on the island, has given rise to some misgivings.

As early as 1956, after the Soviet withdrawal from the Pokkala naval base in Finland, the Icelandic Parliament, Althing, passed a resolution demanding the withdrawal of the American base from the island.

Although at present, under the Caretaker Government, the whole matter seems to have been put in abeyance, it is difficult to foresee what the situation will be after the election due this spring: at any rate, qualified observers are rather pessimistic.

Further, no one can say at this juncture whether there will be complications of a similar nature in Japan, where there are several American air and naval bases.

Finally, in the event of any change in the political status of Formosa, the fate of the American bases can again become doubtful: this is probably one of the main reasons why the United States prefers the *status quo* in the Far East, which gives them a possibility of relying on Chiang, who is completely dependent on Americans to, for instance, support the policy of two Chinas.

As Mr. P. Nitze has pointed out, the larger the number of bases, the smaller would be the chance that the Russians would be able to stage a grand-scale Pearl Harbour and incapacitate them all at once.

However, as a result of the steady development of the Soviet intermediate ballistic missiles, some American bases have become much too close to the territory of the Soviet *bloc* and, consequently, some of them have been gradually abandoned as air bases, the bombers returning to the States, and the bases reduced to refuelling stations.

Finally, as a result of technological progress in the field of intercontinental missiles and submarine-fired missiles, the importance of the overseas bases will gradually tend to diminish. All these facts and trends show once again the fluidity to a *status quo* based upon a balance of military power.

Disintegration of the Alliances

On August 8, 1959, *The Economist* commented on a pamphlet published in the United States by the Advisory Council of the Democratic Party. *The Economist* challenged the whole basis of the strategy adopted by Eisenhower's Administration and stated:

> . . . the pamphlet does not discuss the third consequence of the new strategic thinking but this may well prove to be the most important for the West's foreign policy. It rests on two premises: first, the Russians' undoubted superiority in medium-range missiles means that the American bases which lie under their nose in Europe will soon be (if they are not already) virtually worthless.

As Mr. Harold E. Stassen, Assistant on Disarmament to the President, said in a statement before the Sub-Committee on Disarmament of the Senate Foreign Relations Committee on January 27, 1958:

> As to military bases abroad, about which the Soviet Union has frequently expressed concern, we reconfirm that such bases are the product of the times and tensions in which we have lived; on our side they have been developed as part of the effort of the free world to protect itself and advance the cause of

freedom. If the circumstances that brought them into being are mitigated, then the need for the defences decreases and the need for the bases would also decrease.

It would be wrong to believe that the two military systems opposing each other along the Iron Curtain represent alliances full of harmony, cohesion and unity of purpose: both systems, and in particular the Warsaw Pact, have also been undergoing, in various forms, a process of erosion.

Like the West, the Soviets have set up a system of military alliances: one, which was intended as an answer to NATO, culminated in the Warsaw Pact and into this the satellite armed forces have been integrated; the other is with Red China.

Stalin's decision to integrate satellite armed forces into the Soviet military system has proved to be one of his biggest mistakes.

Like Hitler, who in 1941 failed to understand the feelings of millions of Russian, and especially of Ukrainian, peasants, who greeted German soldiers as their " liberators," Stalin failed to grasp the state of mind of peoples in Eastern Europe. Despite an oriental and suspicious mentality, he concluded that the Communist puppet régime, established with the help of the Soviet bayonets, was firmly in the saddle, and that he could therefore integrate their armed forces into the Soviet military machine.

The result of this momentous decision was that all those national armed forces, who had hitherto been poorly armed with weapons from the last war and whose air forces were allowed petrol for not more than for some twenty minutes flying time to prevent pilots escaping to the West, began gradually to transform themselves into a modern and formidable fighting force, able—due to the setting up of vast para-military organisations—to expand very considerably in the event of war.

This process of integration culminated in a fully fledged military alliance, under the name of the Warsaw Pact,

which was signed in Warsaw in May 1955, two months
before the Summit conference at Geneva, which was supposed to bring about the reduction of international tension.
That alliance was joined in January 1956 by Eastern
Germany, and her armed forces, which until then had been
carefully camouflaged under the label of " People's Police,"
became known as " The National People's Army." All
these armed forces, numbering—according to *NATO Year-
book*—some seventy to eighty divisions with modern naval
and air forces integrated into an alliance with Russia with
the Soviet Marshal, Koniev, as their Supreme Commander,
became yet another nightmare in the eyes of the Western
political leaders and military planners. They realised that
the whole of Eastern Europe has become a vast military
Soviet base. This applies particularly to Eastern Germany
where, in addition to the picked twenty divisions, there are
many Soviet airfields for their interceptor-fighter squadrons,
which constitute the outer ring of the Soviet air defence
system.

In addition to these airfields, there are airfields for the
Soviet heavy bombers and increasing numbers of launching
sites which will be used for the Soviet intermediate ballistic
missiles; finally, in the area of Kaliningrad (formerly
Königsberg) in Eastern Prussia—which, under the Potsdam
Agreement has been ceded to Russia—a huge supply depot
has been set up, most probably as an advance base for the
Soviet troops located in Eastern Germany; in case of war
these probably would serve as a strategic spearhead, thrust-
ing as deep as possible into Western Europe.

Theoretically speaking, these armed forces with their
potential were, in the eyes of the Soviet High Command, a
very valuable asset, as was also the territory of Eastern
Europe, either as an important base for offensive operations
against the West or, equally, a defence glacis in the event
of an attack from the West.

At the same time, in the eyes of the Western military
leaders, these forces increased the discrepancy between the

conventional forces of both sides, compelling them in their plans to rely even more on deterrence in order to achieve the balance of forces and thus to maintain the *status quo*.

The uprising in Eastern Germany in 1953 was the first warning to the Soviet leaders that the captive nations of Eastern Europe did not want to become docile satellites or colonies of the new Russian Empire. If, at the time of that uprising there had been a strong Bundeswehr in existence in the Federal Republic, no one knows how the situation would have developed: as it was, the West sat still while the Soviet tanks crushed the revolt of an exasperated people.

In his article " Our Captive Allies "—in which he developed the thesis that the most effective deterrent is not " our arsenal of atomic and hydrogen bombs " but " the hatred which the peoples behind the Iron Curtain feel for their tyrannical régimes . . ."—Senator Thomas J. Dodd wrote:

> If the Soviet Union could have the wisdom to withdraw to its pre-war frontiers, tensions would disappear overnight and the whole world would sleep better. To ease the way for the Communists, we should make it clear in advance that, in exchange for liberation, we would be prepared to make some concessions to the Soviet desires in other areas. If Khrushchev truly wants a reduction of tensions, there is no more effective measure he could take than to negotiate a package agreement with the West in which liberation is exchanged for such concessions as a European Security Pact, increased East-West trade, partial disarmament, and, conceivably, even some long term credits.[27]

Mr. W. Lippmann, in an inspiring article in *The Observer*, has expressed the view that the reasons for the uprising in Eastern Germany and subsequent upheaval in Hungary could be found in the atomic race:

> The breaking up [by Russia] of the American monopoly meant the beginning of a race in nuclear armaments. This was a terrifying prospect. It set in motion a strong tendency towards disintegration inside both the Stalinist empire and the

[27] *New Leader*, July 27, 1959, p. 7.

Western coalition. . . . No doubt there were other reasons. But the trigger which set forces of disintegration in motion in both spheres was the race in nuclear armaments and the danger of atomic war. . . . Politically and psychologically these gigantic explosions [H-bombs] have jarred loose, they have dislocated and pulled apart much of the political structure of the post-war world.[28]

The events in Poland of October 1956, when Polish armed forces were ready in support of Gomulka, staging a *coup*, to open fire at their " comrades in arms "—the Soviet troops stationed in Poland, for all formal purposes under the terms of the Warsaw Pact—and, above all, the Hungarian uprising, in which the Hungarian troops actually fought the Russians, produced a terrific shock for the Soviet High Command, which after a sober reappraisal must have decided to write off from its plans perhaps the greater part of the satellite armed forces.

The Soviet military and political leaders, being cynical realists, with all their understanding of the methods of psychological warfare and subversion, must undoubtedly have realised that, in the event of war—as one leading Communist has been reputed to have said during the Hungarian uprising—many satellite troops " would shoot in another direction."

These events clearly suggest the disintegration of a military alliance and, consequently, a considerable shift in the balance of power in Europe.

As we know, no decision of any kind was taken in the West when Soviet influence in Eastern Europe was in the balance, although, as became evident during Professor Habich's trial in Eastern Germany, a general revolt in Eastern Germany and Roumania was at that time a matter of touch and go.

Obviously, if there had been a general revolt in Eastern Europe, the Russians would have had two alternatives: either to have drowned the whole of Eastern Europe in

---

[28] " The Crumbling Alliances," *The Observer*, July 7, 1957.

blood, which would not have been so easy since the revolt could perhaps have spread even to Russia itself, or to have withdrawn from that area altogether.

In either case the West, which had no policy towards Eastern Europe except to maintain the *status quo*, would have been rather embarrassed, as indeed it was during the Hungarian uprising, which threw a challenge to Western statesmanship.

As far as the Western coalition and other alliances on this side of the Iron Curtain are concerned, they also have undergone severe strains and stresses from time to time.

However, the main difference between the Atlantic Alliance, which unites all the free nations of the West of their own free will, and the Warsaw Pact, which is an alliance under the Soviet knout, and which all its members, if only they could, would leave at a few hours' notice, is the unity of purpose which cements the Western coalition.

The main purpose of setting up NATO in April 1949 was the need to establish a barrier against the danger of open Soviet aggression: that fear of Soviet aggression has linked together all nations of Western Europe ever since. Nothing could illustrate this better than the words of Monsieur P. Spaak, then Belgium Foreign Minister and Delegate to the United Nations Assembly in Paris in 1948, when looking into the face of the Soviet delegate, Mr. Vishinsky, he said: " I'll tell you what is the basis of our policy; fear of you, fear of your Government, fear of your policy."

General L. Norstad, in a short statement published in a special issue of *The Scotsman* devoted entirely to NATO, wrote:

> This threat remains and continues to make the military quality of the alliance an important one. . . . Very real progress has been made in providing for our defence in a purely military sense, but the most important factor in our security—the greatest single element in the deterrent to war—is the spirit of unity and

common purpose that has developed over the past nine years of NATO's existence.[29]

However, the Soviet offensive of smiles after Stalin's death, removed the fear of Soviet aggression and produced a sort of complacency and happy-go-lucky attitude towards the problems of defence: further, the popular idea that the safety of Europe rests under the shadow of an American H-bomb, brought a slackening of effort in the countries of Western Europe in building up a defence system in Europe: as General Norstad said in his speech before the American Council for NATO in New York in January 1958: " . . . the most perishable asset is the will to resist. . . ."

Further, the British cuts in conventional forces and the announced intention to withdraw from Germany a considerable part of British contingents—in spite of vehement protestations by all other members of the Atlantic Alliance —produced a lot of hard feeling on the Continent: hardly had those feelings been somehow ironed out, when the Anglo-French action in Egypt in the autumn of 1956 produced a profound rift between the United States and her major allies in Europe.

No sooner had the cracks in the façade of Western unity been patched up and covered by the glossy paint of " interdependence," after the Eisenhower-Macmillan meeting in Bermuda, than Anglo-American arms shipments to Tunisia as well as squabbles with Germany about the maintenance cost of British troops again damaged the spirit of unity of purpose and cohesion within the Atlantic Alliance.

But these frictions were rather insignificant compared with the other troubles which had been brewing on both flanks of NATO for some time and which deserve to be described more fully.

Although Scandinavian statesmen such as Trygve Lie, Lange and Hammarskjold, have played a prominent role in

---

[29] *The Scotsman*, June 17, 1958.

the process of European integration, and Mr. Lange, the Norwegian Foreign Minister, played a particularly active role in NATO, yet according to Mr. Lycon Burbank NATO has never been too strong in Scandinavia.[30] In fact, both Norway and Denmark became members of NATO only after the refusal by the American National Security Council in 1949 to supply arms to the planned joint defence organisation in Scandinavia, which would have consisted of Norway, Sweden—in spite of all her policy of neutrality— Denmark and Iceland. This decision was strongly criticised by the Danish Foreign Minister, Mr. G. Rasmussen, as dividing Scandinavia. As a result of that decision, Norway joined NATO and, after a time, she was followed with little enthusiasm by Denmark. Sweden, as could be expected, stayed outside.

Meanwhile, another organisation came into being in Scandinavia in 1952, the Nordic Council—for political and cultural purposes—which was joined by all the Scandinavian countries, except Finland, who was forbidden by Russia to join the Council in 1952 but was allowed to do so in 1956.

In the long run, the Nordic Council became, so to speak, a sort of competitor to NATO, contributing to the spirit of " revolt against NATO's predominantly military character." [31] It was for these reasons that Denmark in 1953–54 resisted the stationing of foreign troops on her soil, and a similar attitude has been adopted by Norway; both these countries will allow the stationing of foreign troops on their territories only if they are attacked or threatened by an attack.

For the same reasons, the Icelandic Parliament, Althing, began making difficulties for the United States over the stationing of a combined air and naval base on the island.

The Russians were quick to exploit these feelings and contributed to the process of erosion of the Atlantic Alliance

[30] See his article " Scandinavia's Integration with Western Defences," *Foreign Affairs*, October 1956, p. 150.
[31] Burbank, *supra*.

in that area; they concentrated first of all on Iceland: in 1952, the Americans, having that year established their bases in Iceland, bought 25 per cent. of the Icelandic catch of fish, by 1955 their purchases fell to 15 per cent.; on the other hand, the Soviet purchases have increased from 7 per cent. in 1952 up to 28 per cent. in 1955, according to figures supplied by the Icelandic Legation in London. The figures for 1956 and 1957 are equally enlightening: whereas in 1956 and 1957 the United States bought Icelandic fish for 128 and 91 million Kroner respectively, the U.S.S.R. paid 203 and 213 million Kroner respectively—these figures are further proof of the extent to which the Soviet Union is using its trade relations for political ends.

Besides these commercial manoeuvres, intended to increase friendly feeling in Iceland towards Russia, the Russians did everything they could to antagonise the Icelandic people towards the American bases on their soil; there is no doubt that the Soviet withdrawal from the Pokkala naval base in Finland was, to a very great extent, intended to produce a psychological impact in Scandinavia and, in Iceland in particular, to encourage neutral sentiments.

In this context, the Russians brought into play another trick, namely, the concept of a special régime for the Baltic. The general idea was not new because just after the war Russia tried to induce Sweden to sponsor this plan, the basic idea being that the Baltic should be treated as a private preserve of all riparian States. The Swedes, refusing to act as a Trojan horse, politely but firmly turned down the whole idea. However, after Stalin's death, the idea was revived and a series of approaches has been made during the last few years, *e.g.*, the exchange of courtesy visits by Swedish and Soviet warships, the exchange of visits on ministerial level between the Russians and all Scandinavian countries, with the Soviet satellites following the Soviet footsteps. Thus, Mr. Rapacki, the Polish Foreign Minister, has also been in Oslo, where his plan has met with approval and support.

Apart from this subtle and pervading Soviet penetration into Scandinavia with the ultimate purpose of bringing about the erosion of the Western Alliance, it is important to remember recent friction in the NATO Council which resulted from German suggestions concerning the reorganisation of NATO's northern flank. It was suggested that Denmark should be placed under the orders of Central European Command, with General Speidel as Commander of Land Forces. Denmark, mostly for psychological reasons, objected to the German suggestion that the Danish Navy should be placed under the orders of the German Navy.

On another NATO flank, until February 1959, the situation which resulted from increasing tension over Cyprus, was developing in a way which created serious misgivings.

This issue, which flared up sharply after the evacuation by Britain of the Suez Canal Zone, was rapidly poisoning relations between Greece and Turkey and between Britain and her Balkan allies. As a result of the bloodshed in Cyprus, the danger of an open conflict between Greece and Turkey was a distinct possibility; this would have meant the complete collapse of the NATO southern flank.

Against this background the Zurich and London agreements on Cyprus can be seen as acts of statesmanship of a high calibre; apart from settling this controversial issue, these agreements have foiled Soviet plans to take advantage of the dangerous situation which the Cyprus crisis had created.

This catalogue of frictions within NATO would not be complete if we omitted General de Gaulle's recent demand for full control of the French Mediterranean naval forces, in war as well as in peace. At present, these naval forces, consisting of a strong squadron based on Toulon, would, in war, be subordinated to "Allied Forces Mediterranean Command," under a British Admiral, which is answerable to SHAPE. The French maintain that they have a much stronger naval force in that area than the British and, furthermore, that their interests in North Africa are more vital than British commitments in the Mediterranean.

This demand is being considered, partly because of de Gaulle's protest against the lack of NATO solidarity towards France's difficulties in North Africa, and partly because of his opposition to the principle of integration: he very much prefers the principle of co-operation, which preserves the national character of the troops and their *esprit de corps*.

Hardly had this trouble been patched up when General de Gaulle came forward with a new demand, making difficulties in granting permission to the Americans to base atomic warheads on French territory. In fact the whole trouble had begun in September 1958, when General de Gaulle wrote to President Eisenhower and Mr. Macmillan calling for a global NATO strategy in which France would have an equal say with Britain and the United States. He asked at the same time for atomic secrets to be shared with France and for diplomatic support on the Algerian question. De Gaulle's policy aroused strong criticism within NATO, rooted as it was in a sort of mystical nationalism which sees in membership of the " nuclear club " a claim to the rank of World Power. It could have consequences disastrous not only for NATO but for the whole world.

If General de Gaulle gets his way, nothing can stop other countries, in Europe and in other parts of the world, from putting forward their own claims. Such a development will seriously jeopardise the present slender chances of reaching agreement with the Russians on a ban on nuclear tests. The whole situation is the more paradoxical in that France which, within the Atlantic Alliance, takes the most uncompromising attitude towards any attempt to find a compromise solution with the Russians and which, together with Dr. Adenauer, is pushing the West towards the policy of "brinkmanship," is in point of fact contributing extremely little to the defence of Western Europe. The cohesion of the alliance has been exposed to very severe strains.

At any rate, this attitude, apart from creating political difficulties, has necessitated serious replanning of all existing arrangements, both in peacetime as well as for war.

Finally, one must not omit from this catalogue General Kassem's recent announcement of the withdrawal of his country from the Baghdad Pact. Although, since the revolution Iraq has been only a " sleeping partner," its nominal adherence contributed to the continuation of the *status quo* in that area. Its withdrawal means that, in the case of Soviet aggression against Persia, it will be more difficult for Western reinforcements or supplies to reach Persia by land. Iraq's defection—a typical example of the erosion of an alliance—produced in the system of alliances a shift in the balance of power.

Having dealt with the particular lights and shadows in the Western Alliance, it is also important to examine another matter of a more general nature which cannot but affect adversely the structure of the Alliance, namely, the constant vacillations in American policy towards the use of deterrent weapons in the event of Soviet aggression on any member on the periphery of the alliance. These heart-searching American considerations of the automatic functioning of the mechanism of the " Big Deterrent," can be found in Mr. Henry Kissinger's remarkable book, *Nuclear Weapons and Foreign Policy*:

> . . . if we examine the alliances on which United States policy is based, we find that some of them do not share a common purpose. . . . In such circumstances, a system of collective security runs the danger of leading to a dilution of purpose and to an air of unreality. . . . In short, our system of alliances can thrive only if we curb our penchant for pushing principles to their ultimate conclusion.[32]

This book which, like Professor Carr's wartime book, *Conditions of Peace*, has become almost a sort of a Bible in the State Department, has been widely read in many countries outside the United States and, in particular, in

---

[32] *Nuclear Weapons and Foreign Policy*, pp. 239, 254.

those where Mr. Kissinger's ideas have created profound misgivings and doubts as to the value of the American guarantee against Soviet aggression. Obviously, the Russians have been quick to exploit these feelings, trying to apply their favourite method of diplomacy, namely, the "stick and carrot" policy, which involves intimidating countries lying on the periphery of NATO, for example, the Scandinavian countries and Turkey, while simultaneously offering them various financial and economic advantages to lure them away from their military alignment with the West. At the same time, the Soviet campaign against rocket bases in some NATO countries, especially in Norway, Italy and Greece, has made some impact. In this context, note must be made of the support given to Khrushchev's idea of a Balkan "atom-free zone" in Greece, which will be dealt with in later chapters.[33]

NATO is this year entering its second decade. The background has changed considerably since it came into being ten years ago; and with its plate full of difficult problems, one could say that it is a remarkable phenomenon that it is generally taken for granted that NATO must and will endure another decade. In spite of the internal frictions and the process of erosion on all sides to which it has been exposed during the past ten years, NATO seems at times like a weather-beaten ship, manoeuvring adroitly amidst the underwater rocks, well able to survive the most severe storm.

One could not use the same metaphor of the Warsaw Pact. Unlike NATO, where the fear of a Soviet aggression has always been its strongest link, an equivalent event, as far as the Warsaw Pact is concerned, would not only endanger its cohesion, but most probably produce its collapse. Only if the Bundeswehr were foolishly allowed to enter Polish or Czechoslovak territory would, as we have already noted, the Warsaw Pact work; Polish-Czechoslovak troops might then fight alongside the Soviet Army in a spirit of genuine alliance.

[33] See Chap. 9.

3

The Dangers of the Status Quo

THE *status quo*, besides being the reason for the uneasy tension in Europe which can always trigger off a major conflict, heralds other dangers, particularly the growing problems of Red China and German militarism. In both cases bold and creative initiative, leading to a change in the *status quo*, could create a new balance of power and, by implication, prevent the further growth of the Chinese danger or the resurgence of German militarism.

The Growing Menace of Red China

The targets of the second Five Year Plan in Red China are: steel, coal and atomic weapons.

According to press reports from the Far East, plans for the eventual use of atomic weapons are included in a comprehensive scheme for the reorganisation of China's armed forces, which has been finally approved by the Chinese Communist Party and military leaders and is now being put in hand with Soviet military advice.

The aims are to modernise the army, to combine Mao Tse-Tung's guerrilla traditions with Russian tactical theory, to enforce military efficiency inside the people's communes, and to develop the thirty million partly trained and poorly armed militia as an effective army auxiliary. Marshal Lin Piao, vice-chairman of the Central Committee, is collaborating with a Soviet military mission of four generals in modernising the army. The basis of the reorganisation of the regular army, which has been estimated at three million men under arms, is the streamlining of the " human sea " of infantry which fought in Korea into smaller, more

compact, composite divisions, modelled on the American
" Pentomic " pattern. In addition, it is believed that there
are fifteen million in reserve and, according to unconfirmed
claims, a further ten million discharged men who could be
swiftly remobilised.

If and when Red China, after completion of her second
Five Year Plan, approaches the level of one of the big
Western Powers, and when she has atomic weapons issued
to her formidable infantry mass, trained in the use of these
weapons, the West, especially the United States, will have
to face a new and very real menace to peace not only in
the Far East but also perhaps in the world at large.

Already China's attitude towards the West is touched
with contempt: the United States is known in China as a
" paper tiger." Reliable Western observers, returning from
China, report having seen maps of the world with the
frontiers of the future China extending in the West up to
the River Oder, and in the Middle East up to the Red
Sea.

Because of China's small regard for the sanctity of
human life, the prospect of a thermonuclear war, in which
some 200 or 300 million Chinese may perish, will in no way
prevent her leaders from sabre-rattling or indeed, perhaps,
from sabre-drawing. An American journalist, John
Strohm, described in *Reader's Digest* his impressions of his
recent visit to China.

> The war-spirit is fomented everywhere. I was told that
> more than six million former fighting men have volunteered to
> lead militias. Most factories and communes have organised
> militia units " to repel the American invaders."
>
> The answer is that the Chinese have a fatalistic attitude
> towards war—as towards everything. If war results from their
> efforts to take what they believe rightfully belongs to China,
> then war it must be, and the United States will have been at
> fault. Party Chairman Mao has said that China is the only
> nation that can afford a war: " We can lose 300 million Chinese
> and still 350 million will be left." [1]

[1] March 1959. " How Hatred Builds Tomorrow's China," p. 99.

This contrast between China's readiness to risk a major war and the growing reluctance of the United States to face it will make China's blackmailing tactics more brazen and consequently more successful, with the result that far-reaching changes in the *status quo* in the Far East may occur within the next decade. If this happens consequences in other parts of the world where the *status quo* is already crumbling will undoubtedly be very grave.

Chinese Communist leaders must undoubtedly draw some satisfaction from current trends in Western strategic thinking: they may well have studied Kissinger's book which, recognising the potential fear of mutual destruction, makes nuclear war an unlikely choice, perhaps even at the tactical level. They also realise that tactical atomic weapons —the so-called graduated deterrent—would be of a limited advantage against China: at the same time, they are probably aware that the West is becoming less willing or able to assist the smaller States of South-East Asia bordering on China with substantial numbers of infantry prepared to fight an attrition-type warfare. Against the background of this knowledge, present events in Tibet constitute a test case for both sides.

Those in the West who indulge in what is at present only wishful thinking about a possible split between China and the Soviet Union usually overlook the strong ideological ties which have existed between Soviet and Communist leaders since the very beginning of Communism in China. The two-camp view of the world is strongly embedded in every aspect of China's régime. During his second visit to Moscow in November 1957, Mao, as head of Red China, declared before the Supreme Soviet:

> We share the same destiny and the same life-spring with the Soviet Union and the entire socialist camp. We regard it as the sacred international obligation of all socialist countries to strengthen the solidarity of the socialist countries headed by the Soviet Union.

In implementation of this commitment to the Soviet camp, the Chinese Communist leaders have followed unflinchingly the line laid down by Moscow through crises in which their national interests would seem to have dictated otherwise: the Hitler-Stalin pact, the Japanese-Soviet treaty and the Soviet plundering of Manchuria.

Equally, after the war, in supporting the Soviet decision to crush the Hungarian uprising, which shocked many peoples in South-East Asia, in attacking Tito, in supporting the Soviet policy of penetration into the Middle East, Mao has given further proof of his loyalty to the primacy of Soviet aims and the necessity for Soviet leadership.

In implementation of this policy, he cancelled his promised visit to Poland, where, in view of the tacit support given by him to Gomulka in 1956, he had been anxiously awaited.

On the other hand, in spite of China's attitude towards the Soviet Union, it is interesting to note that during his conversation with Senator Humphrey in Moscow last autumn Mr. Khrushchev spoke very critically about some aspects of China's developments. The Soviet leaders are fully aware of the growing Chinese menace, and this is one of the reasons for the Soviet suggestion of an " atom-free zone " in the Pacific, which would prevent China becoming an atomic Power.

It is equally only fair to add that the Soviet military mission in China, while training Chinese fighter pilots, has done very little to develop the Chinese bomber force. One could assume that the Russians are not anxious to strengthen the Chinese bomber potential any more than the United States, for quite different reasons, wishes to strengthen Chiang's bomber force.

At any rate, these Soviet feelings, though not displayed too openly, could in due course become a platform for an understanding between Russia and the West. Any reduction of tension in the West could contribute considerably to such a development, however remote and unlikely it may seem today.

However, for the time being Sino-Soviet co-operation is in all fields a reality, adding additional weight to the impetus of China's expansion. One must remember that China's régime is perhaps even more dynamic than the Soviet one. It cannot and never will accept a *status quo*, either inside its own territory or abroad.

The Danger of German Military Power

Kennan, in his Reith Lectures, rightly said:

> . . . the German question still stands at the centre of world tensions; . . . no greater contribution can be made to world peace than the removal of the present deadlock over Germany. . . .[2]

And yet even Kennan, who sees in the division of Germany a potential cause of conflict with Russia, does not seem to realise that Germany—if the present situation is allowed to continue—may become one day, and perhaps fairly soon, a new danger in Europe and a menace to world peace.

Few people in the West realise that the German Federal Republic has already, except for Turkey, the strongest national contingent in NATO.

The situation has changed out of recognition since the war days, when endless official declarations and statements solemnly proclaimed that Germany should be totally disarmed and demilitarised for a long time to come. It would be interesting and enlightening, before coming to any conclusions, to recall those days and to give a very brief review of the evolution of the problem of German rearmament from complete disarmament up to full membership in NATO.

As a result of the agreement reached during the Conference of Foreign Ministers in Moscow in November 1943,

[2] *Russia, the Atom and the West*, p. 37.

the European Consultative Commission, created after that conference, in a document dealing with German surrender terms, formulated a clause (Article 12 (a)) ensuring the " complete demilitarisation " of Germany: this document, which expressed the policy of the Big Three towards the problem, was signed by their representatives in July 1944.

Likewise, during the conferences in Yalta and Potsdam, it was solemnly agreed to " destroy German militarism " for ever.

Immediately after the war both American Secretaries of State, Mr. Byrnes in 1946 and Mr. Marshall in 1947, strove to reach an agreement with Russia on a peace treaty with Germany, which would implement these decisions and guarantee the continued demilitarisation of Germany.

Even after the Soviet coup in Czechoslovakia in February 1948, which gave the West a terrible shock and led to the setting up of the Brussels Treaty, the participation of Germany was not contemplated. It was only during the Berlin blockade that the Americans began to ponder the possibility of rearming Germany. Mr. James Warburg, former adviser of the American Administration on German affairs during the war, gives a very interesting account of feelings at that time:

> The real crisis was not in Berlin but in Washington. American policy in Europe was drifting rapidly into a dilemma composed of two alternatives: either the programme for rearming Western Europe would involve the remilitarisation of Western Germany, or else it would turn out to be the most cruel hoax ever perpetrated. If Western Europe was to be placed in a position to defend itself against Russian military attack, there was only one arsenal and one source of manpower which could be employed to bolster France, the Low Countries, Scandinavia and Italy. Unless we remilitarise the Ruhr and draw upon 48,000,000 people in the western zones of Germany, we should be rearming Western Europe merely to fight a delaying action, to be once more overrun and occupied and perhaps eventually to be once more liberated. On the other

hand, if we did rearm Western Germany, what would be the result? [3]

Not unexpectedly, the strongest opposition to any rearmament of Germany came from France: as we know, the French attitude, as well as that of the United States, has undergone a complete change.

The American attitude towards German rearmament could be best illustrated by the testimonial of Mr. Dean Acheson, then Secretary of State, before the Senate Foreign Relations Committee in April 1949, when he said:

> We are very clear that *the disarmament and demilitarisation of Germany must be complete and absolute.*

It was the same Mr. Acheson who, a few months later, was instrumental in drawing up the Petersberg Agreement, signed there on November 24, 1949, between the three High Commissioners and the German Chancellor, Dr. Adenauer, who pledged the young Federal Republic to *maintain strict demilitarisation and to prevent the re-creation of armed forces of any kind.*

It was the same Dr. Adenauer who, a year later, declared in the Bundestag:

> I confirm that I have objected on many occasions to the rearmament of Germany, wanting in that way to express the feelings of the German nation, and above all of German youth. . . .

Soon after the signature of that document the American Secretary of Defence, Johnson, visiting Germany in the company of General Bradley, made the following statement in Frankfurt:

> President Truman said that the United States had no intention to rearm Germany. This is official United States policy with no hedging and no dodging. . . .

Yet, in spite of these statements, reports which reached Paris that American generals, like Bradley and Clay, were

---

[3] *Germany: Key to Peace*, p. 69.

talking of the need to use, in one way or another, the German potential produced serious misgivings in France. It was the opposition of the French National Assembly a few years later which made the European Army still-born because the plan would have involved the revival of German militarism.

However, the idea of German rearmament found a powerful crusader in the person of Mr. Winston Churchill, who, speaking in Parliament in March 1950 as Leader of the Opposition, moved for a secret session, and said " there could be no defence of European frontiers possible without a German contribution."

When Mr. Bevin said that any thought of " arming Germany " was " frightful," Mr. Winston Churchill denied that he had said anything about rearming Germany, but continued:

> I see no reason why the Germans should not aid in the defence of their own country and of Western Europe, nor why British, American, French and German soldiers should not stand in line together on honourable terms of comradeship as a part of a combined system of defence.[4]

The outbreak of war in Korea and the hysterical fear of Russian aggression which swept across Western Europe helped to soften the Western attitude towards German rearmament. At this juncture Dr. Adenauer, who turned out to be a brilliant tactician, began, as Warburg writes:

> . . . playing a very shrewd game. . . . Sensing that there would be now a frantic search for ways and means to hasten up the build-up of West European defences, he began dropping hints that West Germany might, on certain conditions, be willing to contribute to that defence. . . . Openly the Chancellor went no further than to demand a West German police force capable of offsetting the East German " Bereitschaften "—a demand which now encountered much less opposition in France in view of the events in Korea.[5]

---

[4] *Hansard*, 1950, Vol. 473, Col. 155.
[5] *Supra.*, p. 140.

However, the main part in the game was allocated to Dr. Schumacher, the leader of Socialist opposition, who stated that West Germany should not consider contributing to Western defence unless, as Warburg writes:

> (1) At least twenty American divisions were stationed in Germany as a shield behind which the rearmament could be undertaken; (2) Germany was to have its own national army under German command; and (3) the purpose of rearmament was clearly understood to be to defend all of Germany—not just that part of Germany which is under the control of the Western Powers.[6]

How far these words represented Dr. Schumacher's own views or how much they were part of a prearranged move which, by representing Schumacher as an " enfant terrible " in the eyes of the West, made Dr. Adenauer's position easier, we shall never know.

The Soviet reaction, apart from a strong Note protesting against any Western efforts to rearm Germany, was expressed in the resolution of the Conference of the Foreign Ministers of Eastern Europe, in Prague in October 1950, which called for " *withdrawal of all occupation troops* a year after the conclusion of a peace treaty with Germany. . . ."

This was already the second Soviet " indirect " overture; the first one took the form of a similar resolution, approved at the Conference of Foreign Ministers in Warsaw in June 1948. Both of them were ignored by the West. If one compares these two resolutions with the demand put forward later on by Mr. Khrushchev, calling for the dismantling of all American overseas bases, one can see that in those years the price for the reunification of Germany and the liberation of Eastern Europe was very much cheaper than it later became.

The die was now cast; Mr. McCloy, the American High Commissioner in Germany, said after his conference with President Truman in September 1950:

---

[6] *Ibid.*, p. 141.

> In some manner, in some form, the Germans should be
> enabled to defend their own country. . . . If that sounds like
> rearmament, then it is rearmament.

It is worthwhile describing very briefly a few early episodes in German rearmament which show the tactical skill with which the German political leaders took full advantage of the Western quest for manpower for the defence of Europe, in order to restore the position of their own country from the status of a beaten enemy to that of an equal partner.

When General Eisenhower arrived early in January 1951 in Europe to make a survey of the problems he was about to take over as Supreme NATO Commander, he was struck with the divergence of views between France and Germany on the methods of Germany's rearmament.

Whereas the French "Pleven Plan" provided for twenty brigades of 6,000 men each to be integrated into mixed divisions under a non-German command, the German generals Speidel and Heusinger, accompanied by Herr Blank, future Defence Minister, submitted in a secret conversation with the American High Commissioner, Mr. McCloy, a plan which provided for twelve German divisions of 12,000 men each, organised in six army corps, under German command with a German tactical air force.

It was also reported to General Eisenhower that during the elections held in several Länders in Western Germany in the previous autumn, a popular demand had been voiced for equality in command and for a strong shield of Anglo-American troops behind which Germany could rearm. The Social Democrats were the most vociferous and incurred the strong disfavour of the Americans, who preferred the more restrained and accommodating attitude of Dr. Adenauer.

Having acquainted himself with these developments, General Eisenhower recommended the postponement of German rearmament and efforts were renewed to put into effect Pleven's plan of a European Army. But Eisenhower soon realised that, in view of the drain on French contingents, due to the war in Indo-China, and in view of Britain's refusal to participate in the European Army, resort to German manpower on a larger scale was unavoidable.

The Germans were quick to realise that their chances were rapidly improving. When Herr Blank went to Paris to negotiate the details of the Pleven Plan, he declared, as far as Germany was concerned, acceptance of the above-mentioned Speidel-Heusinger plan. Several months later, on February 8, 1958, the Bundestag voted the following conditions, among others, to German participation in a European Army: the return of the Saar to Germany and an equal voice for Germany in NATO decisions. Soon afterwards, a right wing deputy, Herr Eule, speaking in the Bundestag, added to these conditions a demand for restoration to Germany of the 1937 frontiers. These words were preceded a few months earlier by a statement made by Dr. Adenauer in December 1951 in Hanover, when he said:

> Our chief reason for wanting to enter the European Army is to be able to recover our Eastern territories. . . .

We shall not pursue further details of the history of the European Army, which was supposed to allay French fears, nor of the events leading to full German partnership in the Atlantic Alliance: enough has been said to suggest that German rearmament proceeded strictly in accordance with German plans.

As a result of the reversal of Western policy towards the rearmament of Germany, the new West German army is, according to Liddell Hart,

> . . . rapidly becoming the most powerful force in Western Europe. Few people seem to realise that fact or foresee the natural results. . . . In terms of divisions, the new German Army is now the strongest national contingent in NATO. When the twelve divisions are complete, it will be as strong as all the others put together . . . moreover the weight of the

German Army will be all the greater because of its superior state of readiness.[7]

This uneasy situation, of which, as Liddell Hart has justly remarked, too few in the West are fully aware, came, so to speak, as a surprise even to those who had been planning the rearming of Germany. After all, when the decision to rearm Germany was contemplated—after the outbreak of war in Korea—it was planned to integrate German contingents into the projected European Army in units not stronger than brigades, which would have made up into mixed divisions under non-German command.

Furthermore, according to the plans which stipulated the establishment of twelve German divisions, there would have been also fourteen French, five Belgian, two Dutch, four British and five American divisions under SHAPE in Western Europe. One must also remember that, at the NATO Council meeting in Lisbon in 1952, it had been decided that all members of NATO should raise within five years 100 divisions in Western Europe alone. Against this background, the planned twelve German divisions seemed to present no special problem. But, as already noted, the withdrawal of French troops to Indo-China, and later on to North Africa, the cuts in the British contingent in Western Germany, and the melting-away of other NATO troops, changed the situation so that it developed quite at variance with expectations.

Dr. Strauss, the German Defence Minister, in his speech at the Fourth NATO Parliamentary Conference in November 1958, said that the total strength of the Bundeswehr at present is approximately 157,000 men: its peacetime strength, according to planning goals for 1960, will be approximately 350,000 men organised in twelve divisions, making thirty-four brigades: together with the Air Force and the Navy, the total military force would amount to approximately 430,000 men.

---

[7] "The Truth about Adenauer's Army," *Reynolds News*, April 20, 1958.

The method of intake shows only a small preponderance of raw recruits over ex-soldiers of all ranks, including generals. According to Dr. Strauss, out of 250,000 applications from ex-soldiers about 50,000 were accepted, and from some 200,000 applications from young men without previous military service about 75,000 could be drafted. Consequently, this method (undoubtedly based upon lessons learnt of the expansion in similar conditions of the Reichswehr and Wehrmacht), with the Territorial Army added in, would ensure that in case of war the Bundeswehr would easily be able to double, if not treble, its strength. Since all men born between 1926 and 1936 who were not in the army undergo reserve training, the intake amounts to some 150,000–300,000 men yearly. This means that within five years of its existence the Bundeswehr will be able to raise for a war a reserve army well over one million men, with modern war material waiting for them.

In order to make clear the technique of expanding armed forces by using a large percentage of regular soldiers—as was the case with the Reichswehr after the First World War—it is helpful to quote Mr. Schwarzschil's book:

> The German army, theoretically 100,000 men strong and in fact much stronger, had assumed a character different from that of any other army. Ten years before Marshal Foch had vainly recommended that Germany be allowed a conscript army of 200,000 men with one or two years of compulsory service rather than a professional army with twelve years' service. The British and Americans, prejudiced against the very word "conscription," had stubbornly insisted on a professional army. The Marshal's fears proved even more correct than he had foreseen. The 100,000 members of the German army of 1926 were not soldiers: they were 100,000 drill sergeants.[8] . . .
>
> And what was the state of the army? The Reichswehr had never limited itself to 100,000 men as the treaty demanded. General J. Morgan, former member of the Military Control Commission, revealed that as early as 1922 the commission discovered that by an ingenious system of organisation the Reichswehr comprised 250,000 instead of 100,000 men. When

[8] *The World in a Trance*, p. 269.

he made a report to this effect, he received a telegraphic order from Lloyd George to resign, and only Marshal Foch's personal intervention saved him from outright dismissal.[9]

Obviously, the Bundeswehr which, even in peacetime is becoming a formidable force, is a powerful card in the hands of skilful politicians, and Germany certainly has plenty of the latter.

Kennan wrote in January 1959:

> No longer having any great need for the presence of Western garrisons on their territory, possessed themselves of a national armed force which would alone constitute a formidable obstacle to any attack launched by the Soviet forces now in Eastern Germany [the West Germans] will not have that same concern for the general superiority of Soviet ground forces which plays so prominent a part in Western thinking. They will be then free to trade, if they can, the severance of their ties with NATO, a relinquishment of the tactical atomic weapon, acceptance of the present Polish border, and perhaps the assurance of a gradual adjustment in the political and military status of Eastern Germany, for a retirement of Soviet forces beyond the Polish-German frontier and for the privilege of bringing about a general reunification of their country.[10]

A similar view has been expressed by Warburg:

> In our fear of Russia and ignorance of Europe we have pushed and strained to create a so-called " United Europe " as a bulwark of democracy and freedom . . . this weak and fundamentally disunited Little Europe will soon, if we continue to have our way, be dominated by the " new " Germany which we shall have brought into being, supported and rearmed. The one purpose of this " new " Germany will be to regain the lost East Germany. It will seek to accomplish this purpose by any and all means. It may sell out the West and make a deal with Moscow. It may drag or manoeuvre the West into war with Russia if no deal can be made.[11]

His views are especially interesting when he compares the Weimar Republic and the Federal Republic:

9 *Ibid.*, p. 335.
10 " Disengagement Revisited," *Foreign Affairs*, January 1959, pp. 204–205.
11 *Germany : Key to Peace*, p. 6.

As an intimate friend of the late Gustav Stresemann, Adenauer had a thorough schooling in the art of playing off Russia against the West [12];

and in commenting on Professor E. H. Carr's book, *German-Soviet Relations between the Two World Wars, 1919–39*, he writes:

> For the time being the Bonn Republic is in a different position from that of the Weimar Republic. It is, like the Weimar Republic, dependent upon the West for financial assistance, but unlike the Weimar is dependent upon the West—not upon Russia—for its chance to rearm. Once rearmed and with recovery still further advanced, the Bonn Republic will be in a position far more favourable for playing the Stresemann game than that which existed in Stresemann's own time. It is even truer than it was in the 1919–39 period that while German industry must look westward for its capital, it must look eastward for its markets, and—more important—it must look eastward for the reunification of the German nation.[13]

To venture further analogies and comparisons with Stresemann who, in only a few years, owing particularly to his tactics at the Locarno Conference, created a key position for Germany in Europe, so his brilliant pupil, Dr. Adenauer, managed in a few years to lift Germany from the position of a ruined and beaten enemy into the position of an equal and fully fledged partner in the Atlantic Alliance. In both cases the German Chancellors shrewdly played the same game—fear of Russia.

It was thus Russia, especially after the last war, which contributed indirectly to the rebirth of German military might. But it is this same military power, which almost destroyed Russia in the last war, of which Russia must now be apprehensive.

It is a natural reaction to the views of Kennan and Warburg to try to shrug them off as unfair and not corresponding to the real feelings of Germans today. It is quite true that there are many millions of Germans, especially of

[12] *Ibid.*, p. 120.
[13] *Ibid.*, p. 121.

the younger generation, who are content to be good
Europeans: but it is impossible to ignore some very vocal
political organisations, especially among the so-called
" Expellees," which cultivate revisionist tendencies and act
as a pressure group on the Government and Opposition.
According to *Der Deutsche Soldaten Kalender* of 1958, there
are some 1,200 various paramilitary organisations, many of
which are actively engaged in political activities, advocating
the restoration to Germany of the frontiers, not merely of
1937, but of 1914! Obviously, consciousness of increasing
military might adds to these exhilarating dreams a touch of
reality.

The revisionist campaign increased considerably in 1959,
and manifested itself in several public gatherings of former
" Expellees " at which resolutions were passed demanding
not only the return of the frontiers of 1937 and Sudetenland, but of Memel, Danzig and Silesia and some territories
in the West, too. During Whitsun several such meetings
took place in different towns throughout Western Germany:
during such a meeting in West Berlin, organised by the
East Prussian " Expellees," speeches were made extolling the
heroic memories of " the best sons of the German nation
who gave their lives in defence of East Prussia," including
the heroic soldiers of Hitler's Wehrmacht! During a similar gathering in Karlsruhe, the " Expellees " were told not
to give up hope of regaining their homelands in Yugoslavia,
Rumania and Hungary. The peak of these gatherings was
the Congress of " Expellees " in Vienna: some 2,000 delegates participated, including some former close collaborators
of Henlein, Hitler's *Gauleiter* in Sudetenland, who have
obviously in their time been rabid Nazis. The congress
approved the text of a telegram to be sent to Geneva to the
Conference of Four Foreign Ministers demanding the right
to return to their former homelands.

It would take too much space to quote the various books
and articles which are published in ever-increasing numbers

under the auspices of various East European Research Institutes. However, some of them are worth mentioning individually: the monthly *Nation Europa*, published in Coburg, contained an article by J. Gildon called " Do we forget West Prussia? ", stating that Hitler wanted nothing more than the return of Danzig and the right to build an extra-territorial *Autobahn* through Polish territory and that as a result of his peaceful efforts a war was launched by Polish adventurers assisted by the Western Powers." Another publication, *Schlesische Rundschau*, which specialises in stories from former German territories, talks of " our German " towns and places in reference to areas which, except for the last war, were never occupied by the Germans; this publication, as well as many others, dwells extensively on the favourite theme of the German " cultural mission " in the East. According to the quarterly *Deutsche Ostkunde*, during geography lessons in Western Germany, children stick small flags into maps on the places of birth of their ancestors: and the publication continues: " Every German land and province is shown in our classes from the Rhine to the Vistula . . . from the Baltic to Odessa."

A recent publication, *Die Deutschen Trümpfe*, by Johann Barnick, makes remarkable reading: according to the author, the Eastern frontiers of the future German State should run from Kolberg down along the " Curzon Line ": this future State will include, of course, the present States of Austria and Czechoslovakia, and in the south Trieste, with the surrounding area and South Tyrol. In order to achieve these breath-taking goals, the author recommends: (a) rearmament; (b) faith in the Western Allies—for the time being; (c) patience. The author believes that Russia will have to accept such a design as a lesser evil than war.

It is possible, of course, to dismiss Barnick's book as irresponsible rubbish, but it ties up with the conversation— which sounds like something out of a thriller—between one of the most prominent German industrialists, Professor Heinkel, and the British Air Vice-Marshal Bennett:

> When Heinkel drank more and became more talkative, on my question why so many German aircraft designers went voluntarily to Russia at the end of the war, Heinkel said that this was all the result of a "Plan." He said that when the collapse of Germany was drawing nearer a conference was held in the Hartz Mountains with many senior officers and industrialists at which a programme for the period between the surrender and next war was approved. The plan was that defeated Germany would gracefully accept the defeat and would co-operate with the Allies to achieve the most rapid and extensive rehabilitation; when their strength was sufficient they would gradually come more and more into the defence picture and would be willing to share the burden. In sharing that burden they would gradually acquire units of their own and they would grow into a responsible German army and air force.
>
> When these units became sufficiently large, an increasing measure of independence would be gradually obtained until the day arrived when Germany would be able to say: "We are independent, and we will do what we like," and have the military strength to back up her assertions.
>
> After Germany had declared her independence militarily, she would then make a pact with Russia and this great alliance would face the world—the greatest industrial and military power ever known on earth.[14]

After the publication of Air Vice-Marshal Bennett's book a storm broke out in Germany, and an official spokesman did his best to deny Professor Heinkel's utterances, attributing them to drunkenness. But even assuming that Professor Heinkel's tongue was loosened by drink, *in vino* there is supposed to be some *veritas* and he certainly said what many Germans have in mind.

Although the percentage of " Expellees " in the Bundestag is fairly insignificant, this vocal minority still exercises a considerable influence over the Bonn Government, quite out of proportion with its voting strength. This is illustrated by certain recent events:

14 Air Vice-Marshal D. C. T. Bennett, *Pathfinder*, p. 267.

During the first Geneva conference Herr von Brentano put before his Government a suggestion for an exchange of documents between the Federal Republic on the one hand and Poland and Czechoslovakia on the other, containing an undertaking not to use force in their mutual relations. He resumed his initiative during the second Geneva conference, and enlarged his suggestion into a draft to be put before the Governments in Warsaw and Prague. This draft was to propose a joint declaration to renounce force, a non-aggression pact and negotiations for the resumption of diplomatic relations; it would have amounted to a cautious retreat from the so-called " Hallstein Doctrine," by which the Federal Republic does not maintain diplomatic relations with any other countries which have such relations with the Pankow régime. His initiative was approved by the government, but being not only an experienced diplomat but also a shrewd politician Herr von Brentano wished to ensure the support of the " Expellees." Dr. Oberländer, Minister for the " Expellees," and Dr. Krueger, Chairman of their central organisation, declared their agreement but made it dependent upon the attitude of the majority of their members. After a heated debate, under pressure from extremists, the " Expellees " took a negative attitude towards the idea.

As a result of this opposition, one of the politicians of the " Expellees' " organisation—despite the fact that these conversations were of a confidential nature—made a deliberate " leak " and presented von Brentano's plan as an intention to resume diplomatic relations with Poland and Czechoslovakia at the expense of the lost German terri-tories in the east.

In view of the 1961 elections, Dr. Adenauer met a dele-gation of the " Expellees " and decided that it would be wiser to abandon the whole idea. This political skirmish, which ended with the capitulation of the Government to the pressure of the " Expellees," gave them further encourage-ment to intensify their revisionist campaign.

Before closing this chapter, perhaps overloaded with quotations, one more must be added: Mr. Aneurin Bevan, during the debate on Foreign Affairs in Parliament on December 4, 1958, said:

> I now come to foreign affairs debates with increasing depression, because I feel exactly as the House of Commons felt before the war when listening to speech after speech from the Right Hon. Gentleman the Member for Woodford [Sir Winston Churchill]. It was like seeing a film, which one had already seen made, unfolded again, with the inevitability of an ancient Greek drama.
>
> Mr. Khrushchev is quite right when he says in his Note that the increased rearmament of Western Germany is a source of profound alarm to Poland and Russia. It alarms me. It ought to alarm right hon. and hon. gentlemen opposite, if they have learnt anything. . . . Years ago, we on this side of the House were saying that the rearmament of Germany would be not a source of strength to the West but a source of alarm to Poland— and a source of weakness to the whole European system.

And at a Press Conference on January 18, 1959, President Eisenhower stated:

> In its own self-interest, the United States recognises that it would be unwise to build up German strength in a way which might legitimately allow Russia to consider Germany as a menace to her own security.

4

The Alternative Solutions

WE have tried in previous chapters to examine the *status quo* and to demonstrate the precarious nature of the military stalemate which support it.

Of this stalemate Kissinger has well stated:

> Of course, stalemates have occurred frequently in the history of warfare. Normally they have been brought about by the emergence of a balance between offence and defence on the battlefield. The distinguishing feature of the current use of the term is that it refers not to a balance on the battlefield, but to a calculus of risks. With each side possessing the capability of inflicting catastrophic blows on the other war is said to be no longer a rational course of action. To be sure, even if a nuclear stalemate does exist, it would not make for stability in the present volatile state of technology, much less for a sense of harmony.[1]

We have also tried to present the dangers involved in the present state of affairs; as far as Europe is concerned, the dangers of the *status quo* boil down to the perpetuity of the division of Germany, the enslavement of Eastern Europe and, above all, to the rising military might of Germany.

The *status quo* turns a temporary solution, the halt which was reached in Europe in 1945, when the troops of both sides met on either side of the river Elbe, into a permanent one; in short, it transforms a military demarcation line into a political frontier. Raymond Aron puts the point clearly:

> Wherever a frontier is identical with a military demarcation line, it is almost impossible peacefully to alter it. . . . Though militarily they may lose their value, frontiers remain a political

[1] *Nuclear Weapons and Diplomacy*, p. 86.

issue of the first importance. . . . As long as these two Germanies are occupied, the one by the Russians and the other by American troops, the course of history remains, so to speak, invisible. The diplomatic game is reduced to a minimum.[2]

It is misleading to call this freezing of the existing state of affairs a *status quo*, since Russia has been able to integrate a large area into both her military and economic systems. Despite trouble in Poland and Hungary, the Communist puppet régimes have been able—due to various measures—to strengthen their grip on their armed forces and to get rid of unreliable factions.

Equally, in the economic sphere the integration of the economies of the countries of Eastern Europe into the economic system of Russia is progressing according to plan, and what is more important, their industries are working increasingly for export markets in the so-called non-committed area, thus taking part in the Soviet economic drive in that area.

These trends confirm the Soviet view, quoted by Walter Lippmann after his conversation with Mr. Khrushchev, that for the Russians the *status quo* is not something static but part of the working out of their plans.

Finally, the *status quo*, being based upon military stalemate, leads to increased reliance on German rearmament: this in turn portends another danger, German military power, which we have already examined and to which we shall later return.

We must now examine, one by one, the alternatives to the *status quo*.

War

Lord Salisbury once said: " war is always the result of bad diplomacy." These words have a special application to war in our nuclear age, which makes another celebrated

2 *On War, Atomic Weapons and Global Diplomacy*, pp. 89–91.

saying, " war is a continuation of politics," somewhat out of date.

There is no need to go into details of the destruction which all-out nuclear war would bring, nor to foretell the damage which our civilisation would suffer. But in spite of the growing understanding of the horrors of thermo-nuclear war, and even of the dangers of continuing atomic tests which pollute the atmosphere by increasing radiation and the load of Strontium, the arms race goes relentlessly on, and, of course, neither side dares to abandon it: humanity, as Oppenheimer has put it, begins to resemble two scorpions locked in a bottle with their poisonous tails raised, neither daring to make the first move.

But it is convenient at this point to make clear that this book holds no brief for unilateral disarmament of the Bertrand Russell or King-Hall variety. On the contrary, it is *imbalance in armaments* which has twice been one of the main reasons for war in this century between Germany and Britain. Before the First World War, Kaiser Wilhelm was assured by his General Staff that his land forces, in spite of the Royal Navy, would secure victory for him: Hitler acted on similar information.

The present arms race has become for the West a dire necessity, imposed by the Soviet policy of expansion and control.

Unfortunately, Western strategy—as opposed to Soviet strategy, which is much more flexible—has become increasingly dependent upon the use of weapons of mass destruction, thus making war an instrument of mutual suicide.

The evolution of Western strategy seems, briefly, to have been as follows. At the start, when NATO was having its teething troubles, Western strategy was a balanced one, resting upon co-operation between the conventional forces, to which were allocated the task of fighting a delaying manoeuvre, and S.A.C. Even at the time of the Lisbon Conference in 1952, when it was decided to raise some 100 divisions, sixty in peace-time and forty as reserves, that concept of a balanced strategy still held good.

Unfortunately, partly due to the influence of the Pentagon and partly to the error of Western military planners in adopting as a prototype for Continental divisions a heavy American division of the 1944–45 period, the cost of raising more divisions to implement the decisions of the Lisbon meeting became astronomical: higher, certainly, than any national economy could possibly bear. It was Churchill who at that time said: "No security at the cost of bankruptcy."

It is not for the first time that Western military planners have erred in their preparations for war. In this respect the history of the years preceding the last war is pathetic. The pattern of Blitzkrieg was becoming increasingly evident, but the Western military leaders still thought in terms of the 1914–18 War. The result of such myopia was the disastrous campaign in France in 1940, where:

> *The German Army was actually inferior to the Allied Armies not only in numbers of divisions but particularly in the number of tanks.* While the combined Anglo-French forces had about 4,000 tanks, the German Army could field only 2,800. Nor did we have any preponderance in quality. . . . The Allied military leaders, and particularly the French, still thought in terms of the linear tactics of the First World War. . . .[3]

Captain B. H. Liddell Hart wrote:

> Anyone who really understood this new tempo could easily have foiled the German break-through, for the Allies at the start had six mechanised divisions at hand (with two more available) and seventeen motorised divisions against the German ten mechanised and seven motorised. Both the break-in and break-through were achieved by the small fractions of mechanised divisions before the mass of the German infantry divisions, marching on foot and with horse transport, came into action.[4]

---

[3] There is much authority for this proposition. The particular source used is *Panzer Battles*, by Major-General F. von Mellenthin, p. 12.
[4] "Defence Against the Odds," *Manchester Guardian*, June 16 and 17, 1959.

After the war, the American mistake in not supplying enough arms to the South Korean forces resulted in the initial defeat of the American forces. However, the most strikingly inaccurate assessment occurred in the Suez affair. The fighting quality of the Israeli troops was underestimated and the worth of the Egyptian forces overestimated, in particular the value of their air force. This error of judgment resulted in a heavy and cumbersome plan, almost a replica of the Normandy landing, with the difference that at Normandy the Allies had to deal with a tough enemy under the orders of first-class generals like Rommel and Rundstedt, and in Egypt with a half-trained rabble. Instead of a lightning operation conducted by airborne troops, supported by a task force of aircraft carriers which would have taken the defence by surprise, an elephantine operation was mounted and eventually launched against rising public resentment at home and all over the world.

And today a wrong assessment is again being made. Western military planners, basing their strategy on a comparative estimate of forces, included in the *Ordre de Bataille* of the enemy, the satellite forces, without taking into consideration the possibility of an armed uprising in Eastern Europe in the event of open, major Soviet aggression. This basically false assessment was strengthened by the signature of the Warsaw Pact in May 1955. But this is a compulsory alliance, the precarious nature of which was exposed a year later by events in Poland and Hungary; it is in no way comparable to the Atlantic Alliance. The same yardstick or criterion has been wrongly applied by the Western military planners to two quite different sorts of alliances.

In Chapter 3 this view was supported by extracts from the official document, *Report on the Present State of European Security*, stating that Western Europe and, in particular, the Central Sector, can be attacked by fifty to sixty divisions, including some twenty odd satellite divisions "of varying reliability." What in fact this boils down to is that twenty Soviet divisions, deployed in Eastern Germany, would be used for a major offensive against Western Europe on a front of some 500 miles. The remaining twenty divisions would be reserve and administrative forces.

Since, according to the same document, the number of NATO divisions would amount to fifteen, which " can be considered combat-ready," the ratio of force, 20 : 15, would amount to, say, 1·2 : 1, which is really almost parity; and this assessment does not take into consideration all the advantages which are at the disposal of a defence force operating on its own ground. Furthermore, as the Report adds:

> . . . This overall figure will increase when more German divisions and the second Netherlands division come into being and when the French divisions return from Algeria.

A comparison of the probable figure of twenty Soviet divisions to be used in a hypothetical offensive against Western Europe on a frontage of 500 miles, with the figure of twenty-nine German divisions, which were used in 1940 against Belgium as a feint manoeuvre, and forty-four divisions deployed in the Ardennes for a single thrust against the 1st French Army,[5] supports the view expressed on various occasions by Montgomery—that in the present circumstances the Russians do not visualise any major overland aggression in Europe.

Unfortunately, the consequence, first, of the failure of the Atlantic Alliance to provide the number of troops which was agreed at Lisbon and, secondly, of the wrong assessment as to the alleged Soviet overwhelming superiority, was that SHAPE had no option but to rely increasingly on atomic, and later, on thermo-nuclear weapons.

The erosion of the NATO land forces, to which French commitments in Indo-China and North Africa contributed very considerably, continued until the NATO "shield" degenerated gradually into a " trip-wire " whose only function is to create a *casus belli atomici*; the drift towards

---

[5] See David Divine, *The Nine Days of Dunkirk*, p. 25.

preparation only for a nuclear war had become almost irreversible.

Furthermore, in view of the horrifying nature of thermo-nuclear war, Western strategy has, simultaneously with the melting down of the " shield " to a " trip-wire," degenerated from a constructive strategy of defence into a negative strategy of deterrence.

We must be clear what we mean by the term " deter-rent." General Le May, General Commanding S.A.C., has defined it thus:

> A deterrent force is one that is large enough and efficient enough that no matter what the enemy force does, either offensively or defensively, he will still receive a quantity of bombs or explosive force that is more than he is willing to accept. Therefore he never starts a war.[6]

Unfortunately, the Russians seem inclined to believe that they will be able to stomach a degree of devastation which would, perhaps, for some Western countries be unbear-able.[7] The booklet, *Defence of Great Britain*, written in 1954, soon after details about the H-bomb became known, makes pertinent reading:

> Great Britain is the most inviting, the most vulnerable and the most easily located target on earth. . . . Over eighty per cent. of British industry and over a quarter of her population are contained in the first ten major towns. . . . Fifty per cent. of her shipping enters six ports. Virtually all her armaments industries and machine-tool manufacturing centres are centred in five towns. . . . If it comes to an atomic slogging match, ten H-bombs cast down on our ten major cities would wreak infinitely greater damage to this country than the combined United States Air Force and the Royal Air Force were able to achieve in five years of continuous bombardment of Germany.[8]

To this must be added the findings of the special sub-committee of the Congress Joint Committee on Atomic Energy, which heard expert views of the results to be

---

[6] Quoted by Kissinger, *Nuclear Weapons and Foreign Policy*, p. 96.
[7] See Garthoff, *Soviet Strategy in the Nuclear Age*, p. 91.
[8] Connor and Jacobson, *Defence of Great Britain*, p. 4.

expected from a nuclear attack. According to the dispatch of the Washington correspondent of *The Times*, it appeared that:

> An attack on the United States with atomic and hydrogen weapons would kill about 49 million Americans. Nearly half of them could be expected to die instantly, killed by blast or incinerated in the fire-storms caused by the explosions: the remainder would linger for perhaps a few hours or days, dying of their injuries or from the effects of radioactive fall-out. Another twenty million would be injured, but might recover.[9]

In view of the prospects offered by a thermonuclear war, the only hope is that the strategy of deterrence will really be able to fulfil its fundamental task, namely, to deter the Russians from aggression. But what happens if the deterrent fails to deter?

In a previous chapter, the precarious nature of the balance of mutual terror was emphasised. The growing understanding of this fact, or rather process, has led to an agonising re-appraisal of the whole problem, both in Russia and, above all, in the United States, and the conclusions of this mental exercise are fatal to the whole concept of a *status quo* based upon a balance of terror. The logical conclusions to be drawn from the uncertainty of the balance are, first, that *one side, fearing that it is losing the race, may be driven to a desperate decision to launch a preventive war*, in order to prevent a situation in which she would be completely outgunned by the enemy; secondly, the side which has achieved an overwhelming superiority, or a technical break-through, may also decide to deliver the first blow, in order to paralyse the enemy's counter force. The strategy of the " first-strike "—for which a new word has been coined, " pre-emptive strategy "—has become a subject of serious study in Russia.

In his recent comprehensive book, *War and the Soviet Union*, in the chapter on " Surprise and the Initiation of War," Herbert S. Dinerstein quotes Marshal Rotmistrov, a

[9] June 25, 1959.

leading Soviet military writer who, in several of his articles, emphasises the importance of strategic surprise. For example, in an article, " On the Role of Surprise in Contemporary War," [10] Marshal Rotmistrov writes:

> Surprise attack, employing atomic and hydrogen weapons and other modern means of conflict, now takes on new forms and is capable of leading to significantly greater results than in the past wars. . . . Surprise attack with the massive employment of new weapons can cause the rapid collapse of a government whose capacity to resist is low as a consequence of radical faults in social and economic structure and also as a consequence in an unfavourable geographic position.[11]

Dinerstein makes the following comments:

> Rotmistrov felt that surprise attack played an important part in the strategy of the United States and Great Britain, and that American and British leaders would expect, by bombing the deep rear of the Soviet Union to put her war facilities and industrial centres out of commission, to paralyse transportation and to demoralise the population. . . . Rotmistrov brought to its logical conclusion the discussion and controversy of 1953–54. If surprise attack could indeed determine, or even seriously affect, the outcome of a war it was even more necessary to surprise and avoid being surprised than in the past. A surprise attack could be frustrated if the enemy were himself surprised as he prepared to strike: " The duty of the Soviet armed forces is not to permit an enemy surprise attack on our country and in the event of an attempt to accomplish one, not only to repel the attack successfully but also to deal counter-blows, or even pre-emptive surprise blows, of terrible destructive force." [12]

It is interesting to note that Soviet military doctrine is attaching increasing importance to the " forces-in-being." In the chapter, " The Conduct of a Nuclear War," Dinerstein writes:

> As time passed, increasing emphasis was placed on the importance of forces-in-being deployed for immediate action, an obvious consequence of the doctrine that the first phase of nuclear war can be decisive. Colonel Petrov, in an article

[10] *Voiennaja Mysl*, No. 2, February 1955, p. 14.
[11] Quoted in Dinerstein, *op. cit.*, pp. 187–188.
[12] Dinerstein, *op. cit.*, p. 186.

published in May 1958, pointedly emphasised the importance of
forces-in-being. . . .   Forces-in-being now have the same
importance that mobilisable potential once possessed. . . .

Although according to Col. Petrov the fate of a war is determined by the fierce clash of the armed forces and although the
most useful definition of war potential is forces-in-being, mobilisation after the outbreak of hostilities and reserves are accorded
great importance. . . . The novelty of [Col. Petrov's] presenta-
tion is this: whereas formerly victory was to be won mainly by
resources, arms and troops mobilised after the outbreak of
hostilities, now victory depends mainly on forces-in-being
properly deployed to deal with (or perhaps deal) a surprise
nuclear attack.[13]

In view of the growing understanding on both sides of
the Iron Curtain of the importance of forces-in-being and
their role in the first phase of war, as well as of the enormous difficulties in putting into effect plans of mobilisation,
the present ratio of force in Europe does not warrant the
obsession in the West with the danger of a Soviet surprise
attack on the ground. The real danger, and on an increasing scale, lies in the propensity of military pundits in the
Soviet Union—and perhaps in the Pentagon—to ponder the
advisability of a pre-emptive strategy.

The strategy of deterrence leaves to the West the very
limited choice between an atomic holocaust or capitulation, between, in effect, everything or nothing. The effect
is that, in point of fact, nobody in the West really believes
that such a war will ever take place. After all, nobody
wants to fight it; the idea seems incredible. Now the
obvious result of such an inner conviction is that, for all
practical purposes, almost nothing or—in order not to
offend Civil Defence organisations—very little is being done,
in view of the amount of devastation which could result
from an all-out war, to protect the civilian population; still
less to organise the dispersal of industry all over the country.

A *total* war, then, certainly cannot be regarded as a
practical alternative to the *status quo*.

[13] Dinerstein, *op. cit.*, p. 221.

However, our analysis would be incomplete if we omitted the evolution in military thinking on both sides of the Curtain concerning limited nuclear war and conventional warfare.

One of the most striking phenomena of this evolution is the growing criticism of the Great Deterrent as well as of the strategy which depends on it. The *Report on the Present State of European Security*, to which we have already referred, contains strong criticism of official British doctrine:

> The NATO shield in Europe is not a trip wire. This theory has by now been proved wrong. The ground forces have much more important functions. The 1958 British White Paper on Defence described only their role in the event of all-out war when it is proclaimed in paragraph 12 that the role of the Allied defence forces in Europe will be to hold the front for the time needed to allow the effect of the nuclear counter-offensive to make itself felt.[14]

The Dutch Defence Minister, in disagreeing with the tendency to increase the nuclear potential at the expense of the shield, gives a correct appreciation of the situation:

> If the military effort of NATO were to be aimed exclusively in that direction the possibility of combating aggression by conventional means might be so restricted that nuclear weapons would have to be used immediately under conditions where the use of such extreme measures would not be justified.[15]

In a recent article Mr. Kissinger wrote:

> A basic cause for Allied disunity is the weakness of NATO and the ambiguity of its strategy. It is no doubt correct that we need not match the Soviets in *every* strategic category. But we are reaching a situation, where we are not keeping up in *any* category. Against the background of that weakness, declarations of firmness ring hollow, and the sense of insecurity of our allies must inevitably increase. . . .
>
> Two sets of measures are therefore required: (1) an immediate strengthening of the United States overall deterrent . . .

---

[14] p. 7.
[15] *Statement on Defence Questions, 1957–1958.*

(2) a common effort to devise a defence of Europe which does not have the aspect of suicide. . . .

A defensive alliance which cannot protect the territory of its members without destroying them is immensely brittle. There is no reason why the United States and Western Europe, whose combined resources, human and material, still far exceeding those of the U.S.S.R., cannot create an adequate force for local defence of Europe. The obstacle is not capability but lack of will.[16]

Certainly the Russians, contrary to the Americans—

. . . do *not* regard nuclear and thermonuclear weapons as *all-decisive* . . . the Soviets retain the flexibility of a strategy without the use of the intercontinental thermonuclear striking force, and maintain the strong ground and tactical aviation forces to fight such wars. . . .

The Soviet view that future wars, general and local, *may or may not* include the use of nuclear weapons, was stated most authoritatively by Marshal Zhukov in early 1957.[17]

These few thoughts lead us on to the dangerous ground of the controversy raging on both sides of the Curtain about the Graduated Deterrent and limited nuclear war; without going into the details of this mental exercise, we may say that both General Norstad and, some time ago, Marshal Zhukov, doubted whether it was possible to draw a line between the use of the Graduated Deterrent in the form of tactical atomic weapons and the use of the ultimate weapon. Yet, at the same time, both General Norstad and the Soviet High Command seem to believe that tactical atomic weapons are becoming a part of the organic armament of conventional forces.

It would seem that the truth lies somewhere in the middle; it will probably be possible, without danger of sparking off an all-out war, to wage a limited nuclear war on the peripheries fighting with limited means for limited objectives. On the other hand, it seems very unlikely that

---

[16] " As Urgent as the Moscow Threat," *New York Magazine*, March 8, 1959.
[17] Garthoff, *supra cit.*, pp. 100, 101, 102.

a limited nuclear war in Europe could remain limited for long.

In view of this very real danger, it is rather difficult to understand West German inhibitions against any suggestion for the " denuclearisation " of a large area in Europe which would at least prevent Germany from becoming an atomic cemetery. The arguments put forward by West German politicians in favour of the equipment of German troops with atomic weapons, although of course couched in military terms, have a very strong political flavour; they have much to do with political ambitions and prestige, but little with the strategy of defence. According to recent press reports the small island of Montebello in the Pacific, where the first British H-bomb was exploded in 1954, is still dangerously radioactive. If things come to a war, Germany will be the first main battlefield. Whatever the result of such a war, Germany would remain for many years to come a radio-active desert.

It would appear, after all, as Liddell Hart has said, that:

> . . . the safest course of all in defence would be to rely on conventional forces using purely conventional weapons. . . . Now that the Russians are matching America in nuclear weapons, the paradoxical consequence is to revive the danger of invasion in a conventional way.[18]

And Raymond Aron writes:

> Once more, common sense and public opinion rebel against this military doctrine which threatens each time to force the West into a choice between capitulation or suicide. . . . The layman persists in attaching importance to the numbers of soldiers under arms, even though the experts continue to harp on the futility of these remnants of a bygone age. There is no alternative to peace, reiterated President Eisenhower, who agrees with his advisers that a war between the great Powers would be thermonuclear war. But the chorus of the simple and the wise comes echoing back to him: should we not maintain a substitute for thermonuclear war?[19]

---

[18] *Basic Problems of the Defence of Europe, supra cit.,* p. 13.
[19] Aron, *supra cit.,* p. 40.

Obviously, a conventional war, even on a major scale, would still be a better and safer proposition than an atomic holocaust. Equally, a limited nuclear war, if the species of arms to be used could be kept under control so as to prevent a slide into an all-out war, would also be a better alternative.

At any rate, both these forms of war could provide much more "elbow room" both for a flexible defence strategy and for a constructive diplomatic policy.

Again Mr. H. Kissinger's penetrating views throw light on this subject:

> Reliance on all-out war not only reduces the credibility of our deterrent but also dooms us to a fundamentally irrational diplomacy. . . . In the era of nuclear plenty, the defence of Europe can no longer rest on the threat of all-out war alone." [20]

He has support in the statement in the *Report on European Security*, by Mr. Mulley, M.P., Rapporteur, " As credibility as to its use diminishes, so the effect of the strategic deterrent loses force." [21] Kissinger continues:

> The line of demarcation between limited war and all-out war in Europe need not be determined in the abstract. The stronger the local forces of NATO the less likely it will be that the Soviet Union will be tempted to adventure. The more effective the military establishment on the Continent, the larger must be the Soviet attack designed to overcome it. The more the required effort approaches the scale of all-out war, the clearer the challenge to our security and the more plausible our overall deterrent. In short, as the horrors of all-out war multiply and cripple the will to resort to it, the minimum objective of the forces in Europe must be to raise the scale of the Soviet effort required to defeat them to a level that can leave no doubt about its ultimate objective. In the age of atomic plenty a capability for a local defence is required to give validity to the over-all deterrent.[22]

General Norstad's insistence on the number of thirty divisions, so as to make the forces in Europe under his

---

[20] " In Search of Stability," *Foreign Affairs*, July 1959, p. 546.
[21] Submitted on behalf of the Committee on Defence and Armaments, Document 128, p. 3.
[22] " In Search of Stability," *Foreign Affairs*, July 1959, p. 547.

command a real shield, able to hold even a major conventional attack, seems to signal on the one hand a step forward in military thinking, and on the other hand a retreat from the rigid strategy of deterrence. His ideas are finding also growing understanding and support both in Britain, especially in Labour Party circles, as well as on the Continent.

This trend in military thinking suggests also the possibility of a new approach towards the *status quo*.

What is quite clear is that any war, whether conventional or nuclear, into which the West and Russia may slip by miscalculating the intentions of the other side, or in implementation of the reckless policy of preventive war, or of its even worse version, invented in the Soviet Union, pre-emptive war, or by pursuing a stupid policy, will be a catastrophe.

Objective research into the history of the First and Second World Wars shows that both were the result of miscalculations: Germany never wanted to fight a full-scale war, but hoped to win easily a limited conflict. If things come to a Third World War, it will only be as the result of miscalculation or stupidity. As a *calculated* policy, war is no alternative to the *status quo*.

Re-unified Germany, Allied with the Soviet Union

This is an alternative which undoubtedly once was—and perhaps still is—an integral part of the Soviet plans for Europe.

A political and military alliance, regardless of the colour of German banners, between Germany and Russia was a reality before the last two wars, and certainly a similar situation was, *mutatis mutandis*, contemplated again by Stalin and also by his successors in the Kremlin.

The history of German-Soviet relations gives valuable

food for thought to Western statesmen. Thus, Dallin
wrote in 1942:

> . . . before the revolution of 1917, Germany had a special place
> in the Bolshevist philosophy. . . .

After the revolution,

> . . . staking everything on Germany became the first principle
> of the Russian Grand Strategy of world revolution. . . . Back-
> ward Russia and advanced Germany would together create the
> first socialist structure capable of survival.[23]

This was the Communist "Schlieffen Plan" for world
revolution. Furthermore, Lenin wrote quite plainly that:

> The principal link in the chain of revolution is the German
> link, and the success of world revolution depends more upon
> Germany than upon any other country.[24]

A similar view has been expressed by a prominent
American, Paul Nitze, Director of the Foreign Policy
Association:

> The history of the Soviet Party in Russia and its attitude
> towards foreign relations in general have been deeply moulded
> by their historic experience with the German question. These
> go back to the early days of Lenin's seizure of power. He and
> many of his associates thought that the Russian revolution was
> of minor importance to the Communist movement in com-
> parison to the German Communist revolution which they
> anticipated would shortly follow. Their initial experience with
> foreign relations was with the negotiations of the Brest-Litowsk
> Treaty. Their first collaboration with a non-Communist country
> was with Germany. With General Seekt they developed secret
> arrangements for the manufacture of armaments and training
> of military cadres by Germany in Russia in circumvention of
> the provisions of the Treaty of Versailles. Their first diplomatic
> relations were with Germany. These led to the Rapallo agree-
> ment. In 1939 they negotiated the Hitler-Stalin Pact which led
> to World War II. In 1941 they felt the full force of German
> military power in Hitler's attack. As a result of these experi-
> ences, the Communist leadership has consistently given full

---

[23] Dallin, *Russia and Post-War Europe*, pp. 50–52.
[24] Lenin, *Report on Tactics*.

weight, and perhaps excess weight, to the importance of the German problem.[25]

Unfortunately, Poland lay as a barrier on the road to Germany and an obstacle to the realisation of the ambitious Soviet plans; when the Soviet troops marched in July 1920 towards Warsaw, Trotsky stated openly: " We will give decisive battle to the troops of the Entente on the Rhine." At that time, as after the last war, the conquest of Poland was not a primary aim of the Soviet Union, since Poland held only a secondary role in Soviet plans. As Dallin wrote:

> If Warsaw fell Soviet troops would have reached the German border, a German-Soviet Government would have been formed and kept in readiness and Communist and semi-Communist forces inside Germany would have been able, in view of the widespread dissatisfaction with the terms of the Versailles Treaty—so it was reasoned in Moscow—to overthrow the weak government in power.[26]

Marshal Pilsudski's victory in August 1920 completely frustrated the Soviet schemes and for nineteen subsequent years Poland prevented fully fledged Soviet-German military co-operation. The history of 1920 and 1939 is a memento and a warning for today when Soviet troops are on Polish soil.

The history of German-Soviet relations is worth dwelling on:

> The rapprochement of the two nations, both outcasts from the family of nations, was cemented by the Treaty of Rapallo in 1922. This was the start of close economic and military co-operation. Their treaty of commerce, signed in 1925, was presumed to serve as a working model for subsequent arrangements between the capitalist and socialist camps. By signing the Locarno Treaty in 1925 and negotiating for entry into the League of Nations in 1926, Germany seemed to reorient her policy in favour of the Western Powers. But she immediately

---

[25] Speech at the Third Annual Meeting of the Institute of United States Foreign Policy, February 21, 1959.
[26] Dallin, *supra cit.*, p. 54.

propitiated the Bolsheviks with the 1926 Treaty of Amity, by which Russia was assured that German soil would never serve for the passage of a League army in execution of Article 16 of the Covenant. . . . Germany aided Russia to emerge from quarantine, and at the same time used her as a club to shake in the direction of Britain and France.[27]

These views coincide remarkably with those of Dallin:

German Governments were invariably convinced that close ties with the eastern colossus added weight to any negotiations and bargaining by Germany with France and England. Co-operation with the Soviet Union became a fixed concept of German policy.

Such a policy admirably suited the Soviet Union:

As seen by the Soviet Government, the object of its close co-operation with Germany was to create a strong counterweight to the French and British mastery on the Continent.[28]

When, in the early thirties, Soviet Russia began emerging as a great Power, German military circles thought it worth while to increase their collaboration with Russia. Heiden put the position succinctly:

On the German side the object of understanding was: with Russia against the Versailles. And on the Russian side: with Germany against Western capitalism.[29]

The advent to power of the Nazis in 1933 did not at first change Moscow's policy towards Germany; in spite of Hitler's hostile tirades, and the revelations of *Mein Kampf*, the Soviet leaders on various occasions professed their desire for continued good relations with Germany.

The Molotov-Ribbentrop pact of 1939 merely restored the familiar pattern of Soviet-German relations: it was only for a short period that this pattern had been broken when Litvinov tried to steer Soviet foreign policy Westwards.

The German aggression in June 1941 was a bitter disappointment for Stalin, and his right hand man, Molotov.

---

[27] Bruce C. Hooper, "Narkomindel and Comintern," *Foreign Affairs*, July 1941.
[28] Dallin, *supra cit.*, p. 75.   [29] Heiden, *One Man against Europe*, p. 116.

And yet, even during Russia's most difficult days, Stalin never (in his public speeches) condemned the German people but only Hitler.

At the same time, when Russia's Western allies had no other ambitions but to defeat Hitler, Russia, in the line of her traditional long-term policy, was grooming a potential government for post-war Germany. Indeed, some members of the " Free Germany Committee " and of the " Bund der deutschen Offiziere " emerged immediately after the end of the war in Eastern Germany, playing an important role in the administration of the Soviet zone, in the police (which was formed the next day after the armistice) and later on in the armed forces.

It was on those Germans who had been converted to the Communist creed that the Russians relied—and still do—in their plans to expand their influence in post-war Germany.

The battle for Germany began immediately after the war. In point of fact, the opening shots had already been fired over the wartime conference tables when the leaders of the West and Stalin were shaping the " new order for Europe." The situation in Europe, with Communist parties everywhere—and especially in ruined Germany—seemed to be favourable for the cautious realisation of Soviet plans : in addition, the over-hasty Western demobilisation, which squandered the greatest military potential in history, left Western Europe open to Soviet aggression, with Fifth Columns waiting in every Western country for the appearance of the Red Army. Dallin wrote in 1942 with exceptional foresight :

> Should stabilised political relations fail to be quickly estab-
> lished in post-war Europe, and should Germany, for instance,
> become a scene of stormy popular movements, then the old
> cherished dreams of a great Soviet coalition from Vladivostok
> to Aachen are certain to awaken and the old ideas, put aside
> many years ago, may be revived.[30]

[30] Dallin, *supra cit.*, p. 218.

In those schemes armed forces in Eastern Germany undoubtedly played a considerable role, and the Russians proceeded to create them almost the day after the war ended. According to a French expert, R. J. Boutard, the " People's Police " (*Volkspolizei*) was already established on June 3, 1945, and by September next year its strength amounted to 50,000 men; formations of so-called " Barracked Police " (*Kasernierte Volkspolizei*), an equivalent of regular armed forces, were set up in June 1948, and in September 1949 a mission consisting of 150 generals and senior army officers, under General Rentsch, left for Russia to attend Soviet military exercises and lectures at the Soviet Military Academy in Moscow and at Privolsk, near Saratov.[31] At that time the rearmament of Western Germany was not even contemplated.

Yet, in spite of the overwhelming Soviet superiority at that time, with thirty Soviet divisions in Eastern Germany and huge land forces in Western Russia (only very slowly being demobilised) against a completely disarmed West, Stalin was too careful to risk a major war over Germany. The main reason for his hesitation was probably fear, not of an atom bomb but of a mass uprising in Eastern Europe, which was then in a state of turmoil and confusion; in the prevailing circumstances, the uprising would have spread first of all to Eastern Germany, the contemplated base for Soviet operations against the West.

Furthermore, Stalin must have realised that Western Germany would never accept Communist rule, even imposed by the Soviet bayonets, because memories of horrors perpetrated by the Red Army in its advance into Eastern Germany in the last stages of the war were too fresh and vivid to be forgotten.

However, encouraged by the February coup in Czecho-slovakia, Stalin took the risk of imposing a blockade on Berlin : this was, however, a " calculated risk," because the

[31] *L'Armée en Allemagne Orientale*, pp. 32–36.

blockade was carefully not called a "blockade." It was—as far as Russia was concerned—simply a matter of "technical difficulties," which could as easily be resolved, if necessary. We have already pointed out that the policy of "brinkmanship" is foreign to Soviet policy; where, for instance, Russia entangled herself, although indirectly, in the Korean war, it was only because she miscalculated American intentions.

The real reason for the blockade became clear when Marshal Sokolovsky, a few days after its imposition, declared that it would immediately be lifted if the governments of the West abandoned their plans for a separate West German Government, clearly foreshadowed by the resolutions adopted at the meeting of the Council of Western Foreign Ministers in London on November 25, 1947.

The Russians took advantage of the mistakes which the West committed during the war in the settling of the essential problems of post-war occupation in Germany. General Lucius D. Clay has expressed astonishment that in the plan for three-zone arrangement, proposed in the European Advisory Commission late in 1943 by the British delegate, Sir William Strang, supported by the American delegate, Ambassador Winant, no attempt was made to have the western boundary of the Soviet zone run through Berlin instead of 100 miles west of the capital.[32] Although the division of Berlin was envisaged from the start, it never seems to have occurred to the British and American representatives that the Western zones should be contiguous to the Western sectors of Berlin. Equally, as General Clay comments, no provision was made for a corridor of communication between the Western zones and the Western sectors of Berlin.

Professor Philip E. Mosely, of Columbia University, former political adviser to Ambassador Winant, has said

---

[32] Clay, *Decision on Germany*, pp. 26–27.

that the War Department in Washington took the view that the matter of communications between the Western zones and Berlin was a purely military matter and no concern of the European Advisory Commission.[33] At any rate, as Warburg rightly remarked in *Germany, Key to Peace*, a clear agreement with the Russians about this matter could easily have been secured by holding up the withdrawal of American troops from that part of the Russian zone which they had liberated. It seems that the Americans at that time did not want to raise the matter in order, as General Clay remarked, " not to offend the Russians."

By imposing a blockade on Berlin, Stalin wanted to compel the West to agree to the Soviet plan for a Four-Power Government in Germany, which in his view would gradually lead to Communist infiltration into the projected Central German Government, thus preparing the ground for a repetition of the coup in Czechoslovakia. It was, indeed, due only to General Clay and to the Berlin Burgo-master, Professor Reuter, that the West had the courage to face the Soviet challenge. Even so, the decision of an air-lift was only a compromise and an evasion of the *direct* Soviet challenge.

If the West had taken the risk of sending an armed convoy, Stalin, in spite of the numerical superiority of his conventional forces, would have retreated before the double threat of an American A-bomb and the danger, if war had broken out, of a mass uprising in Eastern Europe. A Soviet retreat would have been a heavy defeat for Soviet prestige and diplomacy with far-reaching implications in Europe.

The Berlin blockade, which, for all practical purposes, put an end to the era of wartime co-operation with Russia, opened the eyes of public opinion in the West to the real intentions of Soviet Russia; it marked the beginning of the cold war, and led to the policy of containment and of

---

[33] " The Occupation of Germany: New Light on How the Zones were Drawn," *Foreign Affairs*, July 1950, p. 580.

military blocks. Again, Dallin showed a remarkable gift
for prophecy:

> As soon as one of the great states of Europe enters upon a
> course of expansion at the end of the war, whether impelled by
> high purposes or by bad ones, and whether the expansion is
> open or veiled, that state will inevitably contribute to the forma-
> tion of international coalitions directed against itself, which will
> at the same time provoke a rapid restoration of the military
> power of Germany.[34]

The Soviet Note on Berlin of November 27, 1958, was
the opening of the second round in the struggle for Berlin
and consequently for Germany, although in circumstances
very much different from those of 1948. In accordance with
Russia's usual policy of indirect aggression and action by
proxy, an important role in this new scheme was allocated
to the Soviet Communist puppets in Eastern Germany.
Kissinger writes:

> The Soviet Union obviously sees in the consolidation of its
> East German satellite not only a means to destroy the cohesion
> of the West but also a first step in the Communisation of
> Germany. "On what foundations should Germany be re-
> united?" Khrushchev said in Leipzig on March 7. "Can we
> agree when the capitalist world proposes to achieve the reunifi-
> cation of Germany at the expense of the German Democratic
> Republic and thus narrow down the front of socialism? The
> question can also be put thus: Why not reunite Germany by
> abolishing the capitalist system in West Germany and estab-
> lishing there the power of the working class? But it would be
> unrealistic today." . . . The Soviet draft of a peace treaty is
> not an end but the beginning of a process: it is a measure to
> consolidate a tactical base.[35]

A resolute, determined and united stand by the Western
Powers has again made realisation of the Soviet plans—at
least for the time being—impossible. On the other hand,
the Soviet position is at present much stronger than it was

---

[34] Dallin, *supra cit.*, p. 221.
[35] "In Search of Stability," *Foreign Affairs*, July 1956, p. 540.

ten years ago and the appalling prospects of nuclear warfare
make it imperative to find a solution.

It must be remembered that the realisation of Russia's
plan (which, as we have pointed out, was formulated before
the last war) would extend Communist influence right up to
the French frontier, giving a tremendous boost to the
Communist Party in France, and coming dangerously close
to Great Britain. At the same time, a Communist régime
in Germany would be a great encouragement to the Communist Party in Italy. In other words, Germany, as a
satellite of the Soviet Union, would become a stepping-stone
to the conquest of the whole of Western Europe.

Another version of such a plan, which is undoubtedly
also contemplated in the Kremlin and unfortunately by
some West German politicians as well, is for Germany—
while retaining her full sovereignty and internal structure,
with Communist influence reasonably under control—to be
politically and militarily allied with Russia. In view of Air
Vice-Marshal Bennett's report of his conversation with
Professor Heinkel, the possibility of such a danger—however
remote at present—cannot be excluded. This would equally
represent a mortal danger for Western Europe.

It is obvious that this solution—like the previous one of
war—is not a good alternative to the *status quo*.

Reunified Germany, Free to be Allied with the West

Theoretically speaking, there can be two versions: (1) Germany alone, free to be allied to the West, with Eastern
Europe remaining in the Soviet sphere, and (2) both
reunited Germany and also Eastern Europe, freed from
Soviet troops, free to be allied with the West.

(1) There was a time, especially in the early days of
the build-up of NATO, when it seemed that Russia would
one day recoil before the rising might of NATO. Those
were the days when Mr. Dulles spoke of Russia " rolling

back." Schütz, a prominent German political writer, has written:

> For years our policy was based on the assumption that the Western world's power and weight could be decisively increased, partly through the six-nation merger in Europe, partly through the Atlantic Pact. In other words, the West would become so strong and cohesive that a Russian retreat would be inevitable. For a time this way of thinking was understandable: today it is anachronistic.[36]

However, whereas the official policy of the Federal Republic, dominated by Dr. Adenauer, saw the fulfilment of German dreams only through Germany's alliance with the West, and took for granted that if it came to the formation of an all-German Government, that Government would decide on adherence to NATO, the Social Democrats, the main party in opposition, have developed different ideas.

The Western Powers naturally welcomed and gave their full support to the official policy of the Bonn Government: the United States, especially, is strongly biased against any form of Socialism, whether it is the British Labour Party, the German Social Democrats or a kindred party on the Continent.

Sir Anthony Eden, then Foreign Secretary, speaking at the Foreign Ministers' meeting in Berlin from January 25 to February 18, 1954, introduced his famous " Eden Plan," and, in summing up, emphasised that a future all-German Government, resulting from free elections, must be free, among other things, to " associate with other nations for peaceful purposes."

Sir Anthony, being adroit at diplomatic verbiage, did not say what, in fact, he had in mind, namely that freedom of choice for the future all-German Government would amount to a decision to join NATO.

His successor, Mr. Macmillan, at the meeing of Foreign

---

[36] Schütz, " New Initiative for a New Age," *Foreign Affairs*, April 1958, p. 466.

Ministers which met at Geneva from October 17 to November 16, 1955, in order to debate the issues connected with the reunification of Germany, was much more frank about this issue. In his speech on October 28, he said: " . . . the final stage will come into effect when a reunified Germany decides to enter NATO. . . ."

The next day, he said: " . . . as far as Western Powers are concerned, a reunified Germany will have its freedom to choose whether she should join NATO or not. . . ." And again, in his speech on November 8, he said: " . . . Of course, the Western Powers are not dictating a choice to the Germans."

Finally, the draft of a peace treaty with Germany, submitted by the French delegation on behalf of all three Western delegations, contained a clause worthy of Talleyrand, to the effect that the future all-German Government should have authority to " . . . conclude such other international agreements as it may wish."

Kennan, in his third Reith lecture, made a penetrating comment:

> I think we cannot scrutinise too closely or too frequently in the light of the developing situation the position our governments have taken in the question of Germany in recent years. . . . The [position] . . . is one that has insisted, and with very good reason, that the modalities of German unification, as a domestic programme, must flow from the will of the German people, expressed in free elections. But it has gone further than that. It has also insisted that no restrictions whatsoever must be placed in advance on the freedom of a future all-German Government to determine its own international orientation and to incur military obligations to other States. Specifically, the Western governments have insisted that such an all-German Government must be entirely free to continued to adhere to the NATO Pact, as the German Federal Republic does today; and it is taken everywhere as a foregone conclusion that an all-German Government would do just that.
>
> Now the question at once arises as to what would happen in such a contingency—that is, in the contingency that a future united Germany should choose to adhere to NATO—what

would happen then with the garrisons of the various Allied Powers now stationed on German soil? The Western position says nothing specific about this.[37]

However, if Kennan had read closely Mr. Macmillan's speech on October 29 at the Geneva Foreign Ministers' meeting, he would have found several details relating to the "safeguards" offered to Russia in case Germany should decide to join NATO. Incidentally, a comparison of that speech with Mr. Macmillan's proposals put to Mr. Khrushchev during the recent conversations in Moscow and later repeated to the Western leaders, shows considerable consistency in his approach to the problem of a unified Germany, free to be allied to the West.

The Western attitude towards this problem crystallised into the so-called Berlin Declaration of July 27, 1957, which in clause 9, on the assumption that "If the all-German Government in the exercise of its free choice, should elect to join NATO," states quite clearly that:

> . . . Western Powers, after consultation with the other members of this organisation, are prepared to offer, on a basis of reciprocity, to the government of the Soviet Union and the governments of other countries of Eastern Europe which would become parties to a European security arrangement, assurances of a significant and far-reaching character. The Western Powers are also prepared, as part of a mutually acceptable European security arrangement, to give an assurance that, in the event of a reunified Germany choosing to join NATO, they would not take military advantage as a result of the withdrawal of Soviet forces.

The Berlin Declaration was preceded by a statement by Dr. Adenauer at his press conference in Hamburg only a few weeks earlier that he would be prepared, in the event of reunification taking place, to demilitarise the area of the Soviet Zone. He said that, in such an event, neither NATO nor German troops would be stationed in that area. If it were demanded that that area should be exempt from

[37] *Russia, the Atom and the West*, p. 38.

military service, he would agree to the demand. It was his intention, said Dr. Adenauer, to show that the release of the Soviet Zone by Russia would not lead in any way to the strengthening of the potential of the West.

This coincidence of views seems clearly a case of " les beaux ésprits se rencontrent."

Kennan's view of the Soviet reaction to this line was:

> . . . The Soviet leaders are not likely to be impressed with such paper assurances as the Western Powers may undertake to give, to the effect that a unilateral withdrawal would not be exploited to Russia's disadvantage. . . .[38]

It would seem that the reunification of Germany and her freedom to associate herself with the West, which in plain language would mean membership of NATO, in the manner envisaged by the Western Powers and the Federal Republic, is under present circumstances a fairly remote possibility.

In this respect, the difference between the Bonn Government and the Social Democrats is fundamental, and the gap is unbridgeable.

The Social Democrats gradually came to the conclusion that German entanglements in NATO would make any agreement with Russia on reunification increasingly difficult. Herr Ollenhauer, the leader of the Social Democrats, and Herr Erler, one of the leading members of the party, have now become outspoken. Herr Ollenhauer, in his press conference in Bonn on May 23, 1957, at which he put forward his own " Ollenhauer Plan " for the reunification of Germany, said:

> Every step towards the integration of the Federal Republic into the Atlantic Alliance has only stiffened the Soviet attitude in this matter. The insistence on such a policy does not lead to reunification; on the contrary it makes it more difficult.

Herr Erler, in various speeches and articles published in the world press, has consistently expressed a similar view:

[38] *Ibid.*, p. 39.

I deplore the argument that for strategic reasons West German military participation in NATO is a higher necessity than the establishment of a free united Germany which is protected and limited by other instruments than the actual NATO solution: . . . Neither is a unification of Germany possible as long as each of the two power *blocs* insists on having the whole of Germany as its military ally. . . . The West cannot allow, and the German nation does not wish, the Red Army to establish itself at the border of the Rhine—but neither will Russia tolerate a United States command at the Oder.[39]

This attitude made the Social Democrats very unpopular in Western capitals, and especially in Washington. For this reason Dr. Adenauer's victory in the elections in 1957 was greeted in Western capitals with great relief.

However, Western public opinion is not necessarily united behind government policy towards Germany: for instance, a prominent Senator, John Kennedy, has written:

. . . partly out of appreciation and admiration for the outstanding reinvigoration of German politics, American policy has let itself be lashed too tightly to a single German Government and party.[40]

Aneurin Bevan, during the debate on foreign affairs in Parliament, on December 4, 1958, said:

If, therefore, we are to have a reunification of Germany, which would assimilate the Berlin problem, it must be assumed that such a reunited Germany should not join the NATO alliance.

Equally, Lord Henderson, a former Parliamentary Under Secretary in the Foreign Office, said in the debate in the House of Lords on December 18:

. . . it is useless to go on thinking that the Russians will agree to a united Germany joining NATO.

As mentioned before, both the Adenauer Government and the Social Democrats are concerned only with the reunification of Germany, and are not especially concerned

---

[39] Erler, "The Reunification of Germany and Security for Europe," *World Politics*, April 1958, p. 369.
[40] Kennedy, "A Democrat Looks at Foreign Policy," *Foreign Affairs*, October 1957, p. 49.

with the situation in Eastern Europe. Unfortunately for the long-term interests of the West such a solution would be even worse, and potentially more dangerous than division of Germany—the present *status quo*.

Reunification of Germany, irrespective of what happens later, can only be achieved as a result of withdrawal of Soviet troops from Eastern Germany.

There is no point in dwelling too long on the concept of a unilateral Soviet withdrawal from Eastern Germany, for this, under present circumstances, can be only regarded as unrealistic.

Yet, accepting for the sake of argument such a highly hypothetical solution, it would mean that the greater part of the twenty Soviet divisions now stationed in Eastern Germany, together with the air force and various establishments, would be moved to Poland.

Such a heavy concentration of Soviet forces could portend several dangers: first of all, it could increase tension in Poland and Eastern Europe, a development which could only favour further integration of the whole area into the Soviet *bloc*.

> Things cannot be expected to remain this way for long. There must either be further violent efforts by people in that area to take things into their own hands and to achieve independence by their own means, or there must be the beginning of some process of real adjustment to the fact of Soviet domination. In the first of these contingencies, we in the West could easily be placed once more before the dilemma which faced us last year at the time of the Hungarian uprising. . . . As for the second alternative, which at this moment seems to be the more likely of the two, it seems no less appalling. . . . The failure of the recent popular uprisings to shake the Soviet military domination has now produced a state of bitter and dangerous despondency throughout large parts of Eastern Europe. If the taste or even the hope for independence once dies out in the hearts of these peoples, then there will be no recovering it; then Moscow's victory will be complete. Eastern Europe will then be permanently lost to Europe proper.[41]

41 Kennan, *Russia, the Atom and the West*, pp. 35–36.

Should such an unthinkable solution really materialise and this sort of psychological process occur, then—and only then—the satellite divisions, so rightly described by Colonel Fens in his report on "The State of European Security" as "of various reliability," may one day become fully reliable instruments in the hands of the Soviet High Command. Thus, a partial solution, such as reunification of Germany would, by implication, merely increase the Soviet military potential.

Once again Kissinger's views on this subject are profoundly important:

> Nevertheless, a proposal to neutralise Germany in return for unification has tempting aspects, since unification would undoubtedly contribute to political stability in Europe. Even if rejected, such an offer would demonstrate once and for all that German membership in NATO is a response to Soviet intransigence. The temptation is all the greater when it is considered that were Moscow ever itself to make such an offer it would be next to impossible for a German Government to refuse. It is important to be clear, however, as to what is meant by neutralisation. It could mean that Germany would leave NATO and Western troops withdraw from the Federal Republic, while Poland, Czechoslovakia and Hungary would leave the Warsaw Pact and Soviet forces retire from these countries. Or it could mean the departure of Soviet troops into Poland only. . . .
>
> If Soviet troops retire only to Poland and if German forces are limited along the lines of the Soviet proposals in the draft peace treaty, Russia would be able to exert an enormous pressure on an independent Germany. With self-defence against Soviet attack impossible, Soviet influence would be likely to grow relative to the West, even if NATO could be satisfactorily based in the Low Countries and France—a possibility which, in the absence of careful study, cannot be taken for granted. On the other hand, Germany's capability to protect herself against a Soviet attack might increase European tension. A militarily strong Germany without the restraint of NATO would surely disquiet the Soviet satellites and drive them closer to the Soviet Union, thereby increasing the cohesion of the Eastern *bloc*.[42]

---

[42] "In Search of Stability," *Foreign Affairs*, July 1959, p. 553.

Furthermore, the presence of Soviet troops in Poland could encourage the Communists in a reunified Germany in their efforts to undermine that unity and to create endless internal difficulties and unrest. The shadow of the Soviet soldiers stationed just across the border would always mean the danger of a replica of the 1948 Communist *coup* in Czechoslovakia.

Likewise, if in the meantime the thorny problem of the German-Polish frontier is not definitely settled, and internationally guaranteed—not as until now only by Russia—it could either be the cause of a major conflict between Germany and Poland, or a pretext for a deal between Germany and Russia, on the pattern of so many previous deals, at the expense of Poland. Such a development would bring us nearer to the greatest danger of all, namely, *the possibility of a new German-Soviet rapprochement.*

In any case the immediate proximity of Russia to Germany, in spite of the purely nominal sovereignty of Poland, would become a temptation for German politicians to revive the old game—which was played so successfully by Bismarck, von Seekt, Stresemann and others—of playing off East against West, and West against East.

In this context it is extremely interesting to quote Dallin's book, remembering again that it was written as long ago as 1942:

> Soviet policy will pursue these objectives: . . . it will seek a common frontier with Germany and will try to prevent Poland from gaining a position which, as in 1920, would be able to keep the forces of Russia and Germany apart. . . . in case of a favourable development of German domestic affairs Soviet policy will endeavour to convert the probable collaboration with Germany into a hard-and-fast military alliance.[43]

Viewed in this light, the mere reunification of Germany would seem to play right into Soviet hands. Consequently, the first version of the alternative under study, regardless

[43] Dallin, *supra cit.*, p. 299.

of whether Germany chose to join NATO, or did so by implication, presents more dangers than the present *status quo*.

These possible dangers might, however, be prevented if reunified Germany were separated from Russia by a broad belt of countries of Eastern Europe which were also freed from the presence of Soviet troops on their soil. In fact, it would amount to the revival of one of the wisest concepts of our era, that of the *cordon sanitaire*, conceived by Georges Clemenceau, submitted by him before the Supreme Council in Paris in December 1919, and sponsored by Marshal Foch. Komarnicki, in his comprehensive study, *Rebirth of the Polish Republic*, relates a conversation between Marshal Foch and Lloyd George at the session of the Supreme Council in Paris in December 1919, at which Lloyd George asked Foch the following question:

> Do you propose a military entente between those different States with the object of attacking Soviet Russia, or on the contrary, with the object of common defence in case the Bolsheviks attack?

Marshal Foch answered:

> The first thing to be done is to stop the advancing Bolshevism and to consolidate the states which have just been founded. It is a matter of establishing a defensive organisation, a safety belt to protect Central Europe against the advances of the Bolsheviks.[44]

Komarnicki comments on this dialogue—quoted only in part:

> Mr. Lloyd George did not understand all the implications of the Bolshevik advance for the security of Europe. Such assumptions obviously stood in the way of his policy of gradually removing all the obstacles to a rapprochement with the Soviet State.

Unfortunately, Lloyd George was not the only one to underestimate the potential danger of the Bolshevik menace

[44] Komarnicki, p. 515.

to Europe and to misunderstand the purely defensive nature of the *Cordon Sanitaire*. At a Press Conference soon after the Hungarian uprising, on December 18, 1956, Dulles said:

> The United States has no purpose at all to turn (the) satellite countries into our allies; in the same sense that we have no desire to surround the Soviet Union with a band of hostile States and to revive what used to be called the *cordon sanitaire*, which was developed largely by the French after the First World War with a view to circling the Soviet Union with hostile forces.[45]

(2) All this brings us to the second version of the alternative under study: Germany reunified, as a result of the withdrawal of Soviet troops, and Eastern Europe also freed from Soviet troops; both free either to associate non-militarily with the West or committed to remain neutral.

As a matter of fact Soviet leaders, and, in particular, Marshal Bulganin, expressed on various occasions their desire to see the situation return to the *status quo ante*—without, of course, venturing into further detail.

Although such a solution, under present circumstances, seems a wild dream, it was one of the main features of the war aims of the Allies, embodied in the Atlantic Charter of April 14, 1941. The clauses of that historic document now make ironic reading:

> 1. . . . Their countries seek no aggrandisement, territorial or other . . .
> 2. . . . They desire no territorial changes that do not accord with the freely expressed wishes of the peoples concerned.
> 3. . . . They respect the right of all peoples to choose the form of government under which they will live.

Yet any agreement with the Russians which would result in the withdrawal of Soviet troops from Eastern Europe, or at least from part of it—the terms will be the subject of subsequent chapters—would carry far-reaching psychological, political, military and economic implications.

[45] Department of State Press Release No. 624, December 18, 1956.

Even if the efforts of the West did not bring about the fulfilment of such a plan, the psychological impact on Eastern Europe would be enormous: such efforts would restore hope and, above all, confidence in the West, so badly shaken by the West's inactivity during the uprisings in Eastern Germany and Hungary.

One of the few Western leaders who has expressed similar views has been Monsieur van Zeeland, who in his numerous lectures and leaflets, for instance, *Réflexions sur les Fondements de la Paix*, has emphasised the need for a show of initiative which would produce a profound psychological impact on the peoples of Eastern Europe.

It seems that Western statesmen have ignored or forgotten the valuable lessons and experience of psychological warfare of the last two wars. Professor Charles Seymour, of Yale University, in his article " Woodrow Wilson in Perspective," wrote:

> Wilson's programme [Fourteen Points] as an instrument of political warfare thus achieved resounding success. It became a determining factor in the Allied military victory in 1918.[46]

And Georges Clemenceau commented in moving tones on Wilson's Fourteen Points:

> Suddenly, when the war was raging at its fiercest, the whole scheme of military aims was completely changed. We had started as allies of Russian oppressors of Poland, with the Polish soldiers of Silesia and Galicia fighting against us. By the collapse of military Russia Poland found herself suddenly set free and re-created, and then all over Europe oppressed people raised their heads and our war of national defence was transformed by force of events into a war of liberation . . . the problem of military power is bound up with the problem of moral power to build up, by their mutually supporting forces, strongholds of invincible force against which the savage onrush of aggressors will exhaust its strength.[47]

---

[46] Seymour, " Woodrow Wilson in Perspective," *Foreign Affairs*, January 1956, p. 181.
[47] Clemenceau, *The Grandeur and Misery of Victory*, p. 180.

Equally, during the last war, both Hitler and the West paid a very high price for ignoring elementary lessons of psychological warfare: Hitler by neglecting the feelings of millions of Russian, above all of the Ukrainian peasants who in 1941, when the German armies were advancing towards Moscow, greeted them as their liberators from the hated Communist régime [48]: at the same time, the Allied slogan of " unconditional surrender " unnecessarily prolonged the war, giving Goebbels a priceless card.

Obviously, the withdrawal of Soviet troops from Eastern Europe would give a great moral uplift to all that area. Even if under the corresponding clauses of the agreement stipulating Soviet withdrawal, which we shall examine in subsequent chapters, Eastern Europe were prevented from military co-operation or alliance, as between the two wars, it would still be free to associate itself in many other fields, returning slowly to the family of Western Europe to which, by virtue of history, Christian culture and civilisation, it belongs. And yet, in view of the fact that any Soviet attempt to re-enter under any pretext would be most fiercely resisted, the whole area, by implication, would become a defence glacis of the West. Further, and for the long-term interests of the West perhaps equally important, this belt of States, free from Soviet troops and free to have their own independent policy—apart from possible limitations on military alignments—would amount to a physical barrier between Germany and Russia.

> The most persuasive scheme has therefore coupled the neutralisation of Germany with that of Poland, Czechoslovakia and Hungary—the original Gaitskell Plan.[49]

[48] See the testimony of former Wehrmacht officer Baron von Herwarth, quoted by Senator Thomas J. Dodd in " Our Captive Allies," *New Leader*, July 20–27, 1959: " With an intelligent political policy, we could have won the war in the East simply because the Russian people themselves would have overthrown the régime. Especially in the first months of the war, surrenders were on a mass scale and were political, not military. At one time I would go out as a cavalry officer on a patrol and would come back with thousands of altogether voluntary prisoners."

[49] " In Search of Stability," *Foreign Affairs*, July 1956, p. 554.

There will, of course, be many who would say that, in view of the recent shift in Soviet policy and its emphasis on the maintenance of the Soviet conception of the *status quo*, which means further consolidation of Soviet influence all over Eastern Europe, any talk of the withdrawal of Soviet troops from Eastern Europe is completely unrealistic. But Walter Lippmann's conclusions from his long talk with Mr. Khrushchev in Moscow in October, 1958, as reported in the *New York Herald Tribune*, are not unhopeful:

> The Soviet system does not work and there is no reason to think that it will work in Eastern Europe. I feel sure that the Soviet domination of Eastern Germany, of Poland, Czechoslovakia and Hungary is precarious and impermanent. Moreover, I think that the rulers of Russia know this and that if they could think, which they have not, of any safe way to disengage, they would eventually accept some such settlement.

Obviously this alternative, in its second version, would be the best one could imagine: it would bring about the reunification of Germany and the liberation of Eastern Europe, together with the reduction of international tension, creating the conditions for general disarmament: it will turn the word "co-existence," which at present is as unrealistic and misleading as the idea of the perpetuity of the *status quo*, into something really practicable.

Disengagement

We have examined in the previous sections various alternatives to the *status quo* and we have come to some conclusions not always in accordance with generally accepted views.

(1) *War*, especially nuclear war, is such an appalling solution that, as Mr. Macmillan said in the United States, " no efforts should be spared to avoid it."

Unfortunately, it would seem that there is a dangerous tendency—this time in the West—towards a policy of military " brinkmanship " and even towards a " limited show-down " with the Russians. The time for a show-down was in 1948, during the Berlin crisis, when the United States had a monopoly of the A-bomb and when Eastern Europe was in a state of a profound confusion; but at that time the Pentagon was pursuing a timid policy in order not to offend the Russians.

Nobody can guarantee that a limited show-down could not easily get out of control and turn into an all-out nuclear war: any sabre-rattling, which so far has been the monopoly of the Soviet marshals, is extremely dangerous.

(2) *Germany allied with the Soviet Union.* This would be a stepping stone towards the conquests of the rest of Western Europe and perhaps of the whole world. Any attempt by Russia to achieve it by force is ruled out in the present set-up because it would lead to a major war, which Russia does not want to fight. However, an attempt by Germany to reach a rapprochement with Russia which could eventually lead to a Soviet-German alliance cannot theoretically be ruled out. It is a possibility to be guarded against.

(3) *First, Germany reunited and free to choose her political association, but with Eastern Europe remaining in the Soviet sphere; and, secondly, Germany reunited and Eastern Europe also freed from Soviet troops, both free— under certain conditions to be agreed—to be associated with the West.*

Although reunification of Germany has been the paramount national aim of West German politics, as well as one of the major aims of the Western Powers, it must be clearly understood that these two aims are not identical. For Germany, the build-up of NATO and German participation in it were only the means to change the *status quo*, that is, the division of Germany, and to achieve reunification on German terms. For the West, the build-up of NATO and German participation in it have been the means to maintain the *status quo*.

The days in which a strong NATO was supposed to achieve German reunification by "rolling back" Russia were short-lived. NATO has become for the West, especially after the development by the Soviet scientists of the H-bomb, a sort of modern version of a three-dimensional Maginot Line, with the problem of German reunification slowly receding into the background. Siegler, in a very comprehensive study, wrote:

> . . . a divided Germany means retaining the present state of affairs as it has developed since the war. This is not really a solution to the German problem but the evasion of the solution in view of the risks entailed by any genuine solution. Any such retention of the present unsatisfactory state of affairs is a very real danger which has to be reckoned with and which both the Federal Chancellor, Dr. Adenauer, and the Leader of the Opposition, Herr Ollenhauer, characterised in the words: "The world at large could grow accustomed to the present fact of the division of Germany." [50]

Patrick O'Donovan, the Washington correspondent of *The Observer*, reporting Mr. Macmillan's visit in Spring, 1959, to the United States and the American reactions to his initiative, wrote:

> It is hard to avoid the impression that the *status quo* has an ideal quality in the thinking of the Administration. They are being forced to change by the pressure of their enemies and friends abroad, by Congressional criticism and military realities. . . . It is a difficult time for an Administration devoted to the erection of a position of massive and unassailable immobility. The *status quo* has never looked so pleasant. It is like a native land being left for ever. The ties that bind Americans to the post-war policy that they created and directed, that their strength and wealth maintained, are not easy to break in favour of something untried and uncertain. There is an inertia here and revulsion from change which is being reinforced from many quarters. The wonder is that they can even contemplate it. [51]

It is also quite likely that this Maginot Line mentality has become part and parcel of French military and political

---

[50] *The Reunification and Security of Germany*, p. 172.
[51] Dispatches dated March 21 and 28, 1959.

thinking: the breasts of Bundeswehr soldiers are slowly becoming in French eyes a substitute for the earthworks of the old Maginot Line. France's implacable hostility towards any form of disengagement could perhaps be explained by the fear of a "vacuum" and of the necessity to accept increased responsibilities for the defence of Western Europe.

If ever the *status quo* is broken and an agreement with the Russians is reached on German reunification —and the history of the negotiations on this issue, which is the concern of Part Two, shows that at some occasions it seemed not impossible to reach it—international tension in Europe will be, at least for a time, reduced.

But, of course, the solution of the German problem alone would be insufficient; as Kennan pointed out in a letter to the author in December 1957:

> Suffice it to say that I should see no advantage at all in a mutual withdrawal from Germany that did not include a similar withdrawal from Poland and Hungary.

This brings us to the second version of this alternative. If both Germany and Eastern Europe were freed from Soviet troops, the conditions for a real peace would be created, a peace not based upon a delicate balance of mutual terror but upon constructive co-operation between East and West. Obviously such a comprehensive solution can be achieved only as the result of the withdrawal of Soviet troops: such a withdrawal can take place either as a result of pressure by the West, backed by the threat of use of force, or as a result of a negotiated agreement.

The first alternative has ceased, since the discovery by the Soviet scientists of the H-bomb, to be even remotely possible. There remains, therefore, the second alternative, namely, withdrawal as a result of negotiations, which could lead only to a further negotiated mutual withdrawal.

As Mr. Denis Healey has written:

> . . . you can produce any change in the *status quo* by agreement with the Russians. Any agreement with the Russians has got

to involve concessions by the West parallel to those made by the Soviet Union. Consequently, the answer must involve a reciprocal withdrawal of Western forces and Soviet forces from the existing Iron Curtain with mutual control of the area thus exposed.[52]

At first glance, both sides appear to have reached stalemate. M. Spaak, Secretary-General of NATO, writes:

> . . . in the present state of affairs . . . an agreement on Germany appears almost impossible. I am convinced that the Soviets will never accept the West's terms for reunification of Germany, while we on our part will find it impossible to agree to theirs. The West says: " Let us organise free elections—free according to our understanding of the word." The Soviet Union replies: " Recognise that there are two Germanies. Decide that they must confederate and that this confederation is to be neutralised and demilitarised." The two sides have adopted the course of action—each with its own logic—which can never be fused, because they are based upon irreconcilable points of view.[53]

And yet, even M. Spaak sees some possibility of coming to terms with the Russians, which, in view of his reputation as an implacable enemy of any concept of disengagement, is extraordinary:

> I see only one possibility of compromise. We must convince the Russians that once Germany is reunified, our concept of European security will be wholly different from what it is today. For the purposes of this hypothesis, it would matter very little how the reunification has been brought about, whether by free elections, a joint decision or a process involving several stages. Many of the things which the Russians are either protesting or proposing and which today are difficult to accept—*a qualified disengagement, a controlled demilitarised zone*, a non-aggression pact between NATO and the Warsaw Pact—all these would then become conceivable and practicable.[54]

Another statesman who, even more than M. Spaak, has the reputation of being opposed to a flexible approach towards Russia is Herr Josef Straus, Federal German

[52] *A Neutral Belt in Europe?* p. 4.
[53] " New Test for NATO," *Foreign Affairs*, April 1959, p. 361.
[54] *Ibid.*, p. 362.

Minister of Defence; but in an article, "Soviet Aims and German Unity," published in the same issue of *Foreign Affairs* as M. Spaak's article, he writes:

> . . . I do not share the opinion that the West should not or cannot negotiate with the Soviets, because their conception of faithfulness to an agreement is in practice different from ours. On the contrary, we must negotiate with them whenever, wherever and on whatever subject possible.[55]

These extracts suggest a shift in the attitude of the West —except that of Dr. Adenauer—from a position of diplomatic immobility and atomic stalemate towards greater flexibility. It is this shift in attitude which may eventually lead to some form of regional disarmament or security agreement in the form of area limitation and area control, which may in turn give rise to disengagement or, strictly speaking, to a mutual withdrawal of troops, accompanied by a political settlement.

[55] p. 376.

PART TWO

IN SEARCH OF A SOLUTION

5

First Attempts, 1945-1949

As few things are more enlightening than the lessons of history we shall precede the analysis of the problem which forms Part Three of this study by a review of the various plans which have been put forward by both sides since the end of the last war.

The history of what is called disengagement will be a fascinating study for future historians. They will, having charted their way carefully through the dense jungle of statements, speeches, articles, books and official documents, see that in fact the differences of opinion, especially in the early stages, were not great, that the gulf separating both sides was not so wide that it could not be bridged and that a solution was almost within reach.

The issue of disengagement was opened by Roosevelt during the conference in Yalta in 1945. As Sir Winston Churchill writes [1]:

> Stalin now asked how Germany was to be dismembered. . . .
> At Teheran Mr. Roosevelt had suggested dividing Germany into five parts, and he had agreed with him. I, on the other hand, had hesitated and had only wanted her to be split into two, namely Prussia and Austro-Bavaria, with the Ruhr and Westphalia under international control. The time had now come, he said, to take a definite decision. . . .
>
> Mr. Roosevelt . . . made a momentous statement. He said that the United States would take all reasonable steps to preserve peace, but not at the expense of keeping a large army in Europe, three thousand miles away from home. The American occupation would, therefore, be limited to two years. Formidable questions rose in my mind. If the Americans left Europe Britain would have to occupy single-handed the entire western

[1] *The Second World War; Vol. VI, Triumph and Tragedy*, p. 308.

portion of Germany. Such a task would be far beyond our strength.

At the opening of our second meeting of February 6, I accordingly pressed for French help in carrying such a burden. To give France a zone of occupation was by no means an end of the matter. Germany would surely rise again, and while the Americans could always go home the French had to live next door to her. A strong France was vital not only to Europe, but to Great Britain. She alone could deny the rocket sites on her Channel coast *and build up an army to contain the Germans*.[2]

The contrast between Churchill's misgivings and the present Franco-German rapprochement is striking.

The Root of the Trouble

Charting a successful course of policy in peacetime is in itself a difficult task for a statesman. Planning for the future amidst the changing fortunes of war, especially within the framework of a haphazard coalition, is an almost superhuman task and a severe test of statesmanship. It appears that one of the major mistakes in planning for the immediate post-war period was the decision to dismember Germany, a decision which, since 1945, has lain at the root of our present troubles. The fact that the division of Germany took place at the same time as the division of the world into two opposing *blocs* which gradually became two armed camps, and that the political dividing line coincided with the military demarcation line, made this dismemberment part of a universal problem.

Consequently, attempts which have been made on several occasions since the war to return, *mutatis mutandis*, to a *status quo ante* have immediately acquired the dangerous significance of a shift in balance of power either in favour of or to the disadvantage of one of the opposing *blocs*.

---

[2] Author's italics.

Against the background of atomic stalemate, all attempts to find a solution for the reunification of Germany, which is, first of all, a political issue, have been frustrated by considerations of security. Thus, partition of Germany which was contemplated as a temporary measure became permanent, laying the foundations of the present uneasy *status quo*.

It is interesting to read Sir Winston Churchill's account of the decision to partition:

> The occupation of Germany by the principal Allies had been long studied. In the summer of 1943 a Cabinet meeting, which I set up under Mr. Attlee, in agreement with the Chiefs of Staff, recommended that the whole country should be occupied if Germany was to be effectively disarmed, and that our forces should be disposed in three main zones of roughly equal size, the British in the north-west, the Americans in the south and south-west, and the Russians in the eastern zone. Berlin should be a separate zone, occupied by each of the three major Allies. These recommendations were approved and forwarded to the European Advisory Council, which then consisted of M. Gousev, the Soviet Ambassador, Mr. Winant, the American Ambassador, and Sir William Strang, of the Foreign Office.
>
> At that time the subject seemed to be purely theoretical. No one could foresee when and how the end of the war would come. The German armies held the immense areas of European Russia. A year was to pass before British and American troops set foot in Western Europe, and nearly two years before they entered Germany. The proposals of the European Advisory Council were not sufficiently pressing or practical to be brought before the War Cabinet. Like many praiseworthy efforts to make plans for the future, they lay upon the shelves while the war crashed on. *The common opinion about Russia was that she would not continue the war once she had regained her frontiers,* and that when the time came *the Western Allies might well have to try to persuade her not to relax her efforts.*[2] The question of the Russian zone of occupation in Germany, therefore, did not bulk in our thoughts and in Anglo-American discussions, nor was it raised by any leader at Teheran.[3]

[3] *Churchill, op. cit.,* p. 443.

To contrast the common opinion of which Sir Winston writes, that Russia would not pursue the beaten German armies and would call a halt at her former frontiers with Eastern Europe, with the real facts is to understand the bewilderment and bitter feelings of Western leaders as they gradually saw the frustration of their plans for the post-war settlement.

Warburg is extremely critical of the original decision for the partition of Germany, in which he sees the seeds of all further evils:

> In the opinion of this observer, we made a series of disastrous mistakes in our German policy. It is true that Russian intransigence has driven us further and further into the wilderness, but we were headed for that wilderness before the wartime honeymoon with Russia ended.
>
> Instead of building, in Germany and Austria, a bridge between East and West—a neutral half-way house, where at least the two halves of a divided Europe might meet and exchange their products—we permitted these two countries to become a no man's land: then we allowed them to become partitioned, with one-third of Germany locked into the Soviet orbit and two-thirds loosely and precariously attached to Western Europe.
>
> In our ignorance of Europe and our fear of Russia we have created or helped to create a new, truncated German nation of 48,000,000 restless inhabitants—an unnatural state which threatens the future of the German people no less than it jeopardises the peace of Europe and ultimately the security of the United States. To contain Russia we have brought into being a new unpredictable Germany, which may prove to be more difficult to contain than Russia itself.
>
> The new Germany has been shaped exclusively by the West under our leadership. It is not the " new," peaceful, democratic Germany which we talked about creating years ago. It is the old Germany—not the Germany of Hitler, but the Germany which produced Hitler—the Germany of industrial magnates and political bureaucrats who somehow survive all political change, of hardworking people too apathetic or too immature to govern themselves, and of well-meaning but essentially undemocratic leadership. It is a Germany very like that of Gustav Stresemann and General von Seekt, which in the early

twenties worked its way back to power by playing off Russia against the West.[4]

The evil consequences of the partition of Germany might have been avoided if by the implementation of either of two British plans the war had taken another course. Unfortunately these plans were rejected by the Americans.

First of all, if Churchill's plan for an Allied landing in the Balkans had been agreed upon, it might have produced a mass uprising all over the wide area of Eastern Europe, completely paralysing the overstretched German lines of communications with the main armies bogged in Russia. American objections to this plan, stemming purely from logistical considerations, showed not only a lack of understanding of the political issues involved, but also ignorance of the lessons of the First World War, namely, the paramount importance of President Wilson's Fourteen Points.

An Allied landing in the Balkans, the news of which would have spread with lightning speed all over Eastern Europe, could have set fire to the whole area, engulfing German troops and establishments in a violent explosion: such an operation would have meant the imminent collapse of German armies on the Eastern front, shortening the war very considerably at a time when the Russians were hundreds of miles from the frontiers of Eastern Europe.

A more modest British plan, devised by General Wilson, might eventually have produced similar results. General (later Field-Marshal) Wilson suggested an offensive through the Pisa-Rimini [Gothic] Line into the Po Valley, supported by an amphibious operation against the Istrian Peninsula, " for exploitation through the Ljubljana Gap into the plains of Hungary."

> It was possible that such a course might achieve decisive results by striking at the heart of Germany and thereby provide the most powerful kind of indirect support to General Eisenhower's operations in France by inducing the Germans to withdraw formations from the West to meet the new threat.

[4] *Germany, Key to Europe*, pp. 5–6.

But General Marshall informed me that General Eisenhower required operations to clear additional French ports in order that Allied formations might be deployed in France more rapidly and on a broader front; that there were between forty and fifty divisions in the United States which could not be introduced into France as rapidly as desired or maintained there through the ports of North-west France.

I admitted that General Marshall's emphasis on the necessity of seizing a major port in Southern France was to me a new factor of paramount importance, but a shift of our operations for this purpose seemed to me to imply a strategy aimed at defeating Germany during the first half of 1945 at the cost of an opportunity to defeat him (*sic*) before the end of 1944. . . .[5]

Major-General J. F. C. Fuller's comments are very critical:

Technically and administratively, the invasion of Southern France was an overwhelming success: strategically, it was a blunder. The war was in its last lap. As to this there could be no doubt, and because war is an instrument of policy, then the nearer the termination of the war was approached the more should its political ends have been considered by the Americans and British, if only because for months past it had been by the Russians. This was essential because the political aims of the Russians differed diametrically from that of their two major partners.

General Wilson and his Commanders-in-Chief would appear to have seen this when they suggested the Ljubljana operation: but General Eisenhower did not because, so it would seem, he was too much of a soldier and too little of a statesman to realise that already for months past the war problem had shifted from a tactical on to a political basis. The defeat of Germany was now certain in any realisable set of circumstances, therefore the political problem had become paramount . . . strategically, the decisive point in the West ceased to be politically the decisive area. This area was Austria and Hungary, for were the Russians to occupy those two countries—the strategic centre of Europe—before the Americans and British could do so, then the two Western Allies would have fought the war in vain: for

---

[5] See "Report by the Supreme Allied Commander, Mediterranean, to the Combined Chiefs of Staff on the Operations in Southern France, August 1944," p. 18.

all that would happen would be the establishment of a Russian Lebensraum in Eastern Europe instead of a German.[6]

As we know, the Russians occupied not only Austria and Hungary but the whole of Eastern Europe.

Unfortunately, instead of accepting one of the imaginative British plans with their profound political implications which might have completely changed the present world balance of power, a decision was taken to open the Second Front, thus creating the conditions for the present state of affairs in Europe.

This is not the place to go into the intricate details of the discussions of the partition of Germany at Teheran, Moscow, Yalta and even Potsdam, except to note that, according to Churchill, Mr. Truman referred to Germany in terms of " Germany of 1937." But it is interesting to note that, as a result of the exchange of views during the war between the Anglo-Saxon Powers and Russia, unanimity were reached on their concept of a " neutralised "—completely disarmed and demilitarised—Germany.

This concept, of course, rested on the understanding that the wartime alliance between Russia, Britain and the United States would continue after the cessation of hostilities. As a result of post-war developments, especially the growing estrangement of Russia and the West and the gradual formation into two armed camps, the policy of the neutralisation of Germany has been gradually abandoned, especially by the West.

The Declaration of Surrender which followed the military surrender on May 8, 1945, and which was mentioned in page 5 of the Instrument of Surrender, stated that the assumption of occupation powers by the four Great Powers did not mean the annexation of Germany and that the four Governments would at a later date establish the boundaries of Germany or part of Germany and her legal status.. It was decided that Germany should be divided

---

[6] *The Second World War*, pp. 324–325.

into four zones of occupation within her 1937 boundaries, each of which was to be allotted to one of the four Great Powers, the city of Berlin, however, being occupied by all four Powers. Furthermore, it was decided that the supreme authority was to be exercised in Germany by the four Supreme Commanders, each acting on the instructions of their respective governments in their own zones; in respect of questions concerning Germany as a whole they would act jointly through the agency of the Control Council, consisting of the four Supreme Commanders. These were the provisions which laid the foundations for the partition of Germany.

However, the agreement reached between the Allies during the war on the future running of Germany was not without several flaws.

The Potsdam agreement of August 2, 1945, which established the political and economic basis for the treatment of Germany, was intended to ensure a uniform policy on the part of the four occupying Powers. The basic economic principles laid down in that agreement envisaged that the whole of Germany would be treated, during the period of occupation, as a single economic unit. These principles were the cause of friction not only between Russia and her Western Allies, but also among the Western Allies themselves. Furthermore, these principles were thwarted by the division into zones of occupation—a contributing cause of the later split.

Thus it was that differences arose continually in the Four-Power Control Council and especially at the Four Powers Conference held in Paris from April to July 1946.

Reparations and the question of the Ruhr were important bones of contention, especially the question of Soviet participation in the international control of the Ruhr.

The question of the demarcation of the frontiers of the zones of occupation was not settled definitely until July 1, 1945. The lack of provision for the delimitation of those boundaries gave reason for further friction from the very start. In his memoirs Field-Marshal Lord Montgomery gives a very vivid account of these matters, though he is none too complimentary to the British Government of that time:

> The boundaries of these zones had been agreed by the European Advisory Commission in London on September 12, 1944, and its findings had been approved by the three Governments.
>
> At the Yalta Conference the following statement had been issued by the Prime Ministers, President Roosevelt and Marshal Stalin on February 11, 1945:
>
> "Under the agreed plans the forces of the Three Powers will each occupy a separate zone of Germany. Co-ordinated administration and control has been provided for under the plan through a Central Control Commission, consisting of the supreme Commanders of the Three Powers with the Head-quarters in Berlin.
>
> "It has been agreed that France should be invited by the Three Powers, if she should so desire, to take a zone of occupation and to participate as a fourth member of the Control Commission. The limits of the French Zone will be agreed by the Four Governments concerned through their representatives on the European Advisory Commission. . . ."
>
> But in spite of these international agreements, the British Government considered, and instructed me accordingly on the day before I went to Berlin, that *de facto* occupation by British and American armies of large parts of the Russian Zone was an important bargaining counter for obtaining satisfaction from the Soviet Government on a number of outstanding questions, such as our policy towards Germany and its treatment as one whole economic unit, the problems of Poland, the Balkans and Austria and other related matters.
>
> I knew that the Prime Minister [Churchill] attached the utmost importance to the British and American armies standing firm on the existing tactical boundary line reached by VE-Day; he reckoned that they should not withdraw until the impending meeting of the three Heads of Governments in Berlin [the Potsdam Conference], when these and other questions could be discussed and settled.
>
> I also knew that the attitude of the American Government was different. While they would have liked to reach settlement of the German and Austrian problems before withdrawing the

American armies, they were not prepared to link any outside question such as Poland or the Balkans with the question of withdrawal: nor would they give any assurance to stand firm until the Heads of Governments had met. Indeed, the American Government had said that if the Russians insisted on an immediate execution of the zones agreement they would not delay their own withdrawal.[7]

Field-Marshal Montgomery ends this account with the following words: " All this looked a bit awkward to me."

With regard to the Ruhr, France was predominant in insisting on political and economic separation of the Ruhr from Germany. Britain, too, was in favour of this territory being placed under a separate economic régime. The Soviet Union, however, demanded four-Power control of the Ruhr, to which, theoretically speaking, she was entitled under various agreements: substantiating her demand by stressing the eminent significance of the Ruhr to Germany's military potential.

From the Western point of view, any concession to the Soviet demand would have meant that Russia gained a considerable say in the heart of the Western zones and the extension of her sphere of influence from the Elbe to the Rhine and Ruhr.

These difficulties led to an agreement between Britain and the United States to amalgamate their zones on December 2, 1946. After the London Conference, the French zone was also included. This " Trizonia " laid the foundation for the creation of the present Federal Republic in July 1948. A year later, in October 1949, the Soviet zone was transformed into the German Democratic Republic.

During these developments, the Ruhr became increasingly a bone of contention, due not only to the Soviet intention of participating in its control (to which under the Potsdam agreement they were entitled) but also to France's

---

[7] *Memoirs of Field-Marshal Lord Montgomery*, pp. 377–378.

attitude. Byrnes, then American Secretary of State, throws some light on this:

> France was not represented at Potsdam and, therefore, did not feel bound by the agreements made there: in fact, it objected strongly to some of them. These objections were placed before President Truman by General de Gaulle and M. Bidault during their visit to Washington a few weeks after our return from Germany.
>
> Their worries centred on the plan to establish central German administrative agencies and on the disposition of the Rhineland, the Ruhr and the Saar. General de Gaulle feared that these acts were the prelude to the reconstruction of a centralised German State. *To re-establish German unity, he contended, would be even more dangerous than in the past, because Germany might come under the influence of a strong and powerful Slav* bloc *rising in the East. . . . The extension of Poland into Eastern Germany, both of the French leaders argued, shifted Germany's centre of gravity towards the West and therefore endangered the security of France.*[8]
>
> They asked for the separation of the Rhineland from Germany for administration by France, for the annexation of the Saar, and the transfer of the Ruhr to an international régime.[9]

In view of France's present attitude towards Germany this quotation from Byrnes's book is most interesting: it shows that France's foreign policy at least has not lacked flexibility.

The process of crystallisation into zones of occupation, set against a background of haggling over the Ruhr and reparations, ended with the formation, as mentioned above, of the Federal German Republic and of its counterpart in Eastern Germany, the German Democratic Republic. This latter is referred to in Western Germany as the " Soviet Zone," and its administration as the " Pankow régime."

The Byrnes Draft Treaty

During his visit to Moscow in December 1945, Mr. Byrnes, then Secretary of State, in conversation with Stalin about

---

[8] Author's italics.   [9] F. Byrnes, *Speaking Frankly*, pp. 169–170.

the draft peace treaty with Germany made an important
statement at the suggestion of Senator Vandenberg, Chairman of the Senate Foreign Relations Committee:

> " Such a treaty would give all European States assurance that
> the United States would not return to a policy of isolation," I
> told him. " I have often recalled how you expressed at Yalta
> your fear of another invasion by Germany. You then asserted
> that the continued co-operation of the four Allies in keeping
> Germany demilitarised would relieve your fears and perhaps
> influence your actions in the Balkan States."
>
> Stalin replied that it was the best proposal he had yet heard.
>
> " The United States has always been reluctant to enter into
> such treaties," I added, " but our experience in trying to stay
> out of Europe's wars has been so disastrous, I am confident
> our people would support a treaty under which the major
> Powers would join forces to keep Germany disarmed."
>
> " If you decide to fight for such a treaty," Stalin said, " you
> can rely on my support." [10]

With this conversation in mind, Byrnes started drafting
a peace treaty with Germany, which included a proviso for
inspection teams. President Truman, to whom Byrnes had
shown his draft, was so pleased that he said that if it was
accepted, it would be called the Byrnes Treaty.

This draft, containing a proviso for the complete
demilitarisation of Germany and for a four-Power treaty
of mutual assistance as guarantee against any further
German aggression, he put before the Foreign Ministers in
Paris in April 1946.

He immediately agreed to Mr. Molotov's objections to
twenty-five years instead of forty years.

During these negotiations in Paris, Byrnes received
strong support from Ernest Bevin, then British Foreign
Secretary, and from M. Bidault: the attitude of both these
statesmen must be recalled:

> Mr. Bevin and M. Bidault made strong statements in general
> support of our position. " The British people regard resurgence
> of Germany as the greatest menace to peace," Mr. Bevin said,

[10] *Op. cit.*, p. 169.

and although he might have some amendments to offer later, his Government warmly approved the treaty for the long-term disarmament and demilitarisation of Germany.

M. Bidault, in his statement, declared it was necessary that measures be undertaken to destroy the " militaristic Prussian character " of Germany, and the American treaty should constitute " the crown of the edifice." It would not be an obstacle to reparation, denazification or any of the other essential tasks of the occupation, he insisted, but would make more concrete the solidarity of the Allies against the danger of a resurgent Germany and would guarantee the security of Europe with the indispensable support of the United States.[11]

As a result, however, of Molotov's filibustering tactics, Byrnes came reluctantly to the following pessimistic conclusion, which could equally be applied to Soviet attitudes on some later occasions:

> I have been forced to the conclusion that following Stalin's promise in December 1946 to support the treaty, the Soviet High Command or Politburo concluded they did not want the United States involved in the maintenance of European security for the next twenty-five or forty years. The pressure of the American power would restrict the freedom of action which the Soviet Union, as the predominant military power in Europe, might otherwise enjoy.[12]

The Russians were quick to take advantage of the failure of the conferences of Foreign Ministers in Paris and Moscow. In July 1947 Molotov went on record as opposing any attempt at French annexations of German territory, and proposed the early creation of an anti-fascist Central German Government.

In adopting such an attitude Molotov antagonised French public opinion and put the strong French Communist Party in a difficult position, but at the same time he made Russia appear in the eyes of many Germans as the champion of German unity and Germany's protector against French encroachments.

[11] *Op. cit.*, pp. 175–176.
[12] *Op. cit.*, p. 176.

George Marshall Tries his Hand

The next attempt was made by Mr. Marshall, the new American Secretary of State, at the conference of Foreign Ministers which took place in Moscow between March 10 and April 26, 1947. The conference in Moscow took place in an uneasy atmosphere, created to a great extent by President Truman's announcement of U.S. help for Greece and Turkey—the Truman Doctrine.

Thus, the United States which had already almost completed the headlong demobilisation of its tremendous armed potential, had begun afresh to adopt a " military posture." It is doubtful whether the timing of the declaration of the Truman Doctrine, obviously directed against Russia, was particularly propitious for the success of the conference attended by Marshall.

Marshall was hampered by lack of unity within the Western camp, in particular by the different approaches to the German problem, the main issue of the conference. Whereas the British and Americans were in favour of a federal constitution for Germany and therefore envisaged the setting up of a central government with fairly restricted powers, the main preoccupation of the French delegation was to put forward demands for the separation of the Ruhr and the Rhineland from the remainder of Germany and for the permanent Allied occupation of the left bank of the Rhine. The French asked for the establishment of a Rhenish State with restricted autonomy, something on the lines of the old concept after the First World War, and as far as the Ruhr was concerned, they suggested a status similar to the Free Territory of Trieste. A most interesting suggestion was made by the French delegation concerning the Ruhr coal and steel mines, which were to pass into the hands of the nations which had fought against Germany. That suggestion was rejected outright by the United States, Britain and Russia. The ghost of Poincaré clearly leaned over the French delegation.

As far as the Soviet Union was concerned, Mr. Molotov, while objecting to Anglo-American suggestions for a flexible federal constitution, favoured the establishment of a central government with greater powers. He substantiated his arguments by saying that the Allied idea of a federated Germany could lead to a revival of German chauvinism.

In order to meet Soviet complaints that demilitarisation and denazification were not being carried out in the Western zones, Marshall put forward a forty years draft treaty—as suggested a year before by Byrnes—to guarantee complete German demilitarisation under international control. This draft was supported by Mr. Bevin and M. Bidault; even Mr. Molotov agreed in principle with Marshall's proposals for the demilitarisation of Germany. He put forward Soviet counter-proposals, containing provisions for the demilitarisation of Germany and the withdrawal of all troops of occupation. But he included so many provisions, in particular one dealing with the Four-Power control of the Ruhr, and strongly laced with statements of a political flavour that they were completely unacceptable for the West. After six dreary weeks of debate and banqueting the conference ended in failure.

In May, 1947, the former President Hoover paid a visit to Germany. After his return to the United States he suggested making a peace pact between the West German State and the West: his suggestion was supported a few months later by Byrnes and Senator Vandenberg. These statements further crystallised the partition of Germany. At any rate, as a result of various measures introduced by the Western Powers and by Russia in their zones of occupation, which gradually changed the economic and social structures of both parts of Germany, the problem of the neutralisation of Germany and of joint guarantees by the Great Powers as to her future status began slowly to fade away.

The London Conference, 1947

The next attempt was made at the meeting of Foreign Ministers which took place in London from November 26 to December 15, 1947. The chances for its success were even slighter than before. Both sides were more unwilling to make any concessions in order not to weaken their position in the power struggle which was now clearly about to start in earnest. The " Cold War " was in full swing.

From all points of view the weakness of the West was at this time acute. Europe, and especially Germany, was in the throes of an economic crisis, infested with strong and active Communist parties who fomented strikes and labour unrest; from the military point of view, except for the American monopoly of the A-bomb, Europe was almost completely undefended. In the circumstances it was rightly considered in the West that to concede to Soviet demands for participation in the control of the Ruhr would be tantamount to giving Russia a key to Europe's back door.

At that time Russia, who had not disbanded her huge land armies, was apparently bent on further expansion, if possible in all directions of the compass. The situation in Europe, especially in Germany, seemed to favour her plans.

The London Conference, like the Moscow Conference, was preceded by a public statement of American policy: Marshall made a momentous speech on November 18 announcing his Marshall Plan, aimed at whatever part of the world was in need of American assistance. Warburg makes an interesting comment on this idea:

> The great unanswered and probably unanswerable question as to the year 1947 is whether the Truman Administration had actually changed its mind between March 12 and June 5, or merely its method of procedure. Was the Marshall Plan a repudiation of the Truman Doctrine or just a more subtle version of the same policy? On the face of it, the Marshall Plan represented a reversal of the anti-Soviet crusade. The reversal seemed explicit in Secretary Marshall's already quoted, " Our policy is not directed against any country or doctrine."

It seemed fully demonstrated by the subsequent offer of participation to Russia and the countries in the Soviet orbit. On the
other hand, could one really assume that President Truman
believed that the Congress, which he himself indoctrinated with
the spirit of anti-Soviet crusade, would consent to a plan which
made American dollars available to the Soviet Union and its
satellites? [13]

Molotov misunderstood and misread the altruistic intentions underlying the Marshall Plan, participation in which
was open to all. He took the attitude that its main purpose
was the rebuilding of Western Germany into the arsenal of
the West. Unfortunately subsequent events have demonstrated that, as far as results are concerned, his criticism was
not entirely without foundation.

At the London Conference, Marshall put forward
Byrnes's offer of a forty-years peace treaty with Germany,
containing guarantees of complete demilitarisation: again,
due to Molotov's tactics, the conference ended in the usual
failure.

The Berlin Blockade

The failure of the previous conferences of Foreign Ministers
to find a solution to the German problem intensified the
cold war, and both sides were again busy consolidating
themselves as military *blocs*.

On January 24, 1948, Mr. Bevin revealed that conversations were already under way between Britain, France and
the Benelux countries for the formation of a sort of
" Western Union."

Lord Montgomery takes up the tale:

> The scene now changes to December 1947. The Foreign
> Ministers of the occupying Powers in Germany had been
> engaged in conference in London on the subject of that country,
> and it became obvious that no agreement with Russia could be
> reached. When I arrived back from my African tour, Ernie
> Bevin sent for me [on December 23, 1947] and said that he
> suggested to the Foreign Minister of France [M. Bidault] that

[13] *Germany, Key to Peace*, pp. 56–57.

the time had come to begin the formation of a Federation or Union in Western Europe, and if possible to bring the Americans in. . . . On the initiative of the Foreign Office, General Revers, Chief of Staff of the French Army, was invited to London and I had long talks with him on the whole problem. Meanwhile Bevin pushed ahead with the project of a Western Union. . . . He then approached General Marshall, Secretary of State in President Truman's Administration, who warmly welcomed the idea of a political and economic union of the Western European and Mediterranean countries on the lines suggested. Encouraged by this, Mr. Bevin suggested that we should now begin private talks with the Americans, with a view that they might eventually join with the alliance. *This was not agreed by the Americans. They were not prepared to face up to Congress at that time on the question of a military commitment to fight in Europe.*[14]

Field-Marshal Montgomery then relates the contents of the plans for military strategy prepared by the Chiefs of Staffs:

They considered three courses of action in Europe:

1. An air strategy.
2. A Continental strategy.
3. A semi-Continental strategy, involving holding Spain and Portugal and liberating Europe by an offensive through the Pyrenees.

The paper dismissed the Continental strategy in a few lines, and the choice was left between the air strategy and the Pyrenees strategy. I blew right up, saying that I disagreed completely with the conclusions of the report. What was meant by the expression "the best strategy appears to be air strategy"? We must defend Western Europe, not liberate: if we allowed it to be overrun from the East, there would be all too little to liberate. . . . I said it would be mighty difficult to achieve an effective Western Union if we could not promise support on land in the event of war. *The Prime Minister [Mr. Attlee] then weighed in strongly against a commitment to send our Army to the Continent.*

I replied that we had already an army there, the British Army of the Rhine. Did he propose we should withdraw it [through Dunkirk] if the Russians attacked? . . . It was

[14] Montgomery, *supra cit.*, pp. 498 *et seq.*

finally agreed to consider the implications of the strategy I advocated, including the effect on the shape and size of our armed forces, consequent on the adoption of such a strategy. At any rate, I had routed the Pyrenees strategists. . . .

My great point was that, if France or the Benelux countries suspected that the British troops then in Germany were to be withdrawn in the event of war, there would be no hope of our bolstering them up to play their part. . . . If we held back, France and the Benelux countries and Western Germany would all collapse against the growing Communist pressure from the east.

On September 20, a few months after the start of the Berlin blockade, Field-Marshal Montgomery was appointed Chairman of the Western Union Commanders-in-Chief Committee.

As in this book we are dealing very much with the military aspects of the problem, we have purposely quoted at such length from Field-Marshal Montgomery's book to show the absurdity of military thinking at that time.

The Soviet coup in Czechoslovakia on February 25 and Masaryk's mysterious death were a shock for the West and a rude awakening to the real menace of Soviet policy in Europe. Western reaction was very swift indeed: within a month all preliminary negotiations between Britain, France and the Benelux countries were completed and the Brussels Treaty was signed, pledging economic co-operation and military assistance.

Russia showed her displeasure by Marshal Sokolovsky's walk-out from the Allied Council, a sign of protest at the London Conference, which was dealing with the German question, being held without any invitation having been issued to the Soviet Union. It is interesting to note, by the way, that the resolutions of the London Conference were strongly criticised in the French National Assembly as not having taken into account French claims in many important respects—the Assembly took a firm stand against any efforts to reconstruct " an authoritarian and centralised Reich."

In spite of these differences of opinion inside the Western camp, events moved further towards the creation of a West German State and towards the crisis over Berlin.

On June 18, the Western Powers introduced in their zones the reform of German currency, which had been long delayed by French obstructions. The Berlin municipal administration repeatedly expressed their misgivings both before and after the separate currency reform in the West, since such a measure was bound to lead to a split in Berlin: the only other alternative was economic fusion of Berlin as a whole with the Soviet zone or with the Western zones, both of which courses were impossible. The Berlin municipal authorities did everything in their power to bring about a currency reform throughout Germany, and appealed to the Allies even after the reform was completed to allow Berlin to retain her political status as a city subordinated to all four Powers.

Marshal Sokolovsky declared that by carrying the currency reform in Berlin, the Western Powers had practically eliminated the Komendantura as a body responsible for the administration of the city. As this measure placed the Soviet zone at a great disadvantage, the Russians not only proceeded to introduce a similar measure in their zone, but on June 24 cut off all land communications westward from Berlin on the pretext of " technical difficulties." This was the beginning of the Berlin blockade, a landmark in the cold war, which brought both sides to the brink of a hot war: this was also the beginning of the airlift, which continued until the end of the blockade on May 12, 1949. During that time 1,500,000 tons of goods were transported in the course of nearly 200,000 flights: the operation was carried out with 380 planes, staffed by 57,000 flying personnel belonging to the three Western Powers.

While developments in Berlin were leading to a crisis, an important event took place which could have had far-reaching effects on the whole situation in Germany: a few days before the beginning of the Berlin blockade, a

conference of Foreign Ministers of the countries of Eastern
Europe took place in Warsaw. The communiqué, the
Warsaw Declaration, published at the end, on June 24,
expressed strong criticism of the London Agreement and
of Western intentions to split Germany, and demanded a
return to the Potsdam principles: it also suggested that a
four-Power conference be called at an early date to discuss
not only the restoration of four-Power government in Germany, but also—and this was more important—the withdrawal of all occupation forces from Germany as soon as
possible.

Point Four demanded:

> The conclusion of a peace treaty with Germany, in accor-
> dance with the Potsdam decisions, so that the occupying troops
> of all the Powers should be withdrawn from Germany within
> one year after the conclusion of the peace treaty.

As Mr. W. Phillips Davison remarks:

> . . . withdrawal of Soviet troops meant withdrawal only to the
> river Oder, forty miles from Berlin. Withdrawal of American
> troops probably meant withdrawal across the Atlantic.[15]

As at that time there was no Atlantic Alliance and the
United States was under no commitment to defend Europe
it is quite likely that Mr. Davison's misgivings were
justified.

This was, however, the first time that the Soviet Union,
applying a " strategy of indirect approach," had come
forward with the suggestion of a mutual withdrawal of
troops. At that time the word " disengagement " had not
been invented.

Warburg makes an interesting comment on these proposals, viewed against the background of the situation in
Europe:

> The Western Powers ignored this interesting overture,
> partly because the defection of Jugoslavia suggested that further
> weakness might develop within the Soviet system, and partly

[15] *The Berlin Blockade*, p. 26.

because they were quite properly unwilling to discuss anything under duress. The vicious circle was now established.

. . . It would have seemed that this moment in the summer of 1948 called for a reappraisal of the deadlocked position and the display of a little ingenuity on the part of Western diplomacy. The Russian indication that the Kremlin would even consider a withdrawal of any part of the Soviet troops stationed in Eastern Europe introduced a new and potentially important element into the picture. Rather than continue to wrestle with the deadlock itself, why not outflank it by a new approach dealing with the causes out of which the deadlock had arisen?

Such an approach might, for example, have taken the form of proposing a wholly new type of agreement as to Europe between the non-European Powers—Russia, Britain and the United States—an agreement under which the three Powers would guarantee the neutrality of the entire Continent west of the Soviet frontier and withdraw their armed forces from the area so neutralised. Such a treaty would not have prevented the United States from maintaining powerful forces in the British Isles or in North Africa. It might have even provided for the maintenance of certain Anglo-American bridge-heads on the Continent, to facilitate a quick return in the event of Soviet encroachment.

Some such broader attack upon the whole problem of Europe might or might not have borne fruit. It might even have failed and yet resulted in relaxing pressure at the point of deadlock to a degree sufficient to make possible at least the discussion of an all-German settlement. . . . Yet no such move was undertaken. The door opened by the Warsaw communiqué was not entered. The Western statesmen were so preoccupied with winning a relatively minor victory that they gave no thought to anything else.[16]

A similar overture—as we shall see later—was again made by Russia, by proxy, a few years later and was again completely ignored by the West.

On May 12, 1949, an agreement was reached at the four-Power conference in New York lifting all traffic restrictions between Berlin and the Western zones. Thus, after ten months, the airlift ended, its primary purpose successfully accomplished.

[16] Warburg *supra cit.*, p. 66.

Davison writes:

> The Soviet decision to lift the blockade has been ascribed to
> a combination of factors. Ambassador Smith wrote that it was
> based in part on the fact that the counterblockade was hurting
> the East far more than the blockade was hurting the West. . . .
> U.N. Secretary-General Trygve Lie believed that the propa-
> ganda effect of the triumphant lift, possibly combined with the
> force of public opinion, played a large role, in addition to the
> counterblockade. . . . Moscow's reasons for ending the crisis
> appear in somewhat different perspective. . . . One advantage
> was that the airlift constituted an appreciable drain on Germany
> and Western Powers: . . . disadvantages of continuing the
> blockade were substantial . . . it was furthering the very develop-
> ments in Western Europe it was intended to block.

> The end of the blockade signified a change in Soviet strategy,
> but not in Soviet aims . . . behind the decision to lift the
> blockade was the fact that it showed no prospect of achieving
> either of the gains to which they [the Russians] had apparently
> aspired in June 1948: incorporation of West Berlin into the
> Soviet zone, or further delay in the recovery of West Germany.[17]

Careful study of this well-documented book suggests
that, although the Soviet blockade ended in defeat, the
margin of the Western victory was rather narrow. It is,
on the other hand, very likely that, if General Clay's suggestions to send an armed convoy—ready if necessary to shoot
its way through—had been accepted, the Russians would
almost certainly have withdrawn before Western determination. The Soviet retreat would have amounted to a
major diplomatic and psychological defeat with far-
reaching implications.

The " Nauheimer Kreis "

Against the background of tension created by the Berlin
blockade, mention must be made of the indefatigable
activities of Professor Ulrich Noack, Professor of Modern
History at the University of Würzburg. In August 1948
he set up an organisation, which he called " Nauheimer

---

[17] Davison, *supra cit.*, p. 139.

Kreis," which had as its main purpose to discuss on a high level the problems of Germany and in particular reunification.

Professor Noack's predominant aim, for which he tried in vain to enlist support in both parts of Germany, was complete neutralisation of Germany. In various outlines of his plan, and in particular his most comprehensive work, the " Witzenhausen Proklamation," formulated on May 18, 1950, he advocated the creation of a completely neutralised and unarmed Germany, freed from troops of occupation. In view of her status, he also advocated an international guarantee.

He gradually enlarged the extent of the territory to enjoy the status of " unarmed neutrality ": at first it should be a narrow strip, stretching from Finland to Trieste, separating the Soviet Union from the Western Powers. Later on, in the summer of 1950, he combined the idea of a " Third Force " with the idea of neutrality. According to him, the whole of Europe should remain neutral between East and West.[18] As a result of his strongly pacifist attitude (in this respect he differed from a similar organisation set up at the same time by a former German Ambassador, A. Nadolny, called the " Gesellschaft für die Wiedervereinigung Deutschlands " also supporting a policy of neutrality, but an armed neutrality), he met with increasing hostility, both in Eastern Germany, where he had talks with Communist leaders, and in Federal Germany. In spite of his efforts, Dr. Adenauer refused to see him.

Prof. Noack's activities slowly faded away, leaving no lasting impact on German political thinking.

The Warburg Plan

Against the background of the Berlin blockade and the Allied airlift the new American Secretary of State, Mr. Dean Acheson, took up his office early in January, 1949.

[18] W. Cornides, *Europa Archiv.*, April 20, 1951, p. 3890.

The situation in which he found himself was not enviable. In the Far East Communist influence was increasing and it was already impossible for the Americans to check it: there was no alternative but to save the remnants of Chiang Kai-shek's routed forces and withdraw gracefully from the mainland of China. As far as Europe was concerned, crucial problems lay unsolved in Germany, which again became a battlefield—this time in the cold war.

Acheson faced a difficult problem, whether to try by determination and patience to unite Germany and thus eliminate it as a bone of contention and danger to peace —or alternatively to accept as a *fait accompli* the partition of Germany as a basis for a more or less permanent solution, based upon a balance of military power. In view of the development of the cold war, the setting up of the Brussels Treaty Organisation and, above all, the policy of containment which was slowly becoming the principal dogma of American thinking, it seemed that division of Germany as part and parcel of the division of the world into two hostile *blocs* was becoming a permanent reality.

The die was cast and only one question remained to be solved, namely Germany's participation in the joint defence system of the West. The talks preliminary to the formation of the North Atlantic Treaty Organisation were a further factor with which the new Secretary had to contend in trying to formulate his policy.

Against this background Mr. James Warburg, in his capacity as former adviser of the U.S. Administration on German affairs, submitted to Mr. Acheson on February 26, 1949, and, a week later, to members of both Houses of Congress, a memorandum of recommendations for the modification of the North Atlantic Treaty, which was then in preparation and a draft Treaty of Europe, which contained among others the following suggestions:

1. *The permanent demilitarisation of Germany* and the control of the Ruhr.

2. *The withdrawal of American, British and Russian troops from all Europe west of the Soviet Union frontiers,* except that Russia, on the one hand, and Great Britain and the United States, on the other, would have the right to maintain not more than two divisions in Germany and Austria. The United States would not be prevented from stationing forces in the British Isles under agreement with Great Britain.

3. *A guarantee to all nations of Europe between the Soviet frontier and the Atlantic against aggression.*[19]

Warburg followed his memorandum with an eight-point argument emphasising that such an agreement " would get the Russian Army out of Europe " and:

> Once the Continent of Europe were neutralised by the proposed treaty, it would become possible for the Western Powers and the Soviet Union to discuss realistically the reduction of their armaments and the transformation of the United Nations into an organisation under which universal enforceable disarmament would be realistically possible.

Mr. Warburg's memorandum did not influence the realisation of the North Atlantic Treaty, which was signed on April 4, 1949. Stalin retaliated a few weeks later by his decision to integrate the national armed forces of the satellite countries into the Soviet military machine, entrusting Marshal Bulganin with the realisation of this plan, which laid the foundations for the Warsaw Pact, to be signed six years later.

At that juncture, the West was still determined not to integrate West Germany into its defence system and neither to use her manpower nor to rebuild her industry for the purposes of war.

Acheson, in a statement before the Senate Foreign Relations Committee on April 27, declared: " . . . there was no thought of bringing West Germany into the alliance. . . . "

---

[19] See Warburg, *supra cit.*, p. 86.

Acheson's Alternatives

At the conference of Foreign Ministers which took place in Paris in May 1949 the German question was, of course, again the bone of contention, not only between Russia and the West but also inside the Western camp.

Paul Nitze, Director of the Foreign Policy Association, has given a very vivid account of the American attitude at that conference:

> As a condition of lifting the blockade we had agreed with the Russians to convene a meeting of the Foreign Ministers in Paris to discuss matters arising out of the situation in Berlin and matters affecting Germany as a whole.
>
> George Kennan, who was then Director of the State Department Policy Planning Staff, was in charge for the upcoming meeting. I was among those who worked with him at that time. We were uncertain as to what it was the Russians wanted to accomplish at the meeting or what they would propose. One possibility was that they may consider or possibly propose withdrawal of foreign forces from Germany and the reunification of Germany. We developed two alternative proposals for consideration by the Western delegation. One was called Plan A and contemplated the phased withdrawal of foreign forces from Germany, the reunification of Germany under free elections and the limitation of German rearmament under four-Power control. Plan B contemplated no commitment to withdraw Western forces from Germany. It endeavoured to go as far as might be practicable within that limitation towards German reunification, the limitations of unilateral control by the individual occupying Powers in their respective zones and the substitution therefor of four-Power control operating by majority vote—except for certain basic limitations on German rearmament which could be changed only by unanimous agreement among the occupying Powers.
>
> It was finally decided to base the Western negotiating position on Plan B and not Plan A. This was done because few people believed that the Russians would in fact agree to any plan requiring the withdrawal of their forces from the Eastern zone.
>
> The negotiations completely confirmed this view. General Chuikov, Soviet High Commissioner in the Eastern zone, said

one day at lunch: "Anyone who suggests the withdrawal of our forces from Germany is mad. These people hate us." [20]

Acheson, probably on the advice of Kennan, decided to negotiate on the lines of Plan B. Mr. Bevin was undecided about the attitude to take towards German reunification: on the one hand he was against partition; on the other he was afraid that a strong reunified Germany might become a powerful competitor for Britain in the export markets, thus worsening the position of British workers.

The French delegate, M. Schuman, was also on the horns of a dilemma: he was afraid that German reunification, as envisaged by Mr. Acheson, might provoke war with the Russians and also that a reunified Germany would become a danger for France.

The Soviet delegate, Vishinsky, instead of pressing for the acceptance of the resolution of the Foreign Ministers in Warsaw the previous year, which demanded a peace treaty with Germany and the withdrawal of all occupation troops (obviously such resolutions could not have been taken without previous blessing from Moscow) simply limited himself to the reiteration of the old Soviet demands for a return to the Potsdam principles. Stalin was still bent on the expansion of Soviet influence over the whole of Germany.

Thus this conference, like several others both before and after, ended in failure, where with more goodwill on both sides it could have ended in success.

The Brecht Plan

A few months after Warburg had submitted his draft "Treaty for Europe," Professor Arnold Brecht, of the New School for Social Research in New York, published an

---

[20] Lecture delivered at Second Annual Meeting of Institute of United States Foreign Policy, Milwaukee, February 2, 1959. See Congressional Record, 1959.

article entitled " The Idea of a Safety Belt." [21]   He suggested the establishment between the Soviet Union and the Western Powers of a broad belt of neutral countries, stretching from Scandinavia to Iran.

Under this plan the Soviet Union and the Western Powers would conclude a pact guaranteeing that the armed forces of one of the signatories would not be allowed on any pretext to enter the territory of any of the countries of the " safety belt ": any attempt to do so would be considered open aggression.

The countries of the belt would be free to associate themselves with Russia and the West, politically and economically: they would be free to enter into any defence alliances among themselves, in order to organise their defence in the case of aggression. Professor Brecht's views are especially interesting for his distinction between the terms " neutrality " and " neutralisation "; in his view, neutrality does not mean a passive attitude, even in case of an aggression; on the contrary, the countries of the " safety belt " could contribute, by their readiness to defend themselves against any aggression, to the security of the West.

Similar views appear in the books and lectures of the distinguished British military writer, Sir John Slessor, who put forward the idea of a Germany committed to a state of " military non-alignment " but having strong national armed forces.

The area of the safety belt would, in the first stage, have consisted of Scandinavia, Germany, Austria and Switzerland and, in the second stage, of Yugoslavia, Greece, Turkey and Eastern Europe.

Professor Brecht was of the opinion that membership of countries of Eastern Europe in the safety belt would be of importance not only to them but also to Germany: as under this plan Soviet troops would have withdrawn from

[21] *The American Political Science Review*, October, 1949.

the countries of Eastern Europe which belonged to the safety belt, they would be prohibited from re-entering, thus removing any danger of Soviet aggression against German territory.

These views support the conclusion reached in an earlier chapter, that reunification of Germany alone, with Eastern Europe remaining in the Soviet sphere of influence and consequently with Soviet troops stationed in Poland, is not, in the long-term interests of the West, a good solution.

Almost as soon as the Berlin blockade came to an end a lively election campaign started in Western Germany, culminating in the victory of the Christian Democrats, headed by Dr. Adenauer. The Russians, having vehemently protested against the setting up of a separate West German State, retaliated one week later by setting up an East German State, the German Democratic Republic, with Moscow-trained German Communists as its leaders.

On November 23 an agreement was signed in Petersberg between the three High Commissioners and Dr. Adenauer conceding to Germany the right to construct ships and to end the dismantling of certain industries, but maintaining the principle of German demilitarisation.

In spite of this, rumours spread, from an unknown source, that German rearmament was only a question of time. An American weekly, *U.S. News and World Report*, on November 27 quoted Kennan as saying that:

> . . . the United States had better put faith in Germany rather than in France as the bulwark against Russia. Mr. Kennan's view is that France will never regain her old position of leadership in Western Europe.

6

Lost Opportunities, 1950-1953

A DRAMATIC reversal in the Western attitude towards German rearmament and consequently the settlement of the German question took place in 1950.

Theoretically, the Western leaders were still determined, at the beginning of the year, to proceed with plans for the defence of Western Europe without German participation. Mr. McCloy, the American High Commissioner, speaking in Stuttgart on February 6 stated emphatically:

> . . . Germany cannot be allowed to develop political conditions or a military status which would threaten other nations or the peace of the world.

At the same time, in view of doubts expressed in the German press as to the efficiency of the Western defence system, in so far as it was aimed at the protection of German territory, M. Schuman, the French Foreign Minister, stated that the Western Powers should guarantee the defence of Germany.

His statement was brought about by the rising demand, voiced by several former German generals, for fully fledged German participation in the defence of their homeland: Warburg writes of Dr. Adenauer's talks with

> . . . the Brüderschaft, a group of German generals, under the leadership of General Kurt von Manteuffel, who openly demanded the creation of a West German army. Their plans—in January 1950—were for one infantry division to be organised by June and an armoured corps in 1951. Moreover, the Brüder-schaft frankly demanded the recapture of the German East.[1]

However, a massive breakthrough against united Western opposition to German rearmament was made in a public

---

[1] Warburg, *Germany, Key to Peace*, p. 29.

statement by Mr. Churchill who, speaking in Parliament as leader of the Opposition on March 16, 1950, suggested that Britain and France should jointly raise Germany to an " equal rank and lasting association."

With these words Mr. Churchill, who before the war had warned his compatriots in vain against the danger of German rearmament, completed the full circle in his political thinking.

Against this background, on April 11, 1950, the famous American columnist, Walter Lippmann, put forward a suggestion for the reunification of Germany and for the mutual withdrawal of Allied forces from West Germany and of Soviet forces eastwards up to the Soviet frontier.

Unfortunately, these counsels, which reappeared a few years later in various proposals, and especially in those of Mr. Gaitskell, were, in 1950, cries in the wilderness.

In the meantime the Schuman Plan, conceived by a prominent French economist, M. Monnet, forecast a significant change in France's attitude towards Germany. Although, originally, it gave opportunities—as did the Marshall Plan in 1947—to the countries of the Soviet *bloc* to take part in it, the Western political leaders did not appear to grasp its value as a weapon in the cold war.

The Soviet leaders, on the other hand, were quick to realise the potential dangers for Russia which stemmed from the Schuman Plan and reacted very quickly: no doubt under instructions, Walter Ulbricht went to Warsaw where he signed a treaty which recognised the Oder-Neisse Line as a permanent frontier—a " frontier of peace " between Poland and Eastern Germany. By this shrewd move Russia put herself in the position of champion of Poland's aspirations and defender of her frontiers.

A week later, on June 13, a senior member of the German Parliament, Paul Loebe, protested against this treaty and declared that the territory east of Oder-Neisse " remains part of Germany."

The outbreak of war in Korea had dramatically speeded up the rather slow evolution in Western thinking towards German rearmament: at the conference of Foreign Ministers in New York on September 12, Acheson suggested an increased British and French armaments effort, a bigger American contribution to the defence of Europe, and, above all, the integration of German contingents into the defence system of Western Europe.

As usual on these occasions, there was a considerable difference of opinion between the delegates of the United States, Britain and France: whereas Acheson was in favour of German participation on an equal basis, the French thought rather in terms of a police force, which would balance the increasing build-up in Eastern Germany of the so-called " Volks-Polizei," which had been set up by the Russians as long ago as 1946.

The Soviet Union protested very strongly on October 18 against Western intentions to revive " German militarism," and a few days later, on October 21, Moscow Radio released the text of the communiqué issued on that date at the end of the conference of the Ministers of Eastern Europe which had met in Prague. This communiqué, having condemned the West for its plans to restore the German army, suggested:

> A peace treaty with Germany in accordance with the Potsdam principles, *a withdrawal within one year after the signature of the treaty of all occupation forces* [author's italics], the setting up of a body to represent both Eastern and Western Germanies in the form of an all German Council, with the task of forming a provisional, democratic, sovereign government. The Council was to submit to the four occupying Powers appropriate proposals, and was to be called in, until such time as an all-German Government was formed, to attend consultations on peace treaty negotiations. There might be even the possibility of going to the German people directly and holding a referendum on this proposal.[2]

[2] See H. Siegler, *The Reunification and Security of Germany*, p. 83.

If the Soviet Union really wanted to achieve reunification of Germany, and first of all to bring about a mutual withdrawal of troops, the best opportunity would have been at the Paris conference in 1949, when it would have coincided with the American Plan A, which Kennan, Acheson's right-hand man, was holding in his file.[3]

Unfortunately, the Soviet Union launched into a " war of notes," complicating the issue and stiffening Western determination to go on with the building up of its defence potential.

As one might have expected, the Soviet Note of October 18 was rejected by the West: in the first place by the United States and a few days later by Dr. Adenauer in Bonn, who stated that any Four-Power conversation with Russia would be futile until the West was strong enough. This line of thought became a rather familiar feature of statements by many Western politicians and military leaders.

Walter Lippmann, however, commented in the *New York Herald Tribune*, soon after his return from a routine trip to Europe:

> It was absurd to make a military ally out of Germany before we had made peace with Germany. More concretely, it was in vain to think that the French and German infantry— the bulk of the ground forces of the proposed Western army— could be " integrated " or would fight loyally side by side, unless France and Germany had first ended their historic quarrel and had become, in law and in fact, partners in Europe.

This eventful year ended with the debates of the NATO Council in Brussels which approved the nomination of General Eisenhower as Supreme Commander in Europe. Again, because of the diverging views towards German rearmament, a compromise solution was adopted to allay French misgivings, the so-called " Pleven Plan " of the " European Army," which provided for the integration of German contingents in the form of brigades of 6,000 men

3 See above, p. 143.

in mixed divisions under the command of non-German generals.

As subsequent events have shown, this plan has remained an unrealistic fiction.

It is interesting to note that it was in this same year of 1950 that Soviet diplomacy for the first time officially put forward a suggestion for mutual withdrawal—until then it was thought better in Moscow to employ a " strategy of indirect approach," and to put forward the same idea through the mouths of the Soviet satellites.

Background to the Soviet Draft Peace Treaty

One of the purposes of this Part is to consider the history not so much of German rearmament as of the various unsuccessful efforts to prevent it. During the whole of 1951, no serious attempt in this direction was made by either side, nor was any suggestion put forward by any politician or writer of repute. We shall therefore limit ourselves to a brief survey of the events leading to the further integration of Germany into NATO.

In an earlier chapter we mentioned General Eisenhower's " reconnaissance " trip to Europe early in January 1951, when he learned of the differences between France and Germany over the question of German rearmament and of the fluctuations in German public opinion. As a result, he recommended a " go slow " on German participation in Western defence.

Meanwhile, the diplomatic exchanges between the West and Moscow continued until the Foreign Ministers Conference in Paris, which began in March and lasted until the middle of June, ending in the usual failure.

It is interesting to analyse briefly and to speculate on the reasons for that failure, which, as was the case with the previous conference in Paris, might have been avoided.

During these latest negotiations both sides piled up

difficulties, filling up the agenda with additional items and procedural technicalities, without hoping to solve them. The Western delegation brought in matters irrelevant to the main issue, such as general disarmament, the Austrian Treaty, etc.; for their part, the Russians retaliated by putting on the agenda such delicate questions as American overseas bases and NATO.

Warburg writes on the failure of the conference:

> Ostensibly, the conference broke up over Russian insistence that the Atlantic Treaty and the question of American overseas bases be put on the agenda. The Russian demand could not very well have been made at all if the Western Powers had been willing to confer primarily on Germany. . . . The essential fact was that nobody wanted to discuss German reunification. . . . Where the Western Powers made their mistake was in failing to take the determined initiative with a concrete proposal for German unification and a peace settlement once the Russians had committed themselves to a four-power conference designed to bring about these results. Had they done so, they would either have achieved a German settlement or placed the onus for a continued partition of Germany squarely upon the Kremlin. Two factors probably caused this Western failure: the stubborn adherence of the American Government to its pet project of including West Germany in NATO; and the vocal opposition to a four-power conference expressed at this time by the West German Government. . . . This apparent contradiction between the German desire for unification and German opposition to a four-power conference to discuss unification was not too difficult to understand. Chancellor Adenauer's policy of exerting constant pressure upon the Western Powers for more and more concessions had proved itself highly profitable. . . . A four-power conference, even if its results should prove to be inconclusive, would make Germany once more the object of negotiations, instead of being one of the major participants.[4]

We have quoted Warburg's comments on the German attitude at such length, because in the light of recent events, in particular the second Berlin crisis, his views have lost nothing in topicality.

---

[4] Warburg, *op. cit.*, pp. 162–163.

Meanwhile, on September 15, the Prime Minister of Eastern Germany, Otto Grotewohl, wrote to Dr. Adenauer, referring to the resolutions of the Prague conference in the previous year (mentioned above) and to his subsequent approach to Dr. Adenauer with a suggestion for the formation of an all-German Council with equality of membership from both Germanies. He repeated the proposal but dropped his demand for equality of membership. The Government of the Federal Republic again rejected Grotewohl's overtures on September 27: after all, Bonn was not too keen, at that juncture, to press for reunification, and time was running in its favour.

It is against this background that we must examine the Soviet draft for a German peace treaty, which was submitted to the three Western Powers on March 10, 1952, together with a suggestion that it should be discussed at a conference of the four major Powers.[5]

This draft, which was a major feat of Soviet diplomacy, showed that Russia was willing to agree to the establishment of a reunified Germany, democratic in the Western sense; the Russians even went as far as to agree to mutual withdrawal of troops from Germany, dropping their demand for the dismantling of all American overseas bases, which would obviously have been unacceptable to the United States. As the price for her concessions, Russia demanded German military neutrality.

If one compares this draft with previous Soviet proposals it is obvious that Russia was prepared to pay a heavy price, including the dropping of the East German Communist régime, in order to prevent the imminent integration of Germany into NATO.

Unfortunately, this Soviet overture was made at least two years too late: the die was cast, and nothing, except perhaps a complete capitulation of Russia, tantamount to an unconditional acceptance of Western terms, would

[5] For full text, see Appendix 1.

have changed the Western determination to push through the plans to use Germany's manpower and resources, as well as its territory, for the benefit of NATO.

The Western Powers, as expected, rejected the Soviet draft and this war of notes lasted for all practical purposes until the conference of Foreign Ministers of the Four Powers in Berlin in January–February, 1954.

In the meantime two important events took place: on May 26, 1952, the three Western Foreign Ministers and Dr. Adenauer signed the agreement in Bonn which restored full sovereignty to the Federal Republic; after that historic ceremony they went to Paris to sign another important document, the deed setting up the European Defence Community with its European Army.

The United States Government was the first to recognise and—on July 1, 1952—ratify these two treaties which, as Warburg pointed out, " would make the Bonn Republic the dominant partner in the West European community." [6] But the United States' example did not galvanise other Western European governments into following suit. It took more than a year for Dr. Adenauer to push ratification through the reluctant Bundestag, and in France the National Assembly, after a bitter debate, rejected it.

These delays are the best proof of how strongly public opinion in the West was opposed to German rearmament. History may show that the peoples of Western Europe understood by instinct the dangerous implications of re-arming Germany better than did their governments.

A few months later, after a lively exchange of diplomatic Notes, the Soviet Government renewed its offer of a mutual withdrawal of troops and of a peace treaty with Germany, suggesting that a conference of Foreign Ministers of the four Powers be convened. But the Western Powers rejected the Soviet proposals on the ground that there could be no discussion of a peace treaty until an all-German

[6] Warburg, *op. cit.*, p. 211.

Government existed with which such a treaty might be negotiated. Mr. Warburg writes:

> The weakness of the Western position lay in the obvious sophistry of the contention that the four Powers could not profitably discuss what sort of a treaty they would wish to negotiate with Germany until such an all-German Government existed. Suppose that an all-German Government did exist. Would its existence resolve the differences between Russia and the West—the differences which would have to be resolved before there could be any four-Power negotiations with Germany? Why should not the four Powers seek to reach agreement in order to be ready to negotiate with an all-German Government? [7]

The history of diplomatic exchanges between the Soviet Union and the West is a tale of lost opportunities. The West had in its hands a strong bargaining card, namely, the rearmament of Germany and her integration into NATO. At that time, when German troops did not exist and were only vaguely contemplated, it would have been much easier than it is today to barter the whole idea for the comprehensive settlement with Russia of European problems. Unfortunately, the United States embarked on a rigid policy of rearming Germany, which neither France nor Britain nor the great majority of Germans wanted at that time. This decision was based upon a wrong assessment of the Soviet military threat in Europe, which in fact never seriously existed: after all, if Russia wanted to invade Europe she could have easily done so before NATO came into being or even when NATO was being formed and the French contingents were melting away to Indo-China. The Soviet Union was deterred from an aggression—if it had ever seriously contemplated it—not merely by the A-bomb but by fear of a mass uprising in Eastern Europe, which was a more serious danger to Russia than a few German divisions in West Germany.

Another reason for the determination of the United

[7] Warburg, *op. cit.*, p. 227.

States to press for German rearmament was the appraisal of the strategic situation made by the Allied senior commander at that time. At the end of the NATO manoeuvres in 1952 Marshal Juin—then Commander of the Central European Front—declared that the forces under his command would not be able to defend Western Europe before the Rhine was reached, which meant, by implication, that the whole territory of Western Germany would be abandoned, perhaps after some sort of delaying action. This utterly pessimistic and, in fact, unjustifiable statement, which produced an outcry in Western Europe, and especially in Germany, who would have been the main victim of such strategy, made a contribution from Germany appear more important than ever.

Karl Pfleiderer's Plan

Apart from the plans for the solution of the German problem which were put forward by the Soviet Union and by the West, several statesmen, politicians and political writers of repute also contributed ideas and suggestions which undoubtedly made their impact on public opinion, and perhaps also on official policy.

We have already mentioned the Warburg and Brecht plans in the United States. One of the first European politicians was Dr. Karl Pfleiderer, a member of the Free Democratic Party and a former diplomat, who had seen a lot of service in the Soviet Union.

He had the courage of his convictions and did not hesitate to present his views, in spite of the fact that they differed greatly from the policy of the Bonn Government, and in particular from the firmly accepted dogma that free elections and Soviet withdrawal must be interlocked together. For him—and this seemed like heresy in Bonn at that time—the primary object of the policy of the West was to get Soviet troops out of Eastern Germany at any price. He had the courage to state in his public speeches and leaflets that EDC and NATO were an obstacle to the reunification of Germany—a thesis which was later adopted by the Social Democrats—and that the maintenance of the *status quo* meant the continuation of the enslavement of eighteen million Germans in the Eastern Zone.

In his speech of June 6, 1952, in Waiblingen [Würtemberg] in which he presented his plan, he said, *inter alia*:

> . . . we want the peaceful reunification of our Western and Eastern halves. What is the new system of States to be? I should think that, if those areas of Germany which are under Polish administration remain occupied by the Soviet forces, the Western Allies could, with good cause, keep corresponding portions of Western Germany under occupation. Both parties could strengthen and make sure of their positions by bridgeheads. Between these occupied parts of Germany would be a third part, the largest, provided with its own forces of fixed strength. No German would recognise the Oder-Neisse frontier as final, but all Germans would recognise that in this matter there was to be no question of applying force. . . . This would be a kind of compromise between the NATO and EDC systems on the one hand, and the Russian system on the other.

On September 2 of the same year he published a memorandum, *Treaty Machinery and Eastern Policy*, which is worth quoting at greater length:

> All thought of neutralisation of the Federal Republic through a third Power, of her voluntary neutrality based upon self-protection, can be just as easily left out of consideration as the Soviet proposals for negotiations, according to which the Federal Republic is not to attach itself to any Western system. . . . The best example by far which could be considered for mutual security, and which may serve as a point of departure because it worked excellently for years, is the former European treaty system as it was created in 1925–26 by the Locarno Pact, by the entry of Germany into the League of Nations and by the Berlin Treaty signed between Germany and Russia on April 24, 1926. In this connection, however, the fundamental question remains open, whether the peculiarity of a middle position today applies only to Germany or to a whole group of European States. . . .[8]

---

[8] H. Siegler, *op. cit.*, p. 106.

Although Dr. Pfleiderer's views caused great annoyance to the Bonn Government, in view of his high personal standing he could not simply be sent into the political wilderness, and he was offered the post of an ambassador in Belgrade, which he accepted: he died of a heart attack shortly before the recognition by Marshal Tito of the East German régime.

The Second Warburg Plan

We mentioned earlier Warburg's memorandum of 1949, submitted to the Secretary of State and members of both houses of Congress, which contained recommendations for the modification of the North Atlantic Treaty—then in process of negotiation—and suggestions for a treaty for Europe.

On December 18, 1952, he submitted another memorandum to General Eisenhower's personal chief of staff, Sherman Adams, to John Foster Dulles and to President Conant of Harvard University, designated as the new High Commissioner for Germany.

Before mentioning the essential points of that memorandum, which was published by the author in a pamphlet entitled *France, Germany and NATO*, and which appeared in a German translation under a more appropriate title, *The Warburg Plan*, we should offer a rough picture of the political situation at that time.

General Eisenhower was elected President of the United States in the November elections of 1952: during the election campaign, attacking Truman's policy of containment, he coined the fiery slogan " liberation," which resulted in millions of votes in his favour by many Americans of East-European extraction. One would have expected that the policy of the New Administration, if truly based upon this slogan, would have meant a re-shaping of the policy of the Truman-Acheson era and consequently some modification of the attitude towards the problem of German rearmament.

At the same time it was well known in Washington that public opinion in Western Europe was not unanimous in support of the American initiative for closer integration of Germany into the joint defence system of the West. Thus during the debate on the ratification of EDC in the French National Assembly in October, 1952, which ended with its rejection, a prominent French statesman, M. Herriot, took a very strong stand against the proposed treaty, demanding stronger guarantees against the dangers of German domination; the de Gaullists and some smaller parties—including the Communists—rallied to the stand of the French Radicals, headed by Herriot. At the same time similar misgivings were voiced in Britain.

Unfortunately, despite the slogan of " liberation " and despite the doubts of millions of Europeans, no fundamental change in American foreign policy, and especially in the American attitude towards Europe, took place.

Warburg put forward the following suggestions: a peace treaty with Germany, to be preceded by negotiation with the Soviet Union which, *inter alia*, ought to

> (1) properly determine Germany's frontiers; (2) decide whether Germany should or should not be given the right to maintain armed forces and to manufacture arms; (3) decide whether Germany shall or shall not be given the right to join alliances.[9]

In elaborating these proposals, he suggested (1) that Germany should be permanently deprived of East Prussia and Upper Silesia, but that the remaining former territories annexed by Poland in 1945 be returned. As regards German rearmament he suggested (2) that

> . . . Germany shall be kept disarmed and demilitarised for a period of five, perhaps ten years, with the explicit provision that if universal disarmament shall not have been achieved at the end of that period all restrictions applicable to Germany alone shall be lifted.

[9] Warburg, *op. cit.*, p. 253.

The Western proposals should further provide for continuous inspection by a United Nations Commission to enforce German disarmament and demilitarisation, with any violations to be reported at once to the Security Council. The United Nations Commission should take over its duties as soon as the occupation forces of the four Powers are withdrawn; this should be not later than one year after the signature of the peace treaty.

Concerning Germany's right to enter into military alliances, he suggested:

The Western Powers should propose a guarantee of German neutrality by all signatories of the peace treaty for the period during which Germany is denied the right to rearm; if at the end of that period German rearmament is permitted (by reason of failure to achieve universal disarmament) then the guarantee shall lapse and Germany shall have the right to enter whatever military alliances it may wish.

In summing up his proposals Warburg comments:

What is suggested here is not an unarmed neutrality freely chosen by a fully sovereign German nation but neutralisation by four-power agreement and German consent, co-terminous with a period of demilitarisation enforced by the United Nations.[10]

Dulles, to whom Warburg submitted his memorandum, in his speech on the radio on January 27, 1953, clearly indicated that no revision of American policy towards Europe was being contemplated, unless the European reluctance to carry out the NATO plan compelled a reorientation.

The death of Stalin on March 5, 1953, and the conciliatory attitude adopted towards the West by Stalin's successor, Malenkov, opened new vistas and possibilities for imaginative Western policies and for the settlement of European and, in particular, German problems. Indeed, President Eisenhower was willing and prepared to consider such reorientation in American policy: in his Press Conference on April 2, he said that he would welcome an honest step on the part of Russia and repeated his willingness to meet Malenkov.

---

[10] Warburg, *op. cit.*, p. 265.

Unfortunately, the next day John Foster Dulles, at his own Press Conference, declared:

> "Nothing that has happened or seems to me likely to happen has changed the basic situation of danger in which we stand."

Sir Winston Churchill's Proposal

In describing Dr. Pfleiderer's plan for setting up a sort of middle zone in Germany, we mentioned that in planning the future European security system he recommended that advantage be taken of the experience of the Locarno Pact of 1925–1926.

It is doubtful whether Sir Winston Churchill was ever acquainted with Dr. Pfleiderer's ideas, but he also based his proposal on the basic principles of the Locarno Pact. Speaking in Parliament on May 11, 1953, Sir Winston Churchill, then Prime Minister, expressed the view that after Stalin's death one of the main problems of his successors was to bring the security of Russia into line with the security and freedom of Western Europe. The 1925 Locarno Pact, as he said, had been based upon the elementary provision that Great Britain would side with the French in the event of a German attack, or with Germany in the event of a French attack. And that idea, on which the Locarno Treaty was based, might well play its part between Germany and Russia. He added that "Russia had every right to the certainty that the dreadful events born of Hitler's invasion would never be repeated."

By putting forward his constructive idea of a European settlement based upon the principles of the Locarno Pact, Sir Winston took the sting out of Dulles's favourite idea— although purely academic and meant for rhetorical effect only—of "liberation." In the same speech Sir Winston Churchill suggested high-level talks in order to settle all the differences between Russia and the West. It is important to note the views of a foremost Soviet expert, Boris

Nicolaevsky. In an article, "Khrushchev's Foreign Policy," he wrote:

> Today, it is obvious from available documents that in April and May 1953, Soviet foreign-policy makers, in the confusion following Stalin's death, were prepared to seek agreement with the West even at a price of substantial concessions. Sir Winston Churchill saw this: in May he pleaded in the House of Commons for a Summit Meeting. Unfortunately, just at that time sickness prevented him from pushing the issue. The heads of the other West European Powers, moreover, failed to grasp the urgency of the situation.[11]

President Eisenhower, however, responded very favourably to Churchill's initiative and suggested a conference in Bermuda in early June to precede the Four-Power Conference which was to follow at a later date.

In order to convince the West that there had been a fundamental change in Soviet foreign policy, Russia, during May and June, had relaxed its occupation régime in Austria, withdrawn all territorial claims against Turkey and introduced a series of far-reaching economic measures in Eastern Germany which were already much overdue, thus admitting its past mistakes. These Soviet moves produced something like panic in Bonn: Herr von Brentano, the Federal German Foreign Minister, speaking in the Bundestag, said that these moves must be considered only as "tactical attempts to spoil Western unity," but that they must be taken seriously. In a nervous atmosphere in Germany, Dr. Adenauer sent a cable to President Eisenhower on May 29 warning him against any attempt to settle the German question with the Russians by negotiation. Obviously, Dr. Adenauer realised that any settlement of the German question by negotiation—and at that time such a settlement was feasible—would have meant the end of Germany's dreams of becoming a dominant power in Europe.

[11] *New Leader*, May 4, 1959.

A Secret Western Plan ?

It is very likely that in this situation, created by a far-reaching change—at least on the surface—in the Soviet attitude and foreign policy, the Western Powers began seriously to consider a plan for the settlement of the German question. The existence of such a plan was disclosed for the first time by the spokesman of the SPD at the press conference of the Party in Bonn.[12]

According to the SPD spokesman the three Western High Commissioners, including the new American High Commissioner, James B. Conant, were, in 1953, preparing a plan for the formation, by stages, of an interim all-German Government with severely limited powers, to act until a peace treaty was signed. Until then the two existing East and West German Governments were to function. Foreign policy, defence and internal security would be exclusively reserved to the jurisdiction of the two separate governments, the " supra-government's " responsibility being limited mainly to internal administration.

So far it has been impossible to secure from the SPD in Bonn any further details of this alleged plan, and, of course, even more difficult to obtain confirmation from official Western quarters.

Obviously, to put this plan into effect would require an agreement between the Western Powers before an agreement with Russia could be attempted: unfortunately, the Bermuda conference, at which this plan, or its basic principles, would have been debated was delayed for a considerable time owing to the ministerial crisis in France.

A new French Government was formed on June 26, but on the next day Sir Winston Churchill, following his doctors' advice, asked for an indefinite postponement of the conference.

[12] Reported by the Bonn correspondent of the *New York Herald Tribune*, March 25, 1959.

In the meantime, a completely unexpected event had dramatically, if only temporarily, changed the whole atmosphere, namely the uprising in Eastern Germany. The harshness with which this uprising—due to some fairly minor grievances of an economic nature—was suppressed by the Soviet tanks came as a moral shock to the West; it played straight into the hands of those who advocated intensified military effort and a closer integration of German resources.

Yet the conference of the three Western Foreign Ministers, following Sir Winston's suggestion, sent an invitation to Russia to take part in top level talks, which after the exchange of many notes eventually took place in Berlin in January–February, 1954.

The Van Zeeland Plan

Having described Churchill's suggestion for the European settlement on the basis of the Locarno Pact, we cannot, of course, omit another plan which was put forward at the end of the same year by a prominent Belgian statesman, M. Paul van Zeeland, who was then the Belgian Foreign Minister. He submitted his plan to the NATO Council meeting in Paris on December 11, 1953, and expounded it at his press conference at the Palais Chaillot the next day.

Before putting his plan before the NATO Council, M. van Zeeland discussed it with President Eisenhower and Dulles during his visit to Washington in October. In his conversations with the American leaders he did not fail—according to the despatch from Washington of the Belgian paper *Le Soir* of October 1—to inform them of the misgivings which the European nations had as a result of the rigidity of American foreign policy towards some aspects of the European problems.

The essence of his plan is as follows:

(1) The reunification of Germany as a sovereign State will take place on the condition that Soviet troops withdraw

from Eastern Germany, which should remain completely demilitarised.

(2) On both sides of this completely demilitarised zone, two partly demilitarised zones should be set up: (i) Poland, in which Soviet troops would withdraw to east of the Vistula, and which would have her own national armed force, and (ii) the Federal Republic, which would also be allowed to have its own national armed forces and from which all NATO troops would withdraw to west of the Rhine.

American troops should be deployed on the left bank of the Rhine and on the territory of the adjacent countries.

Such a settlement should be covered by a European Security Pact on the lines of the Locarno Pact, and any attempt at aggression would be dealt with by the necessary sanctions. This Security Pact would guarantee the existing frontiers and, among others, the present German-Polish frontier along the Oder-Neisse Rivers. Van Zeeland did not entirely approve this frontier and was of the opinion that Germany should negotiate with Poland for some modifications of it through diplomatic channels.

The result of such a settlement would be that Western Europe would be divided from the Russians by three defensive glacis.

Although M. van Zeeland's plan has never been put before the Russians and consequently never been put to the test, it made a certain impact on Western thinking. It can be found in the Berlin Declaration of July 27, 1957, with which we shall deal later.

The Spaak Plan

Brief mention should also be made of the suggestions put forward in the same year by another prominent Belgian statesman, former Belgian Foreign Minister and at present Secretary-General of NATO, M. Henri Spaak, who said, during the debate at the Council of Europe in Strasbourg:

> It is not the question whether we are for and against German reunification, because we are for it—the question is only of the price.

According to an article in *Aussenpolitik*,[13] M. Spaak rejected the idea of Germany's neutrality. He is of the same opinion now, and in his speech he put forward the following proposals: (a) that there should be a multilateral security pact in which the United States and U.S.S.R. should participate; (b) that a demilitarised zone should be set up on both sides of the eastern frontier of the reunited Germany. (He did not go into further detail on this proposal.)

V. V. Tilea's Memorandum

In December, 1953, in view of the forthcoming Four Foreign Ministers Conference in Berlin, Mr. V. V. Tilea, former Rumanian Minister in Great Britain from 1939 to 1940 and now a political exile, submitted to the Foreign Ministers of the United States, Great Britain and France a Memorandum drawing their attention to the situation of the countries of Eastern Europe under Soviet occupation. He suggested mutual withdrawal of troops from Germany and Eastern Europe; according to him, the whole area, freed from foreign troops, should become a neutral area, covered by guarantees under the terms of a European Security Pact.

---

[13] Schmieden, "Europaeische Zusammenschluss und Deutsche Vereinigung," June 1957.

7

Marking Time, 1954-1956

THE year 1954, which began with the Four-Power Conference of Foreign Ministers in Berlin, abounded in diplomatic exchanges between the Soviet Union and the West, and several constructive plans, both official and unofficial, were put forward by both sides.

The conference of the four Foreign Ministers in Berlin, from January 25 to February 18, which was the eventual result of Sir Winston Churchill's suggestion for top level talks, overshadowed everything. The conference took place against the background of a considerable change of heart in the Kremlin, especially in the attitude of the then Soviet Prime Minister, G. Malenkov. In this context it is worth quoting Boris Nicolaevsky once again:

> Only Stalin's death saved the world from catastrophe, . . . others in the dictatorship's top rank, including Molotov, Malenkov, Beria and many professional soldiers, headed by Marshal Zhukov, were dubious about Stalin's last policies. . . .
>
> The first one to urge a more moderate course was Lavrenti Beria. The long-time secret police [MVD] chief was in a better position than anyone else to appreciate the gravity of the situation inherited from Stalin, both within the U.S.S.R. and in the European and Asian satellites. *He feared an explosion, particularly in the satellites and was prepared to make concessions.*[1]

In his speech preceding the elections to the Supreme Soviet in February 1954, Malenkov declared that any future war would be a nuclear one and would spell the doom of all civilisation. This was the very first time that a top leader addressed an anti-war declaration to the Soviet public with the idea of stirring up opposition to a war policy. Before this, all anti-militaristic slogans voiced by Soviet leaders had been strictly for export. It was not until Molotov's speech at the Supreme Soviet session in

---

[1] Author's italics.

February 1955, and the appearance of the fourth issue for 1955 of the magazine *Kommunist*, that the strong impact of Malenkov's words on the war faction of the top leadership became apparent.[2]

It was during that conference that Mr. Anthony Eden, in his speech on January 29, put forward his first Plan for the reunification of Germany by all-German elections,[3] free and supervised.

As there exists a great deal of confusion about the Eden plan and its real contents, it is essential to point out at this juncture that for all practical purposes there were three Eden plans. The first one was put forward during the Berlin conference and dealt primarily with free elections and Germany's right to associate herself with other States; the second was put forward at the Summit meeting in Geneva in July, 1955, and related to security and regional disarmament; and, finally, the so-called "amended Eden plan" put forward by the British delegation at the Foreign Ministers' conference at Geneva in the same autumn dealt with free elections and problems of security.

The essence of his proposals, called officially "A Plan for German Reunification in Freedom," describes the mechanism for five stages of German reunification: (1) Free elections throughout Germany, under adequate supervision, in accordance with electoral law.[4] (2) The convening of a National Assembly resulting from these elections. (3) The drafting of a constitution and the preparation of peace treaty negotiations. (4) The adoption of the constitution and the formation of an all-German

---

[2] *New Leader*, May 4, 1959.

[3] For full text, see Appendix 2.

[4] In this context Eden said " . . . both the West German Bundestag and the Assembly of the Soviet Zone have prepared drafts of an all-German electoral law. These contain much valuable material. A Four-Power draft, therefore, should draw very largely upon them. . . ." (See his speech on January 29, 1954: *Documents relating to the Meeting of Foreign Ministers of France, the United Kingdom, the Soviet Union and the United States of America*, p. 35). Eden's reference to the electoral laws originating in the East German Parliament and the possibility of their being considered by the West met with resentment from Bonn.

Government responsible for negotiating the peace treaty. (5) The signing and entry into force of the peace treaty.

In summing up he emphasised the fact that the future all-German Government

> . . . must be free to assume any international rights and obligations of the Federal Republic or of the East German régime which are consistent with the UNO Charter,

and

> . . . to associate with other nations for peaceful purposes.

Not surprisingly, these stipulations, which are the substance of the Western policy towards Germany and aim at its integration with the Western defence system, evoked strong and determined criticism from the Soviet delegate, Mr. Molotov.

Although he expressed his approval of the idea of free elections by saying on January 30,

> . . . the Soviet Government always attached great significance to the holding of free elections,

he also declared:

> Germany should not be bound by any agreements with any group of Powers . . . but she should have free decision not only in internal affairs but also in external affairs.

He developed his point of view in his next speech on February 1, suggesting some additions to the original Soviet draft of a peace treaty with Germany, which had been submitted in 1952. And in his speech on February 8, in answer to Mr. Dulles, he reiterated:

> We consider it wrong that united Germany should be included in any military *bloc* of Eastern European countries directed against Western Europe. We consider it equally wrong that united Germany should form part of any military *bloc* of Western European States directed against Eastern Europe.[5]

Mr. Molotov summed up his ideas in the official proposals put forward by the Soviet delegation. These ideas embodied the following principles:

[5] See *Documents, etc., supra cit.*, p. 104.

(1) That all foreign troops should withdraw from Germany not later than one year after the date of the coming into force of the peace treaty. All foreign bases on German territory would be liquidated simultaneously.

(2) That the frontiers of Germany should be determined in accordance with the Potsdam agreement.

(3) That Germany should undertake not to enter into any coalitions or military alliances directed against any Power whose forces took part in the war against Germany.

(4) That Germany should be allowed to have her own national armed forces, their strength to be limited in accordance with internal requirements, defence of the frontiers and anti-aircraft defence. Germany should also be permitted to manufacture military supplies and equipment.

All these arrangements should be covered by a " European Security Pact" containing "adequate guarantees against aggression," with U.S.A. and U.S.S.R. as its signatories. [This was a new concession on the part of the Soviet Union.] In spite of these concessions by Mr. Molotov, the conference broke down due to the unbridgeable gap in the attitudes of each side towards Germany's right to enter into an alliance with NATO. It was obviously understood in the West that a reunited Germany would enter into such an alliance although this point was not openly admitted.

The Soviet Government made its position clear once again on October 23, the last day of the Paris conference, when it envisaged the accession of Germany to NATO in the same year. In a Note to the three Western Powers it stated that *it would be willing to re-examine the Eden Plan.* If, however, the decisions taken at the Paris conference were put into effect, Russia would no longer be able to regard Germany as a " peace-loving nation." This Soviet statement implied that Russia was at that time ready to jettison its puppet régime in Eastern Germany in order to prevent Germany's integration into NATO.

The Soviet attitude was endorsed by the resolution of the heads of the Eastern European governments at a conference in Moscow from November 29 to December 2, which, after condemning the intended rearmament of Germany, expressed the hope that:

> If the plans to remilitarise Western Germany were forgone, the main obstacle to reunification would be removed, and an agreement could be reached on the holding of all-German free elections in 1955 and the formation of an all-German free government, which would be followed by the conclusion of a peace treaty.[6]

M. Bohy's Suggestions

The failure of the Berlin conference was discussed on various occasions at the sessions of the Council of Europe. During the September debate, one of the Belgian delegates, M. A. Bohy, a Socialist, suggested the following compromise formula:

> Germany shall be free to be associated politically with the West, and to have a special military status of non-alignment. These provisions could bring about security by setting up between the Soviet *bloc* and Atlantic *bloc* a sort of European middle zone.

which was to be strong enough to defend itself although too weak to be able to commit an act of aggression.

In his next speech, in December, M. Bohy suggested the following three stages: (1) a gradual thinning out of forces on both sides of the present demarcation lines; (2) the fixing of a " ceiling of forces " in the countries neighbouring Germany, combined with free elections in Germany, and (3) a gradual limitation of arms in the Soviet Union, Great Britain and the United States.

It is interesting to note that some of M. Bohy's views reappeared the following year in Sir Anthony Eden's famous

---

[6] See H. Siegler, *The Reunification and Security of Germany*, p. 88.

plan for "thinning out" and, again, in Mr. Macmillan's suggestions for a freezing of arms in Europe.

Colonel von Bonin's Plan

The Western plans for the defence of Western Europe and for the use of German resources for that purpose were strongly criticised in German military circles at that time.

German strategists strongly objected to the basic principles of Western classic strategy, which consisted of fighting a delaying battle in Germany near the Rhine, until the effects of the counter-stroke by the American Strategic Air Force were felt by the Russians, and until the mobilised reserves enabled the West to regain the lost ground. They called it derisively "a retours offensive," and were especially opposed to the so-called "scorched-earth" policy, which had been inadvertently advocated by some Western military leaders.

One of the most outspoken critics of Western strategy was Colonel B. von Bonin, head of the planning department in the so-called Blank Office, which is known now as the Federal Ministry of Defence: as a result of his attitude, which was certainly not in accordance with the long-term policy of the Bonn Government, Colonel von Bonin was dismissed from his post and retired.

His views have been presented by a leading German military writer, A. Weinstein, in his book, *Keiner kann den Krieg gewinnen*. Colonel von Bonin maintained that the defence of Germany should be entrusted to German national forces alone, and the classic Atlantic strategy of a delaying manoeuvre, which would transform Germany into a battlefield, should be replaced by a strategy of absolute defence ("die absolute Verteidigung"). A fortified zone, some fifty kilometres deep should be established along the whole of the present political frontier, approximately 800 kilometres (500 miles), and this should be manned by eight frontier divisions, heavily armed with anti-tank weapons: these divisions would be formed entirely of volunteers, and supported by four armoured divisions, acting as mobile reserve.

The full strength of these national armed forces would not exceed some 150,000 men, which differs considerably from the figure of 500,000 anticipated by the Western military planners.

Colonel von Bonin, looking at the question from a military standpoint, did not realise that the larger the German contribution to the joint Western defence effort, the greater would be her political importance in international counsels.

The NATO troops, according to this concept, should withdraw to the left bank of the Rhine and could be called upon only as a strategic reserve in case of major Soviet aggression.

Colonel von Bonin's plan came under an increasingly heavy fire of criticism from German military circles. For example, in an article, " Strategie des Wunschtraumes," [7] J. Rogge, after a minute analysis of the plan, came to the devastating conclusion that the forces to be allocated, by von Bonin's plan, to the defence of the fortified area along the frontier would be completely inadequate for the job. " One Panzerbattalion and one Panzergrenadier battalion with 12 field guns " on " a frontage of 30–70 klm." could hardly be expected to prevent a breakthrough by the Soviet massed armour. Furthermore—and this argument seemed to appeal even more to German readers—German troops defending, according to von Bonin, the fortified zone, would constitute in fact a German army " de couverture," thus " sacrificing themselves in defence of others " and constituting a shield which would be too weak to halt the enemy's major thrust.

---

[7] *Wehrkunde*, May, 1956, pp. 177–179.

Sir John Slessor's Views

Similar views on the defence of Western Germany, and the role of NATO troops, were expressed in the same year—and repeated on several occasions later on—by Marshal of the R.A.F. Sir John Slessor, the former Chief of the Air Staff. In his book, *Defence for the West*, he expressed the view that, as soon as German armed forces are organised and ready to act, NATO troops should withdraw from West Germany (though not from Berlin), whether the Red Army leaves Eastern Germany or not. Such an agreement could be covered by a mutual security pact, with Anglo-American nuclear power as a deterrent against aggression. In addition, Eastern Germany, after Germany's reunification, should be demilitarised as an additional guarantee for the Russians.

Sir John Slessor's ideas on the demilitarisation of Eastern Germany reappeared in the Berlin Declaration of July 27, 1957. For the sake of accuracy, it is necessary to add that a year earlier van Zeeland was also advocating the complete demilitarisation of Eastern Germany as a guarantee for the Russians.

These plans and proposals were put forward in 1954 against a shifting political background.

Roughly speaking, Russia was still passing through the period of relaxation which began after Stalin's death in March 1953. In her attitude towards the West, Russia was willing—as we have already seen [8]—to come to an agreement, especially on Germany, which had been a bone of contention since the end of the last war—provided that Germany did not become part of a Western military *bloc*.

In the West, on the other hand, there was a period of consolidation and expansion of the system of military alliances, both in Europe and in the Balkans, where Greece, Turkey and Yugoslavia, which had broken off

[8] *Supra*, p. 153.

relations with the Soviet Union, signed the Balkan Pact on June 7.

In Western Europe a few months later, a new military alliance was established, namely, the Western European Union, supplementing the old Brussels Treaty Organisation, and assuring automatic military aid in the event of aggression. In addition to the old partners of the Brussels Treaty, the Federal German Republic and Italy were admitted. The French National Assembly had rejected EDC approximately eight months previously. The admittance of Germany into the WEU was therefore considered as a device to by-pass the decision of the French National Assembly.

The protocol of establishment of the WEU fixed the German contribution at twelve divisions—the same figure as had been fixed by the stillborn EDC—and explicitly prohibited Germany from manufacturing atomic, biological and chemical weapons and conditionally prohibited the manufacture of other types of heavy equipment. (According to the press reports of March 1959, Herr Strauss, Minister of Defence, intends to ask for a lifting of restrictions on the German war industry.)

The most important event in 1954, the impact of which was felt only some time later, was the discovery by the Soviet scientists of the means to manufacture the H-bomb. This discovery, for all practical purposes, turned thermo-nuclear war into suicide and slowly transformed the defensive strategy of the West to one of deterrence.

The Warsaw Pact

1955 began with a renewed effort by Russia to prevent German integration into NATO: in a statement published on January 15, 1955, the Soviet Government declared that, if the Paris Agreements were ratified by the Bundestag, it would perpetuate the partition of Germany for years.

Russia was ready at that time to pay a heavy price for German neutrality. She was ready to agree to free all-German elections being held in Germany the same year, as well as to their international supervision—in other words, to all the terms stipulated by Eden at the Foreign Ministers' conference in Berlin in January–February, 1954.

The official Soviet statement was supplemented by a resolution, adopted on February 6, 1955, at a session of the Parliamentary Union in Warsaw, which called for the first time for the withdrawal of all occupation troops from both parts of Germany and of Soviet troops from Poland, and also recommended " free, all-German elections *in accordance with the Eden Plan*." [9]

The most important feature of that session was that it was attended by a delegation of the Supreme Soviet, headed by Mr. A. Puzanov, President of the Russian Republic of U.S.S.R., and a personal friend of the then Soviet Prime Minister, Malenkov.

As Mr. Puzanov arrived in Warsaw direct from Moscow, where he had been attending a session of the Politburo, it seems most likely that this was another indirect Soviet overture. It was, however, completely ignored and possibly even unnoticed by the West. Yet it was obvious that at that time Russia was prepared to jettison the Pankow régime without any hesitation in order to prevent Germany's integration into NATO.

Only two days later Mr. Molotov, addressing the Supreme Soviet, declared that the ratification of the Paris agreements by the Bundestag would make German reunification impossible for a long time to come, and announced that the Soviet *bloc* would take necessary counter-measures. At the same session changes in the Soviet hierarchy were announced. Malenkov was replaced by Mr. Khrushchev and Marshal Bulganin; thus began the gradual evolution of the present Soviet attitude towards the West.

Following Mr. Molotov's announcement at this session of the Supreme Soviet of imminent counter-measures, a

---

[9] Author's italics.

military alliance between the Soviet Union and the countries of Eastern Europe—with the exception of Eastern Germany—was signed in Warsaw on May 14, 1955, under the title "The Warsaw Pact." The Soviet Marshal, Koniev, was appointed its Supreme Commander. And yet, by keeping Eastern Germany outside the Warsaw Pact, Russia probably kept the door open for a possible agreement on German reunification. Eastern Germany was only admitted in January of the following year.

The "Summit" Conference

The so-called "Summit" conference at Geneva in July, 1955, was one of the most important international meetings between the Soviet Union and the West. It represented a major effort to find a way out of the dangerous impasse into which both sides stumbled after the last war.

President Eisenhower, opening the session, began his speech with these simple and moving words:

> We are here for a simple purpose. We have come here to find a basis for accommodation which will make life safer and happier not only for the nations we represent but for people elsewhere.

In his speech, indicating the issues to be discussed, he said:

> First is the problem of unifying Germany and forming an all-German Government based on free elections

and put the predominant idea of Western policy:

> . . . we insist that a united Germany is entitled at its choice to exercise its right of collective self-defence.

The French Prime Minister, Edgar Faure, took a strongly negative attitude towards the idea of German neutrality and reaffirmed his conviction that a reunited Germany should remain in WEU and NATO. However, in order to dispel Soviet misgivings, he suggested the following safeguards: (1) the armed forces of the reunited

Germany should not exceed the strength of those held by the Federal Republic; (2) that the Western Powers must be ready to prove by every means at their disposal the purely defensive nature of the agreement; and (3) Germany should be included in a general security organisation which would be superimposed on the existing defence organisations.

Sir Anthony Eden, in his speech on the same day, came forward with several constructive proposals which together constituted his famous " Eden Plan." Features of this plan constantly reappear in later proposals. In view of the great importance of his speech, it is quoted in full in Appendix 3.

The essence of his proposals was as follows: (1) a mutual security pact; (2) an agreement to limit the forces and armaments in both parts of Germany, subject to reciprocal supervision, and in the countries neighbouring Germany; (3) *the setting up of a demilitarised zone between East and West.*[10]

In summing up he said that his ideas were " not a complete plan but an outline sketch " and a " practical experiment in the operative control of armament."

Marshal Bulganin in a long speech put forward several counter-proposals, some of which overlapped with those proposed by the West, such as his concept of a collective security pact between the U.S.A. and U.S.S.R. He suggested two stages for putting this pact into effect: in the first stage the countries of the Warsaw Pact and of NATO would retain their membership of the respective alliances but " will be bound to refrain from the use of armed forces and to settle by peaceful means all disputes between them." In this stage both sides would agree to " freeze " the existing armed forces.

In the second stage, the Warsaw Pact and NATO would be dissolved and replaced by an all-European security system.

[10] Author's italics.

Marshal Bulganin introduced a new idea. When dealing with the problem of the mutual withdrawal of troops the Soviet leaders had until then referred to this measure as the withdrawal of troops from Germany alone. Marshal Bulganin, however, spoke of "withdrawal of foreign troops from the territories of European States and the re-establishment of the situation which existed prior to the Second World War." No American troops, of course, were stationed in Europe before the last war.

It is obvious that he was driving at the withdrawal of American troops from Europe, which could well have endangered the very existence of NATO at that stage.

Marshal Bulganin also objected to the question of the countries of Eastern Europe being raised, and called it an "interference in the internal affairs of these States." Lastly, in his final statement he spoke of the necessity of a rapprochement between the two parts of Germany, one of the favourite themes of Soviet policy.

The conference ended with the drafting of the " Directives of the Heads of Governments to their Foreign Ministers," which included among others the following points :

1. " A security pact for Europe or for a part of Europe."

2. Limitations, control and inspection with regard to armed forces and armaments.

3. *The establishment between East and West of a zone in which the disposition of armed forces would be subject to mutual agreement.*[11]

These points emerged in various proposals put forward by both sides later on, in particular in the Rapacki Plan and in Mr. Macmillan's proposals for a " freeze " of armed forces. The most important fact from the point of view of the present study is that all four Heads of State, including President Eisenhower, agreed to instruct their Foreign Ministers to study the problem of a zone of " controlled

[11] Author's italics.

armaments." This was the proposal revived by Mr. Macmillan after his talks with Mr. Khrushchev in March 1959.

Unfortunately had such a plan been put into effect as Sir Anthony Eden suggested, it would have run along the present demarcation line and as a result the whole idea met with a very strong opposition from Bonn. During the ensuing Conference of Foreign Ministers at Geneva, the issue was quietly shelved.

The Conference of the Four Foreign Ministers, Geneva, October 27–November 16, 1955

Above all, the ideas embodied in the Directives reappeared at the conference of the Foreign Ministers at Geneva from October 27 to November 16, particularly in the speeches of the then British Foreign Secretary, Mr. Macmillan.

At that conference Mr. Macmillan repeated that a reunited Germany " must be free to ally herself with the Western Powers or enter into NATO." On safeguards, he said:

> . . . in order to establish a military balance and thus to contribute to a sense of security we should work out arrangements for the limitation of force and armaments in a zone, the precise limits of which are to be determined, lying on either side of the line of demarcation between a reunified Germany and Eastern European countries.

The Conference ended, as could have been predicted, with failure to reach any concrete results; it dealt at great length with the problems left to it by the Summit Conference according to the " Directives " of the Heads of State, although the issue of a zone of controlled armaments was cautiously avoided.

Four years later the same ideas can be found in Mr. Macmillan's proposals put before his Western colleagues, and probably before Mr. Khrushchev in the Spring, 1959, " reconnaissance " trip to Moscow.

The Western proposals were presented in an official document under the name of " The Eden Plan."

The Soviet delegate, Mr. Molotov, in his speech on October 28, strongly criticised Western intentions to integrate a reunited Germany into NATO:

> . . . This [Western] proposal simply envisages only such a unification of Germany whereby all Germany would be remilitarised, since it has been decided in advance that such Germany must indispensably be a member of the North Atlantic Treaty Organisation. . . . On the one hand, the Three Powers' proposal contains the so-called " Eden Plan " for free all-German election. On the other hand, it is decided beforehand that regardless of what the German people may say at these elections it must already be concluded that a reunified Germany should be remilitarised and, in addition, be required to participate in the West European military groupings. The proposal of the Three Powers can be so interpreted since their draft treaty goes into effect only " when a unified Germany would agree to join NATO and W.E.U."

As it was tacitly accepted in the West that, in the case of free elections, the majority of Germans would vote in favour of association with the West, Dulles's answer on the same day: " . . . There is nothing in the treaty proposal that requires Germany to become a member of NATO. . . . This is a complete freedom, and nothing in our proposals is in any way contrary to that " was deliberately ingenuous.

Speaking on November 8 about German reunification, Dulles said:

> The problem of German reunification can be solved at present only gradually, step by step, through bringing closer together the German Democratic Republic and the German Federal Republic and through their co-operation.

In view of the importance of the Soviet proposals put forward on October 28, the full text is given later.[12]

The conference ended, as usual, in failure, due to

---

[12] See Appendix 5.

fundamental differences on two main issues, Germany's membership of NATO and the means to reunification.

A comparison of the Soviet attitude during the 1955 Summit conference and the 1955 Conference of Foreign Ministers, with her attitude at previous Conferences, demonstrates that the price of withdrawal of Soviet troops from Eastern Germany had gone up. Whereas in the draft peace treaty submitted by Russia in 1952 and in 1954 the expression " all the armed forces of the occupying powers shall withdraw from Germany " was used, in the similar draft of 1955 the Russians spoke of withdrawals " from the territories of European countries."

As to the means to reunification, whereas the West insisted on free elections, Mr. Molotov, in his counter-proposals, suggested an all-German Council.[13]

Again, if one compares the Soviet readiness during the Malenkov era to agree to the holding of free all-German elections (which, it is obvious, would have meant the end of the Pankow régime) it is clear that at that time the Russians were ready to sacrifice their puppet régime in order to come to an understanding with the West over Germany. This was really the period when the chances of an agreement with the Russians were at their best.

The three Western Ministers, after the end of the conference, issued a Tripartite Declaration on November 16:

> . . . they made a proposal for the reunification of Germany by free elections in 1956 and for a Treaty of Assurance giving the Soviet Union far-reaching safeguards against aggression when Germany is reunified. . . . The Soviet Foreign Minister refused to agree to the reunification of Germany since that would lead to the liquidation of the East German régime. He made counter proposals which would have involved the continued division of Germany as well as the eventual dissolution of the Western security system.[14]

---

[13] In the Soviet draft of 1954, the Russians spoke in terms of setting up a Provisional All-German Government.

[14] *Documents relating to the Meeting of Foreign Ministers of France, the United Kingdom, the Soviet Union and the United States of America*, H.M. Stationery Office, Cmd. 9633.

The Russians made no secret of their attitude towards the method of reunification, as they indicated to Dr. Adenauer very bluntly on the occasion of his official visit to Moscow between September 9th and 13th: reunification was a business for the Germans themselves—a matter of a joint effort by the Federal Republic and the German Democratic Republic. In order to emphasise their attitude, the Russians, only one week after Dr. Adenauer's departure from Moscow, signed a treaty with the Pankow régime on September 19, recognising its sovereignty and independence in foreign policy, including its relations with the Federal German Republic.

It would be wrong to assume that the Bonn Government represented the unanimous opinion of the German nation: shortly before the Foreign Ministers met at Geneva the SPD in Germany published a long statement formulating its views on the forthcoming conference and putting forward a number of suggestions, including:

> The Federal Government must demand that the Soviet Government state unequivocally its views on the military status of a unified Germany and that the Western Powers declare their preparedness to negotiate changes in clauses concerning military commitments in the Paris Agreements, in order to guarantee a solution of the problem of European security and German national unity either at the same time or in consecutive inter-dependent action.
>
> Since the Foreign Ministers were empowered by the terms of the Directives issued by the Heads of Governments " to make whatever arrangements they may consider desirable for the participation of, or for consultation with, other interested parties," the Federal Government should not reject such co-operation, regardless of its declaration that it rejects any *de facto* or *de jure* recognition of the Government of the Soviet Zone as having equal status and rights.[15]

Furthermore, the SPD supported limitation on arms and a European security pact—as already proposed both by the West and by the Soviet Union on previous occasions.

[15] pp. 2–3.

Hermann Rauschning's Plan

Of the unofficial plans put forward in 1955, only that of Hermann Rauschning, the former Nazi President of Danzig, is worthy of mention. Dr. Rauschning, who broke with the Nazis some time after Hitler came to power and lived in exile, returned to the limelight when he published in the *Rheinisch-Westfalische Zeitung* in June his detailed 16-point proposals for the reunification of Germany, which can be summed up as follows:

1. Mutual withdrawal of foreign troops from both parts of Germany. As the territory to be evacuated by the Western troops would be larger than the area of astern Germany, the withdrawal should be matched by the evacuation by the Soviet troops of Eastern Europe.

2. Limitation of Germany's arms potential.

3. Guarantee of Germany's territorial integrity.

4. The Oder-Neisse Line to be revised.

5. A commission consisting of members of the old Reichstag to supervise the preparations for free elections to be set up by the Governments of both parts of Germany.

6. Elections to be held under international supervision.

The crystallisation of the military *blocs* went one stage further by the integration into the Warsaw Pact of the armed forces of Eastern Germany. This decision, taken at a conference of the Foreign Ministers of countries in Eastern Europe held in Prague on January 28, 1956, indicated that the Soviet attitude towards the German problem was hardening.

Mr. Khrushchev, speaking at the Twentieth Congress of the Communist Party in Moscow on February 16, reasserted Soviet policy: the signing of a collective security pact and the abrogation of the Paris and Bonn Agreements were a condition precedent to the solution of the German problem.

Guy Mollet's Views

An interesting, imaginative and constructive view of the German problem was expressed by M. Guy Mollet, the French Prime Minister, in an interview with the *U.S. News and World Report* on April 6, which provoked a storm in Bonn.

Speaking on disarmament, M. Mollet said that in the first stage existing alliances should remain, but that armed forces and armaments should be limited to an agreed level.

Further international negotiations could then be conducted in the less strained atmosphere which would result from the agreement on arms limitation. Such talks might well induce the Russians to agree to free elections in Germany. Such a development might also bring about Germany's renunciation of her NATO membership. He concluded his interview by saying:

> There is a place for united Germany in a European Union just as there is for the German Federal Army. But one thing is clear. It will be easier to integrate Germany, united or not, into Europe—economically, socially and perhaps even politically —if it is envisaged in the framework of disarmament. If it is a question of having a fully rearmed Germany, its integration into Europe poses such problems that the possibility of German reunification is much lessened.

M. Mollet's views, as one might have expected, met with strong criticism in official circles in Bonn, and in a statement issued by the German Ministry of Foreign Affairs it was said:

> The French Prime Minister has now designated the policy followed by the three Western Powers at Geneva as a mistaken one. He has expressed the opinion that the solution of the reunification and security problems should be preceded by disarmament. *These statements seem to indicate a certain willingness on his part to accept the sequence demanded by the Soviet Union* [16] . . . the French Premier has hinted that there is an alternative: either a united or a divided Germany as part of an integrated Europe. This alternative cannot even

[16] Author's italics.

fall within the realm of serious political consideration for the Federal Government and the West German Parliament.

A few days later Herr von Brentano elaborated in public Germany's attitude in this matter, and at the same time answered M. Mollet. At his Press conference on April 13 he said:

> . . . disarmament was naturally a consequence of and not a prerequisite of a political decision. . . . Any agreement on disarmament based on the partition of Germany was unthinkable, since such an agreement would, from the very first, harbour the seeds of fresh entanglements.

A few days later, in his speech before the Consultative Assembly of the Council of Europe, on April 18, he said:

> The Bundestag and the Federal Government have constantly stressed the inseparability of the German problem and of the problems of security and disarmament . . . the Federal Government feels bound to stress the inadequacy of a purely mechanical reduction of existing military strength. . . . The order of importance may largely be a matter of sentiment. But the basis of the political decisions now before us should always be the common conviction that these problems are *indissolubly linked*.

Herr von Brentano's speech at the Council of Europe was undoubtedly an indirect answer to the Soviet disarmament proposals, put forward by Mr. Gromyko, the Soviet Foreign Minister, at the UN Disarmament Sub-Committee in London on March 27, in which they suggested the setting up in Europe of a zone with limited armaments, under international supervision, which would include the territories belonging to both parts of Germany and her neighbouring States. Under this proposal, the stationing in that zone of units armed with atomic weapons would be also prohibited. There is some similarity between these proposals, Sir Anthony Eden's proposals of the previous year and the Rapacki Plans.

In continuing this somewhat dry narrative it is important for the record to quote statements made by British political leaders, which show that the British attitude did not coincide with that of the Federal German Government.

Mr. Anthony Nutting, the British delegate at the UN Disarmament Sub-Committee, in answering in Parliament on May 7, 1956, Mr. Shinwell's question as to whether one had to accept the fact that the reunification of Germany was so vitally important that it was obstructing disarmament which would be of great benefit to other countries, said that the Western Powers were prepared to take certain steps towards partial disarmament, *prior* to the settlement of either the German or some other open question.

Also Sir Anthony Eden, speaking in Parliament on July 23, in answer to a question from a Labour member asking whether the offer of a security pact, which he mentioned at Geneva, was made only on condition that Germany joined NATO, said:

> I am quite clear in my mind what my mind now is, and that is that a security agreement in Europe, as we see it, would not be conditional in any circumstances upon Germany joining NATO.

In his speech he expressed the hope that it might be possible in due course for East and West to discuss what other mutual undertakings might be given to reduce tension in Europe, and whether an agreed limitation of forces in certain areas would be helpful to an agreement.

Unofficial German Views

Several members of the Bundestag came forward with their own proposals, some of which are worth mentioning briefly:

Herr Erich Mende, a member of the Free Democratic Party, speaking in Stuttgart on March 1, suggested:

(1) The withdrawal of NATO troops from the territory of the Federal Republic to positions behind a general line, marked approximately by the Rhine. Thus, the B.A.O.R.

and the R.A.F. would have their bases in the Eifel area and the American land and air forces would retain their bases in the Palatinate, where, in any case, the focal points of their defence systems are located.

(2) The withdrawal of Soviet armed forces to the territory beyond the Oder-Neisse Line. Herr Mende added: " Thus the Powers of the Western and Eastern *blocs* would still remain on German territory since by international law the territory east of the Oder-Neisse Line still forms part of Germany."

(3) The defence of German territory between the Oder-Neisse Line and the Rhine by German armed forces with a " ceiling " to be agreed at somewhere between twelve and twenty divisions.

(4) A Five-Power Pact, the other Powers, apart from Germany, being the United States, the U.S.S.R., Britain and France.

(5) An alternative solution would be an all-European security system, including also countries of Eastern Europe.

(6) On the coming into effect of either of these systems, the Federal Republic would leave NATO and the Soviet Zone would leave the Warsaw Pact.

(7) Free and internationally supervised elections to be held in 1957.

Herr Fritz Erler, who has also published several articles in leading American periodicals, speaking before the Consultative Assembly of the Council of Europe on April 20, 1956, said:

> We must speak the plain unvarnished truth: a reunited Germany as a member of NATO will be impossible because the Soviet Union does not want to extend the Atlantic Pact to what is now the Soviet Zone of Germany. Similarly, we do not want the Russians on the Rhine—the Germans do not want it and the West would not tolerate this, and in the same way the Russians do not want an American Supreme Command on the river Oder. . . . The greatest illusion, however—and Herr von

Brentano, the German Foreign Minister, has uttered a note of warning to the same effect—would be to believe that effective disarmament is possible without the reunification of Germany: Why? . . . Anybody making serious efforts to reach agreement on disarmament is, in fact, endeavouring to put an end to the cold war.

On the other hand, Professor Ferdinand Friedensburg, a member of the Christian Democrats, speaking in Cologne on April 19, said:

> Of course, reunification means that Western influence would advance as far as the Oder . . . nothing would be more mistaken than to dissociate ourselves from NATO and our Western Allies.

He suggested that Germany should return to the role of mediator between East and West, following Bismarck's model, but with unequivocal dependence on the West.

George Kennan, 1956

Mr. Kennan, in an article published in *Aussenpolitik* in Bonn in June and reproduced simultaneously in *The New Leader* in New York, wrote:

> I have always felt that the release of Eastern Europe from the abnormal sort of bondage in which it has been held in these recent years will be best facilitated if the line that divides American and Russian military power in Central Europe is not too strongly accentuated and if there can be an increase, rather than reduction, in the neutral zone that stands between . . . I have always doubted the wisdom of the decision to rearm Western Germany and to bring her into the Atlantic Pact. It seems to me that American policy should be aimed at the reunification of Germany and the earliest possible re-establishment of that country as a neutral factor that can blunt the sharp edge of military bipolarity in Europe.

This extract foreshadows the famous 1957 Reith Lectures, which have left an indelible impression on political and military thinking.

The Official American Attitude

It is of interest to note the shifting attitude of the American Administration at this time towards the German problem. President Eisenhower, at his Press conference on June 6, dwelt on the advantages of neutrality, as compared with the risks resulting from the membership of military alliances. However, a few days later Dulles, at his own Press conference, took a very strong line: "Neutrality," he said, "is an immoral concept and of short duration."

After Dr. Adenauer's visit to Washington in June, where he was reassured that no change had taken place in German-American relations and in America's attitude towards Germany, he received a severe shock when he read in the American Press after his return home of the so-called "Radford Plan," the essence of which was a considerable reduction in the American armed forces in Germany and their gradual withdrawal to "Fortress America." Dr. Adenauer felt resentful that during his visit to the United States he was not told about such a plan, which, if put into effect, would considerably modify the whole situation in Europe, and imply also a change in American policy towards Germany.

Events in Eastern Europe

Although the Berlin uprising in 1953 was caused by grievances of a minor nature, it nevertheless provided evidence of a spirit of rebellion smouldering under the surface.

Three years later, another uprising, also in protest against life under the Communist régime, took place simultaneously in Poznan and in Pilsno (in Czechoslovakia). However, events this time took place against a rather different background.

Mr. Khrushchev's condemnation of Stalin and of his methods, made in his famous speech at the Twentieth

Congress of the Communist Party in Moscow in February, 1956, had wide repercussions all over the satellite area. Such denigration of Stalin's hitherto unchallenged authority and of the dogma of his rule considerably weakened both the Soviet grip on the countries of Eastern Europe and the authority of the Communist puppet régimes.

Consequently, in 1956 expressions of unrest combined a growing resentment at the deficiencies of the local régime with a nationalist resentment of Soviet overlordship.

It was fortunate for the Poles, who had already badly burnt their fingers during the Warsaw rising in 1944, that Gomulka's coup in October did not lead to Soviet armed intervention, which would undoubtedly have led in turn to an armed revolt. It was also fortunate for the Russians that both Mr. Khrushchev and Marshal Zhukov, who arrived hastily in Warsaw in order to get the situation under control and, if possible, to kidnap Gomulka and take him to Moscow, realised that any harsh measure would most certainly lead to a revolt of the whole country. Not that the revolt could have succeeded: before the Soviet leaders took their decision, part of the Soviet troops stationed in Eastern Germany were moved towards the Polish frontier ready to cross it if necessary. These troops would have acted as one arm of a pincers movement, which the Poles could not have withstood.

When on October 24, 1956, the Hungarians revolted and the wave of unrest spread all over the satellite area, the danger of an explosion was very great indeed. Yet, before using military force to suppress the uprising, the Russians carefully watched Western reactions and only when they were sure that they would be left unhindered did they send their armoured divisions to crush the rebellion.

At that time there was a serious split in the West over the unfortunate Suez affair, and Anglo-American relations were at their lowest ebb. However, it is possible to surmise that, even if there had been no quarrel between the major Allies, the West would not have acted.

In his booklet, *The Challenge of Co-existence*, Mr. Gaitskell writes:

> In our defence planning and its political framework, we did not envisage such a situation developing out of a rising behind the Iron Curtain. Our flash points were such events as the blockade of Berlin, the threat to Yugoslavia, and always the possibility of Russian troops advancing directly into Western Germany. But for us to take the initiative in breaking through the Iron Curtain to help people on the other side of it was a prospect for which we had never really provided.[17]

The roots of the Western attitude lay in the policy of containment, and its will was paralysed.

Any constructive initiative on the part of the West would have placed it in a position of strength, because Soviet prestige was at that juncture very low. It is likely that the Russians would have been only too glad to take advantage of any face-saving formula to get out of Eastern Europe.

This was an unearned opportunity for the West to settle the problem of Germany and of Europe quickly and cheaply. When Mr. Khrushchev spoke to Polish journalists on November 18 at the reception in honour of Gomulka in the Kremlin, he declared that, if British and American troops were withdrawn from Germany, he would withdraw Soviet troops from Hungary and Poland. While he was speaking, Soviet guns were firing on the Hungarian troops who were supposed to be Russia's allies under the terms of the Warsaw Pact.

Unfortunately his offer was completely ignored: not the slightest notice was taken of it in the West.

Mr. Khrushchev's speech was followed by an official statement of the Soviet Government, in which, having noted that " an armed attack on Egypt by Britain, France and Israel has created a solution threatening peace and has sharply placed before the peoples the danger of a third

[17] p. 53.

world war," it put forward several suggestions relating to disarmament in Europe.

The Russians suggested: (1) a considerable reduction during 1957 in the armed forces stationed in the NATO and Warsaw Pact area; (2) the closing down within two years of foreign bases in the territory of other countries; (3) the setting up of control posts and the re-examination of the proposal for aerial inspection up to 500 miles on each side of the demarcation line; (4) a non-aggression pact between the NATO and Warsaw Pact countries; and (5) a summit meeting, as suggested by the President of Switzerland.

Although these proposals contained several concessions, and especially a positive interest in President Eisenhower's favourite idea of " sky-inspection," the West at that juncture ignored them. At no time did the West take the initiative.

President Eisenhower, at his Press conference on November 14, said:

> I must make one thing clear: the United States does not and never has advocated open rebellion by an undefended populace against a force against which they could not possibly prevail.

On December 14 and 15, Senators Knowland and Humphrey put forward proposals which involved the withdrawal of troops from Germany. But they produced no impression on Dulles. At his Press conference on December 18 he denied that the United States was contemplating any negotiations with Russia for the withdrawal of Soviet troops from Central Europe.

Dulles's words provoked strong reaction in Congress, and a group of twelve Democrats, including James Roosevelt, Jr., and Henry S. Reuss, contended for a more vigorous and constructive foreign policy. They sent a letter to President Eisenhower suggesting some concrete goals for U.S. policy in Europe, based upon the American ideals of Life, Liberty and the Pursuit of Happiness.

1. Life—to bring an end to the threat of war in Central and Eastern Europe. A road toward that goal: creation of a demilitarised area without the capacity to make aggressive war for 1,000 miles from the Rhine to Russia's historic frontiers, with the demilitarisation and the security of the area guaranteed by East and West.

2. Liberty—to free the peoples of Central and Eastern Europe from foreign occupation or domination, to confirm their right for free elections.

3. The pursuit of happiness—to hasten the economic and social progress of the liberated areas.

In Europe, at the same time, Mr. Gaitskell, Leader of the Opposition, spoke in Parliament during the debate on Hungary, and put forward his plan for the setting up of a neutral zone in Europe, to follow the withdrawal of foreign troops from Germany and some countries of Eastern Europe. He elaborated what is now known as "The Gaitskell Plan" in the course of numerous lectures in the United States and on the Continent, in his booklet, *The Challenge of Co-existence*, and in an article in *Foreign Affairs* in April, 1958.

8

Gaitskell – Rapacki – Kennan, 1957-1958

THE Hungarian uprising—like the second Berlin crisis two years later—galvanised public interest in the problems of Germany and Eastern Europe, and the search for a solution began again. The year 1957 was one of lively diplomatic exchanges between Russia and the West and produced a fresh crop of plans and proposals.

The Gaitskell Plan

One of the most comprehensive plans, which laid the foundations of present political thinking in the West in this matter and is still relevant, is the so-called " Gaitskell Plan," which we have already mentioned.

In his book, *The Challenge of Co-Existence*—the text of the Godkin Lecture delivered at Harvard University—Mr. Gaitskell put forward his views [1]:

> The path to be followed seems to me an extension of the Eden Plan put forward in 1955. It was at that time proposed that there should be a withdrawal of forces from the frontier between East and West Germany, leaving within Germany itself a zone in which there would be no foreign troops. Would it not be possible to extend the area of such a zone until it covered, say, the whole of Germany, Poland, Czechoslovakia and Hungary, and, if possible, Rumania and Bulgaria?
> . . . [The withdrawal of troops] could be a gradual one taking place over a period of time. It would have to be subject to control, as would also the size and character of whatever national forces it was agreed that the countries in question should possess.

[1] pp. 56–58.

. . . In the early stages it might be advisable to leave the alliances unchanged. To begin with both NATO and the Warsaw Pact might continue. But, if foreign troops withdraw, it is doubtful whether this situation could last long. Indeed, the Russians might refuse to contemplate the plan without the neutralisation on both sides from the start.

Especially interesting are Mr. Gaitskell's views on Germany: " I was myself never favourable to the idea of a neutralised Germany as the condition for reunification alone." He then analysed the dangers which could result from such a solution, and concluded: " But none of these dangers would be serious in a plan involving a much wider neutral *bloc*, and the withdrawal of the Red Army to Russia. Moreover, the weakening of the Communist Party in Eastern and Central Europe would greatly reduce any risk of this kind." He did not forget " . . . the permanent controls on arms in those territories " and " a multilateral European security plan, in which the various States in the neutral zone would have their territories guaranteed by the Great Powers as well as by each other."

He showed a statesmanlike approach to the thorny question of the German-Polish frontier, and wrote:

> It seems to me unlikely that any substantial change can be made in the existing frontiers. The populations have moved and settled down, and I do not believe that either the Poles or the Russians would agree to drastic revision. Both Dr. Carlo Schmid and Herr von Brentano deserve much credit for their courage in facing the issue in recent speeches. I hope that the Germans themselves would feel that the renunciation of claims to the pre-war 1945 territories would be a price worth paying for reunification. . . .

Finally, and in view of the claim made by some opponents of disengagement that it would entail the withdrawal of American troops from Europe, especially important is Gaitskell's strong attitude on this final point.: " I must underline that in any plan of this kind American troops should stay in Europe—in the Low Countries, in

France and in Britain. In short, NATO should not retreat further back than the frontiers of Germany."

Mr. Gaitskell summed up and dealt with various criticisms and objections, in an article in *Foreign Affairs* in April, 1958, under the title "Disengagement: Why? How?" In the same article he put forward a modified plan which would "involve a reduction in foreign forces and a pilot disarmament plan in the area." In point of fact, his modified plan is very similar to the Eden Plan, put forward at the Summit Conference in July, 1955, and to the second version of the Rapacki Plan (with which we shall be dealing later), and, indeed, even to Mr. Macmillan's latest proposals—as far as they can be gauged on the strength of the scanty Press reports.

The real criticism which can be advanced against the Gaitskell modified plan, as against all similar plans, such as the Rapacki or Macmillan Plans, is that they may tend to "freeze" the *status quo* rather than modify it as they are primarily military measures of limited regional disarmament. On the other hand, it could be said that if such a "practical experiment in the operative controls of armaments" (as Sir Anthony Eden phrased it at the Summit Conference) were successful it could create a political *détente* and a climate favourable for a successfully negotiated political settlement.

Denis Healey's Plan

Although chronologically inexact, it is appropriate to mention at this stage Mr. Denis Healey's plan, not only because it resembles and supplements Mr. Gaitskell's, but also because Mr. Healey took an active part in formulating Mr. Gaitskell's ideas.

According to Mr. Healey, a mutual withdrawal of troops should not be limited to Germany alone but should take place in Eastern Europe as well. He rightly remarked:

> If you had a neutral Germany which was actually next door to the Soviet Union—which had Soviet power, the Soviet policy, the Soviet empire, immediately on its Eastern flank—then I think it would be too easy for some future German governments to make a deal with the Soviet Union. . . . It is vital, I think, if you have a neutral zone which includes the whole of Germany, that it should also include countries east of Germany, which could form a counter-weight to Germany inside the neutral area and would constitute a *physical as well as a political barrier to direct contact between Germany and the Soviet Union.*[2]

The neutral zone, according to Mr. Healey, would consist of both parts of Germany, Poland, Czechoslovakia and Hungary, and " then, in addition, as many other States as you could get in by bargaining. It might be, for example, that you could bring in Denmark against Rumania and so on."

As far as sanctions against Soviet re-entry were concerned, in which respect his plan supplemented Mr. Gaitskell's, Mr. Healey suggested a method of limited retaliation, also known as " graduated deterrence."

His view that the various Russian proposals have never been properly taken up by the West were of especial interest in view of a similar statement by Mr. Khrushchev in his American television broadcast, to which we shall later refer.

Dr. Adenauer's Views

In view of the rising public interest in the various schemes for the easing of tension in Europe, Dr. Adenauer expressed his views at a Press conference in Bonn on January 11, 1957. He said that the establishment of a thinned-out European zone was not by itself capable of removing tension. In his opinion, it was doubtful whether negotiations regarding such a zone would succeed in furthering discussions between East and West on the reunification of

---

[2] Healey, *A Neutral Belt in Europe*, p. 7. The italics are the author's.

Germany. However, he added that the Federal Government would revert to this problem of a thinned-out zone after it had been examined by all experts, including, of course, the military experts.

However, with the flexibility of the great tactician, Dr. Adenauer, at a Press conference on May 15, 1957, expressed the opinion that he would after all be quite willing to agree to the setting up of a zone of military inspection in the heart of Europe, adding, however, that this had nothing to do with disarmament.

He further stated that, as far as synchronisation between disarmament and reunification was concerned, he favoured the so-called *pari passu* method, which meant a step-by-step progress in which *it was not absolutely necessary for all steps to be taken simultaneously*. [It is of interest to add that only one month previously Herr von Brentano, speaking at the Council of Europe on April 15, declared that the German problem and disarmament were inseparable.]

It was at the same Press conference that Dr. Adenauer put forward his own plan regarding the military aspects of reunification (should it take place): namely, that he would be prepared in such an event to demilitarise the whole of Eastern Germany, which would amount to the disbanding of the units of the National People's Army and various para-military formations, strongly permeated with Communists. He added that neither NATO nor the Bundeswehr units would then be stationed in Eastern Germany, which should give the Russians proof of the purely defensive attitude of the West. It is interesting to note that Dr. Adenauer's ideas reappeared soon after in the so-called Berlin Declaration on July 29 of the same year.

The Council of Europe

The resolution of the Consultative Assembly of the Council of Europe in Strasbourg in January of the same year called for the withdrawal of Soviet troops from Hungary and

Eastern Europe in accordance with the resolution of the
United Nations recommending the neutrality of Germany
and of Eastern Europe. If the Soviet Union agreed to such
a plan, NATO troops would withdraw from Western
Germany as well. Furthermore, the whole area covered by
the agreement about the withdrawal of troops should also
be covered by a European Security Pact, with the Soviet
Union as one of its signatories.

The Polish Freedom Movement

Among the many plans put forward during 1957 one,
certainly based to a great extent on Mr. Gaitskell's ideas, is
worthy of mention, namely, the resolution, a comprehensive
plan, by the Polish Freedom Movement in Great Britain,[3]
the gist of which is as follows:

(1) withdrawal of all foreign troops from the Federal
Republic, on the one hand, and from Poland and
other countries of Eastern Europe, on the other
hand;

(2) withdrawal of the countries covered by the plan
from their respective military alliances;

(3) arms limitations and denuclearisation of the zone;

(4) a European security pact to guarantee the external
and internal frontiers as well as to prevent external
interference into the internal affairs of the countries
in the zone.

The Soviet Attitude

The Soviet Government had also been busy, from the
start of the year, restating its attitude towards the German
problem.

During the visit to Moscow of the East German
Government delegation, headed by Walter Ulbricht, a

[3] March 30, 1957.

communiqué issued after talks with the Soviet leaders on January 8, 1957, said:

> The prerequisite to solving the German question on a democratic basis is understanding between the two German States, which is first and foremost a matter for the Germans themselves. The main obstacle in the way of reunifying Germany . . . is their [West Germany's] policy of remilitarisation, their participation in the aggressive, belligerent NATO *bloc*. . . .

The communiqué ended with this warning:

> In the light of their alliance and their obligations in accordance with the Warsaw Treaty, the Government of the German Democratic Republic and the Government of the Soviet Union declare that any attempt to resort to force as a method of solving the German question, and any attempt by way of hostile action to undermine the German Democratic Republic will be crushed.

A few days later, Mr. Kuznetsov, the leader of the Soviet delegation at the Political Committee of the United Nations General Assembly, repeated in a speech on January 14, 1957, the Soviet suggestions for immediate suspension of nuclear tests, considerable reduction of foreign troops in the NATO and Warsaw Pact areas, the dismantling of all military bases in foreign countries within two years, and a non-aggression pact between the NATO and Warsaw Pact countries.

Speaking again on January 25, Mr. Kuznetsov put forward concrete proposals to reduce foreign troops in the NATO and Warsaw Pact areas by one-third in 1957, and considerably further during 1958.

The Soviet Prime Minister, Marshal Bulganin, in a message to Dr. Adenauer on February 5, warned him against the dangers of military alliances:

> Every fresh million spent on armaments, every new division raised, will only complicate the international situation of the Federal Republic and increase the mistrust and the fears which other States, particularly Western Germany's neighbours, feel towards her. . . ."

Marshal Bulganin's message to the British Prime Minister, Mr. Macmillan, on April 20, deserves special attention:

> It seems to me that the Soviet Union and Britain have similar interests in safeguarding peace and security in Europe. It is not accidental that our two countries for many centuries have been drawn in one way or another into every major conflict in Europe. Such a step as the inclusion of the Federal Republic of Germany in NATO has further worsened the situation in Europe . . . a very dangerous situation is created merely by the very fact that large armies equipped with up-to-date and highly destructive weapons are facing each other . . . the Soviet Government would be willing to resume discussion on the proposals made some time ago by *Sir Anthony Eden the former Prime Minister of Britain on the establishment in Europe of demilitarised zones and also of areas with restrictions of armaments.*[4]

In view of the Bonn Government's intention to arm the Bundeswehr with tactical atomic weapons, the Soviet Government, in a Note of April 27, said:

> . . . the course towards the atomic arming of the Bundeswehr is incompatible with the restoration of the unity of Germany and those statesmen in the Federal Republic who now pursue this course assume thus a most grave responsibility to the German people.

A few days later, the Soviet Ambassador in Bonn, Mr. Smirnov, asked Dr. Adenauer for a promise that the Bundeswehr would not be armed with atomic tactical weapons.

Dr. Adenauer's answers to the Soviet Ambassador and to the Soviet Note did not in fact overlap, in order perhaps to reserve freedom for manoeuvre. In his answer to Mr. Smirnov, on April 28, he said that the Federal Government neither possessed nor had sought supplies of atomic weapons of any kind whatsoever. In the answer to the Soviet Note of April 27, Bonn stated:

---

[4] *Soviet News*, Nr. 3616, April 24, 1957.

Every government with a sense of responsibility will be confronted with the necessity . . . of seriously examining ways and means of taking modern weapons developments into account in equipping its forces. . . . It is generally known that the Western forces stationed on the territory of the Federal Republic are there for purely defensive purposes. . . . The territory protected by NATO forms a unit. The same applies to joint defence planning in that territory. This alone suffices to persuade the Federal Government that the *proposal to renounce*, prior to the conclusion of a general disarmament agreement, *stationing atomic weapons in both parts of Germany is not conducive to guaranteeing the security of the Federal Republic.*[5]

Dr. Adenauer received—as usual—strong support from President Eisenhower, as appears from the communiqué issued on May 28, after Dr. Adenauer's visit to Washington, in which it was stated:

The President stressed that the idea of extending disarmament measures to Europe would be accepted by the United States only if her Allies in NATO were to agree, and if the connection between European security and German reunification were taken into due consideration. He assured the Chancellor that the United States would take no steps in the field of disarmament which might lead to rendering the reunification of Germany more difficult.

The American Attitude

Dr. Adenauer's visit to Washington was most likely prompted by President Eisenhower's remark at his Press conference on May 8, 1957, in which he spoke sympathetically of Soviet desires to revive and resume discussion on Eden's plan, as suggested by Marshal Bulganin in his letter to Mr. Macmillan.[6] Only one week later President Eisenhower was disavowed by his Secretary of State, who said at his Press conference on May 14 and 15:

. . . the setting up of a demilitarised zone along the Iron Curtain is not the policy of the United States. . . .

[5] Author's italics.   [6] *Soviet News*, April 24, 1957.

and the next day:

> I don't think we favour any plan for neutralised zones. Chancellor Adenauer suggested that with a reunified Germany he would be willing to agree that NATO forces would not be put into the Eastern Zone . . . anything that Chancellor Adenauer wished in this respect would be given very careful and sympathetic consideration by ourselves.

During Mr. Macmillan's visit to Bonn early in 1959 after his visit to Moscow, Dr. Adenauer is reputed to have said: " I am not so completely mad as to think that I can influence British policy. . . ." But it would seem that he has been able to influence American policy for quite a few years.

Mr. Khrushchev's Television Interview

In one of his most outspoken public appearances, an interview with three American journalists which was televised in the United States, Mr. Khrushchev gave his views on several problems and in particular on Germany and on mutual withdrawal of troops.

In answer to a question about the progress of negotiations on disarmament he said:

> We are prepared to be satisfied with something less than a comprehensive solution of the disarmament problems at once. We are prepared to start with small things which might lead to something bigger.[7]

In reply to a question as to what, in the opinion of the Soviet Government, were the conditions under which the Soviet Union would feel itself secure to withdraw its forces, he stated:

> Why could not the United States and other countries withdraw their troops from Western Germany and from the Western countries, that is to say, from France, Italy, Turkey, Greece and from other places where your troops are stationed and of which I do not know? We, on the other hand, could

[7] *Soviet News*, June 2, 1957.

withdraw our forces from Eastern Germany, from Poland, Hungary and Rumania. We do not have troops in other countries.

In answer to a question as to whether the countries of Eastern Europe would remain Communist if the Soviet troops were withdrawn from them, he said:

> The Communist system must be based on the will of the people and if the people do not want this system let them establish the way of life they most prefer. That is why we will unhesitatingly withdraw our troops from all the countries in which they are stationed—from Poland, Hungary, Rumania and Eastern Germany, and I am sure that the peoples of these countries will defend their system even better then.

Then Mr. Khrushchev added:

> Let us put this to the test. You withdraw your troops from Germany and France, while we withdraw ours from Germany, Poland and Hungary. Then we shall see that Kadar's régime, which is a régime of the Hungarian people, will live and prosper for ever.

Answering a question as to what major steps the Soviet Government was ready to take to ease tension, he said:

> I believe that we are all the time thinking of steps to take and are actually taking them. But if one side takes such steps and the other does not, this will not get us anywhere, because the relaxation of the world tension depends not only on one side but on the other as well. We are waiting for America to take such steps, and also Britain and France, and we declare that we shall not lag behind and we shall not be found wanting.

Unfortunately, Mr. Khrushchev's challenge to put the issue to the test remained unanswered. As Van Zeeland, Denis Healey and Sir John Slessor have emphasised on different occasions, the West has never taken up the Soviet Union on that proposal to withdraw their troops.

There was, however, one reaction in the United States, unfortunately a rather mistaken one, from Senator Knowland. In a letter to Dulles on June 20 he suggested putting Russia to the test. He came up with a proposal that in exchange for Norway's becoming a member of a neutral Baltic *bloc*, the Hungarian people should be given the right to free elections under international supervision: failing this he suggested that Russia should withdraw her troops from her Baltic States

> to live up to her previous treaties of friendship and non-aggression pacts with those three Baltic Republics, return thousands of Latvians, Lithuanians and Estonians from Soviet prison camps, and to agree to United Nations supervision of free elections in these three Baltic Republics. The Free World and the Soviet Union thereafter jointly to agree to guarantee the frontiers of the Baltic Neutral *Bloc* against any aggression.

Senator Knowland added:

> Khrushchev has given an opening which should not be ignored. It would give us an opportunity to test his words against Soviet deeds.

Unfortunately, Senator Knowland's suggestions were not aimed at solving any major problems: first of all, his proposal about Norway was made without prior consultation with the Norwegian Government and was strongly resented in Oslo; secondly, by putting forward this idea, Senator Knowland played right into the hands of Soviet diplomacy which, since the end of the last war, has been trying to sell the idea of a neutral Baltic *bloc* to all the Scandinavian countries.

As far as his alternative suggestion was concerned, it had nothing to do with either the reunification of Germany or the liberation of Eastern Europe, and dealt only with a sector of minor importance as compared with the magnitude of the German problem. Dulles did not waste much time in brushing Senator Knowland's suggestions aside; at his Press conference on June 12, 1957, he said:

> Well, I fully share Senator Knowland's feelings that every proper effort should be made to get the Soviet troops out of Hungary. And I believe that if we can find a way to test the sincerity of what Mr. Khrushchev said in that respect, we should try to find out. But I feel this about our mutual security: these

arrangements . . . are not military alliances . . . and I do not consider it is appropriate to suggest that any free country in the world which wants to participate in collective security should withdraw from it.

Herr Ollenhauer's Views

It is now essential to deal at some length with Herr Ollenhauer's views.

Speaking in the Bundestag on January 31, 1957, he emphasised that the SPD,

> while advocating the Federal Republic's withdrawal from NATO, had never abdicated an adventurous . . . policy as a possible means towards German reunification.[8]

In a broadcast on February 7, a few days before leaving for Canada and the United States, he said:

> A European security pact should include a reunified Germany and its neighbours in the East and West.

He emphasised that a reunited Germany would have a military contribution to make within the scope of such a security system. He added:

> It has become general knowledge that NATO and reunification are incompatible. The Western Powers will never agree to a reunited Germany entering the Warsaw Pact. The Soviet Union will react similarly if they learn that the whole 70 million Germans will walk into the Atlantic Pact.

Into these few words Herr Ollenhauer compressed the essence of the SPD doctrine as regards methods of reunification, and at the same time he exploded the myth that the SPD intends to have a neutralised Germany, which would mean in actual fact a demilitarised and disarmed country.

As a result of long internal deliberations on May 23, 1957, the SPD produced its comprehensive views on reunification and security which have become known as

---

[8] H. Siegler, *The Reunification and Security of Germany*, p. 117.

the Ollenhauer Plan. The essence of this Plan is as follows:

(a) European security and German unity form a joint problem.

(b) Reunited Germany should be incorporated into a European Security system, which should be recognised as a regional agreement within the framework of the United Nations.

(c) A system of armament restriction and control throughout the whole area would have to be put into effect.

(d) The U.S.A. and U.S.S.R. would have to agree to "its creation [the European security system] in place of the Eastern and Western military alliances. Once political agreement has been reached, the question of the manner in which the two Powers intend to guarantee the system is capable of solution."

(e) It would be advisable to proceed step by step, with the view of achieving an intermediate goal: a pact in which the four major Powers guaranteed the frontiers of Germany. (The SPD did not go into the details of this delicate problem.)

Herr Ollenhauer restated his views in a Circular just before the Fifth International Socialist Congress, which took place in Vienna from July 2–6, 1957, with the participation of several leading Socialists from Western Europe, including Mr. Gaitskell. In that Circular he repeated his suggestions for the integration of a reunified Germany into a European Security Pact, which would include her neighbours, and for a declaration by the NATO and Western Pact States of

> their willingness to release the two Germanies from their contractual obligations when the European Security System comes into being.[9]

---

[9] *SPD Circular*, No. 51/57, June 15, 1957.

The Fifth Socialist International Congress

The Congress of the Socialist International, which was attended by 139 delegates, met in Vienna, July 2–6, 1957, in an atmosphere of increasing international tension caused by the occurrence of the Hungarian uprising only six months before and growing frictions in the Middle East. Despite speeches by such prominent advocates of disengagement as Mr. Gaitskell, Herr Ollenhauer and Fritz Erler, the Congress by-passed this issue, and adopted instead a vague resolution:

> The peaceful reunification of Germany in freedom would be a substantial contribution to the lessening of international tension. On the other hand, unification depends upon a relaxation of international tension. Relaxation of tension, disarmament and the reunification of Germany are today completely interdependent. This Congress of the Socialist International agrees with the Social Democratic Party of Germany in stating that the German problem cannot be solved by Germany alone. German reunification is a European problem of the first order.

But another resolution of the Congress, on disarmament, to some extent contradicted the ideas on " interdependence " expressed in the previous resolution quoted above:

> The Congress is firmly of the view that agreement on disarmament should not be made conditional on the settlement of outstanding political questions. To do so would be to make agreement difficult if not impossible in both fields.[10]

One of the most ardent supporters of the mutual withdrawal of troops was the prominent Polish Socialist and politician in exile, Mr. A. Ciolkosz, who demanded the withdrawal of Soviet troops from the whole of Central and Eastern Europe, including the Balkans: " only then would a belt be created in Europe—a belt of freedom and peace." Mr. Ciolkosz was not, however, voicing the general attitude of his compatriots. For instance, the Polish Government in Exile, in two memoranda submitted to the

[10] *Socialist International Information.*

Western Powers, one on February 6 and another one on June 6, although favouring a neutral zone in Europe comprising the whole of eastern Europe (except Bulgaria and Albania), expressed the view that Germany should remain in NATO after some " reasonable adjustments."

The Eastern and Central European Commission

The Commission, of which Mr. Macmillan was one of the Presidents at that time, met in London on July 15, 1957, with the participation of several leading politicians in exile as well as some Members of both Houses of Parliament. A resolution was approved, the essence of which was as follows:

1. Support is given for the present disarmament negotiations in the hope that they will lead to gradual military disengagement.

2. The fate of the countries behind the Iron Curtain cannot be treated separately from that of Germany.

3. No real peace is possible as long as the Soviet Union retains her troops in Central and Eastern Europe.

4. The withdrawal of Russian troops from the countries behind the Iron Curtain is an essential condition for any system of mutual security in Europe.

In view of the fact that this resolution supports the idea of disengagement in Europe, it is interesting to note that ACEN—the Assembly of Captive European Nations—consisting of leading European exiles, has adopted a strongly negative attitude towards any suggestions for disengagement.

At the Conference of the Socialists Union of Central and Eastern Europe, which also took place in Vienna, July 29–30, 1957, a resolution was approved recommending the withdrawal of Soviet troops from the Russian Zone of Germany, Estonia, Latvia, Lithuania, Poland, Roumania and Hungary, and a guarantee of the national independence of those countries by the Big Powers.

The Conference expressed the belief that

> the plan for the creation of a neutral belt, partly demilitarised
> under international control and comprising both parts of Ger-
> many as well as the countries which since the Second World
> War have been under Soviet control, could be the basis for a
> development towards the complete independence of these
> countries.

A resolution of the German Free Democratic Party took
a rather different attitude from the SPD on this matter.
The information service of FDP published on February
18 an answer to the SPD proposals, in which it was
stated:

> They demand a European Security Treaty as a necessary
> complement to the existing treaty policy, either tending towards
> a balance of the present Western Alliances by a supplementary
> treaty with the East European countries, or towards a compre-
> hensive treaty to bridge existing regional pacts. . . . Here the
> so-called balance of alliances is comparable to Stresemann's
> procedure between the wars. Stresemann signed the Locarno
> Treaty with the Western Powers and then the Berlin Treaty
> with Moscow, without cancelling or invalidating the Locarno
> Treaty.

The Berlin Declaration

In July a very important statement of policy was made by
the three Western Powers together with the Federal German Government, which for the first time found itself
formally in a position of equality with the Great Powers.
This twelve-point statement was signed on July 29, 1957, in
Berlin by the three Western Ambassadors and by Herr von
Brentano. Emphasis was put on free elections throughout
the whole of Germany; it rejected categorically any suggestions of an imposed status by stating in article 6:

> There should be no discrimination against a reunified
> Germany. Its freedom and security should not be prejudiced
> by an imposed status of neutralisation or demilitarisation. Its
> government should be free to determine its foreign policy and
> to decide on its international obligations.

Article 8 stated that

> The Western Powers have never required as a condition of German reunification that a reunified Germany should join NATO.

It goes without saying that such a decision by the future government of the reunited Germany would, in fact, be taken for granted.

Finally, article 9 contained—in case a future all-German Government should elect to join NATO—assurances of a significant and far-reaching character to Russia and other countries of Eastern Europe, which would become parties to a European security arrangement, namely, that the Western Powers would not take military advantage as a result of the withdrawal of Soviet forces.

Although the above article did not specify Western undertakings, it is fairly safe to assume that they would be identical with Dr. Adenauer's views as expressed by him at his Press conference on May 15, that is, that in the case of reunification Eastern Germany should remain demilitarised and that neither NATO nor Federal German troops should be stationed in that area.

The Soviet Government rejected " The Berlin Declaration " on August 2 in a statement read by a Soviet spokesman :

> The joint statement repeats in its essentials the proposals put forward by U.S.A., Great Britain and France at the Geneva Conference of Foreign Ministers. These proposals proved a long time ago that they were useless as a basis for solving the German question. . . . As regards guarantees, the Soviet Union does not need them.

Frank Aiken's Proposal

In the course of the debate at the United Nations on September 10, 1957, on the Report prepared by the UN Committee on Hungary, Mr. Frank Aiken, Irish Delegate and Minister for External Affairs, put forward his plan for " phased withdrawal of foreign troops from Europe."

> I would urge that we should make every effort to discover whether it is possible to reach an agreement in a fair and reasonable drawing back of non-national forces on both sides from the border of Russian-occupied Europe. . . .
>
> To avoid prolonged negotiations and the great emotional difficulties of deciding what country must be evacuated in exchange for what other, we suggest that the drawing back should take place along a latitudinal line from either side of the border for an equal number of kilometres. This drawing back might be, for example, a few hundred kilometres in the first stage. A second phase might be a further reciprocal drawing back, taking Russian officers and troops out of Hungary and the other captive nations west of the Russian border established at Yalta and Potsdam.

Then Mr. Aiken put forward a very useful suggestion as to the role the UN should play in the realisation of his scheme:

> If that idea is adopted, we would suggest that in the widening zone thus created the Organisation might be able to play a very useful part. Member nations could be invited to contribute to a United Nations inspection unit which could supervise the withdrawal of the foreign contingents; this inspection unit could not only see to it that these withdrawals were complete but also remain in the area to see that no new military infiltrations took place, under the guise of volunteers, technicians, advisers or the like. It could also see that the countries concerned would be left free to govern themselves in their own way without outside interference.
>
> If the suggestion we have put forward is agreed to by the NATO Powers, we do not see what excuse Russia would have for rejecting it.[11]

Unfortunately Mr. Aiken's resolution did not make much headway in the United Nations, and no resolution adopting or recommending his plan was ever approved by the General Assembly.

---

[11] *Weekly Bulletin of the Department of External Affairs*, No. 380, September 16, 1957.

Chivu Stoica's Plan

In the same month, on September 17, 1957, the Rumanian Prime Minister, Chivu Stoica, came forward with a proposal for a Balkan conference with the participation of Rumania, Bulgaria and Albania, on the one hand, and Yugoslavia, Greece and Turkey on the other. The purpose of the conference was to be the signature of a Balkan security pact which would transform that area into a " Balkan zone of peace." The stationing of troops armed with atomic weapons in that area would be prohibited; in this respect, Mr. Stoica forestalled Mr. Rapacki.

Mr. Stoica's overtures, accepted with some reservations by Yugoslavia, were, however, cold-shouldered by Turkey and, above all, by Greece. Greece is to date still technically in a state of war with Albania, for on October 28, 1940, Italian aggression started from Albanian territory; she also still has considerable claims against Bulgaria for payment of the $45 million as reparations fixed after the last war by the Peace Treaty with Bulgaria.

Henry S. Reuss's Proposals

Henry S. Reuss, a Democrat, in a statement issued on November 7, 1957, urged Congress to consider the Administration's forthcoming proposal for an atomic share-out with their NATO allies " not in isolation but in the context of the whole of our foreign and military policy." He asked Congress to consider accompanying any removal of the ban on sharing secrets and weapons with a " Vandenberg type " resolution requesting the Executive " simultaneously to try to evolve a position with our NATO allies for a relaxation of tension in Middle Europe."

Reuss said that the aim was " disengagement in Europe," which

> could range from a withdrawal of the Great Powers' troops to a much wider proposal for the reunification of Germany in

freedom, peaceful liberation of the satellites and the demilitarisation of the whole area with its security guaranteed by East and West.

The Rapacki Plan: First Version

Another important event as far as disengagement is concerned was an official suggestion put forward on behalf of the Polish Government by the Polish Foreign Minister, Mr. Rapacki. He first put it before the United Nations General Assembly on October 2, 1957. It was then followed by Notes in December through the usual diplomatic channels, and finally confirmed by a Memorandum delivered on February 15, 1958, to the diplomatic representatives of the three Western Powers, Czechoslovakia and Eastern Germany.

The plan suggested the creation of an " atom-free zone," which should include Poland, Czechoslovakia and both parts of Germany; in those territories

> nuclear weapons would be neither manufactured nor stockpiled, the equipment and installations designed for their servicing would not be located there, the use of nuclear weapons against the territory of this zone would be prohibited.

At the same time, the plan envisaged that:

> In order to ensure the effectiveness and the implementation of the obligations contained . . . the States concerned would undertake to create a system of broad and effective control in the area of the proposed zone and submit themselves to its functioning. This system could comprise ground as well as aerial control. . . . The system of control established for the denuclearised zone could provide useful experience for the realisation of broader disarmament agreement.[12]

The Rapacki Plan met with a very mixed reception: although the reaction in Canada and in the Scandinavian countries was to show positive interest and the British Government at first found it an interesting basis for further

---

[12] *Polish Facts and Figures,* No. 591, 1958.

discussion, the attitude of the United States and of the Federal Republic was from the beginning negative. The main arguments advanced against the plan were that it would " freeze " the existing numerical superiority of the Soviet *bloc* in conventional armed forces.

The plan was eventually rejected in May of the following year, and we shall deal with it more fully when we come to 1958.

The Memorandum of the ACEN [13]

This five-point Memorandum was submitted to all NATO Powers before the NATO Council meeting in Paris on December 16, 1957.

In analysing Soviet policy, the Memorandum drew the attention of the NATO Powers to the fact that one of the main objectives of Soviet policy is to secure Western acquiescence to what Mr. Khrushchev has called the " historic changes " in Central and Eastern Europe. " It is quite apparent," the Memorandum points out, " that in the judgment of the Kremlin only the unambiguous Western acceptance of the *status quo* would deal a fatal blow to the hopes of the captive people."

The Memorandum continued:

> It is submitted that to render the defence of Europe possible at a lesser price than an all-out war it is essential to deny to the only potential aggressor the use of its present forward bases in Central Europe. This lends the greatest urgency to the problem of helping the captive nations to recover their freedom and independence.

At the same time the Memorandum warns the NATO Powers against

> entering into security pacts with the Soviet Union which would cover the captive countries or comprise among their signatories any of the Communist puppet governments.

[13] Assembly of the Captive European Nations.

In this respect, the ACEN opposed the concept of a European security pact, which had been contained in both versions of the Eden Plan, and has again been broached by Mr. Macmillan's tentative suggestions of April, 1959. It must be added that ACEN is as a whole—unlike the Union of Socialists of Central and Eastern Europe—strongly opposed to any idea of disengagement, which is considered tantamount to " capitulation."

The Reith Lectures

At the end of 1957 Mr. George Kennan delivered over the B.B.C. his six Reith lectures. The broadcasts became an international event and made a profound impact on public opinion all over the world.

As his name has become almost a synonym for disengagement and everything this word stands for, and as we have quoted his views liberally in previous chapters, it will be sufficient to give the essence of his views fairly briefly. German reunification can be secured only as a result of a negotiated mutual withdrawal of NATO and Soviet troops from Germany: if Soviet troops were to withdraw from some countries of Eastern Europe, such as Poland, Czechoslovakia and Hungary—details could be negotiated later—these countries, together with a reunited Germany, would withdraw from their respective military alliances and accept the status of neutrality.

Contrary to general belief, Mr. Kennan does not advocate " neutralisation "—generally understood as demilitarisation—of Germany. He suggests, indeed, that all the countries of the neutral zone should have their own national armed forces. The whole area ought to be covered by a European security pact in addition to the guarantees of the Four Great Powers.

Contrary also to general belief, he does not advocate the withdrawal of American troops from the Continent, although he does not preclude it at some future date:

... if there could be a general withdrawal of American, British and Russian armed power from the *heart* of the Continent, there would be at least a chance that Europe's fortunes might be worked out ...

Mr. Kennan is also of the opinion that European nations must

by the same token accept a higher level of responsibility for the defence of the Continent than they have recently borne.

Without specifically mentioning the Rapacki Plan for an " atom-free zone," he said:

There is a further contingent danger and a very imminent one, as the thing now stands, and this is that atomic weapons, strategic or tactical, may be placed in the arsenals of our continental allies as well. . . . It would inevitably bring about a further complication in the German and satellite problems. . . . If, therefore, the Western continental countries are to be armed with them, any Russian withdrawal from Central and Eastern Europe may become unthinkable once and for all, for reasons of sheer military prudence, regardless of what the major Western Powers might be prepared to do.[14]

Not surprisingly Mr. Kennan's lectures produced a storm of indignation and he was subjected to broadsides from Germany, with Dr. Adenauer firing the opening shot.

The House of Commons Debate, December

In a debate on December 21, 1957, Mr. Selwyn Lloyd claimed that there were three policies open to Britain: first, to abandon the alliance and to decide that each ot the Western Powers should take its chance with Russia. Such a policy would mean, as Mr. Selwyn Lloyd rightly pointed out, " piecemeal absorption into the Russian system."

The next policy would be to maintain the alliances and to keep nuclear weapons but to work for what was called " disengagement."

[14] *Russia, the Atom and the West*, pp. 60–61.

Mr. Selwyn Lloyd found it impossible to believe that a power of the size and geographical situation of Germany could remain neutral or be detached from the East–West struggle:

> A neutral uncontrolled Germany would be an element of instability in Europe. It was unrealistic to think that in the present circumstances there could be some kind of control machinery to keep Germany down.

The third possible policy was the one which was favoured by the Government:

> We have to seek to strengthen our alliances. If we remain collectively strong the Soviets are not likely to attack.

He finished by saying:

> We believe it is our duty to use in concert with our allies every opportunity to probe Soviet intentions and to negotiate with them whenever there is a slightest prospect of such negotiations being fruitful.

For the Opposition, Mr. Aneurin Bevan criticised Dulles for moralising and for having adopted " almost religious positions." Confessing that he had been depressed during his visit to Washington, Mr. Bevan explained that one cause was the attitude of complete hopelessness which he found among official spokesmen there. All of them thought that it was no good trusting Russians or trying to make any arrangement with them. " In fact," Mr. Bevan said, " I did not find inspiration so much as obsession. The present situation cannot be a contribution to peace. It is a contribution to fear and the contagion of fear."

> I am not satisfied that a definite arrangement can be arrived at with the Soviet Union. I am saying we should try to find one. Would it not be part of the arrangement for disengagement in Central Europe that the area would be guaranteed? . . . When I said to the Germans, " Do you regard this as an affront against your sovereignty? " they laughed and said: " We would rather be limited and alive than free and dead."

Soviet Attitudes

The Russians made several important moves in the last few weeks of the year, reaffirming by implication their earlier attitude towards the European problem.

Marshal Bulganin, sending a Note to the members of the United Nations, to the NATO countries, to Switzerland and Spain, gave full support to the Polish plan for an atom-free zone. In these Notes he suggested the setting up of a partly demilitarised zone, consisting of both parts of Germany, Poland and Czechoslovakia. The partial demilitarisation would be the result of the withdrawal of all foreign troops and the dismantling of all foreign bases on the territory of the countries covered by the agreement on an atom-free zone; the countries of the zone would retain membership of their respective military alliances and the whole area would be covered by a European security pact.

In short, Marshal Bulganin's proposal was equivalent to a measure of limited disarmament and, in view of the proposed continuity of military alliances, amounted to a freeze of the political *status quo*.

His plan was, in fact, fully in accord with the new trend in Soviet foreign policy which emerged after Mr. Khrushchev's arrival in power.

Mr. Khrushchev's policy was one of maintaining the *status quo*—that phrase meaning, of course, the consolidation of the Soviet position and of Soviet influence in Eastern Europe. In a speech delivered before the Supreme Soviet on December 21, Mr. Khrushchev dealt at great length with the virtues of the *status quo*.

The Supreme Soviet thereupon drafted and approved the same day a seven-point Peace Plan which suggested : first, considerable reductions in the armed forces of the Big Powers in both parts of Germany, Poland and Czechoslovakia [15]; secondly, the setting up of an atom-free zone in the territory of the above countries, which would at the

15 As a matter of fact there are no Soviet troops stationed in Czechoslovakia.

same time maintain their military alliances; and finally, the signing of a non-aggression pact between NATO and the Warsaw Pact countries.

This Peace Plan endorsed Bulganin's proposals, for it was the expression of the new Soviet policy aiming at the continuity of the *status quo*. Ironically enough, once again the policies of Russia and of the West, as regards the *status quo*, met half way, and the only bone of contention was the problem of Eastern Germany, which now became the pet of Soviet schemes.

It is relevant to recall that until Mr. Khrushchev's arrival in power, and especially during the Malenkov era, the Russians were quite ready to sacrifice the Pankow régime in order to secure a broad settlement of the problem of security in Europe.

1958 opened in an atmosphere of stalemate, and neither side made any effort to change it; on the contrary, in the West the build-up of the NATO military potential was to proceed according to plans approved at a NATO Council meeting in Paris in December of the previous year. During the parliamentary debate mentioned above Mr. Selwyn Lloyd said:

> Our purpose is to create conditions under which it may be possible to achieve relaxation of tension and what is described as peaceful co-existence. . . . We do not regard strength as an end in itself. It is a means to achieve a permanent peace.

At the same time Soviet policy was bent on the realisation of ambitious plans charted by Mr. Khrushchev, which aimed at consolidating Russia's influence and position in Central and Eastern Europe.

Since the focus of attention had moved to the Middle and Far East, it seemed to many that Europe had entered into a period of prolonged stalemate, based upon an equally prolonged arms race.

Since it had been decided at the NATO Council meeting to strengthen NATO by accepting the American offer

to stock nuclear warheads in Europe and to provide bases
for I.C.B.M.s in agreement with the countries concerned,
it seemed that the Soviet initiative which was aimed at
setting up an atom-free zone had very little chance of
success.

The opening gambit of Soviet diplomacy in 1958 was
Marshal Bulganin's personal letters, sent to Mr. Macmillan
and President Eisenhower and accompanied by " Soviet
Government proposals for easing international tension."

In this lengthy document Marshal Bulganin repeated
his suggestion for top level talks. He recapitulated various
Soviet moves, such as the considerable reductions in Soviet
armed forces and the evacuation of bases in Port Arthur
and Porkkala, and he referred to Mr. Macmillan's speech
in Parliament in which the British Prime Minister spoke of
the necessity of coming to an understanding with the Soviet
Union.

At the new top level talks, as suggested by Marshal
Bulganin,

> in our opinion, the proposal of the Polish People's Republic for
> the creation in the central part of Europe of a zone free from
> atomic weapons, the question of the conclusion of a non-
> aggression pact between States belonging to the North Atlantic
> Alliance and the States which participate in the Warsaw Treaty
> and certain other questions should similarly be discussed.[16]

The Soviet Government proposals put forward in Bulganin's letter boil down to the following points: a substantial reduction in the armed forces of the Big Powers,
the withdrawal of foreign troops from and the dismantling
of foreign bases in the territory of the NATO and Warsaw
Pact states, and the replacement of the " existing military
groupings in Europe by a system of collective security."

It goes without saying that the same document endorsed
also the idea of a confederation of both parts of Germany,
which had by then been a dogma in the Kremlin for about
one year.

[16] *Soviet News*, No. 3760, January 10, 1958.

Henry S. Reuss Again

In the meantime, in the United States, Mr. Reuss, the indefatigable champion of a constructive American foreign
policy towards Europe, reasserted in a speech before Congress on January 27, with some modifications, suggestions
put before President Eisenhower by a group of twelve
Democrats in a letter in December 1956. This letter
advocated the establishment of a 1,000 miles wide zone
between the Rhine and the western frontiers of Russia,
from which all foreign troops should withdraw: Mr. Reuss
specifically added that U.S. troops should remain in Europe.
All the countries of that area would have their own national
armed forces, although restricted and subject to international control. A reunited Germany, he continued,
should remain in NATO; territorial integrity of the whole
area should be covered by the guarantees of the Great
Powers.

Sir John Slessor's Views

A slightly different view of these problems was taken by
Marshal of the R.A.F. Sir John Slessor.

In three penetrating articles, " Test the Soviets on
Disengagement," Sir John suggested setting up " between
the frontiers of Russia and those of France, Italy, Greece
and Turkey "

> [a] belt of States uncommitted to any military alliance with
> East or West, having no atomic weapons, with whatever form
> of government they themselves choose and associated economi-
> cally, socially and culturally with whom they like, in short, a
> broad corridor of countries with the standing of Sweden and
> Yugoslavia.
>
> It would be foolish to pretend there are no risks about this—
> of course, there are serious risks: the whole situation is a
> balance of risks.[17]

Yet he was of the opinion that political advantages would
outweigh political disadvantages. He was definitely in

[17] *New York Herald Tribune*, January–February, 1958.

favour of an atom-free zone, and expressed the hope that
" NATO agreement could be secured without undue
delay." Unfortunately, in this respect his optimism was not
justified.

In analysing this policy of " withdrawal," he made the
point that withdrawal of NATO troops from Germany
would not be possible until German troops were ready to
do the same job: in his view,

> Germany, with her armed forces, should accept the policy of
> " military non-alignment." Demilitarisation makes no sense at all.

Sir John is in favour of an atom-free zone:

> There need not be as many as 28 divisions of them [Germans] provided they are properly mobile. And the last thing
> they need for their job is atomic weapons of any kind. That
> is one of the two reasons why I consider the atom-free zone
> acceptable.

His eyes are open to Germany's role in the past:

> . . . let us not permit our new-found enthusiasm for Germany
> as an ally to blind us to the fact that three times in living
> memory German forces have caused aggressive wars in Europe.

He also has strong views on the need for the United
States and Great Britain to undertake binding obligations
in order to guarantee the territory of the area:

> if there is to be any hope of getting NATO agreement to a
> withdrawal policy, it will be *sine qua non* that the United States
> —and, for that matter, Great Britain—should assume most
> binding undertakings, should engage their honour to stand by
> their obligation under a reorganised NATO and under any
> extended security pact, if their troops leave the mainland of
> Europe.

Captain Liddell Hart's International Safety Belt

In February, Captain B. H. Liddell Hart published an
interesting article which received wide circulation at home
and abroad in *Reynolds News*.[18]

[18] *Reynolds News*, February 9, 1958.

First of all, he took the view that although the Rapacki Plan could give the Russians some strategic advantages,

> the Poles have ample reasons of their own to initiate such a proposal. The lines of communication of the Russian armies in Eastern Germany pass through Poland. So Poland would almost certainly be the first country to suffer atomic destruction if the Russians were to advance into Western Germany. For, in countering the Russian advance, the NATO Powers would have no such hesitation about " atomising " the road and rail centres of Poland—to paralyse the Russian communications—as they would have about wiping out the cities and towns of the country, Germany, which they were trying to protect. The Rapacki Plan, while concerned primarily with atomic weapons, accords quite well with the basic pattern of the proposals which Eden put forward in Geneva in 1955.

Captain Liddell Hart expressed some doubts about the effectiveness of control of such a zone due to the development of small tactical atomic weapons. Consequently, he suggested the development of the plan to include limitations on the size of conventional forces in that area; in point of fact, the second version of the Rapacki Plan includes precisely such limitations.

He concludes that it would be better if such a zone of " limited armaments " could be widened and lengthened in space

> to increase the geographical separation between the nuclear-armed giants, the U.S.A. and the U.S.S.R. The closer they are in contact, the greater the risk of friction.

In this respect Captain Liddell Hart's views differ—and not for the first time—from official British policy as expounded by Mr. Selwyn Lloyd during the foreign affairs debate in Parliament on December 4, 1958:

> . . . the world is a much safer place if, in critical areas, there is a direct confrontation of the major parties and not an area of uncertainty where miscalculations can be made as to the consequences of particular actions.

Captain Liddell Hart suggests setting up

an International Safety Belt—more fully defined as a strategic
interspace—between the great nuclear Powers, filled by countries
which by common agreement would limit the size and arms of
their forces, and would not be in military alliance with the
nuclear Powers on either side.

A somewhat similar suggestion, under the title of " a
safety belt," was put forward by Professor Albrecht Brecht
in October, 1949, although the size of the area suggested by
him was much smaller than that suggested by Captain
Liddell Hart.

According to Captain Liddell Hart, such a belt could
stretch

from Spitzbergen to the Himalayas—embracing the four
Scandinavian countries [Norway, Sweden, Finland and Den-
mark], the six central European countries [Germany, Poland,
Czechoslovakia, Austria, Hungary, Switzerland], the five Balkan countries [Yugoslavia, Rumania, Albania, Bulgaria,
Greece], Turkey and the Middle East countries [Persia,
Afghanistan, Pakistan, India]. The belt might be extended
eastward to embrace Burma, Thailand and Indo-China—and
then to Japan and Korea. In the West the three Benelux
countries and others might choose to join it.

Paul Auer's Plan

A prominent exiled political leader, Paul Auer, a former
Hungarian Minister in France and at present a member of
the Hungarian National Committee, wrote an article in
February suggesting the establishment of a neutral zone to
include both parts of Germany, Poland and, perhaps,
Czechoslovakia; after the withdrawal of foreign troops, contingents of UN troops composed of Russian, American,
British and French troops should be entrusted with the task
of ensuring the neutrality of those countries.

Any interference by those UN troops in the internal
affairs of those countries should be strictly forbidden; the
parliaments elected in both parts of Germany, as a result

of free elections, would take a decision concerning the reunification of Germany.[19]

Although it is doubtful whether a plan which would result in Russian troops [although under the banners of UNO] appearing in Western Germany, would be acceptable to many Germans, yet at any rate, Auer is one of the few among his compatriots in exile to be seriously interested in the idea of disengagement.

In a second article some months later, he suggested that the neutralisation of Eastern Europe could be made provisional for the period of, say, five to ten years. He maintained that international guarantees of the neutrality of the area as well as of its territorial integrity would contribute to the peace of Europe.[20]

Herr Strauss's Plan

In the same month, the German Federal Minister of Defence, Herr Josef Strauss, although speaking as a private member of the CDU in the Bundestag on February 22, put forward a five-point plan, the essence of which is as follows:

(1) The establishment of an atom-free zone together with a restriction on armaments in as many countries of Eastern Europe as possible. These restrictions would not apply to Germany.

(2) A certain balance in the conventional forces between East and West.

(3) The setting up of an international control machinery.

(4) An agreement between the Great Powers to refrain from using atomic weapons on the territory of the above zone.

(5) All these measures to be synchronised with the reunification of Germany, which will remain in NATO.

[19] *Le Figaro*, February 8, 9, 1958.
[20] *Le Monde*, August 1958.

Yet, in spite of all the advantages which such a scheme would ensure for Germany, such as her membership in NATO after her reunification and her exemption from all the restrictions to be imposed upon Eastern Europe, Herr Strauss's plan was rejected by the Bundestag. In addition, there were rumours in Bonn that he had incurred, as a result of his initiative, the strong disfavour of Dr. Adenauer who was at the time holidaying in the sun on the Côte d'Azur.

Marshal Tito

Marshal Tito also took an interest in disengagement, and in particular in the Polish plan for an atom-free zone. In an interview with the well-known American journalist Mr. J. Sulzberger, on February 28 (which, by the way, was not published in *The New York Times* and appeared only on March 6 in *Borba*, the official Communist publication in Belgrade) he expressed his interest in the idea of such a zone; however, his interest was motivated primarily by Press reports of the intended setting up of rocket bases in Italy. His approach to the problem was an entirely military one, as he said that such a plan would not result in the neutralisation of the countries of the area and that they would retain their respective military alliances. Apparently he did not grasp the implication that, in the case of the neutrality of such a zone and the withdrawal of Soviet troops, the security of Yugoslavia would be much increased.

The Report on the Rapacki Plan submitted by the Committee on Defence Questions and Armaments

It is interesting to compare the views on the Polish plan for an atom-free zone, expressed by the British military writers above, with its outright rejection by this Committee in a

Report submitted to the Consultative Assembly of the Western European Union on April 14, 1958, by Mr. Goedhardt, the rapporteur.

First of all the Report, probably in order to cast a " psychological shadow " on the Polish proposal—to use Kennan's expression—identified it with Gromyko's proposal put before the UN Sub-Committee for Disarmament in London on March 27, 1956, " for the creation of a zone of limitations and inspection of armaments in Europe." The Report, as opposed to Captain Liddell Hart's article, avoided mentioning that a similar plan had been put forward by Sir Anthony Eden in July, 1955, at the Summit meeting, and in addition by the three Western delegations at the Foreign Ministers' Conference at Geneva in October–November the same year.

The Report was critical of the Rapacki Plan.[21] It would, while offering no compensating advantages, gravely endanger the security of the West, for the following reasons:

(a) it would restore the *superiority of Soviet forces in conventional weapons and in manpower* in this area, depriving NATO of an effective " shield ";

(b) it would lead to the withdrawal of the bulk of Anglo-American forces from the European Continent as the two Governments would not agree to maintain their troops if they were denied modern atomic weapons;

(c) it would deprive the West of satisfactory depth of territory for the effective deployment of forces;

(d) it would commit NATO almost exclusively to a strategy of massive retaliation;

(e) it would deny Germany defensive atomic weapons which may be developed in the future;

(f) it would involve a special status for Germany within NATO.

[21] p. 81.

In elaborating the military arguments against the Plan, which are, of course, of a crucial nature, the Report said:

> There can be no assurance that the relatively small NATO force in the Central European area could hold against numerically superior Soviet forces (6 to 1)

and then stated that from the political point of view

> . . . not only would the Rapacki proposal itself not involve any change in the *status quo* in Central Europe [that is, division of Germany and Soviet control of the European satellites which are the main causes of tension dividing the free world and the Communist world], but for the military reasons stated above, the Rapacki arrangements, by modifying the basic power situation in favour of the Soviets, would make even less likely the settlement of those political issues on a fair and just basis.
> . . . The Federal Republic of Germany would be placed in a special and exceptional position. It would no longer participate as an equal member of NATO, because it would not be sharing equally in the obligations of NATO membership. . . . It would lead to increased neutralist tendencies among the German people and could thus well be an initial step towards German withdrawal from NATO.

That this conclusion was far from unanimous appeared from the Minority Opinion enclosed in the Report, which stated:

> as the Rapacki proposals in their present form are unacceptable, member States should be recommended to formulate counter-proposals based on the view of the NATO military authorities as to what reciprocal concessions could be made without weakening the defensive power of the West beyond the point of an acceptable risk.[22]

French Socialists' Attitude

Contrary to Mr. Goedhardt's condemnation of the policy of disengagement, the French Socialists, SFIO,[23] at their Annual Congress on May 3–4, 1958, passed a resolution fully in favour of disengagement. The resolutions stressed

[22] p. 85.
[23] Section Française de l'Internationale Ouvrière.

that disengagement should be considered as a preliminary step to any general disarmament scheme, it should be put into effect in a zone of political tension, namely in the zone of direct confrontation by troops of opposing sides (a point of view diametrically opposed to that expressed by Oxford historian Mr. G. F. Hudson in his articles in *The Observer* and *New Leader*. They recommended as a means either the reduction of conventional armed forces or the prohibition of atomic weapons. These military measures, to be applied first of all to zones of political tension, should gradually be extended to other areas.[24]

German Criticism of the Rapacki Plan

The official German periodical, *Bulletin des Presse- und Informationsamtes der Bundesregierung*, which appears in Bonn, published on March 11 and 13, 1959, two articles under the title "*Der neue Rapacki-Plan*," commenting on its origin and merits.

In a short preface it stated that the plan had most likely first been conceived at the Conference of the Foreign Ministers of Eastern Europe in Prague on January 27–28, 1956, in order to formulate an answer to Eden's plan, which had been submitted the previous year at Geneva. It was expounded by Mr. Gromyko in his proposals of March 27, 1956, to the UN Disarmament Sub-Committee.

The sympathetic reaction towards the Plan in Scandinavian countries, especially Norway, was due mainly to the "neutralist" tendencies prevailing in those countries. However, during the debate in the Norwegian Parliament reservations were made to the effect that its acceptance should depend upon the simultaneous reduction of conventional forces. It can be assumed that these reservations convinced the Polish Government of the necessity of introducing corresponding alterations in the second version.

[24] *Europa-Archiv*, June 5, 1959, p. 344.

The critical comments made by the *Bulletin*, which amounted to a recommendation for its rejection, were military and political in nature. As far as military arguments were concerned, obviously the alleged overwhelming numerical superiority of the Soviet *bloc* was the key argument.

The *Bulletin* concluded that, from the military point of view, the Rapacki Plan in its second version was certainly a step forward; however, it would result in a shrinking of the NATO bridgehead, whereas the bulk of Soviet troops would be situated relatively near the potential battlefield. Mr. Bevan's views in one of his articles, in which he favoured the Plan, the *Bulletin* called " bucolic " or " idyllic." The main objection to the Plan was that it would prevent Germany's armed forces from having tactical atomic weapons.

After all, the *Bulletin* went on, the Plan was only an isolated measure of disarmament, unfortunately not followed by the third phase of controlled world disarmament.

The main conclusion of the *Bulletin* was that, from the military point of view,

> there can be no middle way between security based upon complete and modern rearmament and real, general, constructive disarmament.[25]

As far as political arguments are concerned, the *Bulletin* said that the Plan could not contribute to the reduction of international tension, which could only be achieved if " military security is increased or the political situation improved."

However, as the *Bulletin* said, the crucial problem and the reason for the tension in Europe is the division of Germany, and the Polish plan could not in any way contribute to the solution of this problem. At the same time, the *Bulletin* quoted the Polish Deputy Foreign Minister, Winiewicz, as saying that the Plan could produce " a

[25] *Bulletin*, March 13, 1959.

better climate " for further negotiations concerning German reunification.

The *Bulletin* came to the conclusion that the main purpose of the Rapacki Plan was to bring about the neutralisation of Germany and to split the unity of the West.

Declaration of the Political Consultative Committee of the Warsaw Treaty Powers

The conference of the Committee of that name which took place in Moscow on May 24 endorsed the Polish plan: at the same time, the resolution adopted can to some extent be considered as an answer to the statements contained in the Report submitted to the Assembly of the Western European Union.

The resolution says:

> If we compare the size of the territory of the States which would be included in the atom-free zone it will be found that the territory of the German Democratic Republic, Czecho-slovakia and Poland is over twice as large as the territory of Western Germany, the fourth country of the proposed zone. Furthermore, the size of the population of the States included in the proposed zone on this side of the Warsaw Treaty organisation is also greater than the population of the States on the side of the North Atlantic Alliance.
>
> It is regrettable that the Government of a non-European Power, the United States, not only hastened to state its negative attitude towards the proposal for the creation of an atom-free zone in Central Europe, but also considered it possible to put pressure on its European NATO allies by placing difficulties in the way of raising this proposition and its further consideration at the Summit Conference.[26]

Mr. Gromyko's Proposals

Mr. Gromyko, the Soviet Foreign Minister, spoke at the Thirteenth Session of the United Nations General

[26] *Polish Facts and Figures*, No. 598, May 31, 1958.

Assembly on September 18, 1958. After condemning
Anglo-American landings in Jordan and the Lebanon as
well as American support of Chiang Kai-shek, he put forward some disarmament proposals, among them the closing
of bases on foreign territory; he added that the " Soviet
Government has always opposed the division of the world
into a military grouping of States " and repeated a suggestion for a non-aggression pact between the NATO and the
Warsaw Pact countries.[27]

The Conference of the Socialist International, June 12–14, 1958

At the conference of the Council of the Socialist International held in Brussels and attended by some sixty-six
delegates, the debate on " The International Situation " was
introduced by Hugh Gaitskell, who reiterated the principles
of his plan for disengagement. Later, a resolution was
approved on the subject of " Collective Security and Disarmament," which dealt in the first part with the problem
of nuclear tests, and in the second with disengagement.
Whereas the first part was passed unanimously, the second
was opposed by the delegates of France and the Netherlands, with Spain, Belgium, Israel and the United States
abstaining. The text of the resolution was as follows:

> Disengagement in Central and Eastern Europe would facili-
> tate settlement of political problems, including German reunifi-
> cation and a change of the present situation in the countries of
> Eastern Europe, through progressive development.
> . . . While it is clear that the balance of security must at all
> stages be maintained, a disengagement plan might as a minimum
> make it possible to establish a pilot scheme of controlled dis-
> armament covering both conventional forces and nuclear weapons
> which would provide valuable experience and greatly facilitate
> the conclusion of a comprehensive, controlled disarmament
> agreement.[28]

[27] *Soviet News*, No. 3916, September 19, 1958.
[28] *Socialist International Information*.

The wording of the resolution was the result of hard bargaining, and even Sir Anthony Eden could have added little or nothing to it, so much did it resemble the plan put forward by him at the " Summit " conference at Geneva in July, 1955.

The Rapacki Plan: Second Version

The Polish Government very carefully studied the reactions to and criticisms of its proposal. In view of the rather sympathetic reactions in Scandinavian countries, especially Norway (where Mr. Lange, the Foreign Minister, on May 14, in Parliament, expressed his interest in the Rapacki Plan), the author of the Plan, Mr. Rapacki, accepted an invitation from the Norwegian Government and paid an official visit to Oslo,[29] where he had talks with Mr. Lange.

Undoubtedly, these talks, together with conclusions drawn from various critical reactions, contributed to the contents of the second version of the Plan, which was announced at a Press conference in Warsaw on November 4, 1958.

Mr. Rapacki in his statement made the following points:

> We have recently considered other arguments and misgivings voiced in the course of the discussion. We are prepared, in agreement with our allies, to take a new step—in our opinion the most far-reaching step—towards meeting the main comments and reservations put forward regarding our proposal.
>
> That is, we are prepared to consider the carrying out of our plan in two stages. In the first stage a ban on nuclear weapons ...
>
> The carrying out of the second stage would be preceded by talks on the appropriate reduction of conventional forces. The reduction would be effected simultaneously with the complete denuclearisation of the zone and again would be accompanied by the introduction of appropriate measures of controls.

Referring to various reservations in the West, Mr. Rapacki said: " It should eliminate major misgivings voiced. . . ." These related in particular to the fears— without considering here whether or not they were well

---

[29] October 27–31.

founded—of " upsetting the existing military equilibrium "
between the two groupings in Europe, of " weakening the
defences of the West " or " withdrawing American forces
from Europe " and so on.[30]

Yet the main principles of the Polish plan—similar
to those contained in both versions of the Eden Plan—
reappeared again in the communiqué published on March
3, 1959, after the Macmillan-Khrushchev talks in Moscow.
There it was said

> they agreed that further study could usefully be made of the
> possibilities of increasing security by some method of limitation
> of forces and weapons, both conventional and nuclear, in an
> agreed area of Europe, coupled with an appropriate system of
> inspection.

The history of Mr. Macmillan's battle with his Western
colleagues to enlist their support for such a study is the
subject of the next chapter.

The Berlin Crisis

The events so far described did not indicate that a dramatic
Soviet move was imminent.

There was an exchange of Notes between the Soviet
Union and the West, dealing with the West German proposal of September 9 for setting up a Four-Power Group
[at least on the ambassadorial level] " with the mandate
to prepare joint proposals for the solution of the German
problem."

On September 18 the Soviet Government informed the
three Western Powers of its agreement to this proposal; at
the same time, it did not miss the chance to reassert that it
supported the idea put forward some time ago by the East
German Government for

> the creation of a commission of representatives of both German
> States, which would examine from the German point of view

[30] *Polish Facts and Figures*, No. 608, November 15, 1958.

all questions connected with the preparation of a peace treaty with Germany.

The British Government, in its answer to the Soviet Note on September 30, reasserted its interest in " free elections throughout Germany " and stated that it

> is ready at any time to enter into discussions with the Soviet Government on the basis of these proposals, or of any other proposals genuinely designed to ensure the reunification of Germany in freedom, in any appropriate forum.

The Soviet reaction came like a bombshell a few days later.

In his speech on November 10, Mr. Khrushchev put forward new demands: he stated the necessity of putting an end to the occupation and proposed to make West Berlin into a Free City: he added that Russia would transfer to the East German régime " its functions, which its agencies still operate in Eastern Germany."

Khrushchev's speech was the opening gambit in a new phase in the struggle for Germany.

Hundreds of articles have been written since all over the world, trying to analyse the background and the motives for the sudden Soviet move.

Kennan gave his views in an article in the *New Leader*:

> The practical reasons that led Moscow to reopen the Berlin situation last fall are not too hard to discern. During the last three or four years it has become clearer and clearer that very few people, either in Russia or in the Western countries, really want a unification of Germany on any terms that would conceivably be negotiable in present circumstances. This means that not only Germany but Europe generally is going to remain divided indefinitely. In these circumstances, it has become a matter of urgent necessity for the Soviet leaders to find some way of consolidating Communist rule in the Eastern European area, of reconciling the people of that area to the fact and the permanency of this rule, and of producing a situation, particularly in Hungary, Poland and East Germany, which would compare much more favourably than what exists there today with the conditions in the non-Communist countries of Europe.

In their effort to solve this problem, the Soviet leaders find themselves up against a major obstacle in the continued weakness of their East German puppet régime. They see no promising prospects for overcoming this weakness unless that régime can gain wider international recognition than it has received to date, and unless something can be done to reduce the constantly unsettling effect of the existence in the very midst of its territory of a free Berlin, protected and supported by garrisons of the Western Powers.

. . . The issue today is whether to alter or not to alter—and if so, how—a most complicated and unusual provisional arrangement governing the status of a single European city. . . .

That the Russians should now have an interest in altering it, in the light of a changing European situation, may be disagreeable to us. But it is in no way surprising. And there is no reason to suppose that the effective way of dealing with it is just to give the firm and simple " no " that ought to have been given to Hitler in 1938.[31]

The Soviet move was made after very careful consideration and assessment of all the possible Western reactions: according to Mr. David Dallin, Mr. Molotov [who was recalled from his semi-exile in Ulan Bator, the capital of Outer Mongolia, where he was serving as Soviet ambassador, to Moscow in July, 1958, and proposed unsuccessfully as an ambassador to the Netherlands Government] took part in the first of the secret plans concerning Berlin.[32]

At the second stage, a method had to be selected, and out of the wide range of direct and indirect moves available the most rigid and most aggressive was chosen—an ultimatum.

Before coming into the open, Khrushchev made another important move by inviting the Polish leader, Gomulka, to Moscow.

Relations between Gomulka and Khrushchev had come a full circle. In October, 1956, Gomulka refused to shake hands with Khrushchev at the Warsaw airport, when he, together with Marshal Zhukov, after their unsuccessful

---

31 " Berlin and the Geneva Meeting," *New Leader*, May 11, 1959.
32 " Khrushchev's Berlin Campaign," *New Leader*, April 6, 1959.

attempt to nip Gomulka's *coup* in the bud, were returning
to Moscow. The West completely missed the opportunity
created by Gomulka's defiance of Moscow, and instead of
giving the necessary financial help to Poland to make
her economically independent of Russia, limited their aid to
a miserable pittance, compelling Gomulka to go cap in
hand to Moscow. His Canossa was not in vain, and eventually his second visit to Moscow in October–November,
1958, was a great success, both for him and for Khrushchev. As Mr. Dallin rightly remarks in an article:

> For Khrushchev, Stalin's heir, one of the situations that had
> to be met was the re-harnessing of Poland under Gomulka.
> The indications had been that Poland, the largest and most
> strategic of the satellites, would go the way of Tito. Unlike
> the régime in Yugoslavia, however, the Communist régime in
> Poland was tied to Moscow by an important factor: Germany.
> As long as Gomulka is able to claim that he alone, with Russian
> support, can protect Poland against German revisionist claims,
> his position will remain unshaken. In spite of the deep-rooted
> hatred of Russia in Poland, a pro-Russian orientation in Poland,
> based upon the sober appreciation of political realities, is the
> direct result of the pro-German orientation of the United States.
> By playing shrewdly on these feelings in Poland, Khrush-
> chev, before making any move over Berlin, made his flanks secure.

Even then, the Russians did not dare to deliver official
Notes without probing Western reactions, and Khrushchev's speech, delivered on November 10, was intended to
gauge Western reactions.

If the Soviet experts on Western affairs had predicted
discord and confusion in the Western capitals, they had
made no mistake. Both official and Press comment on Mr.
Khrushchev's speech, from both sides of the Atlantic,
differed very considerably. Against a background of confusion and disarray in the West, the Soviet Note of
November 27 was delivered to the three Western governments and made public.

In this very lengthy document the Soviet Union, having
accused the West of violating the Potsdam Agreement, of

rearming Germany and of opposing a peaceful settlement in Germany, declared that

> the Soviet Union considers to be no longer in force the Protocol of the Agreements between the Governments of the Union of Soviet Socialist Republics, the United States of America and the United Kingdom on the Occupation Zones of Germany and on the Administration of Greater Berlin of September 12, 1944.

In other words, the Soviet Government unilaterally repudiated an international agreement.

Further, the Soviet Government stated that it would

> enter into negotiations at the appropriate moment with the Government of the German Democratic Republic concerning the handing over to the G.D.R. of functions which were temporarily performed by Soviet organs on the basis of the above-mentioned Allied Agreements. . . .
>
> The best solution of the Berlin question would, of course, be based on the fulfilment of the Potsdam Agreement. Under present circumstances this would mean *withdrawal of the Federal German Republic from NATO simultaneously with the withdrawal of the German Democratic Republic from the Warsaw Pact,*[33] and reaching an agreement that in accordance with the principle of the Potsdam Agreement there would be no armed forces in either of the two German States.

The Note then came to the crux of the new plan:

> In the light of all these considerations, the Soviet Government for its part would consider it possible for the question of West Berlin to be solved at the present time by turning West Berlin into an independent political unit—a free town in the life of which no single State would interfere, including neither of the two existing German States. It would be possible, in particular, to come to an agreement by which the territory of the free town would be demilitarised and there would be no armed forces in it.

Finally, the Soviet Note added—and this was probably done to give necessary assurances to Gomulka:

> Any breach of the frontiers of the German Democratic Republic, Poland or Czechoslovakia, any aggressive acts against

---

[33] Author's italics.

any of the member States of the Warsaw Pact will be regarded by all its participants as an attack against all of them.

Thus the stage was set for a new act in the drama of Europe.

Before proceeding further, we should take a look at the background to the situation.

As in 1948, when the Berlin blockade was Stalin's opening gambit in the game for control of the whole of Germany, so now Khrushchev's present move undoubtedly had a deeper meaning and far-reaching aims.

West Berlin had increasingly become an eyesore for the drab Communist reality of Eastern Germany, a humiliating contrast and a Western challenge to all Communist boasts. The existence of West Berlin and its psychological impact on the whole of Eastern Europe, was certainly one of the biggest—unfortunately, they are very few—victories of the West in psychological warfare. Consequently, if West Berlin, as a result of the changes in its status, could gradually have been absorbed into Eastern Germany, it would have been both a terrific boost for the prestige of the Pankow régime, and a great victory for Mr. Khrushchev personally. After all, it would mean that he had won where Stalin had failed.

Mr. Khrushchev's move revealed the fallacy of the West's belief in the perpetuity of the *status quo*, based upon the balance of military power. As Professor Trevor-Roper wrote in his very interesting article in the *Sunday Times* on April 19, 1959, "after fourteen years, the unlocking pressures of the deadlock are beginning to move." [34]

However, the Soviet move concerning Berlin must be considered only as a tactical manoeuvre within the framework of Soviet grand strategy. The increasing support given by the Russians to their puppets in Eastern Germany —whom they were quite willing to abandon only a few years ago—and the insistence on confederation as the only

---

[34] "Can Germany Stay Divided."

method of reunification of Germany, showed the contours of the " grand design."

A very interesting view of this question was expressed by Mr. Isaac Deutscher, who wrote:

> . . . it is no mere coincidence that Mr. Khrushchev is launching the [Soviet Seven Year] Plan simultaneously with his new scheme for Berlin. Since Stalin's blockade of Berlin in 1948 this is the first time that the Soviet Union has undertaken a trial of strength with the West not in Asia or Africa but in the heart of Europe. In 1949 Stalin called off his blockade, acknowledging defeat. . . . Now after a decade of further intensive industrialisation, when the U.S.S.R. is surpassing Western Europe in productivity and *per capita* output, Moscow feels strong enough to recapture the initiative in Europe. Mr. Khrushchev is now reopening the German question because he hopes that, in the course of the years that its solution must take, Russia's new economic supremacy will have its political impact on Western Europe, including the Federal German Republic. His programme for the coming decade is to gain for Russia the rank of the world's first industrial power and to win the battle of Germany.[35]

If the Russians managed to get an agreement with the West on the principle of Confederation—even without insisting on the principle of equality—it would mean by implication the perpetuity of the enslavement of Eastern Europe and the start of a dangerous phase in Germany.

As Walter Lippmann wrote in his article " The Two Germanys and Berlin," published in the *New York Herald Tribune* on April 7, 1959:

> I am persuaded that if we overestimate the nuisance value of West Berlin, we shall miss the chief significance of the Soviet policy. By seizing the initiative and making the indefinite perpetuation of a divided Germany the basis of their policy, the Russians have a chance to accomplish two large objectives. One to stabilise the East German State and the satellite orbit by extinguishing the hopes of adherents to the West. The other to confound Dr. Adenauer's West State.

[35] *The Soviet Seven-Year Plan—A Summary and Prospect*, pp. 7–8.

There is only one way to counteract these far-reaching Soviet schemes, namely by creating in Eastern Europe a physical barrier between Russia and the German " Confederation." In such conditions, the two German States— separated from Russia by a " broad corridor," to use Sir John Slessor's term—could improve relations and eventually merge without severe strains and stresses, and without any danger to their neighbours. Even if Russia would not agree to withdraw her troops from Eastern Europe in the setting of a plan for mutual withdrawal, the very fact that the West had put forward such a plan would prevent the hopes for independence from being extinguished.

Western Reactions

Herr Willy Brandt, the dynamic Burgomaster of West Berlin, lost no time in declaring the same day that the Soviet plan to turn the Western section into a demilitarised " free city " was " quite unacceptable." He also sharply criticised Dulles's statement that the Western Powers might consider East German officials as " agents " of the Russians and have dealings with them without recognising the régime or abandoning any rights.

The inhabitants of all the Western section of Berlin unanimously supported the stand of their Burgomaster in a vote on December 8, rejecting Khrushchev's plan.

Within the Atlantic Alliance, it was Dr. Adenauer who took the initiative in propping up the attitude of the West, trying to bring about unity and firmness towards the Soviet proposals.

Debate in the House of Commons

On December 4 the House of Commons debated the whole question of Foreign Affairs, but, naturally enough in the circumstances, the accent was on the problem of Germany and Berlin.[36] The course of the debate revealed profound differences of opinion, and these differences were not only between party and party, but even within the ranks of the parties themselves. Mr. Selwyn Lloyd opened the debate for the Government and firmly rejected the notion that disengagement could lead to a lessening of tension: " The world is a very much safer place if, in critical areas, there is a direct confrontation of the major parties and not an area of uncertainty." He also insisted that a reunified Germany remain free to join NATO. This attitude was taken up and amplified by Mr. Sandys, Mr. Fletcher-Cooke and Mr. John Eden, among others, from the Government benches. Viscount Hinchingbrooke, on the other hand, recommended that " the West withdraw half its forces in the area defined by the Rapacki Plan, that is to say, Western Germany, provided the Russians do the same in their half, that is Eastern Germany, Poland and Czechoslovakia." He also made the interesting and unique suggestion that we should " see whether there is any condition on which Russia will allow the sensitive fringe area along the Iron Curtain to be overlapped by the security zones, West and East." For the Opposition, however, Mr. Bevan advocated the establishment of as large an area of disengagement as possible, rejecting the claim that withdrawal behind the Rhine would lead to the withdrawal of American troops from Europe altogether. Mr. Arthur Henderson, also from the Opposition benches, recommended acceptance of the Oder-Neisse line and claimed that entry of a united Germany into NATO would never be accepted by the Soviet Union. But, he continued, " the ultimate solution lies, however, in a European system of security." Mr. Denis Healey summed up for the Opposition and linked disarmament with solution of the outstanding political problems: " It is very difficult indeed to envisage any form of agreement limited exclusively to disarmament which could remain

36 *Hansard*, Vol. 596, No. 28.

effective over a long period, unless it is accompanied, or followed very rapidly, by agreement of some of the political problems."

There was, however, agreement on one point, namely, as Mr. Bevan put it:

> . . . solution for the problem of Berlin is a solution of the German problem and a solution of the German problem is a solution of the European problem.

Debate in the House of Lords

The subject was not neglected by the Upper House either, Some days later—on December 18—Lord Henderson opened the debate in the House of Lords on " The International Situation." [37] In so far as Mr. Selwyn Lloyd had promised that Western troops would not move further East into what is at present Eastern Germany in the event of reunited Germany's entry into NATO, Lord Henderson welcomed the Foreign Secretary's acceptance of the principle of a neutral zone, but he too pressed for a far wider area to be included. In return for the withdrawal of NATO from Western Germany, the Soviet Union should be asked to agree to withdraw from East Germany, Poland, Czechoslovakia and Hungary. " But for the Government to repeat that the first steps towards German unity must be free elections, and that a unified Germany must be permitted to join NATO, is surely futile." Both Lord Birdwood and Lord St. Oswald claimed that the main fear of the Eastern European countries was for the safety of the Oder-Neisse Line, and that this was one point which the Government should settle, removing with one action the basis of Khrushchev's power over those territories. Lord St. Oswald recommended comprehensive disengagement as a means of reaching that end, and Lord Birdwood suggested that the West should make as much effort as possible to meet Russian objections while maintaining Germany's

[37] *Hansard*, Vol. 213, No. 26.

right to join either NATO or the Warsaw Pact. Lord Aberdare, on the other hand, claimed that neutralisation of Western Germany would upset "the delicate military balance that exists at present" and create "a vacuum"; Lord Hastings had two doubts on the subject, firstly, as to what the effect on NATO would be, and secondly, "would Germany, reunified, be safe to leave alone?"

Developments in Europe

The four Foreign Ministers met in Paris on December 14, and having heard Herr Brandt,

> . . . once more reaffirmed the determination of their Governments to maintain their position and their rights with respect to Berlin, including the right of free access.

Two days later the meeting of the NATO Council endorsed fully the decisions of the four Foreign Ministers in its communiqué on December 16, stating:

> . . . no State has the right to withdraw unilaterally from its international engagements. . . . The demands expressed by the Soviet Government have created a serious situation which must be met with determination.

Yet the NATO Council, after rejecting the Soviet demands, did not close the door for further negotiations on Berlin, within the framework of the whole German problem.

One of the most interesting comments on the Soviet proposals appeared in a leader in the *Observer* on November 30, recommending "direct talks" between the two Germanies under the umbrella of four-power negotiations, without committing the West to recognise East Germany. Even a period of Confederation is, according to the *Observer*, by no means out of the question. The very fact that West Germany is so much stronger makes such contact safer.

This should be Western policy: to refuse to negotiate on Berlin [where we are weak] but to offer to negotiate on Germany [where we are strong]. . . . For it is only by reuniting Germany and *disengaging the forces of Russia and the West* [38] that we can hope to solve not merely the problem of Berlin, but the far greater problem of security and disarmament in Europe.

This eventful year ended with the formal unanimous rejection by the West of the Soviet plan. The British Note of December 31—sent simultaneously with similar Notes by other Western Powers—was especially sharp.

Mr. Khrushchev and the Noel-Bakers

Before closing this review of 1958 it is important to quote an interview which Mr. Khrushchev had with Francis Noel-Baker and his father, Philip Noel-Baker, both Labour M.P.s, at the beginning of December. Like his interview given for American television, it contained several important statements which help to define his policy.

He was adamant about the preservation of the present régime in East Germany [only a few years ago the Soviet Government was quite ready to drop it overboard] and he was insistent on the need for the evacuation of all occupying troops from Berlin, but also suggested the possibility of setting up some international system of control.

Speaking about disarmament, he emphasised that Russia still stands by her acceptance in May, 1955, of the Anglo-French plan, involving the fixing of manpower, the partial reduction of conventional forces, nuclear weapon stocks and the establishment of a unified international control system.

The conclusions drawn by the Noel-Bakers are extremely interesting:

For us the most significant conclusion we drew from our talks was that Mr. Khrushchev and his colleagues were glad to

[38] Author's italics.

seek a comprehensive settlement with the Western Powers, if
they could be convinced that the Western Powers would
respond. . . .

This fact, as much as anything they said to us, fortifies our
belief that the West now has everything to gain, nothing to
lose, from a determined new effort to negotiate with Mr.
Khrushchev and his colleagues.[39]

No doubt these words were a further encouragement to
Mr. Macmillan to make the decision to go on a " reconnaissance " trip to Moscow early in 1959—with which we
shall deal in the next chapter.

[39] *The Observer*, December 6 and 13, 1958.

9

From Moscow to Geneva, 1959

RELATIONS between Russia and the West have never been so tense since the Berlin blockade in 1948–49. In the second round of the battle for Berlin the West found itself in 1959 in a much weaker position than ten years ago: in 1948, the United States had the monopoly of the A-bomb; at present there is a dangerous parity and " an atomic plenty." Consequently, any attempt to force a Soviet blockade—should the Russians go so far as to impose one—by sending a convoy ready to " shoot its way through " (as some senior American commanders have suggested) would be a very dangerous proposition: let us remember that in 1948 the Pentagon was definitely opposed to such an idea. On the alternative idea of an escorted airlift the West would again be in a weaker position than in 1948, because now the Russians would be able to shoot down Allied aircraft with guided missiles fired from their launching sites, without incurring the risk of a direct battle in the air.

At the same time, the crucial problem of the reunification of Germany has become more complicated and difficult than it was ten years ago. As this Part has tried to demonstrate, ten years ago the price for German reunification was much cheaper: the Russians did not insist then on Confederation of the two German States; they were quite prepared to abandon their Communist stooges in East Berlin. Furthermore, ten years ago they were speaking in terms of the withdrawal of troops from Germany alone, whereas now they insist on the dismantling of all bases in foreign territories, an impossible condition for the West.

249

Unofficial Suggestions

Before we come to the moves made by the Great Powers, let us deal shortly with various proposals put forward by politicians and political writers on both sides of the Atlantic.

In Britain, two somewhat similar proposals were put forward, although quite independent of one another. Mr. Anthony Nutting, a former Minister of State, in an article published in the *New York Herald Tribune* in December 1958, suggested putting the whole issue before the inhabitants of Berlin:

> If they so desire we will hand over, all four of us, to an all-Berlin Government, freely elected by elections supervised by the UN and properly guaranteed by UNO against aggression, direct and indirect.

Another was put forward by the author in an article entitled " A Solution for Berlin—in the Setting of Disengagement," in which he suggested that the whole of demilitarised Berlin be made a free city, its status guaranteed by all Four Great Powers and its internal security entrusted to an International Police Force. The whole arrangement would be the first stage towards Berlin's becoming the capital of a reunited Germany, a solution which could be achieved only as a result of disengagement.[1]

An extraordinary suggestion was put forward by the Oxford historian Mr. G. F. Hudson, also, like Mr. Nutting, in an article in the United States, but in this case in the *New Leader* on January 19. He advocated the

> transfer to West Germany of everyone in Berlin who wanted to go, and the construction in West Germany, as a matter of top priority and at the expense of all Western Powers, of a new city, called New Berlin or Free Berlin.

The method of carrying this out which Mr. Hudson suggested was to be " an *airlift in reverse*, for the

---

[1] *The Tablet*, December 13, 1958.

evacuation of a civilian population with any movable property that could be taken."

For all practical purposes it amounts to proposing the evacuation by air of two and a half million people, each with one or possibly two suitcases: it would mean ruin and hardship for all those gallant inhabitants of Berlin who look to the West for their protection.

Mr. Hudson concluded his article by saying:

> . . . a withdrawal of such a kind would not be a serious defeat for the West, even though a few square miles of bricks and concrete had to be given up.

It is particularly interesting that such a plan, which would be nothing less than unilateral disengagement, should have been put forward by an outspoken critic of disengagement. It was the same Mr. Hudson who, in an article " Holding the Frontier," published in *The Observer* on January 19, 1958, and reproduced in the *New Leader*, said: " . . . peace will be better preserved if strategically the Western Powers stay exactly where they are."

Sir Ivone Kirkpatrick, former Permanent Under-Secretary to the Foreign Office, in an article " Towards a German Settlement," was of the rather pessimistic opinion that:

> . . . in view of the fundamentally divergent "interests" of Russia and of the West, there is little room for manoeuvre or compromise. . . . Russia cannot afford to sacrifice the Red leaders in Berlin . . . because . . . the establishment of a free Germany would bring freedom to the frontiers of Poland, which would find herself, therefore, in the situation of Yugoslavia, that is to say, a country sustained in the struggle for independence by direct access to the West.[2]

But Sir Ivone would be correct only if the problem of the German-Polish frontier were finally settled and internationally guaranteed, and ceased to be a source of friction between Poland and Germany.

---

[2] The *Sunday Times*, January 19, 1959.

Sir Ivone concludes by stating that he is in favour of " a demilitarised strip across Europe on both sides of the Iron Curtain."

In the United States, General Carl Spaatz, former Commander of the U.S. Strategic Air Force in Europe, published a plan, the idea for which came originally from a former American ambassador, Mr. John C. Wiley. The plan boiled down to a suggestion to *transfer the seat of the United Nations from New York to Berlin*, making it " a diplomatic Bethlehem." [3]

A similar proposal was put forward by Walter Lippmann in a series of three articles under the title " The Two Germanys and Berlin," in which he suggested negotiating a new statute for Berlin

> in which the future of Berlin is put in trust with the United Nations. The new Charter or statute should begin with an explicit declaration that the United Nations trust will last until the two German States agree to restore Berlin as the capital of a reunited Germany. . . . Though it is a complicated thing to do so, it is not an impossible thing to establish a city within a city and within a foreign State. . . . There was the Lateran Treaty which established the Vatican.[4]

Among other plans flooding the front pages of American newspapers, prominence must be given to a plan attributed by *Newsweek*, who published it on January 29, to Mr. Robert Murphy, Under-Secretary of State. According to that plan, authorship of which was, however, most emphatically denied by Mr. R. Murphy, the reunification of Germany ought to take place in the form of a " Confederation," as an interim device, preceding German reunification through free elections. It provided for the transfer of the capital from Bonn to West Berlin and the deployment of units of the Bundeswehr in Western sectors of Berlin, replacing the garrisons of NATO. This

[3] *Newsweek*, January 5, 1959.
[4] *New York Herald Tribune*, April 6, 7 and 8, 1959.

procedure would aim at the establishment of direct relations between the governments of both Germanys.

Mr. L. Sulzberger was very critical of any idea of
forcing the Soviet blockade of Berlin—should it ever come
to that—and at the same time made the rather unrealistic
and dangerous suggestion of putting units of the Bundeswehr into West Berlin.[5]

Mr. George Kennan, in his testimony before the Senate
Disarmament Committee under the chairmanship of Sena-
tor Humphrey, was of a different opinion from Herr
Brandt. In his view

> the first and immediate concern of the Soviet Government with
> respect to Germany is to bring about an alteration in their
> favour of the situation in Berlin.[6]

In view of the impact on public opinion of Kennan's
ideas, it is interesting to quote his assessment of the Soviet
views on this problem:

> With regard to the more long-term problem of Germany,
> in general the main Soviet concern is to ensure:
> 1. That the Eastern Zone is not swallowed up by the
> German Federal Republic in so drastic and violent a way as to
> constitute a major blow to Communist and Soviet prestige; . . .
> 2. That atomic armaments should not be introduced into
> the defences of Western Germany; and
> 3. That the armed forces of Western Germany, or of a
> possible united Germany, should not be allied with, and should
> not constitute an extension of, the U.S. armed forces.

Kennan's views were strongly criticised on the same
occasion by A. Wolfers, director of the Washington Center
of Foreign Policy Research, who said:

> This plan of Mr. Kennan's and all similar plans provide for
> a neutralised Germany, that is a Germany that is under con-
> tractual obligations not to do certain things. Any such plan,
> in my opinion, opens Germany to the rather arbitrary inter-
> vention by its guarantors, and since the Soviet Union is likely to
> be the country that would allege that Germany had committed

---

[5] *New York Times,* January 31, 1959.
[6] Published later in the *New Leader,* February 23, 1959.

violations, a so-called neutral Germany, in my opinion, would be a Germany at the mercy of the Soviet Union.

These arguments will be discussed in a later chapter, but in the meantime it is interesting to note that Mr. Wolfers himself put forward a suggestion for a

> relatively demilitarised zone along the Iron Curtain, [in which] the troops on either side were equalised, thinned out and denuclearised. Under such an agreement—which would require little inspection for its enforcement—the danger of both border incidents and of the immediate degeneration of such incidents into nuclear combat would be greatly reduced. . . . I would like to emphasise, however, that this would have to be a narrow zone for the simple reason that we cannot afford to deprive NATO of the possibility of deploying adequate forces including strong American and German contingents, in a way that will retain for Western Europe the chance of protection.[7]

Mr. Wolfers's suggestion, if accepted, would not amount even to a limited regional disarmament measure, because the narrowness of the zone would nullify the effect of its denuclearisation. It would just be a sort of a " police measure " against possible border incidents, which, in the whole history of the existence of demarcation lines so far, have never occurred. Such a sterile measure could in no way contribute to the lessening of tension in Europe, which was caused not by the fear of non-existent border incidents, but by something more serious—the division of Germany and the enslavement of Eastern Europe.

Senator Humphrey, in an international radio link over the B.B.C. on February 4, mentioned his talk with Mr. Khrushchev in Moscow in 1958 and his firm stand over Berlin. He emphasised Mr. Khrushchev's objections to Germany's having nuclear weapons, and said:

> I had expected all this, but may I say that there's an answer to all of it and the answer to it is for the Soviet Union to be willing conscientiously and responsibly to negotiate for German reunification and for the phased withdrawal of troops in a very broad area in Central Europe.

[7] *Handbook on Arms Control and Related Problems in Europe*, pp. 23–25.

During that broadcast he also said:

> I think we must start, for example, to talk about a phased withdrawal, possibly of opposing forces, maybe some talk of a de-nuclearised zone, maybe some kind of limitations on armaments in the Central European area.

Herr Willy Brandt, Burgomaster of West Berlin, who suddenly hit the headlines all over the world, took a firmly negative attitude towards any change in the present status of Berlin: in his speech at a luncheon given in his honour by the Foreign Press Association in London on April 21, he said:

> . . . any new agreements concerning communications to and from Berlin must not be allowed to replace existing agreements and could never supersede them.

On the same occasion he expressed regret that the West had rejected the Rapacki Plan.

This sketchy review of various suggestions put forward on both sides of the Atlantic shows to what extent the idea of mutual withdrawal of troops has kept reappearing in various shapes and forms in different solutions for Berlin and Germany.

The short chronological review of official moves by both sides which follows shows that an intense search for a solution of the crisis over Berlin, and of the German problem in general, has also been the foremost concern of the governments of the Soviet Union and of the West.

The Soviet Note

The Soviet Union did not waste much time in answering the Western Notes of December 31, 1958. The gist of a Russian Note on January 10, similar to a large extent to Soviet proposals made in 1954, with 25 draft pages of a German peace treaty, boiled down to a Confederation of the two German States, or two independent States. Russia suggested: that Germany should " renounce all territorial claims beyond the present border " along the Oder-Neisse

Line; "that all foreign forces and bases should be with-drawn from German territory within a year of the treaty coming into effect and at least one-third of these troops within six months "; that " Germany should withdraw from NATO, the Warsaw Pact and Western European Union and should undertake not to enter any military alliance directed against a signatory of the treaty."

One of the main differences between this Note and the Soviet proposals of 1954 was that this time the Soviet Government omitted any reference to the need for elections before the formation of an all-German Government.

At the same time, the Note omitted the ultimatum dateline of six months, which had been mentioned by Mr. Khrushchev in his speech of November 10, and later on in the Soviet Note of November 27. This latter Note said only that

> refusal by the Western Powers to enter into negotiations with the Soviet Union . . . will not stop the Soviet Union half-way towards the goal.[8]

The gist of the Soviet Note had been communicated to Mr. Dulles five days earlier by Mr. Mikoyan, who went to the United States on a sort of good will mission, as well as to make soundings of American reaction.

At his Press Conference in Los Angeles on January 11, Mr. Mikoyan said:

> If the Americans were prepared to withdraw their divisions from Western Germany, we should be prepared to do likewise from Eastern Germany.[9]

The Washington correspondent of the *Daily Telegraph* reported on January 16 that during his talks in Washington Mr. Mikoyan had

> revived his old proposal that both sides withdraw their forces 500 miles in each direction from the Elbe river, thereby creating a large demilitarised zone.

---

[8] *Soviet News*, No. 3985, January 12, 1959.
[9] *Daily Telegraph*, January 12, 1959.

On this point Mr. Mikoyan's suggestion coincided almost word for word with similar suggestions put forward by the group of twelve Democrats in their letter to President Eisenhower of December, 1956.[10]

As might have been expected, Western reactions towards the Soviet Note were very critical. First of all, in his Press Conference on January 13, Dulles called it " a stupid approach, because we do not think it will work." On the same occasion he made a remark which produced a storm in Western Germany; he said that there might be other ways of bringing about German reunification. With these words Dulles exploded the dogma of Western policy, contained in the " Berlin Declaration " of July 29, 1957, that is, that *free elections are the only way for German reunification.*

Herr von Brentano is reputed to have said that the Soviet Note offered absolutely no basis for negotiations—a somewhat different attitude from that taken by the most interested party, namely Herr Brandt, who said that in his view it meant a qualified readiness on the part of the Russians to negotiate. He also drew attention to the fact that the Russians wanted to tone down the alarming appearance of an ultimatum. Although Dr. Adenauer also was very annoyed with the Note and called it " a brutal approach," it is not inappropriate to add that the East German leaders did not feel quite happy about it either.

Apart from their suspicions of the possibility of some secret agreement which could be reached by Mr. Mikoyan in the United States, they were worried—*The Observer* correspondent in Berlin, Sebastian Haffner, reported on January 16

> . . . that if some agreement on European security and the military status of Germany should be reached between the Great Powers, the Russians might wash their hands of the East Germans and leave them to fend for themselves.

[10] *Supra*, pp. 193–194.

Herr Ulbricht reasserted his position in an interview
with British United Press on January 24, in which he
categorically rejected the possibility of a Western guarantee,
as suggested by Dulles, that in the event of reunification
Eastern Germany would not be turned into a Western
military base.

However, not only the East Germans were worried
about their masters. It appears from the dispatches of *The
Observer* correspondent in Washington, Philip Deane, on
January 25, that the idea of Confederation, taboo in Bonn,
had for some time been under consideration in Washington.
According to Deane:

> Washington is also studying whether to drop—at a price—
> its insistence on the right of an eventually reunified Germany
> to join NATO; some form of disengagement is no longer
> thought to be impossible.

The report from Washington was substantiated by the
Chairman of the Senate Foreign Relations Committee,
Senator Fulbright, in a speech on January 30 advocating negotiations with the Russians and some form of
disengagement.

Such rumours were very alarming for Bonn, and Dr.
Adenauer dispatched two of his most trusted diplomats
to Washington, Paris and London with the delicate mission
of straightening things out as much as possible.

Mr. Khrushchev's Speech

The XXI Communist Party Congress in Moscow on
January 27 gave Mr. Khrushchev another opportunity to
restate his policy towards the German question in general
and to Berlin in particular. In his six hours' speech he
said that the Berlin situation was " like a burning fuse in
a gunpowder cellar." He attacked American generals and,
in particular, Mr. McElroy, Secretary of Defence, for
saying in his speech that Americans would carry out their
military activities from the territories of their allies.

He reiterated Soviet proposals for a gradual reduction of the armed forces of both sides stationed in Germany, or even for their complete withdrawal. He said emphatically that the Russians were prepared to withdraw their troops not only from Eastern Germany but also from Poland and Czechoslovakia, if other NATO countries would withdraw their troops from Germany and dismantle their bases on foreign territories.

On the third day of the Congress, Mr. Gromyko, the Soviet Foreign Minister, warned the West that if it spurned Russian proposals for settling the German question Russia would " seek other ways " of solving it.

Mr. Dulles comes to Europe

In view of the rising doubt and confusion in Western capitals, Dulles left for Europe on February 8 to try to create a united front towards the Soviet moves. The reason for Dr. Adenauer's entirely negative attitude towards the Soviet plan—and, indeed, to any plan except his own—was that the Soviet draft, if accepted, would, even with far-reaching modifications, put an end to his own ideas of German reunification. Moreover, it would frustrate his schemes for building up Germany's military might and for the restoration of the lost territories in the East. The reasons for General de Gaulle's equally negative attitude were, perhaps, more subtle than Dr. Adenauer's. On the one hand, he opposed any plans which might weaken Germany militarily when France was engaged in a mortal struggle in North Africa and could allocate only a small fraction of her armed forces to the defence of Europe; hence his objection to any scheme for disengagement. On the other hand, in spite of the French-German rapprochement, he did not want Germany to become too strong; hence his recognition of the Oder-Neisse Line as the German-Polish frontier, which came as a bad shock to Dr. Adenauer.

Only in London did Dulles find any willingness to negotiate and to examine various solutions in this field.

Mr. Macmillan goes to Russia

Contrary to both Dr. Adenauer's and General de Gaulle's conviction that the Russians were bluffing, Mr. Macmillan took a much more serious view and "on his own responsibility" decided to make a "reconnaissance" trip to Moscow.

During the debate in Parliament preceding Mr. Macmillan's departure, Mr. Gaitskell, having said that there was no great disagreement between the two sides of the House on the question of Berlin, reiterated his suggestions for mutual withdrawal of troops:

> would it not be better at this point to ask under what conditions could the West agree to the possible sacrifice of a withdrawal of Germany from NATO?

On the subject of a short-term solution, Mr. Gaitskell declared that there was one proposal which offered a chance of agreement between East and West: that was that part of the Opposition proposals which dealt with controlled disarmament in the area.

Mr. Macmillan said in his reply:

> The balance of military security must not be changed to the disadvantage of either side. Any proposals must be consistent with the survival as a defensive organisation of NATO. Nothing must be done which would result, whether logically or in fact, in the withdrawal of the American and Canadian forces from the Continent of Europe.
>
> Within that, nothing ought to be excluded. We must be firm, but we must be flexible. We will not agree to give away our strength and our security except in exchange for effective control.

At the end of his visit, which lasted from February 21 to March 3, the final communiqué about his talks with Mr. Khrushchev stated:

> They agreed that further study could be usefully made of possibilities of increasing security by some method of limitation

of forces and weapons, both conventional and nuclear, in the agreed area of Europe, coupled with an appropriate system of inspection.

In relation to all these matters, the Prime Ministers endorsed the principle that differences between nations should be resolved by negotiations and not by force.

Looking back at the various plans, and in particular at the two versions of the Eden Plan, as well as the Rapacki Plan, it could be said, in view of the wording of the Moscow communiqué, that the gap between East and West had narrowed considerably.

Mr. Khrushchev at the Leipzig Fair

The very day following the publication of the Moscow communiqué, Mr. Khrushchev used the opportunity of his visit to Leipzig Fair to restate, at the Lord Mayor's banquet, the fundamental principles of Soviet policy towards Germany:

> We are in favour of German reunification. Let Dr. Adenauer and Comrade Ulbricht meet and come to an agreement on this question and we shall vote for what they will decide upon.

Looking at Mr. Mikardo, M.P., who was also present at that banquet, he said:

> I see that some gentlemen from Britain are present here. I want to tell you outright, we shall sign a peace treaty with the two existing German States, we shall sign a peace treaty with the German Democratic Republic. Such a treaty will also be signed most probably by other States which took part in the war against Germany. As regards the Berlin question, we want to have it settled not separately but in conjunction with the whole German problem.[11]

Western Press Comment

Although Press comments on Mr. Macmillan's visit to Moscow were, of course, varied, the general opinion which

[11] *Soviet News*, No. 4018, March 6, 1959.

prevailed was that it was worth while, on the grounds that with the information which he brought from his visit it would be easier for the West to decide upon a common policy.

The comments in *The Observer* of March 8 especially deserve to be mentioned:

> Mr. Macmillan seems to have reached the conclusion that at present a real disengagement is impractical, because neither Russia nor some of his own allies are willing to consider it. He is thinking instead of a policy of political and military relaxation, which, if all went well, might make disengagement possible at some future date. This would mean a working arrangement with East Germany—perhaps within German Confederation—and also some plan for disarmament or a thinning out of armed forces in Central Europe. . . . The difficulty would be to translate any military relaxation into a political agreement.

Mr. Macmillan Goes the Rounds— Paris, Bonn, Ottawa, Washington

Most important, of course, were Mr. Macmillan's talks with Dr. Adenauer; according to despatches of British correspondents, the talks ended in agreement. On March 13, the correspondent to the *Daily Telegraph* reported:

> Mr. Macmillan will continue to promote the thinned-out zone proposal when he visits Washington next week. According to British sources, nothing has been said in Paris or Bonn to cause the proposal to be dropped. . . .

and the same correspondent reported that Dr. Adenauer, answering questions at the airport, stated: " They were very good consultations and complete agreement has been reached."

Yet, only three days later, Dr. Adenauer dealt what looked like a sharp rebuff to Mr. Macmillan's plans for a military thinning-out in Central Europe. In a statement published in the Newsletter of the CDU, he flatly rejected any plans for the limitations of arms as " dangerous."

A few days later his Defence Minister, Herr Strauss, declared in an interview that " the idea that the cold war could be eased by thinning out opposing military forces in the heart of Europe is an illusion." [12]

Mr. Macmillan's talks in Ottawa were more successful and, according to Press reports,

> the Canadian view had inclined towards a thinning-out proposal of Allied forces in Germany and a phased disengagement in Central Europe.[13]

In conversation with the author Mr. Lester Pearson, former Canadian Minister for External Affairs and Leader of the Opposition, had stated: " I am not afraid of any disengagement, provided it is not of any advantage to the Russians."

Mr. Macmillan had a much more difficult task in Washington, in view of the rather critical attitude taken towards his decision to go to Moscow: undoubtedly, the President's reference to Munich in his speech a few weeks before was an expression of the opinion prevailing in the United States. Although no communiqué was issued after the two days' talks in Camp David, the well-informed correspondent of *The Observer*, Philip Deane, was able to state in his despatch of March 21 that,

> Mr. Macmillan spoke of a distant stage when the " freezing " could lead to the thinning out of forces and measures even closer to disengagement. His proposals, claimed Mr. Macmillan, represented the greatest common factor of agreement that all concerned could reach.

Deane concluded:

> The Macmillan scheme is also tailored to suit the Americans. They are not required to leave their bases in Germany, do not require to recognise East Germany formally, and do not have to renounce nuclear weapons in Europe. . . . All they have to sacrifice—and not " in principle "—is the reunification of Germany in freedom, which they are not renouncing but merely postponing.

[12] Reported in the *New York Herald Tribune*, March 23, 1959.
[13] *Daily Telegraph*, March 19, 1959.

Yet Mr. Macmillan's talks in Washington aroused grave misgivings in Bonn, and Dr. Adenauer instructed his London envoy to make official inquiries in London about Press reports of Mr. Macmillan's talks in the United States. This move broke down the façade of superficial agreement between Bonn and London on the Berlin crisis and on any solution to the German problem, which had been patched up during Mr. Macmillan's visit to Bonn.

Although this increasing difference of opinion and, in particular, Dr. Adenauer's critical attitude towards Mr. Macmillan's initiative, did not come into the open, it was no secret that relations between Britain and the Federal Republic cooled off considerably. It was without doubt as a result of Dr. Adenauer's stiff and uncompromising attitude that the Western Foreign Ministers lacked the the necessary flexibility during the talks in Geneva.

Dr. Adenauer showed himself increasingly suspicious of the motives behind Britain's policy towards Russia, suspecting an intention to make a deal at Germany's expense. It was out of a desire to exercise a strong influence on the foreign policy of the West—as he had done during the previous years—that he withdrew from the candidature for the Presidency, considerably weakening his personal prestige and casting a shadow by his autocratic methods on the genuine nature of democracy in Western Germany.

Senator Mike Mansfield's Proposals

At the same time as Mr. Macmillan was trying to rally the support of his allies, Senator Mike Mansfield, Democrat, in a speech in the Senate on February 12, 1959,[14] courageously raised some important points and put forward his own constructive proposals.

First of all, he quite bluntly condemned the policy of the West as utterly unrealistic, with its insistence on free

[14] Reproduced in *Aussenpolitik*, May, 1959.

elections in Germany as the only method of German reunification. Such a policy, he said, is no policy at all and is only an excuse for immobility.

Moreover, he expressed doubts as to why the present policy of integrating Germany's military contribution into the Western defence system should be considered sacrosanct. He, personally, was of the opinion that the German contribution could be easily reduced.

At the end of his speech he laid down the following principles:

(1) Western armed forces should remain in Berlin;

(2) The municipal authorities of East and West Berlin should jointly try to run the affairs of the City;

(3) Such co-operation should be developed with the help of the Secretary-General of UNO; in due course, armed contingents of UNO should replace the Soviet and Western garrisons in both parts of Berlin;

(4) Should this plan end in failure, it would be essential that Western troops remain in Berlin;

(5) At the same time, Western troops should be replaced as soon as possible by German contingents;

(6) Both the Federal German authorities and the Pankow régime should establish working contacts with each other in several fields of common interest;

(7) The population of Eastern Germany should be given, in due course, the right to hold free elections;

(8) Both Russia and the Western Powers should guarantee for a period the *modus vivendi* reached as a result of discussions between the Governments of the two Germanys;

(9) It was essential that U.S. policy try to reach an agreement with the Russians, without loosening the various ties which bind Western Germany to

Western Europe, on limitation of armaments in the whole of Germany and in Central Europe. In this connection, nuclear weapons should be withdrawn from various places in Germany and Central Europe.

Summing up, Senator Mansfield was of the opinion that U.S. and NATO policy should take into consideration the recommendations contained in the Rapacki and Eden Plans.

It is quite likely that it was as a result of Senator Mansfield's speech that Dulles, when he arrived in Europe in February, expressed the view that free elections in Germany should not be considered as the only method of reunification. Up to that time, such a view had been the dogma of American policy for years.

The Plan of the German Socialists

Against the background of Mr. Macmillan's trip to Moscow and the capitals of the West, the SPD produced its own plan on March 18, known as the *Deutschlandplan der SPD.*

The publication of the plan was preceded by the talks between Mr. Khrushchev and Herr Ollenhauer in Berlin, and between Mr. Khrushchev and Professor Carlo Schmid and Fritz Erler, both prominent members of the SPD Executive, in Moscow. During a three-hour talk with the German Socialists, Mr. Khrushchev reiterated his view that German reunification is a matter for the Germans themselves. He said that once the treaties were signed, Russia would refrain from any interference in the internal affairs of Eastern Germany, provided that the West did likewise. As regards the disengagement of troops, he expressed the opinion that it could be put into effect by stages, simultaneously with German reunification.

These conversations added some finishing touches to the Plan, which can be summed up as follows:

(1) A zone of reduced tension, *Entspannungzone*, should be set up, consisting of both parts of Germany, Poland, Czechoslovakia and Hungary.

(2) There should be limitation of arms and armed forces in the zone and a gradual withdrawal of all foreign forces of NATO and the Warsaw Pact.

(3) National forces should have no atomic weapons.

(4) All disarmament steps should be under an international control.

(5) A European security pact should be formed.

(6) Countries within the zone should withdraw from their respective military alliances.

(7) The present status of Berlin should be guaranteed until the German question as a whole be solved.

As regards the reunification of Germany, the SPD visualised its settlement either as the result of an agreement between the Great Powers or as the result of an agreement between the two German States: the reunification itself would take place in three stages.

In order to counteract strong official opposition to their plan, the SPD produced some excerpts from a secret plan for German reunification, which was, they maintained, prepared by the three Western Powers together with the Bonn Government in 1953.[15]

General de Gaulle's Views

At a Press Conference on March 25, 1959, in which he refused to recognise the East German régime and—to the great disappointment of Dr. Adenauer—endorsed the existing German frontiers in the East, President Charles de Gaulle took a critical attitude towards disengagement:

[15] *Supra*, p. 163.

As regards turning Germany into a neutralised territory, this " extrication " or " disengagement " in itself says nothing to us which is of value. For if disarmament does not cover a zone which is as near to the Urals as it is to the Atlantic, how will France be protected? How then, in the event of a conflict, could it prevent an aggressor from crossing in one leap the undefended German no-man's land?

How narrow a strip would remain between the Meuse and the ocean to deploy and use the means of the West? Certainly we are supporters of the control and limitation of all weapons of war. But for these measures, apparently humanitarian, not to risk leading to our disappearance, they must cover an area deep enough and large enough for France to be covered and not on the contrary exposed.

General de Gaulle appears to have envisaged a solution by which disengagement would entail the neutralisation of Germany as the result of a withdrawal of Soviet troops only to behind the German-Polish frontier. Were this the case, General de Gaulle's apprehensions would be wholly justified. In point of fact, as previous chapters have shown, such a solution would be even worse than the present *status quo* with all its potential dangers.

However it would be interesting to hear General de Gaulle's reactions to a well-presented, comprehensive disengagement solution, by which Soviet troops would withdraw to behind Soviet frontiers, and a reunited Germany and the countries of Eastern Europe, with national armed forces and a posture of military non-alignment would become not an " undefended no man's land " but a buffer zone, a forward defence glacis for the West in general, and France in particular.

The Plan of the German Free Democratic Party

Only two days after the publication of the plan by SPD, the FDP produced (on March 20) its own Plan, the essence of which was as follows:

(1) Germany should renounce membership of any military *bloc* and prepare to join a European security system.

(2) All foreign troops should withdraw by stages from German territory.

(3) Germany should have her own national conventional armed forces, strong enough for the defence of her territory.

(4) German territory should be an atom-free zone.

(5) Free elections should be held in due course in both parts of Germany.

(6) The eastern frontiers to be delineated in such a way as to become acceptable to the German nation and conform with her desire for reconciliation with her neighbours in the East.

Soviet Proposals for a Non-Aggression Pact

On the eve of the NATO Council meeting to be held in Washington in the last days of March and at the beginning of April, to celebrate the NATO Tenth Anniversary, Russia reiterated on March 30 her proposal for a non-aggression pact between the NATO and Warsaw Pact countries.

This proposal was found during the NATO Council session to be objectionable, because it would amount to the recognition of the permanent division of Germany.

At the end of the session, it was stated in a communiqué that " the basic reasons, which led to the signature of NATO in 1949, remain valid today," which means that the threat from Russia still exists.

The communiqué indicated the following principles for the Western position in the forthcoming negotiations with the Soviet *bloc*:

(1) Any Western concession should bring a corresponding Soviet concession.

(2) The Western Powers should not barter their right as conquerors to be in Berlin to obtain an agreement with Russia to remain there.

(3) There should be no new military arrangement or " freeze " which could upset the present balance of power in Europe.

At the same time, the Council approved the directives for the Four Power working group for the forthcoming Four Foreign Ministers' conference at Geneva on May 11.

According to the Washington correspondent to *The Observer* on April 4:

> Rejected by a NATO majority was the basic British premise that agreement on easing European military tensions should be sought, if necessary as a first step and not made conditional on progress in solving political tension.

This attitude obviously reflected Dr. Adenauer's tactical victory over Mr. Macmillan.

In Berlin, another *Observer* correspondent, Sebastian Haffner, wrote in his dispatch of the same date: " There is obviously some rather bewildered anxiety in British official quarters about Dr. Adenauer's reactions."

Pierre Mendès-France

At a Press conference at the Hotel Lutetia in Paris on April 2, 1959, the former French Prime Minister and former Minister of Foreign Affairs, Pierre Mendès-France, put forward various interesting proposals.

Referring to disarmament proposals put forward by him in 1954 in his capacity as Minister of Foreign Affairs, he suggested the establishment of a broad area, composed of several vertical zones situated symmetrically on both sides of the present demarcation line and subjected to certain restrictions and arms limitations as well as controls. These would relax gradually with reference to each consecutive vertical zone.

According to Mendès-France, these restrictions would not apply specifically to Germany, Poland or Czechoslovakia, and there would be no discrimination between any of the countries situated on the territory of the proposed zone. The restrictions would apply equally to all countries in these vertical zones, which would extend from the Baltic to the Mediterranean.

Going into details, Mendès-France suggested the following scheme. On both sides of the present demarcation line a strip would be established of, say, fifty-one kilometres wide and *completely demilitarised*. It would be manned either by the local police or, preferably, by UN contingents. On both sides of this strip, which he called *la bande zéro*, two further areas would be set up, comprising Zone One, to be manned entirely by national forces with conventional arms only, and subject to arms limitations and controls. To the east and west of Zone One he suggested setting up a further two identical areas comprising Zone Two, in which foreign troops would be stationed, armed with all modern weapons.

By putting forward such a scheme, Mendès-France hoped to avoid the inconveniences of the Rapacki Plan as he conceived them and, furthermore, to prevent the danger of a withdrawal of American troops from Europe.

Although the whole scheme was of a predominantly military character, Mendès-France was of the opinion that the withdrawal of Soviet troops from Zone One in Eastern Europe would contribute to great political changes in the constituent countries. It is difficult to agree with this point of view for, even if only a platoon of Soviet troops remained stationed on a small part of the territory of a given country in Eastern Europe, it would amount to continuity of Soviet influence and would maintain the Soviet grip on that country. Quite bluntly, only a total withdrawal of Soviet troops from a given country, accompanied by guarantees against any attempt to re-enter, can really contribute to a new life in that country—and nothing else.

Proposals by Jules Moch

A few days after the publication of Mendès-France's plan, Monsieur Jules Moch, former Minister of the Interior and French Delegate to the United Nations Disarmament Sub-Committee, published his own plan.[16]   Contrary to Mendès-France, who suggested an initial redeployment of troops from both sides of the demarcation line, Moch concentrated on Berlin, which, in his view, constitutes the focus of tension.

He suggested the following measures:

(1) All four sectors of Berlin (Zone A) should be completely demilitarised and be under the authority and control of the United Nations.

(2) Zone A should be surrounded by a second zone (Zone B) in the form of a ring some 200 kilometres deep, which in the east would run roughly along the German frontier of 1937 and in the west cover some 30 to 40 kilometres of the territory of the Federal Republic. All foreign troops should withdraw from the Zone B.

(3) Zone B should be surrounded by a further one (Zone C), also in the form of a ring and again some 200 kilometres deep, comprising, to the west, Oldenburg, the Ruhr, Nuremberg and Passau, and to the east, Katowice, Brno, Lodz and Danzig. Consequently, and this is a very important point, Zone C would not overlap the territory either of the Federal Republic or of Poland and Czechoslovakia. These countries would maintain their respective military alliances. In other words, this plan—an entirely military measure—could in no way contribute to either the reduction of political tension, the reunification of Germany or the liberation of Eastern Europe. It cannot in any way be considered a scheme of disengagement.

[16] *Le Monde*, April 10, 1959.

Guy Mollet's Views

Monsieur Guy Mollet, former Prime Minister of France, wrote a series of articles, which were published in the Socialist newspaper, *Le Populaire* from April 10 to 25. His attitude towards the problem of Germany was summed up in the article of April 13, in which he wrote:

> . . . German reunification can be considered as the crowning stage of a series of steps aimed at the establishment of military security and disarmament in the interest of all concerned. The West could, undoubtedly, in order to achieve its aim, make a certain number of concessions.

He continued by stating that he believed German reunification to be a matter for the Germans themselves, although he fully realised that the Pankow règime did not represent the German people and acted as a Soviet " Trojan horse."

Mr. Bevan's Speech

In a speech in Copenhagen on April 7, Mr. Bevan, having made reference to his talks with Mr. Khrushchev in 1958, said that the Berlin problem could not be solved if separated from the question of European security. He was worried about German rearmament because one cannot trust " certain German circles."

Turning to disengagement, he envisaged a Central European zone comprising West and East Germany, Poland, Czechoslovakia and possibly Hungary. Disarmament in such a zone should be controlled by the Four Great Powers. " A demilitarised zone would act as a sort of territorial shock absorber."

Montgomery's Talk with Khrushchev

On April 29 Field-Marshal Montgomery, who had gone privately and on his own initiative to Moscow, had an important conversation with Mr. Khrushchev. He described this talk in two articles in the *Sunday Times* on May 10 and 17, and quoted Mr. Khrushchev as saying:

> The overall aim of the Soviet Union is peace. The simplest way to achieve this aim is to dissolve the two military *blocs*, NATO and the Warsaw Pact, and to withdraw national forces back to their own countries. But this is not agreed by the Western Powers. . . . Some steps must be taken to do away with this situation. We must find a formula which would be agreed by both sides. . . . Nobody wants to see the reunification of Germany at present but few people have the courage to say so. Adenauer doesn't want it. The French don't want it, nor do the British. Russia certainly doesn't want it.

> If it could be agreed that national forces should return to their own countries, then Russia would accept a very comprehensive plan of inspection and control of national territories. But a truly comprehensive inspection system is not possible so long as the armed forces of the two armed *blocs* are facing each other in Europe, ready to be alerted for a battle at short notice. To allow inspection of each other's forces and dispositions under such conditions would be absurd. But once all the forces have withdrawn to their own countries, the proper conditions for inspection would be created: the war situation would be then calmed down and an inspection system would gradually remove mistrust and produce a confidence.

Mr. Khrushchev's suggestions would involve the withdrawal of American forces from the Continent and, possibly, in the course of negotiations, the Russians would demand their withdrawal also from all overseas bases. Such a proposition would, of course, be *a priori* unacceptable to the West. In this particular case Mr. Khrushchev did not limit his plan, as he had done previously, to the territory of Germany or Eastern Europe.

In the same article, Field-Marshal Montgomery related Mr. Khrushchev's reactions to his own ideas on the gradual introduction of UN into the problem of Berlin, and the setting up of a zone of controlled armaments. Mr. Khrushchev was generally favourable, but made some qualifications: a beginning should be made in a small defined area in the middle of Europe, which would gradually be extended as mutual confidence was restored, but inspection teams of a truly international nature should be established; the plan, if sound and practical, could well begin at any time, but " care should be taken not to force the Eastern plan down Western throats too quickly."

Mr. Macmillan's Plan

Against a background of intense official and, behind the scenes, diplomatic activities, as well as of leakages and Press speculations, we will now try to formulate the basic principles of the plan attributed to Mr. Macmillan.

As the text of the Macmillan Plan was never made public, the best source from which to glean its recommendations is the American publication, the *Handbook on Arms Control*:

> The British suggestion was also based on two other conditions: (1) that it must not change the balance of military power in Europe, and (2) that NATO's overall strength must not be weakened. At first it was advanced as a measure that could be implemented independently of the unification of Germany, but when this was not accepted by Britain's Western Allies, the London Government agreed that a plan for arms control in Europe should be closely linked with a staged programme for German reunification. The British also suggested that the execution of their plan should be made in two main phases: in the first, there would be established a system of international inspection of Communist and Western forces in the designated area. The principal purpose of this inspection would be to detect preparations for surprise attack. When the reunification of Germany had reached a certain point, the second phase would begin and both sides would become obligated to a limitation of armed forces and armaments.
>
> In an effort to counter charges of discrimination against Germany, the British suggested that the zone should cover only part of West Germany and would extend possibly to the Netherlands, and to all of East Germany, Poland and Czechoslovakia. There would also be a much larger zone of air inspection against surprise attack reaching from Paris to Moscow.[17]

[17] p. 29. Not accepted by British officials. See also Appendix 10.

Probably as a result of a compromise, this plan seems to have reappeared in the Western plan submitted by Mr. Herter, on behalf of the West, at the Geneva Conference.

> Upon the establishment of an all-German Government, . . . in a zone comprising areas of comparable size and depth and importance on either side of a line to be mutually determined, agreed ceilings for the indigenous and non-indigenous forces would be put into effect.[18]

A comparison of the wording of this clause with the similar clause in the Amended Eden Plan submitted by the West during the Four Foreign Ministers' Conference at Geneva, October–November 1955, at which Mr. Macmillan represented Great Britain, leads inevitably to the conclusion that there is a " Macmillan touch " in the wording of the later clause:

> In a zone comprising areas of comparable size and depth and importance on both sides of the line of demarcation between a reunified Germany and the Eastern European countries, levels for armed forces would be specified so as to establish a military balance which would contribute to European security and help to relieve the burden of armaments.

The NATO Working Group

Although the findings of the Working Group have been kept very secret, it is interesting to quote the views of Mr. R. Stephens, Diplomatic Correspondent of *The Observer*, on April 26 that Western proposals would be put forward in the form of a " package deal." He writes:

> There would be no negotiations of a new status for West Berlin or of a zone of limited arms in Central Europe separately from progress towards the political reunification of Germany. There would appear to be little left of Mr. Macmillan's original ideas on a new status for West Berlin or on a controlled zone of limited arms in Central Europe beyond some safeguards against surprise attack.

[18] See also Appendix 9, para. 25.

After eleven days the Working Group completed their study and submitted their report on April 24 to the NATO Council and the Four Foreign Ministers' Conference in Paris on April 29.

The Western and Warsaw Pact Conferences

Before the Conference at Geneva, both sides cleared the decks for action: the Conference of the Four Western Foreign Ministers in Paris on April 29 lasted one and a half days and ended, according to the communiqué, with "complete agreement." Of course the details of the plan to be submitted by the West at Geneva were kept secret.

The Conference of the Foreign Ministers of the Warsaw Pact, which took place in Warsaw under the chairmanship of Mr. Gromyko, Soviet Foreign Minister, restated the familiar Soviet principles, insisting on German confederation. From the Press reports it appeared that the Conference rejected the idea of a "package deal."

The Yugoslav Attitude

On May 10, on the eve of the Geneva Conference, Mr. Popovic, Yugoslav Minister of Foreign Affairs, declared that his government, uncommitted to any military *bloc*, would be prepared to take part in the Geneva talks, where it could possibly play a useful mediating part. He expressed the opinion that the system of making the settlement of one issue conditional upon the settlement of another could lead to nothing, but that "partial and qualified" agreements, made on the basis of mutual concessions, could undoubtedly bring about desirable results.

His views were probably based upon the recent Zürich-London agreement on Cyprus which, by the moderation and willingness to compromise of all parties concerned, had settled a seemingly insoluble problem.

Speaking of the chances of the Geneva talks, Mr.
Popovic foresaw some possibilities of an agreement on the
discontinuance of nuclear tests, the creation of a zone of
diminished tension in Europe and, possibly, some modification in the existing status of Berlin. Within that
framework it would be normal to expect some *de facto*
recognition by the West of the East German régime. It is
interesting to recall that, when Marshal Tito originally
recognised the East German régime, the Bonn Government
broke off diplomatic relations with Yugoslavia.

Mr. Popovic's statement reflected his government's considerable interest in the constructive solution of the problems
of Germany and, above all, of Eastern Europe. It must be
remembered that Yugoslavia has common frontiers with
Eastern Europe, the defence of which is a heavy burden on
Yugoslavia's economy.

The Geneva Conference

The Conference of Four Foreign Ministers opened on May
11, 1959, in Geneva at the Palais des Nations, formerly the
seat of the defunct League of Nations. It was awaited with
very mixed feelings.

It began with bargaining over the seemingly unimpor-
tant details of procedure on seating the representatives of
the two Germanys. The very presence of the Foreign
Minister of the East German régime, which owes its
existence solely to Soviet support and is not recognised by
the West, was in itself a diplomatic victory for the Russians.

After a few days of uninspiring procedural wrangles
Mr. Herter, American Secretary of State and successor to
John Foster Dulles, put forward a comprehensive plan on
behalf of the West: " The outline of a phased plan for
German reunification, European security and a German
peace settlement." [20] It was in four phases, to be spread
over two and a half years, and it provided for the settlement

[20] See Appendix 9 for full text.

of several problems: the thorny question of Berlin; German reunification; and regional disarmament. It was a typical "package" plan, with the accent on German reunification. The basis was Western plans put forward during the conferences of the Four Foreign Ministers in Berlin in 1954, and Geneva in 1955—above all, the "summit" meeting at Geneva in 1955. Also, to meet some previous Soviet objections, it included modifications and flexible diplomatic formulas.

Great credit is due to the Working Party of senior officials from the Foreign Ministries of the United States, Britain, France and Germany. The new proposals, based mainly upon the two versions of the Eden Plan of 1955, were designed to be more flexible and more adjustable to various minor Soviet objections with one major exception—the question of the freedom for a reunified Germany to join NATO. Some of these modifications are very interesting if they are considered against the background of the Western plans of 1954 and 1955.

German Reunification

The 1959 plan suggested a gradual approach—free all-German elections would not take place until two and a half years had elapsed after the signature by the Four Powers of the relevant agreement; by the 1955 plan, free elections would be the starting point of the whole process of reunification. The 1959 plan provided for a Mixed German Committee, to be responsible for the drafting of the electoral law and subjecting it for the approval of an all-German plebiscite; whereas, by the 1955 plan, an electoral law would be prepared by the Four Powers in consultation with German experts. Finally, by the 1959 plan, Germans from both parts of Germany, together with either representatives of the UN or of the Four Powers, would bear responsibility for supervising the elections; according to the 1955 plan this was to be the responsibility of the Four Powers.

A Mixed German Committee

Whereas in the 1955 plan there had been no provision at all for a Mixed German Committee, the 1959 plan dealt very extensively with this issue, providing for such a body, to consist of twenty-five members from the Federal Republic and ten from Eastern Germany. All the necessary reservations were made that such a course of action would not imply recognition of the Pankow régime. However, it is a matter of fact that, in its overtures to Bonn, the Pankow régime had been suggesting such a mixed committee for several years.

European Security

In the 1959 plan there was no definite interdependence of progress towards German reunification and corresponding European security in each stage of the four-phase plan; in the 1955 plan there were parallel proposals for phased reunification and European security, but the exact nature of their interdependence was not defined.

There was a considerable difference in the terms used to denote the establishment of a zone of " controlled armaments." In both versions of the Eden Plan mention was made of a " line of demarcation " which, it was understood, would be the eastern frontier of a reunified Germany; undoubtedly, under strong German pressure, the location of such a dividing line would have to be " mutually determined."

Furthermore, the 1959 plan contained a provision, an inheritance from the Berlin Declaration, that, should Germany join NATO, the forces of the West (including those of Germany) would not advance beyond the existing demarcation line, *i.e.*, NATO would not militarily occupy the former area of Eastern Germany. This would become a completely demilitarised no-man's-land. The 1955 plan contained no such undertaking. Several of these modifications were the token of Western willingness to meet the

Russians and to obtain concrete results. But the Russians rejected the whole plan.

Stripped of all the diplomatic frills, it becomes obvious that the main purpose of the plan—apart, of course, from the desire to settle the problem of Berlin—was to secure for a future all-German Government freedom of choice in its military alliances. For several years it had been accepted that such a choice would be in favour of joining NATO, and for this reason alone the whole Western plan was unacceptable to the Russians. To expect any other result from the Conference would have been utterly naïve. In his Chichele Lecture, delivered in Oxford in May 1959, Field-Marshal Montgomery said: "It is illogical to expect Russia to agree that a united Germany, armed with nuclear weapons, can be integrated into the Western Alliance." Yet nothing appears to convince the governments of the West that their policy in this matter, so persistently pursued for so many years, is doomed to failure.

Another reason for the failure of the Conference was that the West made the wrong tactical approach. Long before the Conference it became obvious that a "package deal," as envisaged and put into effect by the West, would not be acceptable to the Russians. From the very beginning the whole structure of the Western plan gave the painful impression of compromise and of hard bargaining within the Atlantic Alliance; it was like a suit to which too many cutters had put their hands.

It is possible that the whole outcome of the Conference would have been different if, instead of putting forward a "package deal"—*a priori* unacceptable to the Russians—the West had concentrated on a more modest issue, for example on the Macmillan proposal for the establishment of a zone of "controlled armaments." As this issue had already been favourably considered during the "summit" conference and during the Macmillan-Khrushchev talks in Moscow earlier the same year, it is obvious that the Russians would have been ready and willing to discuss it. It is also obvious that any agreement on this issue would have produced a standstill on the question of Berlin; it would have taken out all the stings, and created an atmosphere of *détente*, halting the uneasy drift towards war. Yet this issue—which of all the clauses put forward by the West had the best chance of producing a basis for understanding and agreement—was deliberately pushed in the background by joint Franco-German pressure, and incorporated into the third phase of the plan, where it became completely meaningless.

The Conference ended in failure, although the Foreign Ministers agreed not to break it off but to adjourn it.

The Conference was the first occasion for four years on which both sides had met face to face to discuss both the acute problem of Berlin and the causes of the chronic tension in Europe.

Yet the ambitious plans to find a solution for such problems as German reunification, European security and disarmament had all to be abandoned in the early stages. The gap between the attitudes of both sides was too wide and it soon became obvious that there was no prospect of reaching agreement on any of these issues.

Mr. Khrushchev's Initiative

Independently of the proceedings at Geneva, where Mr. Gromyko was conducting a sparring match with the three Western Foreign Ministers, Mr. Khrushchev became very active on the periphery of NATO.

At the end of May he appeared in Tirana, capital of Albania, the smallest Soviet satellite. Apart from tightening his control on that Soviet outpost, Mr. Khrushchev used the opportunity to make a political move and recommended the setting up in the Balkans of an atom-free zone.

Russia has an important interest in Albania which is equipped as a submarine base. According to the Soviet expert, Mr. W. Poplawski,[21] a feverish effort had been made

21 " The Role of Albania in the Soviet War Plans," *Polish Daily*, June 3, 1959.

in the last few years to protect Albania, considered by the Soviet High Command to be a " soft underbelly," from easy neutralisation by enemy action.   Works were instituted with the purpose of building fortifications and positions for the anti-aircraft artillery, big warehouses and a network of roads along the frontier with Greece.   It was from these warehouses, Mr. Poplawski maintained, that many armaments were shipped to Egypt in summer 1956.

At the end of 1956 work was completed in the mountainous areas of Tomarus and in the mountain range of Griba along the Adriatic, which may have been connected with the construction of launching platforms.   Albania lies, as the crow flies, some 500 miles from Rome and Athens.

In his public speeches Mr. Khrushchev repeated the Soviet proposal to create in the Balkans and Adriatic area " an area of peace."   The communiqué issued after his visit stated:

> The Soviet Government and the Government of Albania consider that it would be in the interest of the peoples of the Balkan peninsula and of the Adriatic if an atom-free zone were created in that area.
>
> A refusal by the countries of that area to allow the stationing of missile and nuclear bases on their territories would be an important contribution to the cause of converting the Balkans into a zone of peace and tranquillity.   The solution of this important problem could be facilitated by calling a conference, as suggested by the Rumanian Government, to discuss the present problems of co-operation among the countries of the Balkan peninsula.[22]

Mr. Khrushchev thus endorsed the initiative of the Rumanian Prime Minister, Chivu Stoica, taken as early as September 1956 and revived at the beginning of 1959.

Strictly speaking, the Soviet move must be regarded as a reaction to the Greek-American agreement signed on May 6, 1959, by which Greek armed forces would be provided by the United States with tactical atomic weapons—Nike

[22] *Soviet News*, No. 471, June 4, 1959.

and Honest John missiles. Greece had not yet decided to agree to the setting up of the American nuclear launching bases on her territory.

Although the Greek Prime Minister, Mr. Karamanlis, rejected the Rumanian and Bulgarian diplomatic overtures and ignored Russia's veiled threats, the Soviet initiative met with an unexpected reaction from the Opposition parties, the Liberals and Progressives, and their respective leaders, Venizelos and Markezinis. They were, in principle, in favour of the setting up of an atom-free zone in the Balkans. Both parties put forward a joint plan, based upon the conversation which Mr. Markezinis had shortly before with Mr. Khrushchev in Moscow:

(1) Greece, Rumania, Bulgaria, Albania, and not excluding the participation of other Balkan States (by which they probably meant Yugoslavia), should agree not to establish missile bases on their territories;

(2) They should accept a system of control on the faithful observation of the agreement;

(3) The agreement should be guaranteed by the Great Powers, in particular the United States and the Soviet Union.

At the same time, an agreement covering such a zone, according to Mr. Markezinis, would not affect the position of the signatories towards their respective alliances. Greece could still remain in NATO and adhere to the obligations assumed under the 1953 Pact granting military facilities to the United States.[23] Monsieur H. Spaak, who was at that time in Athens, commented in a lecture there on the suggestions of the Greek Opposition:

> There is a frightful illusion that the provision of political guarantees could alter the situation. But we have had enough experience of such treaties, providing only political guarantees, and they should be regarded with much scepticism.[24]

[23] *The Times*, dispatch from Athens, May 29, 1959.
[24] *The Times*, dispatch from Athens, June 26.

From the point of view of disengagement the Soviet moves had little value; in fact, by aiming to weaken the West unilaterally on its flanks without any real reciprocal action by the Soviet Union they must be considered with great caution. Furthermore, being *par excellence* military measures, they could hardly bring about any changes in the political situation, except, perhaps, to produce further erosion of the Atlantic Alliance.

A few days later, Mr. Khrushchev appeared in Riga, the capital of Latvia, where he came forward in a public speech on June 3 with a proposal to make the Baltic a " zone of peace."

Mr. Khrushchev's idea of converting the Baltic into a " zone of peace " and an " atom-free " area was not new; it had been a constant subject of Soviet diplomacy since the war.

In a speech at the jubilee session of the Nordic Association in Stockholm, on June 26, the Swedish Foreign Minister, Hr. Unden, firmly rejected the Soviet overtures.

Memorandum of the ACEN

On the eve of the Atlantic Congress in London on June 4, the Assembly of Captive European Nations [ACEN] prepared a Memorandum for the delegates of the Congress, stating that the Soviet Union's sole interest was

> . . . in a settlement which, on the one hand, would formally sanction their conquests in Central and Eastern Europe, and, on the other hand, would pave the way for the expansion of Communist rule and Soviet control throughout Europe.
>
> The nations represented in the Assembly of Captive European Nations are vitally interested in a peace treaty with Germany, as well as in a comprehensive European security system, and are entitled to take part in negotiations to that end. These nations have, however, the indisputable right to insist that such a participation should be reserved to their freely elected governments.
>
> A new approach to the problem of peace-making in Europe is urgently required. The positive aspect of this new approach

should consist of the proclamation of a forthright and comprehensive Western plan for a just and lasting European settlement, to be followed by persistent efforts to put it into practice.

It should provide not only for the reunification of Germany but, first of all, for the restoration of freedom and independence to the captive nations through free and unfettered elections under international supervision, *after the withdrawal of Soviet forces and agents*,[25] and in a condition of complete freedom from fear.

. . . Lastly, it should contain both safeguards against outside attempts at internal interference and provisions for an effective mutual security system which would afford help and protection of all concerned.

Resolution of the Atlantic Congress [26]

Largely as a result of the ACEN Memorandum, and also of the feelings of several of its delegates, the Atlantic Congress, which was attended by several hundred distinguished representatives from the whole NATO area,[27] adopted a resolution at the session of the Political Committee which ran:

> The Atlantic Powers should proclaim their attitude toward the situation of the peoples of Eastern Europe. Such a proclamation would be based on the following principles:
>
> 1. There can never be a settled peace in Europe so long as the Continent is half free and half subject to Moscow.
>
> 2. While it is no part of NATO's purpose to overthrow existing régimes in Eastern Europe by force, the Western countries must support by every peaceful means the right of the peoples of Eastern Europe to achieve self-determination as laid down in many international agreements.
>
> 3. The Soviet Union's own security could be effectively guaranteed if, with the withdrawal of the Red Army, the Eastern European countries were neutralised by international agreement.

It suggested, in fact, unilateral withdrawal by Soviet forces, offering in return neutralisation of the countries of Eastern Europe after their withdrawal from the Warsaw Pact.

[25] Author's italics.   [26] London, June 6–7, 1959.
[27] With the exception of Iceland.

It is to be remembered that Mr. Nagy made a statement to this effect when he assumed power on the first day of the Hungarian uprising, and it was one of the main reasons for Soviet intervention. Russia could not agree to unilateral disbanding of the Warsaw Pact. Noble as the spirit undoubtedly was which inspired these two resolutions, they were of course *a priori* unacceptable to the Russians.

Ben-Gurion's Plan

Although the main purpose of this book is to analyse the various aspects of disengagement in Europe, mention must be made of a bold and imaginative plan for the neutralisation of the Middle East, put forward by the Israeli Prime Minister, Mr. David Ben-Gurion, on June 8, 1959.

In an interview with the correspondent of British United Press, Mr. Ben-Gurion said that Israel would be prepared to consider the neutralisation, or even the total disarmament, of the Middle East to bring peace to that region. He added that he would agree to an arms embargo in the Middle East under either of two conditions:

> Either all armaments should be removed from the region by its total disarmament, accompanied by guarantees of the territorial integrity of all the countries in the area and the signing of peace treaties between them, or both Israel and the Arabs should be equally armed.[28]

Mr. Ben-Gurion chose the timing of his proposal very carefully. The Four Foreign Ministers in Geneva were hopelessly deadlocked over the Berlin issue, and his plan could have given them an opportunity to discuss a solution to the tension on the peripheries of the Atlantic Alliance.

Obviously, Ben-Gurion's plan had its snags. It would involve Western bases in Saudi Arabia, Turkey and Iran; indeed, from the point of view of Western global strategy, it would further erode the ring of American air bases

[28] *Jewish Observer and Middle East Review*, June 12, 1959.

around the perimeter of the Soviet Union and thus to the weakening of the deterrent.

On the other hand, had Ben-Gurion's plan been accepted as a basis for discussion, the West could also have asked for the withdrawal of Soviet military advisers from Iraq and Egypt and the dismantling of Soviet bases in Albania. Although Ben-Gurion's plan was, at first glance, a military measure, if accepted it could have given rise to far-reaching political consequences. It could, therefore, have become a starting point for an increasing volume of discussions on a military and political settlement in the Mediterranean.

Herr Strauss, Federal German Defence Minister, had comments to make on this plan in an interview with Mr. Kimche:

> At this stage of world affairs any regional neutralisation which depended on Soviet participation would be illusory. It would mean, in effect, that Turkey would have to be dismantled as a NATO base, in return for what? Would the Russians abandon their attempts at political penetration from within, either in Iraq or in the United Arab Republic? Nasser's position in relation to Moscow might be equivocal, but not Moscow's in relation to Nasser. Egypt and Syria were geo-political bases of primary importance. But in formal military terms there was no Russian presence there: yet we knew only too well that they were there in strength. What kind of Soviet withdrawal could one ask for if the positions in Turkey were abandoned?
>
> . . . There are possibilities in the suggestion in the context in which I understand the Ben-Gurion proposition: namely, a purely Israel-Arab arrangement which would be guaranteed territorially by the three Western Powers and not dependent one way or another on Soviet actions or intentions. That would be a major step in the *détente* of the region but in a limited sense only.[29]

Senator de la Vallée-Poussin

Even greater evolution of thought, compared with Mr. Goedhardt's Report, can be seen in the Draft Preliminary

[29] *Jewish Observer*, June 26, 1959.

Report prepared on behalf of the Committee on Defence Questions and Armaments for the Fourth Session of the Assembly of the Western European Union, presented on June 10, 1959.

In that Report, entitled " Military Aspects of a Zone of Controlled Armaments in Central Europe," Senator de la Vallée-Poussin, after a short historical preamble, pointed out that

> A comparison of plans considered workable by Western statesmen over the last few years, shows a progressive deterioration of the conditions imposed.
>
> The NATO countries did not avail themselves of the most favourable opportunities for negotiation.

In the chapter on " The Military Situation in Central Europe " he stated :

> . . . the ultimate aim of any agreement with the East must be the complete withdrawal of Soviet troops from Germany and from the countries of Eastern and Central Europe, where only national troops would be maintained. This would prepare the way for a gradual return to independence. . . . This aim could be achieved progressively by a military agreement to reduce the strengths of foreign forces as national armies are built up to form a shield against minor attacks, and by political agreement re-establishing, subject to a special military status in this area, the rights of the Czech, Polish and German peoples and others to self-determination.

Although only the Soviet withdrawal was mentioned, it is safe to assume, by reason of his statement that " only national troops would be maintained," that Senator de la Vallée-Poussin was thinking equally of NATO troops. The expression " a special military status " must mean " military non-alignment " of a neutral Germany and of Eastern Europe. But although both the mutual withdrawal of troops and the special military status, amounting to armed neutrality, are fundamental principles of any scheme for disengagement, this term was purposely not used in deference to the excessive sensitivity Western governments have towards it.

H.D.   19

After comparing the numerical strengths of both sides, the Report recommended reaching a " *de facto* balance with contractual arrangements whereby a ceiling would be mutually set and controlled for the forces and arms deployed in Central Europe. This would ease tension." It did not specify the size and location of the zone covered by such an agreement. The Report stated quite firmly that these recommendations would not weaken the security of Western Europe provided that American troops did not withdraw from the Continent and that a ban on tactical atomic weapons for Western forces was not imposed before reaching numerical parity with the forces of the Warsaw Pact. It also took the view that discrimination against any single country—by which they undoubtedly meant Germany—would be undesirable.

As its last point, the Report stated that:

> The political corollary of the conclusion of a military agreement of this kind would be the simultaneous establishment of a contractual programme which would set the stage for the reunification of Germany, starting from the time the parties to the military agreement reached the common ceiling set for their forces and armaments. A special procedure should enable reunited Germany to reorganise and amalgamate the armed forces from the two sides now existing, under a new ceiling set by common agreement for the reunited country. A special military status previously agreed by international negotiations would then come into force. The Soviets would then have every guarantee that the reunification of Germany would not result in strengthening the Western forces and upsetting the balance.

At this point a novel suggestion was put forward, involving the merger after reunification of the national armed forces of the Federal Republic and of Eastern Germany. Dr. Adenauer had on every occasion expressed the view that on reunification Eastern Germany should be completely demilitarised. That implies that its armed forces should be completely disbanded.

Although it is safe to assume that the term "special status," used in the Report, can mean only a "military non-alignment " it did not elaborate the point. It gave no details either on its claim that " German reunification would not result in strengthening the Western forces," but the phrase could be taken to mean that Germany would not join NATO.

There is no doubt that the Report was a great step forward in the Western attitude towards the problem of disengagement, even though the word itself was studiously avoided.

The Labour Party and Trades Union Congress

A much more realistic and constructive approach was shown by a Declaration by the Labour Party and Trades Union Congress, published in booklet form on June 24, dealing with the controversial question of a Non-Nuclear Club.

According to the Declaration, Britain, to prevent the danger of the spread of nuclear weapons, should take the initiative and set up a non-nuclear club, not only by ceasing to manufacture nuclear weapons but also by depriving herself of their possession.

After referring to the policy statement in April 1958, the booklet confirmed their view that

> . . . the best hope for a long-term solution lies in the kind of plan for disengagement which we have put forward. The first step in our plan would be the establishment of effective international control over arms and armed forces in West and East Germany, Poland, Czechoslovakia and Hungary. It would be followed by the gradual withdrawal of foreign forces from this area, the reunification of Germany, a security pact guaranteeing the frontiers of the countries of the area and, ultimately, the withdrawal of Germany from NATO and of Poland, Czechoslovakia and Hungary from the Warsaw Pact. We greatly regret the failure of the Western Powers to adopt these proposals or even to discuss similar suggestions, such as those put forward by Mr. Rapacki.

Some opponents of disengagement assert that it would bring about a break-up of NATO, and the Labour Party discussed this possibility:

> In present conditions we regard it as essential that the NATO alliance should be maintained and that we should remain loyal and active members of it, providing our full contribution to its forces and accepting also our share of the risks involved.

Sixth Congress of Socialist International

At the Sixth Congress, held in Hamburg from July 14 to 19, 1959, a resolution was passed on " Security and Peace," confirming the

> . . . decision taken at Brussels in June 1958, when the Council placed on record its views that the reunification of Germany could be achieved only as part of a settlement of wider problems in Europe, and that the policy of disengagement would be a contribution to this end. Other parties cannot support disengagement. They consider that the disarmament problem should be examined as a whole and be a subject only of general agreement.[30]

Yet, point 4 of the same resolution showed strong misgivings about the dangers which could arise from any partial measure of disarmament: " Congress emphasises that any disarmament agreements should not alter the balance of military security to the disadvantage of either side." These misgivings and reservations undoubtedly arose from the many arguments advanced by the opponents of disengagement and their militaristic approach to the political problems of Europe. In what was probably the most important speech delivered at the Congress, Mr. Gaitskell suggested that the Western Powers and West Germany itself should accept a " non-alignment " policy for a unified Germany. He argued that this proviso, which would bar a united Germany from NATO, would be the best way to achieve reunification of the two Germanys.

[30] *Socialist International Information*, p. 3.

While the West German Socialists, as well as many other delegations, voiced support for these proposals, the most articulate opposition came from the French delegates, who opposed the demilitarisation of Germany and insisted on Germany's right after reunification to choose her alliances.

The Congress also took the opportunity, in a special " Resolution on Spain," to express its objections to any attempts " by certain governments to accord Franco's Spain entry into Western and European institutions and alliances." This attitude was reflected by Mr. Morgan Phillips, the Labour Party Secretary, in a statement issued in connection with the visit to London of the Spanish Foreign Minister, Señor Castiella, to meet President Eisenhower during the President's talks with Mr. Macmillan. Mr. Morgan Phillips confirmed that the Labour movement was united in opposition to any proposal to admit Spain to NATO.

Mr. Khrushchev in Poland

On the same day as the proceedings of the Socialist Congress began in Hamburg, Mr. Khrushchev, with a dynamic mobility comparable only with that of the late Mr. Dulles, reappeared in Poland. Brimming over with good will, he visited several towns, mixed with the people and made speeches. In an important speech in Stettin on July 17, he reaffirmed strong Soviet support for the existing Polish-German frontier.

The climax of his visit was a speech on July 21, the eve of the fifteenth anniversary of the promulgation, in Lublin in 1944, of the Manifesto of the Polish National Committee of Liberation, which laid the foundations for the present Communist régime in Poland. In his speech, apart from stressing the importance of increasingly friendly relations between the Soviet Union and the new Poland, Mr. Khrushchev developed his favourite thesis of the advisability of setting up atom-free zones in Central Europe, the Baltic and the Scandinavian Peninsula, as well as in the Balkans and the Adriatic coast.

He also introduced a new and interesting argument when he stated that demands put forward by some Scandinavian politicians for Soviet reciprocity in liquidating bases for atomic weapons on their territory,

> . . . are devoid of any practical sense in present conditions. . . . If we consider the range and power of the contemporary rocket and nuclear weapons, a mere 100, 200 or 300 kilometres is of no real importance. Thus rocket- and atom-free zones in a part of Soviet territory will give no guarantee to the Scandinavian countries.
>
> If we speak about the problem of guaranteeing the security of the Scandinavian countries in case they are included in an atom- and rocket-free zone, we should take into consideration that both the Western countries and the Soviet Union should undertake to treat the territories covered by this zone as situated beyond the range of rocket and nuclear weapons and to respect the status of that region. The United Nations could be invited to take part, in some form or other, in the solution of the problem.[31]

On the other hand, the lack of willingness on the part of the U.S.S.R. to agree to reciprocity, recommended in the Rapacki Plan and even in the Soviet proposals for an atom-free zone in the Balkans, amounts in practical terms to a demand for the unilateral weakening of the defence potential of the West, and thus renders them completely unacceptable.

Henry Kissinger's Proposals

In an extremely interesting and penetrating article, " In Search of Stability," an analysis of various aspects of the mutual withdrawal of troops and of different schemes of arms control, Henry Kissinger comes to the conclusion that:

> A preferable solution would be to establish a comprehensive European security system along the borders of a unified

31 " Polish Facts and Figures," No. 625, July 25, 1959, p. 6.

Germany. It could be proposed that non-German forces withdraw the same distance from the Oder as non-Polish forces and that the size of German forces, on the one side, and Polish and Czech forces, on the other, be brought into some relationship with each other, both in numbers and equipment. For example, United States, British and French forces could withdraw to the line of the Weser, while Soviet forces could withdraw to the Vistula. The German forces between the Weser and the Oder would be restricted to defensive armaments, as would the Polish forces between the Oder and the Vistula. To decrease the danger of an attack from the German territory, NATO would agree not to station weapons of more than 700 miles range on German territory. An inspection system could be established. Obviously there are many variations in such a scheme, which could be the subject of negotiations both as to the width of the zone separating Western and Soviet forces and as to types of arms to be stationed in the area. . . . Continued membership in NATO would help protect Germany against Eastern pressure while the deployment of NATO forces would demonstrate their defensive purpose. . . . Such a programme would remove the chief source of political tension in Europe. It would provide protection to both the West and the Soviet Union against offensive operations. It would create a zone of arms controls which, if successful, should bring about a climate of confidence leading to further measures.[32]

But this scheme, although couched in the most convincing terms, would be *a priori* unacceptable to Russia because, as Field-Marshal Montgomery said in the Chichele Lecture at Oxford, " it is illogical to expect that Russia will ever agree to reunified Germany belonging to NATO."

All these elaborate regional disarmament frills, however, do not cover the essential facts: first, that for reunited Germany to remain in NATO would be unacceptable to Russia; secondly, that Eastern Europe would remain under Soviet control, in fact with an increased concentration of Soviet troops withdrawn from Eastern Germany to Poland.

It is difficult to agree with Mr. Kissinger's contention that such a solution " would remove the chief source of

[32] *Foreign Affairs*, July, 1959, pp. 548–549.

political tension." On the contrary, it might well increase it, the result of the direct confrontation of an increasingly stronger Germany, dissatisfied with her eastern frontiers, and a strong concentration of Soviet military forces stationed on a dormant volcano.

Senator Dodd's views on the feelings of the peoples of Eastern Europe reinforce the contention that once the Soviet troops had withdrawn from Eastern Europe, the national forces of that area would, in the event of major overland aggression by the Russians, become a reliable outpost of *Western* defence.

Sir John Slessor's Plan

On July 19 *The Observer* published a comprehensive article on " Redeployment in Europe," by Marshal of the R.A.F. Sir John Slessor, in which he put forward a detailed plan for mutual withdrawal of troops. This he chose to call, not disengagement, but redeployment. He reiterated his favourite concept of setting

> between the frontiers of France and Italy, on the one hand, and of the U.S.S.R., on the other, a broad belt of States militarily non-aligned with either East or West, and with their own political systems.

Although he was sceptical of possibilities of reaching such a solution in the near future, he suggested that it should become the long-term policy of the West.

Contrary to the views of George Kennan, Sir John Slessor favoured " a powerful American military presence on the eastern side of the Atlantic for many years to come." He believed it to be nonsense to consider a military vacuum east of the Rhine, but agreed with Montgomery that German national armed forces should take over the duties of the NATO shield.

He wrote that " when some of the fog engendered by emotion, mutual suspicion among the NATO Allies, muddled thinking and previous rigid and unimaginative attitudes has blown away," he would suggest consideration of the following plan at the Summit meeting:

(1) All foreign troops should withdraw from continental Europe, with recognition of the Oder-Neisse Line as the frontier of Germany;

(2) Mutual withdrawal should take place by stages, initially on a very limited scale, under an effective inspection and control;

(3) Allied troops should remain in Berlin until it was mutually agreed that the situation had reached a stage when they could safely be withdrawn;

(4) The mechanism of an effective inspection and control should be established in the first stage;

(5) German rearmament should proceed according to plan: in addition, semi-static "Home-Guard" troops with light and anti-tank weapons should be formed;

(6) All foreign troops should be withdrawn in the second stage, starting from a narrow strip;

(7) An undertaking should be given by the West that the territory of the present Eastern Germany would be completely demilitarised after German reunification;

(8) Reunified Germany and the countries of Eastern Europe should withdraw from their respective military alliances;

(9) Guarantees should be provided under the terms of a European Security Pact, on the lines of the Brussels Treaty of 1948.

Commenting, Sir John Slessor felt that the withdrawal of reunified Germany from NATO would be acceptable on military grounds. Unfortunately, however, he did not put forward specific arguments, which his great prestige would have supported, to substantiate his views.

The Second Geneva Conference

After a few weeks' interval to allow the Foreign Ministers to report to their governments, they met again at Geneva on July 13. This time the field of discussion had narrowed down considerably, mainly to problems related directly to Berlin, such as the duration of any agreement on that issue, the reduction of Western garrisons and, in addition, the question of a joint German Committee, which had been suggested by the Russians. These frustrating negotiations had nothing to say on the problem of disengagement, and it is enough to say that the communiqué issued after the Conference stated that both parties had come somewhat nearer to each other on some issues, and that the date and place of the next Conference would be fixed in due course.

It could be foreseen from the start that, in view of what the Soviet spokesman called the " substantial divergencies " there was little hope that the Conference would result in any agreement.

The news that President Eisenhower had decided to go to Europe to meet the Allies, as a prelude to his forthcoming talks with Mr. Khrushchev, spelt an end to the Conference, already slowly fading away.

President Eisenhower Visits Europe

Before leaving for Europe, President Eisenhower made a statement to the Press on August 25 in which he expressed his readiness

> to negotiate realistically with the Soviets on any reasonable and mutually enforceable plan for general or special disarmament: to make a real beginning towards solving the problems of a divided Germany: and to help in reducing, otherwise, tensions in the world.

It was generally interpreted that the purpose of his visit was to smooth the existing differences of opinion among America's major allies on the Continent and, by creating a united front, to build up for himself a strong position in his forthcoming talks with Mr. Khrushchev.

It was a wise decision although not easy to implement, and was perhaps influenced by the predictions of the experts on Western affairs in the Soviet Foreign Ministry as to what would be the reactions in the West to the latest Soviet move on Berlin. One of the leading Western experts on Soviet affairs, D. Dallin, wrote in his article, " Khrushchev's Berlin Campaign ":

> The cumulative prediction, it is obvious from the Soviet Press of the last few months, was that the West would react with discord and confusion. . . . With the typical contempt that it has for democracy, Moscow must have been certain that a cacophonous confusion would be the West's answer to the Soviet programme. London would disagree with Washington, and Paris would oppose both of them: . . . the West would not dare to go to the brink: in the end it would surrender.[33]

Faced with great divergencies in the attitudes of the Western Heads of States towards his decision to hold talks with Russia, Mr. Eisenhower's task was indeed not easy. Dr. Adenauer, who had not hidden his criticism of Mr. Macmillan's journey to the U.S.S.R. and was worried by the prospects of Mr. Khrushchev's visit to the United States, had to be tackled first.

The secrecy surrounding the talks between the two statesmen made any conclusions hypothetical, but it is fair to assume that, on the one hand, the President succeeded in dispelling Dr. Adenauer's misgivings by assuring him that any agreement with Russia would not be made at Germany's expense, and that, on the other hand, Dr. Adenauer mollified his opposition towards any attempt to reach agreement with the Russians on a regional disarmament proposal.

President Eisenhower's talks in London were also shrouded in secrecy. The scanty information given to the Press, which gathered in great numbers from all over the

[33] *New Leader*, April 6, 1959.

world, amounted to nothing more than laughably trivial tit-
bits. But something could be gathered from the television
appearance of both statesmen on August 31.

In answer to Mr. Macmillan's statement that: "I have
never concealed from you that I always wanted a summit
meeting and by your initiative we may get it under the best
conditions," President Eisenhower made such a meeting
conditional upon Khrushchev's understanding of the
motives behind the Western attitude, "and if he does
things that show that he recognises [them], just as you and
I do, then I think a summit meeting would be profitable."
Speaking of NATO, President Eisenhower put great
emphasis on the equality of its partners. From this, it is
safe to conclude that he would not agree to any settlement
by which Germany would have any other status or which
would discriminate against her.

If this interpretation was correct, it would mean that the
chances of an agreement with the Russians on a zone of
controlled armaments or, at any rate, one which included
Germany, were somewhat diminished.

Nothing was published on the subject of President
Eisenhower's talks with President de Gaulle either, but in
view of the latter's known hostility to the concept of
German neutrality it is again safe to assume that this question was not discussed in Paris at all.

The Interparliamentary Union Conference

On August 27, 1959, the President of the Interparliamentary
Union, Professor G. Codacci-Pisanelli, and the Secretary-
General of the Union, A. de Blonay, opened their Forty-
eighth Conference in Warsaw, which was attended by the
delegates from forty-eight countries and which lasted until
September 4.

On the second day of the Conference, Mr. A. Rapacki,
the Polish Foreign Minister and author of the Rapacki Plan,
said in his address:

We consider it a just idea to disengage and to thin out the armed forces in the most inflammable areas, that is, where the two main military groupings are facing each other. We see the possibility and the advantage of regional disarmament agreements in various parts of Europe and the world.

In proposing the establishment of an atomic-free zone in Central Europe, comprising Poland, Czechoslovakia, the German Democratic Republic and the Federal German Republic, the Polish Government considered that this area was particularly important from a political and military point of view, that the accumulation of nuclear weapons in that territory and the arming with nuclear weapons of troops which do not yet have such weapons, present special dangers.

We are prepared to continue to discuss that proposal further and to take into consideration all constructive remarks.

The Resolution passed on September 4 noted

. . . with approval the agreement recently expressed by the Heads of the Soviet Union and United Kingdom Governments, [that] further study could usefully be made of the possibilities of increasing security by some methods of limitations of forces and weapons, both conventional and nuclear, in an agreed area of Europe . . .

Mr. Gaitskell Talks with Mr. Khrushchev

Mr. Gaitskell's visit to Russia, planned some time before President Eisenhower announced his visit to Europe, gave the Leader of the Opposition an opportunity to meet Mr. Khrushchev and to discuss with him several outstanding problems, including the problems of Germany and of regional disarmament. These talks were also attended by Aneurin Bevan and Denis Healey. However, as Mr. Gaitskell's visit to Russia coincided with President Eisenhower's visit to Europe, very little appeared in the Press about talks which took place in the Kremlin on September 4. But it did emerge that Mr. Khrushchev had reiterated his readiness to withdraw Soviet troops from Eastern Germany and some countries of Eastern Europe, if NATO troops were withdrawn from Western Germany.

On his return from Russia Mr. Gaitskell made an appearance on television on September 9, and told his audience that during those talks four points had emerged. On the subjects of nuclear disarmament and the spread of nuclear weapons both sides were of the same opinion. On the third point, the Russians were " very much in favour " of a zone of control and disarmament in Europe. This, said Mr. Gaitskell, he considered " the best solution to the rearmament of Germany." Of Berlin, the fourth point, Mr. Gaitskell said that, while there was a wide gap, he thought it possible to get " total agreement."

Anthony Nutting's Proposals

In the summer of 1959 a concise and very informative booklet was published by Mr. Nutting, former Minister of State and British Delegate at various disarmament conferences. In this booklet, entitled *Disarmament*, he proposed the following minimal conditions:

(1) Suspension of tests under adequate control;
(2) An atom-free zone in Central Europe;
(3) A measure of disengagement or thinning out of conventional forces and armaments in Germany and her neighbours, east and west;
(4) An agreement regarding the status of West Berlin;
(5) Possibly some measure of progress towards a German settlement by the establishment of an all-German commission to make proposals for reunification by stages.

However, with all his experience, he was not too optimistic:

> If all concerned are really prepared to make a start with disarmament and disengagement, it should not be impossible to agree upon the minimum requirements for a " partial " package deal. But it is difficult to have great hopes for such agreement. For the sad truth is that in the prevailing climate of mutual

suspicion and mistrust, the Great Powers seem to fear an agreement more than they do a continued deadlock. They prefer the devil they know—and they know that the deadlock means stalemate and a state of armed truce to which they have grown accustomed and which they feel constitutes possibly the least imperfect insurance in an imperfect world against a repetition of the kind of treachery and violence by the aggressors that culminated in the Second World War.[34]

Summary

It is essential to underline that after the end of 1958 the attitudes of both sides towards the problems of the reunification and rearmament of Germany underwent a complete reversal.

It is impossible to relate the various plans and schemes put forward by Russia and by the Western Powers during the 1939–45 War, all of which aimed at the dismemberment of Germany. It is enough to say that discussions had already begun during Mr. Eden's talks with Stalin in the Kremlin in December 1941 when the German armies stood almost at the gates of Moscow.

These talks were followed by the establishment in Washington in February 1942 of an Advisory Committee on Post-War Foreign Policy, under the chairmanship of Cordell Hull, with Sumner Welles as deputy. One of the main tasks of that Committee was to draft plans for dismemberment of Germany into two, three, five or even seven separate entities. In 1944, the Soviet Ambassador in Washington, Mr. Litvinov, reaffirmed Soviet intentions to partition Germany after the war, and the Soviet Ambassador in London, Mr. Maisky, also reasserted the Soviet policy of dismembering Germany, and reorganising her into a federation. A similar attitude had been adopted at the Quebec Conference in 1943, which culminated in the decisions taken at Teheran in December of that year. During that Conference Roosevelt came up with his plan

[34] p. 52.

to divide Germany into five parts, while Churchill, on the other hand, was in favour of a Danube Union.

All these plans reappeared on the agenda of the talks between Churchill and Stalin in Moscow in the autumn of 1944, and led to the decisions taken at Yalta and, later on, at Potsdam.

Thus the urge for the reunification of Germany, which became the cornerstone of the policy of the West, is the exact opposite of the policy pursued by the Great Powers during the War, and is, despite the lofty slogans supporting it, of recent vintage. The Western policy of rearming Germany, on which the West agreed only in the early fifties, is also a complete reversal of the policy of the Grand Alliance during the War, and even after the end of hostilities.

Thus the *status quo*, the maintenance of which is the foundation stone of the policy of the West, is the result of the perpetual evolution of politics. This is true also of the policy of the Soviet Union, although for different reasons.

Examination of the history of various plans, seen against the background of ever-changing circumstances and political interplay, shows that on many occasions the positions of both sides were almost identical, even overlapping at various places: yet, so deeply engrained was the mutual distrust, the result of aggressive Soviet policies and, not least, of the policy of the Bonn Government, that agreement even on the smaller issues, such as partial or regional disarmament, was rendered increasingly difficult.

The positions taken by the Western governments over the problems of Germany, European security, disarmament and Eastern Europe, are basically the same, although, of course, there are differences—some of them difficult to reconcile. But it is the attitude of the Government of the Federal Republic which has been the most inflexible and rigid. The aim of its policies throughout the last years has been the reunification of both parts of Germany as a result of free elections, which it takes for granted would mean the disappearance of the Pankow régime. It has vigorously objected to any measure of disarmament, relaxation of tension or, above all, of disengagement which might have derogated from its aims. Any agreement with Russia, on even the most modest measure of local disarmament, such as thinning out, would have amounted, in German eyes, to the implied recognition of the existing German-Polish frontier, an issue which, for tactical reasons, the Bonn Government preferred to keep open.

One of the reasons for this rigidity is, perhaps, the conviction in Bonn that there will inevitably be Sino-Soviet conflict and that consequently time is playing in favour of the West.

The attitude of France, too, has undergone a considerable evolution since the policy of the dismemberment of Germany and of opposition to her rearmament, until now it has become one of increasing military, economic and political co-operation with her former enemy. Her policy towards Germany, and to the problem of disengagement in particular, has been best summed up in President de Gaulle's statement of March 25 [35]: it implies that for France, embroiled as she is in North Africa, Germany has become a defence glacis, a new version of the Maginot Line. She has, therefore, increasingly lent her support to Dr. Adenauer's policy of opposition to any plan which could alter Germany's present position. This may sometimes be uncomfortable at the present, but from the long-term point of view it is a policy which can give her many advantages. Thus the plans put forward in France by prominent politicians such as Pierre Mendès-France and Jules Moch have had no impact on official policy.

The attitude of the United States has equally undergone many changes. From her war-time policy of the partition of Germany, she has moved to another extreme, that of all-out support for German reunification, now one of the

[35] *Supra*, p. 267.

dogmas of American foreign policy. From the policy of
" complete and absolute " demilitarisation of Germany,
advocated by Dean Acheson in 1949, she changed to one of
vigorous and deeply emotional support for German rearmament. She has steadfastly opposed not only the concept of
disengagement but, despite the presence of President Eisenhower's signature on the Directives of the Heads of States to
their Foreign Ministers after the Summit Conference of July
1955,[36] even to any measure of partial disarmament. The
United States has unflinchingly supported the policy of
the Bonn Government that free elections can be the only
method of German reunification.

But in recent months, especially since the death of Mr.
Dulles and the assumption by President Eisenhower of his
role as effective Foreign Secretary, the attitude of the United
States has become more flexible. Even Mr. Dulles, before
his last trip to Europe, said that free elections are not the
only method of German reunification, and this view had
been supported by several American politicians. It would
appear too that President Eisenhower, perhaps as a result
of his talks with Mr. Macmillan, has modified his attitude
towards plans for partial disarmament: after his return to
Washington he said: " We are prepared to make a real
beginning towards solving the problem of a divided
Germany." [37]

British policy during those years was the most flexible.
It is true that it underwent a similar evolution to that of
the United States in its attitude to the problem of the
dismemberment of Germany and her demilitarisation; yet,
after the war, it was British statesmen who at international
conferences showed the most initiative in pressing for constructive solutions. The Eden Plan became almost a by-
word and was the foundation for several plans of similar
nature. But towards the basic problems of German reunification, the role of Germany in NATO, European security

---

[36] *Supra*, p. 179.
[37] *Daily Telegraph*, September 11, 1959.

and Eastern Europe, the attitude of the British Government is roughly identical with that of the other Great Powers. It supported the policy of free elections in Germany and of freedom of a reunited Germany to choose her alliances. Like all the other Western governments, it opposed the concept of disengagement.

The main difference between Britain and the other Great Powers lies in the fact that Britain, in pursuit of the policy formulated by Eden in 1955, took the initiative in her own hands and tried to hasten the end of the Cold War. Mr. Macmillan's trip to Moscow in the winter of 1958 was the token of this initiative, and it met with a very mixed reception in Western Europe. British plans, vigorously pressed—but probably, for tactical reasons, not formulated in detail—by Mr. Macmillan, amounted to a scheme for " a zone of controlled armaments." In many respects it resembles the second version of the Rapacki Plan, which enjoys Soviet support, and it could become the basis of an understanding between East and West.

Within the Western camp there is a notable difference between the positions taken by the governments, and plans or proposals put forward on both sides of the Atlantic by individual citizens, some of which amount to disengagement in the full sense of the word.

It is, for example, true that Western statesmen in various public utterances have declared themselves to be in favour of the liberation of Eastern Europe: yet, for all practical purposes these were empty words. The policy of the Western Powers towards Europe has been limited: it has been directed primarily towards the reunification of Germany, if possible allied with the West; Eastern Europe has been left to Russia as part of the bargain. Quite a different attitude has been adopted by the advocates of disengagement on both sides of the Atlantic. For example, George Kennan, Hugh Gaitskell, Denis Healey, Sir John Slessor and the German Social Democrats " closely relate the aim of winning greater freedom for the East Europeans to the problem of security and arms control. They contend that disengagement is a key to ultimate freedom for the East Europeans." [38] They have given proof of broad foresight and political vision.

As far as the East is concerned there is, of course, officially complete identity of views within the Soviet *bloc*.

The task of summing up the policy of the Soviet Union towards these issues is not an easy one. It has been a subject of study by various Ministries of Foreign Affairs and experts on Soviet affairs all over the world and there is still no substantial body of agreement.

The policy of the Soviet Union towards all these problems under review has also undergone considerable evolution. Yet, contrary to the policies of the Western Powers, Russia's foreign policy has always had a single unchanging focal point. As D. Dallin put it in his article, "Moscow's Basic Error": "To Moscow, it is Germany which is the threat and the hope—Germany is the pivot. To Moscow, Germany is the Number One political issue of the world." [39]

There are various interpretations in existence as to the tenor of Soviet policy towards Germany. They range from the theory that there exists a Soviet Master Plan by which a reunified Germany must sooner or later be incorporated into the Soviet sphere. With a German ally—and, as Air Vice-Marshal D. Bennett pointed out,[40] this contingency would suit some reckless German politicians—the Soviet Union would have unlimited possibilities for the conquest of the world. There exists also another school of thought which believes that Soviet policy towards Germany stems from fear, and consequently from an obsession for security in the military sense of the word. As Edward Crankshaw wrote:

> Looking back it is easy to see enough to see that Stalin's moves from 1945 to 1947 were concerned with the one overriding

[38] *Handbook on Arms Control and Related Problems in Europe.*
[39] *New Leader*, April 13, 1959.
[40] *Supra*, p. 70.

objective, a limited objective: the killing of the potential threat
of a revanchist Germany, which might form a coalition with
other Powers hostile to the Soviet Union.[41]

There are many good authorities to support the view that
this objective remains the overriding aim of Soviet policy
today, not least among them Mr. Khrushchev himself,
who on various occasions has expressed his deep mistrust of the Federal Republic. He reasserted his views
recently:

> Western Germany is at present in the world arena, not alone
> but within the military North Atlantic *bloc*. She plays a para-
> mount role in this *bloc*. . . .
>
> . . . They have already proclaimed their aggressive plans,
> laying claims, for instance, to lands in Poland and Czecho-
> slovakia.
>
> Will the direction chosen by the modern German revanchists
> for their aggression be any consolation to the peoples of Europe
> if a global war breaks out on that continent? [42]

If one accepts the reasoning of this school of thought it
follows that any agreement with Russia on measures which
would contribute to her security, without at the same time
diminishing the security of the West, would be acceptable
to the Russians. According to Press reports, the Labour
Party plan for disengagement put forward by Mr. Gaitskell
during his talks with Mr. Khrushchev in Moscow aroused
the Soviet leader's interest. In many details Mr. Gaitskell's proposals overlap with plans put forward by the
Russians over the previous years. Agreement with Russia
on some version of this plan appears to be feasible, possible
and desirable.

The main difference, however, between the West and
Russia is that whereas the West closely links any measure,
even of a limited nature, with the reunification of Germany,
the Russians treat such measures as independent of each
other. Western schemes for partial disarmament, such as

---

[41] "The Great Schism," *The Observer*, September 13, 1959.
[42] "Peaceful Co-existence," *Foreign Affairs*, July 1959, p. 309.

a " zone of controlled armaments," *par excellence* a military measure, might well be acceptable to the Russians.

Mr. Selwyn Lloyd's Proposals

A three-stage disarmament plan, culminating in comprehensive disarmament by all States, under international control, was put forward by Mr. Selwyn Lloyd at the General Assembly of the United Nations on September 17:

First Stage

Agreements should be reached on:

(1) Stopping the use of fissionable material for military purposes,

(2) " Ceilings " for the conventional forces, and

(3) The establishment of international control over certain armaments.

Second Stage

(1) Conventional armaments and nuclear weapons should be reduced.

(2) Agreement should be reached on inspection against surprise attack.

Third Stage

Agreements should be reached on:

(1) A ban on the manufacture and use of atomic, biological and chemical weapons,

(2) The final reduction of conventional armaments. There should then be a re-examination of the possibility of controlling, and then eliminating, the remaining stocks of nuclear weapons and other weapons of mass destruction.

Speaking of his own plan, Mr. Selwyn Lloyd was reported by the *Daily Telegraph* on September 18 as saying: " It may seem too ambitious a plan. But once we can get started and get some mutual confidence things could go quickly." At that time he could not realise that the plan, which he considered " too ambitious," would be surpassed by Mr. Khrushchev himself the following day.

To comment on Mr. Selwyn Lloyd's proposals, they were *par excellence* of a military character. They dealt entirely with disarmament and made no attempt to solve any political problems. But it is a sad truth that the armaments race is a consequence of existing political tensions rather than a cause. Unless the tension is removed, or at least decreased, no measure of disarmament will bring us any nearer to peace.

Mr. Khrushchev's Plan

During Mr. Khrushchev's visit to the United States he put before the General Assembly of the United Nations two far-reaching alternatives.

The essence of the first alternative was that

> . . . over a period of four years all States should effect complete disarmament and should no longer have any means of waging war.
>
> This means that armies, navies and air forces would cease to exist, general staffs and war ministries would be abolished, military educational establishments would be closed. Tens of millions of men would return to peaceful creative work.
>
> Military bases on foreign territories would be abolished.
>
> All atomic and hydrogen bombs at the disposal of States would be destroyed and their future production terminated. . . .
>
> Military rockets of all ranges would be destroyed and rocket facilities would remain as means of transport. . . .
>
> At the disposal of States there should remain only strictly limited contingents of police [militia] agreed for each country, armed with small arms and intended exclusively to maintain internal order and protect the personal security of citizens.
>
> *So that no one could violate their obligation, we propose the setting up of international control including all States.*[43]

[43] September 18, 1959.

During the same speech he said: "Such a solution would ensure the complete security of all States. . . . All international negotiations would then be resolved, not by force of arms, but by peaceful means." With these words he confirmed the agreement reached during Mr. Macmillan's visit to Moscow.

However, being a "realist in politics" and understanding that "at present for certain reasons the Western Powers are not prepared to embark on general and complete disarmament," Mr. Khrushchev came forward with a second alternative. This was a more down-to-earth plan for partial disarmament and disengagement.

The most important of these measures were:

(1) The creation of a zone of control and inspection with a reduction of foreign troops on the territories of the corresponding countries of Western Europe;

(2) The creation of an atom-free zone in Central Europe;

(3) The withdrawal of all foreign troops from the territory of European States and the closing down of military bases on foreign territories;

(4) The conclusion of a non-aggression pact between the NATO member-States, and the States which are party to the Warsaw Treaty;

(5) An agreement on the prevention of surprise attack by one State on another.[44]

The suggestion for the creation of a zone of inspection and control had already been put forward by the British Government and an agreement in principle was reached during the Macmillan-Khrushchev talks in Moscow in March 1959. General agreement on this issue could probably be achieved without much difficulty. But the proviso for the reduction of foreign troops should be applicable not only to the foreign troops in Western Europe, as suggested by Mr. Khrushchev, but to those in Eastern Europe as well. The creation of an atom-free zone could also become a possibility, subject to international

---

[44] *Soviet News*, No. 4115, September 21, 1959.

agreement, similar to that mentioned by Mr. Khrushchev in his speech in Warsaw on July 21, to make the area immune from atomic attack. The clause dealing with the withdrawal of all foreign troops from Europe would amount, of course, to the withdrawal of American troops from Europe. This should be avoided in the early stages of any agreement, but it could be that at a later stage the improvement in the political climate resulting from the lessening of tension would warrant it. Similarly, the proviso for the closure of bases on foreign territories would be unacceptable to the West. It would involve scrapping present Western defence strategy completely, with its basis of the Deterrent operating from several bases strung out along the Soviet perimeter. Such a drastic measure, without any equivalent and reciprocal compensation on the part of the Soviet Union, would amount to unilateral Western disarmament. Thus a measure of this sort could be put into effect only at some later stage. The proviso for the conclusion of a non-aggression pact between NATO and the countries of the Warsaw Pact meant that Mr. Khrushchev intended maintaining the present political *status quo*, with the division of Germany and the integration of Eastern Europe into the Soviet *bloc*; such a solution would not contribute to the lessening of tension in Europe for it disregarded the interests of the peoples of Central and Eastern Europe. Joint arrangements on the prevention of surprise attack would become unnecessary if agreement were reached on all the other clauses; that would create a political climate in which surprise attack could be only the product of lunatic stupidity.

As a whole, Mr. Khrushchev's plan, although difficult to accept as it stood, provided a useful basis for constructive negotiation, especially in view of his manifestly sincere desire to end the " cold war." The stumbling block in all such negotiations with the Russians would be not the problem of Berlin but that of Germany as a whole, of which the issue of West Berlin constitutes only one aspect.

For every politician would have to bear in mind that, in the last fifty years, Germany had three times caused a major war; that potentiality remains. Dr. Adenauer was reported to say in comment on Mr. Khrushchev's visit to the United States that " it is clear that the future of Germany is bound firmly with the United States." [45] That, in practical terms, means the continuation of German membership of NATO, which would, if possible, lead to the introduction of united Germany into the Atlantic Alliance. That is, and has been for the last ten years, the policy of the Federal German Government. It has received increasing support from the governments of the West. The tail wags the dog.

[45] *Daily Telegraph*, September 29, 1959. [It was not, alas, possible to incorporate the very recent Lloyd and Khrushchev proposals into the *Summary* on p. 303.]

PART THREE

THE CRUX OF THE MATTER

10

The Pros and the Cons

An attempt at a definition

UNLIKE the phrase *status quo*, which can be found as far
back in history as the Roman Empire, the word "disengagement" is of very recent vintage and has become part
of the political vocabulary, on both sides of the Iron Curtain, only in the last few years.

During its short lifetime it has been thoroughly mis-
construed, misunderstood and misjudged; in fact very few
people know anything about it. As Monsieur Spaak put
it in conversation with the author it is a "mysterious
word."

Sir John Slessor, who has advocated mutual withdrawal
of troops in many books, articles and lectures for some
years, said on the B.B.C. on April 3, 1959, in a transatlantic
radio-link: "I hate the word disengagement. I very much
prefer the words policy of withdrawal." Similarly, Field-
Marshal Montgomery, in his article, "NATO—Past,
Present and Future," having suggested the withdrawal
of Soviet troops to Russia, continued: ". . . I would like
to see it [the Soviet Army] back in Russia, one thousand
miles away." He also suggested the withdrawal of all
NATO troops from Germany: ". . . Why not let all
national forces return to their own countries?" Finally,
not forgetting the "thinning out" process, he added:
"But at least we could begin to discuss it and to negotiate
and both sides to show good faith by beginning to thin out
in certain geographical areas." In the next paragraph, he
said: "Such action involves no question of so-called
'disengagement' . . ." [1]

[1] *Sunday Times*, April 5, 1959.

Yet, after all, if all this redeployment of troops, amounting to mutual withdrawal, is not what is meant by "disengagement" then what is it? Why not call a spade a spade?

Disengagement has gradually become proscribed and a "dirty word." It was studiously avoided—except in a pejorative form—in the many communiqués which followed Mr. Macmillan's discussions in 1959 in various Western capitals. Mr. Gaitskell, in an article entitled "Disengagement: Why? How?" writes:

> Those of us who have tried to put forward reasonably precise proposals which do not involve the withdrawal of American or British forces even from continental Europe may be pardoned if we are mildly irritated when we are grouped not only with Mr. Kennan but with Mr. Khrushchev and subjected to the same attacks from Mr. Acheson's blunderbuss.[2]

In conversation with Americans, especially with high-ranking officers, the name of Mr. Kennan usually brings the same remark, that he "has done a great disservice to the cause of the United States." Naturally, he has become *persona non grata* in Germany, and only his status and very high personal standing have modified the impact of criticism levelled against his views.

The word "disengagement" generally misleads because it conveys the impression, especially to biased and prejudiced minds, that it is a purely military measure which can serve only to wreck NATO. But as Herr Josef Strauss, in an article entitled "Soviet Aims and German Unity,"[3] writes:

> Disengagement is not an end in itself. We must candidly recognise the danger that words and concepts may become fetishes and acquire a life of their own which contradicts reality. *Military disengagement can be regarded as a solution only if both sides are prepared to enter into a political disengagement.*[4]

[2] *Foreign Affairs*, July, 1958, p. 539.
[3] *Foreign Affairs*, April, 1959, p. 373.
[4] Author's italics.

Herr Strauss's views coincide completely with the author's. These final chapters emphasise that disengagement means *a set of military and political measures, closely interwoven in time and space, having as their ultimate purpose the reunification of Germany, the liberation of Eastern Europe and the reduction of international tension.*

Except for those poised for a show-down with the Russians or burning with fiery passion for an armed crusade against Communism, it is difficult to find any objection to those aims, and they are aims which cannot be reached in any other way.

The *Handbook on Arms Control and Related Problems in Europe* gives the following definition:

> The essential idea behind this word, as it is generally used, is that of pulling Soviet and Western troops away from each other and leaving a spatial gap between them. In a sense "disengagement" is not too accurate a term because, strictly speaking, Western and Red Army forces are not now "engaged." . . . The term "disengagement" has sometimes been stretched to apply to a variety of concrete situations. Sometimes it is applied to large geographic areas including several countries and sometimes to very limited zones. At times it is employed to denote a withdrawal of all military troops, at times a withdrawal just of "foreign" troops, and at times to signify merely a diminution of troops. Sometimes the term "partial disengagement" is used to refer to one of the more limited movements. Some of those who oppose the idea of "disengagement" have offered the word "redeployment" as a substitute.[5]

Disengagement, which is a very general term, covers a very wide range of solutions, beginning with modest schemes such as those cautiously put forward by Mr. Macmillan to break the ice and move the West from its position of massive immobility, and detailed plans leading up to the complete disbanding of all military alliances accompanied by general disarmament.

[5] p. 2.

Controversy over Disengagement

The past decade, with the Berlin blockade in 1948–49 as its first milestone, has been an era of incessant efforts on both sides to find a solution to the reunification of Germany and to the settlement of the European question.

The reasons for the failure of these efforts are manifold, but they can be reduced to the following three categories:

(1) The wide gap between the ultimate goals of Soviet and of Western policies, in spite of the fact that on some occasions there was, perhaps, some chance of bridging it.

(2) The policy of Bonn, which aimed at the reunification of Germany on its own terms and at recovering, at some suitable opportunity, her lost territories in the East.

(3) Strong opposition inside the Western camp to any attempt to change the *status quo* by the only feasible method, namely disengagement.

We have dealt fairly extensively with various aspects of Soviet foreign policy as well as of the Western policy of containment, as the background to the unsuccessful efforts to find a solution to the German problem which is acceptable to both sides; in the course of the historical analysis of the issue we have also attempted to examine the reasons for the rigid attitude of the Bonn Government in this matter.

It only remains now to examine the whole group of arguments put forward against disengagement in various quarters of the West.

Opposition to disengagement can be roughly classified as emotional, political and, most important of all, military. During the last few years prominent men on both sides of the Atlantic have lent their weight and authority to this relentless campaign against disengagement.

Emotional Arguments

The emotional arguments are summed up in President Truman's statement some years ago, that: " . . . any agreement which the Kremlin might sign would not be worth the paper on which it had been written." This melodramatic statement which, by the way, is not in accordance with the facts, is a poor testimony to the ability of Western diplomats to hammer out an agreement with proper safeguards.

In his article, " Disengagement: Why? How? ", Mr. H. Gaitskell puts forward strong arguments on this subject:

> It is simply not true that the Russians have been unwilling to make any agreement whatever. . . . The truth seems to be that they are prepared to make agreements if it suits them but that they generally keep strictly to the letter of any agreement and take advantage of any loopholes or lack of precision in drafting.[6]

Here is another authority on this subject. Mr. Anthony Nutting, former Minister of State and British delegate to various disarmament conferences, in his article, " We Need a New Start Now ":

> It is not impossible to turn the Soviets away from a rigid position . . . it had been done before, as the West found out most recently at the Geneva talks on controlling a stoppage of tests, and also in May 1955, when the Soviet delegate in the Disarmament Conference at long last accepted a number of basic disarmament measures, which the West had been pressing upon him from the beginning.[7]

It is indeed true that on other occasions the Soviet record of broken treaties and agreements is a very black one: but for the sake of historical accuracy, it must be said that breaking agreements has not been the monopoly of the Russians.

[6] *Foreign Affairs*, July, 1958, p. 547.
[7] *The Observer*, October 19, 1958.

A few examples from the period between the two last wars will suffice to prove that the Western Powers too, not only once but on several occasions, were guilty of the same breach of faith.

Let us for instance recall the British–German Naval Agreement of June 18, 1935, and the circumstances in which its signature took place: Mr. L. Schwartzschild wrote in *World in Trance*:

> The German fleet did not concern England alone: it concerned all the sea Powers and all the signatories of Versailles. There were no less than seven valid pacts and agreements forbidding England to reach a separate accord with Germany in this question. The most recent of these agreements, concluded with France and Italy, was less than two months old. Sir John Simon—on the very day on which he left the Cabinet—asked the French and Italian Governments whether they would agree to England's concluding a naval pact with Germany.
>
> On June 15, 1935, Rome replied that Mussolini refused to agree to any such thing, that the problem must be solved in common by all the parties concerned.
>
> On June 17 Paris replied that Laval refused to agree and that the problem must be solved in common by all the parties concerned.
>
> On June 18, 1935, Sir Samuel Hoare signed the pact which, in violation of the existing treaties, granted Hitler a larger fleet than France's or Italy's. It was the triumph of anarchy for sake of peace. This time not Hitler but England broke treaties.[8]

In *One Man against Europe*, Konrad Heiden writes:

> A German delegation led by Joachim von Ribbentropp, Hitler's special adviser on foreign affairs, came to England on June 2, and in three days agreement was reached. . . . France and Italy were not informed until June 12. The French were appalled. On the 14th, the French Cabinet instructed Laval and Pietri, the Minister of Marine, to prepare a sharp Note in reply. . . . It was handed to the British Embassy in Paris on the evening of June 17, but on June 18 the Naval Agreement was signed in London.
>
> The French pointed out that that was the anniversary of the Battle of Waterloo. Britain had not only accepted a violation

[8] p. 367.

of the Treaty of Versailles but had violated the Treaty herself by her signature.[9]

Comments by the Diplomatic Staff of the *Daily Telegraph* [10] on the latest volume of official documents on German foreign policy are illuminating:

> In the bilateral naval agreement negotiated in London, Britain accepted that Germany should build up to 35 per cent. of British tonnage. This was four times the tonnage permitted to Germany under the Treaty of Versailles, still judicially valid, and included completely forbidden U-boats.
>
> It astonished a world that was already indignant and alarmed at Hitler's recent announcements that he had created an Air Force (March 1, 1935) and had introduced conscription and a thirty-six division Army (March 16).
>
> Astonishment was all the greater because Britain was playing a leading part in organising international action to stop Hitler. . . .
>
> Such action did much to alienate France, to encourage Mussolini to proceed with his Abyssinian plans on the correct assumption that there would be no common action against an aggressor, and to rekindle Russian mistrust. Countries of Eastern Europe drew similar conclusions.

The history of events during the Sudeten crisis in the summer of 1938, culminating in the shameful Munich agreement, is yet another example of an international agreement broken by the Western Powers. The late Dr. H. Ripka, former Minister in the Czechoslovak Government in Exile, describes how President Benes was dragged out of his bed in the middle of the night by British and French envoys and forced to agree to an Anglo-French ultimatum, demanding acceptance of Hitler's terms:

> The British and French Ministers, Mr. Newton and M. de Lacroix, called on President Benes just after 2 a.m. and remained with him until 3.30 a.m. It was decided to yield to the London proposals. . . . It was generally felt that it would be an inadmissible adventure to embark on a struggle with Germany in the state of absolute isolation to which we had been reduced by the defection of our Western friends and allies.[11]

---

[9] pp. 191–192 (originally published in two volumes under the title *Hitler*).
[10] September 1, 1959.   [11] *Munich—Before and After*, p. 103.

The betrayal of Poland during the war shows again just how the West sometimes honours its solemn pledges and obligations. At the very beginning of the war, in September 1939, it was France who broke the obligations arising out of her treaty of mutual assistance: Hitler was banking on such a reaction by the French, and consequently the Siegfried Line was manned by a few reserve divisions of no value. Thus a German general, Major-General W. von Mellenthin, could write:

> This gave me an opportunity of inspecting the famous West Wall, or Siegfried Line, as it was first called. I soon realised what a gamble the Polish Campaign had been and the grave risks which were run by our High Command. The second-class troops holding the Wall were badly equipped and inadequately trained, and the defences were far from being the impregnable fortifications pictured by our propaganda. . . . . The more I looked at the defences, the less I could understand the completely passive attitude of the French.[12]

Indeed, had France lived up to her obligations and launched an offensive, a breakthrough and invasion of Germany might have terminated the war even before the end of 1939.

Similar statements were made during the Nuremberg trial by Field-Marshal Keitl and General Jodl, among Hitler's closest military advisers.

Hitler, the cynical realist, was so completely sure that Britain and France would not honour their pledges and come to Poland's assistance that he was almost dumbfounded when he heard on September 3 that Britain had declared war on Germany.

So much, then, for the reliability of the West itself.

Another argument put forward by the opponents of disengagement is that the Russians do not in fact want it. Even Mr. Henry Kissinger, in his recent article, " Missiles and the Western Alliance," seems to subscribe to such a view. He writes:

[12] *Panzer Battles*, p. 9.

We must take account of the possibility that the Soviet Union is more interested in negotiating about disengagement than in achieving it. Once negotiations were entered upon, it is more likely that the expectations of disengagement would effectively demoralise NATO planning and undermine any military effort on the Continent. And we can be virtually certain that there will be endless evasions and delays so that the Soviet Union might well achieve one of its primary objectives by default—the dismantling of NATO without any concessions on its part.[13]

In several articles and lectures, Mr. Dean Acheson took a very strong line against any attempts to negotiate with the Russians, especially concerning disengagement. In a recent article in *Time* Magazine he wrote: " There is a good deal of folklore about on the subject of negotiating with the Russians. At the moment, the British, with the authority of those who have just been there, are giving currency to some of its more dubious maxims." [14]

In his hard-hitting article, " The Illusion of Disengagement," he pulls no punches:

The word is a mere conception, which confuses and does not represent any reality. . . . Disengagement . . . it is the same futile—and lethal—attempt to crawl back into the cocoon of history. For us there is only one disengagement possible—the final one, the disengagement from life, which is death. . . . The evils of a timid and defeatist policy of retreat are far deeper than its ineptness as a move in the propaganda battle.[15]

The West cannot expect to discover whether the Russians really want disengagement or simply intend, as Kissinger maintains, to engage in negotiations without wanting to achieve any result, unless the West is prepared to put the numerous Soviet proposals to the test.

The arguments of those critics of disengagement, who say in the same breath both that certain proposals would be too dangerous to the West and that the Russians would never

[13] *Foreign Affairs*, April, 1958, p. 395.
[14] April 12, and quoted by the *Daily Telegraph* correspondent in New York, April 13.
[15] *Foreign Affairs*, April, 1958.

accept them, cannot be accepted. As Mr. Gaitskell wrote in his polemic with James B. Conant, former United States High Commissioner in Germany: " . . . A plan which has real dangers for the West cannot also be to the grave disadvantage of the Russians, and vice versa." [16]

Pace Mr. Acheson, such initiative on the part of the West would have tremendous propaganda value, even if no results were achieved. First of all, the West would demonstrate to millions in Eastern Europe that the West had not abandoned them and that seemingly pretentious statements about the necessity of alleviating the situation of the nations of Eastern Europe were not merely cheap lip-service, but the expression of a real and constructive policy. The realisation that Western policy meant something would maintain the spark of hope for eventual freedom and prevent the integration of those countries into the Soviet *bloc*. Speaking in military terms—and the whole approach of the West towards this problem is based primarily upon military considerations—Western initiative would make the satellite armed forces, to use the expression of the Report, *The Present State of European Security*, of "varying reliability." [17]

After all, should these negotiations end in failure, the blame would rest on the shoulders of the Russians.

Political Arguments

The political arguments are rather more subtle. First of all, one of the most familiar arguments in the West is that the present situation, although uncomfortable and at times even perilous, is still preferable to the unknown dangers that could result from disengagement.

This point of view is best illustrated by Mr. Selwyn Lloyd's words in Parliament on December 21, 1957, on his return from the NATO Council session in Paris: " In my

---

[16] " Debate of the Month," *Western World*, July, 1958.
[17] Submitted at the Western European Assembly, June, 1958.

view the disengagement theory in the present situation and on the present demarcation line might well lead to greater insecurity and a great risk of war. . . ."

Mr. G. F. Hudson has written in *The Observer* [18]:

> The advantage of the present situation, tense though it be, is that neither side can move without a major war, and therefore will not move unless it deliberately seeks a major war. The engagement of the great Powers stabilises Central Europe: they protect their weaker allies but also restrain them, since their own forces would be at once involved in any local clash.

Raymond Aron, in his book, *On War—Atomic Weapons and Global Diplomacy,* writes: " Both Moscow and Washington, equally bent on avoiding a major war, prefer a situation which is deplorable in itself but stabilised to the unpredictability of a process which military disengagement would set in motion." [19]

Obviously the crux of the matter is the problem of Germany. As Mr. Kennan, in his third Reith Lecture, said: ". . . the German question still stands at the centre of world tensions; and . . . no greater contribution can be made to world peace than the removal of the present deadlock over Germany." He added: " There are those in our Western camp, I know, who find in this state of affairs no great cause for alarm. A divided Germany seems, for the moment, to be less of a problem to them than was the united Germany of recent memory." [20]

Indeed, it may be true to say that very few people in the West, and even in Western Germany too, sincerely want Germany to be reunited, and that all this clamour is nothing but so much lip-service in the West and so many empty slogans in Germany. None of the political leaders in Germany would dare to make such a statement in public because it would mean political hara-kiri: but in private conversation they readily admit that reunification, even on

[18] January 19, 1958.
[19] p. 118.
[20] *Russia, the Atom and the West*, pp. 37–40.

Western terms—in other words, on the basis of free elections—would mean that the high standard of living, as it is now in Western Germany, would be considerably lowered: the workers would insist on better wages and improved welfare services and several other complications would arise if these two very different political, economic and ideological systems were amalgamated.

Nobody could claim to foresee exactly what the implications of this difficult process are, but it would certainly mean that those who are now peacefully enjoying the amenities of the comparatively luxurious life in Western Germany would have cause for much grumbling and even for regret.

One must endorse the expression of Mr. Kissinger's views in his article " In Search of Stability ":

> It is said that nobody really *wants* German reunification. But it is surely within our control to set our own goals. If the West understands its interests, it *must* advocate German reunification despite the experience of two world wars and despite the understandable fear of a revived German truculence. The West may have to acquiesce in the division of Germany but it cannot condone it. Any other course will bring, in the end, what we should fear most: a militant, dissatisfied power in the centre of the Continent. To strive for German reunification is not a bargaining device but the condition of European stability.[21]

Up to now this state of affairs has suited Western Germany extremely well from every point of view. By playing an active part in the defence of Europe, Germany was able to climb rapidly from the status of a defeated country into the company of the Great Powers. This miracle would not have been possible for Germany if, as a result of wiser political planning on the part of the West, the war had ended earlier and Soviet troops had halted east of the frontiers of Eastern Europe. Similarly, an agreement for the reunification of Germany might conceivably have been reached, say in 1949, when Mr. Acheson

[21] *Foreign Affairs*, July. 1959, p. 542.

had in his files a plan for the withdrawal of troops from Germany, prior to her reunification; this was during the Conference of the Four Foreign Ministers in Paris. If this had happened, Germany would have remained a country which had lost the war, and was slowly " making her passage home," as Churchill put it.

Unfortunately, Western statesmen have taken a rather too militaristic approach to the problems of Europe. They tend to look at them through khaki-coloured spectacles and forget the lessons of the past. In his second article in the *New York Herald Tribune*, " Test Russia on Disengagement," Sir John Slessor wrote: " But do not let our new-found enthusiasm for Germany as an ally blind us to the fact that three times in living memory Germany has forced aggressive wars in Europe." [22]   And yet even the most cynical believers in the advantages of the so-called *Realpolitik* could not deny that the present division of Germany is, in spite of everything, a source of potential danger: the second Berlin crisis is an obvious example.

The only way to prevent such danger is to reunify Germany; and since it cannot be achieved on Western terms, a price will have to be paid for it during negotiations with the Russians. Mr. Gaitskell, in his article in *Foreign Affairs*, said: " Neutralisation is the price to be paid for reunification." [23]   In Part Two, several German commentators were shown to have taken an identical view.

In considering the political arguments it is also worth mentioning the view that the withdrawal of Soviet troops from the countries of that area—in other words, the setting up of a neutral zone—would bring about the balkanisation of Central and Eastern Europe.

Mr. M. Howard's book, *Disengagement in Europe*, is a case in point.[24]   Yet, he admits that

> . . . there may well be grounds for cautious optimism about the possible developments in Eastern Europe—for believing that the

[22] February 2, 1958.   [23] p. 552.
[24] pp. 49–53.

peoples and politicians have learned their lessons of the past twenty years as well as have the peoples and leaders of Germany. There is a strong movement towards federalism, which might resolve these complex questions of race and frontier as effectively as similar problems have been resolved in Tito's Yugoslavia. . . . The volcanoes of East European politics, like those of German nationalism, may have burned themselves out. . . . But it must be realised that any programme of disengagement will incur considerable political risks, whatever the military consequences may be; and our alarm as to the dangers of the present position must not blind us to them.[25]

Mr. Peregrine Worsthorne, too, described in great detail the dangers which could result from the withdrawal of Soviet troops from Eastern Europe in his booklet, *Dare Democracy Disengage?* He painted a hair-raising picture:

. . . Kadar and Ulbricht would not last long after the Red Army had been withdrawn. They would not in any likelihood be replaced by democratically chosen governments, but at least by less-hated Communist representatives. The process of liberalisation would, let us assume, continue although much less speedily than people seem to imagine: Eastern Europe would be still geared to the Soviet economy, and the Communist parties there would still represent the only organised centres of power. The Red Army's withdrawal might well strengthen rather than weaken them, by allowing them to pose as the agents of liberation, at least for the time being. But at some point, months or years ahead, there would arise a challenge to the Communist Party in one of the East European states. This would be the test moment for the Soviet Union. Could she stand by and see the Communist state slough off Communism? If she decided that she could not, what would be there to prevent her sending back the Red Army?[26]

Unfortunately Mr. Worsthorne shows heart-breaking ignorance of the mood of peoples of Eastern Europe. There is ample evidence to support the claim that, after the withdrawal of Soviet troops, not a single Communist would

25 p. 52.
26 p. 24.

remain. The Lenin-Marxist ideology was imposed from outside and by force upon the peoples of Eastern Europe.

Mr. A. Wolfers, too, testified before the Senate Sub-Committee on Disarmament on February 4, 1959:

> . . . under no circumstances at any time would [the countries of Eastern Europe] become a thorn in the flesh of the Soviet Empire. . . . They might develop very hostile governments opposed to the Soviet Union: there might be trouble of all sorts of kinds which would be much greater than the troubles which have occurred in Berlin.
>
> To imagine that the Soviet Union would sit back and allow these countries to arm to the point where they could defend themselves against the Soviet Union itself, that these countries could be left alone to behave like nice little neutrals, that they could be left alone to keep social achievements, which means Communist régimes, simply on the basis of treaties seems to me to be an exaggerated notion of what treaties can do.
>
> We could not even guarantee that these countries would so behave as to satisfy the Russians, and therefore unless there is power to hold the Russians out, power which we must project in large part into Europe, I can't imagine that this freedom would be worth much. It would be a semifreedom, which is worse than nothing.

To comment on Mr. Wolfers' views, it must be pointed out that the Russians on various occasions suggested that reunited Germany should be allowed her own national armed forces up to 200,000 men, including formations for anti-aircraft defence—in other words, modern armed forces. There is no reason to doubt that they would negotiate the level of national forces in the other countries of Eastern Europe after the withdrawal of Soviet troops. It is an offer which they repeated for years. They realised that the national armed forces of Eastern Europe—which of course would have to be reduced—would, even if combined, never present any threat to Soviet security.

As far as the inability of the United States to " guarantee " their " behaviour " towards the Soviet Union was concerned, that would indeed contradict the very notion of neutrality. Such a suggestion would smack that obsolete concept of Professor Carr, of the division of Europe into "spheres of influence," by which Eastern Europe was earmarked for Soviet control. As Fritz Erler pointed out, Mr. Khrushchev himself expressed readiness to give all necessary guarantees against Soviet interference in the internal affairs of Eastern Germany provided, of course, that the West did likewise.[27]

However, the situation is comparable to that in Western Europe, where fear of Russia has been the foundation stone of NATO. There is no doubt that the same fear in Eastern Europe after the withdrawal of Soviet troops would be able to overcome any petty differences. Furthermore, one can assume that the trend towards some kind of a federation which began even during the war would result in an organisation in which frontier disputes would lose their importance.

It is interesting to recall that Churchill, amidst his preoccupations with the conduct of operations, showed remarkable diplomatic foresight by putting forward a scheme for federation in Central and Eastern Europe. By making his famous statement on March 21, 1943, at a time when appeasement of Russia in this country was rampant, he clearly demonstrated that he alone realised that something had to be done to forestall and check ambitious Soviet plans for expansion and conquest in Central and Eastern Europe.

At this time, *The Times*, in a memorable editorial on March 10, 1943, wrote that, if Britain's frontier is on the Rhine, then "Russia's frontier is on the Oder. Hence, the lands between Russia's frontiers and those of Germany are to be held by governments and peoples friendly to herself." As David Dallin concluded in his prophetic book: "The classic formula of the Soviet sphere of influence demanded no more." [28]

---

[27] *Europa Archiv*, May 20, 1959.
[28] *Russia and Post-War Europe*, p. 188.

In the same period, under Soviet pressure the Polish-Czechoslovak Federation, agreed in 1940, became for all practical purposes a dead letter. Churchill, instead of dividing Europe into sinister spheres of influence, contemplated a formation or confederation of States side by side with the Great Powers.

Naturally, Churchill's plan, which would have created an obstacle to Soviet schemes for expansion in that area, provoked virulent criticism in the Soviet Press. Dallin wrote [29]:

> The Moscow magazine, *War and the Working Class* . . . expressed opposition to "federations, confederations and regional *blocs* of States," concluding that "the project of an East European Federation is directed against the Soviet Union."

Unfortunately, in all his schemes Stalin received most valuable and eager assistance from the late President Dr. Benes who, aware of the trend of events and convinced of the inevitable—as he thought—domination by Russia of Eastern Europe, decided to throw in his lot with her.

An extract from an article written shortly after the Communist *coup* in Czechoslovakia, called "Czechoslovakia and the Soviet Union," by Mr. G. B. Thomas, supports this view:

> What are the facts? This above all: that no independent Government anywhere made more concessions to the Soviet viewpoint than various Governments of Dr. Benes. They went more than half-way to meet Mr. Molotov. It was a very natural thing for them to do since every Czech and every Slovak is conscious of his country's dependence upon Russia: a dependence that will remain absolute until the German problem has been solved in its widest European sense. *It was, in fact, Dr. Benes who laid the foundations of the Soviet security system in Eastern Europe.*[30]
>
> It was the Government of Dr. Benes that signed the first post-war Treaty of Alliance with Soviet Russia—that is to say, the first country outside the Great Powers' circle to do so. Without that gesture of goodwill, without that first Treaty, it

[29] *Op. cit.*, p. 189.   [30] Author's italics.

is doubtful whether the Soviet advance into Europe would have been as rapid as it has been. Some months before its signature —on May 17, 1943 [31]—the Czechoslovak Government formally announced that it had abandoned its attempts to establish a Polish-Czech Confederation. The announcement was made before Sikorski died; it marked another turning point in the history of Poland; it destroyed the only possible alternative to complete Soviet domination of Eastern Europe.[32]

Undoubtedly, the nations of Eastern Europe have now learned their lesson. Their experiences of Soviet domination and their fear of a Soviet re-entry would be a strong enough link in the face of any disruptive issues.

There will, however, be one perennial problem, namely, German ambitions to play a dominant role in that area. As a matter of fact, there are already several Research Institutes in Western Germany studying Eastern European problems and they invariably foresee some sort of leadership by Germany in what is her traditional—as the Germans, since Hitler, have the habit of calling it—*Lebensraum*.

An interesting view in this context, although utterly opposed to any idea of disengagement, has been expressed by a well-known military writer, Lt.-Col. F. Miksche:

> To neutralise only Germany would be more of a disadvantage to the West than to the East. It would reduce still further what remains of free Europe—those who believe in a neutral zone which includes not only Germany but Poland, Austria, Czechoslovakia and Hungary—perhaps even Roumania and Bulgaria—are pure fantasts. Moscow would interpret this as a plan to reinstate Germany in her traditional sphere of influence, where she could inevitably—perhaps even without wanting to— sooner or later resume her role as the leading great Power. . . . Why should the Kremlin accept such proposals, and what has the West to offer in exchange? [33]

Raymond Aron takes the following view:

> In order to avoid any risks, the Western Powers refuse to envisage the withdrawal of Anglo-American troops or even the

---

[31] Churchill's speech was only three days later.
[32] *Time and Tide*, March 6, 1948, p. 242.
[33] *The Failure of the Atomic Strategy*, p. 78.

possibility of a Germany not tied up to NATO. In this way, the *status quo* is crystallised.

The return to a diplomacy of movement does not require the disruption either of the global balance of power between the two camps or of thermonuclear parity. All that is necessary is to forgo the direct confrontation of regular armies, but the dangers of this renunciation would have to be accepted.[34]

These views bring us to the third category, the military arguments, which are the most important.

Military Arguments

It would be necessary to write a special treatise to deal fully with the various military arguments against disengagement, especially in view of the fact that they are endorsed by statements of the highest military authorities.

But these arguments boil down to the view, which has been widely accepted almost as dogma, that disengagement will, first, weaken the West, thereby giving advantages to the Russians; secondly, bring about the withdrawal of American forces from Europe; and thirdly, result in the collapse of NATO.

The most serious argument, of course, was put forward by General L. Norstad, who, in a television interview in the Independent Television programme, "Right to Reply," expressed the view that military disengagement would be absolutely disastrous. Yet even his eloquent criticism was far from being absolute, as he showed at the end of the interview:

> The common denominator of any proposals for disengagement or thinning out is control, which could eliminate or minimise the dangers and consequences of surprise attack. On that foundation, if you have a successful and efficient control and inspection system, then, I think, we might consider other things. On the basis of real security which could be enforced, then we can afford to look over the field and take action, the

[34] *Op. cit.*, p. 92.

action in a particular field which would be most useful, be most consistent with the position of our governments.[35]

He reiterated his views in a statement made to the National Press Club in Washington on April 7, 1959. He said: " I want to see the safeguards considered in the first instance, and safeguards mean, in my judgment, a completely effective control and inspection system which is the common denominator of all the proposals." [36] Expressing his scepticism about the " thinning-out " of forces, he continued:

> I am concerned about any of these proposals because any agreement would be honoured on our side—which would weaken us. And we cannot assume that they would be honoured on the other side.
>
> I am concerned about any of those proposals that is not based upon a solid foundation of something which will guarantee security. Control and inspection itself could be useful. It would eliminate or minimise the dangers, the consequences of surprise attack: it could relieve us of considerable danger. On that foundation, I think, we might consider other things.

Needless to say, an efficient system of control and inspection must be an integral part of any sound scheme for disengagement.

General Norstad's balanced views contrast strongly from those expressed by two prominent military writers, General Pierre Gallois, French expert on nuclear warfare, and General Frido von Senger und Etterlin.

In an article in the April issue of *Nef*, entitled " The Berlin Crisis and the Fear of a Shadow," General Gallois put forward the following views:

(1) disengagement would create a " No-man's land " in Europe;

(2) defence strategy requires a hinterland from the demarcation line to the Atlantic as " elbow-room " for manoeuvre;

---

[35] *Daily Telegraph*, March 31, 1959.
[36] *Handbook on Arms Control*, pp. 22–23.

(3) any possibility of a conventional war would be ruled out;

(4) atomic weapons compensate the West for Soviet numerical superiority in conventional forces;

(5) disengagement would make most unlikely intervention by the United States for the maintenance of the *status quo* in Europe.

Detailed criticism of General Gallois has been given earlier in this book, but one comment must be made now. Any American intervention would have the supreme purpose of defending Western Europe under the terms of the Atlantic Alliance, not solely the maintenance of the *status quo*.

In a very interesting article, " Militärische Probleme einer verdünnten Zone in Europa," General Frido von Senger und Etterlin stated quite bluntly that the establishment of such a zone would be quite " unrealistic," mainly because " the thinning out of a zone as a result of a prohibition on atomic weapons will not make such a zone immune from atomic destruction." [37] Yet Clause 3 of the Rapacki Plan stated unequivocally that " the Powers which have at their disposal nuclear weapons should undertake the obligation not to use these weapons against the territory of the zone or against any targets situated in this zone." A similar clause could easily be incorporated in any similar proposal for a demilitarised zone. Should such a zone ever be established, including, of course, Germany, Germany would be the main beneficiary. It is most difficult of all to understand objections from German sources to the prohibition of use of atomic weapons, for it is Germany which would, in the event of war, become the main battlefield and inevitably the atomic cemetery.

General von Senger und Etterlin claimed further that the setting up of a thinned-out zone would lead to its military neutralisation,[38] but it is interesting to recall the many

[37] *Europa Archiv*, June, 1959, p. 326.
[38] *Ibid.*, p. 331.

Soviet proposals which provided for reunited Germany's right to have national armed forces amounting to 200,000 men. If a similar figure could be agreed upon for, say, Poland, Czechoslovakia and Hungary each, Germany and the countries of Eastern Europe together would have in peacetime a standing army of some 800,000 men, not counting their reserves. The countries of this zone would be allowed to enter into a defensive alliance between themselves; their national armies could therefore offer strong resistance to any Soviet overland aggression. The Russians for their part could not consider that a defensive alliance of those countries could offer a threat to their security. On the other hand, in the event of Soviet aggression, these armed forces would considerably increase the manpower of the West and make good the theoretical disappearance of the Bundeswehr from the *ordre de bataille* of the Atlantic Alliance.

Both General Gallois and General von Senger und Etterlin reasoned from a situation *rebus sic stantibus,* assuming that the Russians would one day launch an offensive from their prepared deployments in Eastern Germany. They both ignored the possibility of an armed uprising in Eastern Europe, which could isolate the twenty Soviet divisions operating on the frontage of 800 kilometres. Yet, as General von Senger und Etterlin wrote, even thirty NATO divisions—General Norstad's target in the event of the setting up of a denuclearised zone—would be " much too weak " to put up efficient resistance to the " overwhelming " Soviet superiority.[39] He ignores the fact that the strength of a Soviet onslaught could not, during the decisive first days, exceed the figure of some twenty divisions.

In his review of Colonel F. Miksche's book, *The Failure of Atomic Strategy,* another prominent military writer, General André Beaufre, expressed the view that the minimum figure for the defence of the territory west of the Iron

[39] *Ibid.,* p. 328.

Curtain would be 120 divisions.[40] Yet General Norstad required only an estimated thirty divisions—and Colonel von Bonnin less than one half of that number—for the defence of a fortified zone from Lübeck to Passau. The discrepancy is strange indeed.

On the other hand, although fully agreeing with General Norstad's wise insistence on a wide measure of inspection and control as a guarantee against the danger of a surprise Soviet attack, it is difficult to understand how the withdrawal of Soviet troops could increase the danger of such an attack. The Strategic Air Force is maintaining twenty-four-hour air patrols over United States territory; for the same reasons astronomical sums of money are spent on the elaborate warning and radar system; and whether there is eventual European disengagement or not it will have no bearing whatsoever on the danger of a Soviet surprise nuclear attack against United States territory.

As to Europe, any attack by conventional Soviet forces against Western Europe must be preceded by a period of troop movements. Western intelligence would have to be extremely inefficient to be unable to detect in time the arrival of Soviet divisions near the frontiers of Eastern Europe (assuming that, as a result of disengagement, Soviet troops withdraw behind the borders of Russia).

Theoretically speaking, in case of war the present state of deployment of troops of both sides is such that it would be difficult considerably to reinforce the Soviet forces in Eastern Germany; hence, perhaps, the increasing emphasis in Soviet strategic thinking on the importance of " forces-in-being," ready for immediate action.

From the Soviet point of view it would be much easier to concentrate troops in their own territory—after a withdrawal behind the Soviet frontiers—in preparation for a massive surprise attack against Eastern Europe in the path of the intended offensive against the West. Such a

---

[40] " La Strategie Atomique a-t-elle Fait Faillite? ", *Revue de Defense Nationale*, June, 1959, p. 982.

concentration would be entirely in accordance with the classic principles of the Soviet strategy. In this context, it is worth quoting the view of General Dittmar, whose voice over the radio, as German military commentator, was known during the war all over the world. In his article, " Masse und Qualität in der sowjetischen Kriegslehre," [41] he claimed that the efforts of the Soviet High Command during the whole war always had been to lay an overwhelming superiority at the point of attack [*überwältigender Schwerpunkt*]. " The use of the ' Mass " during the war . . . was for the Soviets not only the problem of its military purposefulness but in the same degree the keystone of the ideology." Raymond Garthoff, in his book, *Soviet Strategy in the Nuclear Age*, wrote: " The Soviet concept of modern mass armies must be considered in terms of its relation to the doctrine of combined arms operations." [42]

Furthermore, any surprise Soviet attack against the territory of Eastern Europe, which would become a sort of cushion or buffer zone for the West, would be identified and resisted right back on the eastern frontiers of Eastern Europe. In conditions of conventional warfare, the danger of surprise is incomparably smaller than in a thermonuclear war, which, if it comes, will be a global war with Europe reduced to a secondary role from the start.

One of the main reasons for these apprehensions is the false assumption that disengagement would reduce the " strategic depth for manoeuvre " and make the NATO " forward strategy " unrealistic.

Such a view ignores the political and military implications of the withdrawal of Soviet troops from Eastern Europe. It could perhaps be understood before the Hungarian uprising, when it was a generally accepted practice in the West to compute Soviet supremacy on the basis of the total strength of combined Soviet and satellite armies. Yet to continue this mental exercise after the Hungarian

---

[41] *Wehrkunde*, May, 1956.
[42] pp. 149–152.

uprising is really nonsensical. It must be obvious, even to the most obstinate die-hards, that once the Soviet troops left the countries of Eastern Europe, any attempt to re-enter in force would be resisted by every possible means. Consequently, in the event of a Soviet withdrawal from Eastern Europe, despite Mr. Khrushchev's boasts that Communist régimes will survive, any hypothetical Soviet major aggression would be met not along the river Elbe but several hundred miles to the east. In fact Eastern Europe, covered by the guarantees of a European Security Pact containing the necessary military sanctions, would become a defence glacis of the West and an area of troop deployment for the execution of forward strategy. Strategic depth of manoeuvre, far from contracting, would increase very considerably with a corresponding increase in the margin of " warning time."

Thus, the opening phase of a Third World War, which according to Field-Marshal Montgomery is " unthinkable," would be similar to that in 1914 and 1940, when Belgium, neutral in both instances, automatically became a member of the Western alliance on the very first day of German aggression. Similarly, the countries of Eastern Europe, should Soviet Russia invade them, would become members of the Atlantic Alliance, which would come to their assistance in accordance with the clauses of a European Security Pact.

In a war the national armies of Eastern Europe which would be fighting alongside the forward elements of NATO (probably some airborne units) would vastly compensate for the relative loss of German contingents. This loss would indeed be only very relative, because a reunited Germany, although outside NATO, would be permitted to have her own national armed forces. As we have already indicated, even the Russians, in their various proposals for the withdrawal of troops, have always suggested that Germany should have her own national armed forces. Consequently, Germany, which would have to accept the status, as Sir John Slessor has put it, of " military non-alignment," would represent a military factor potentially similar to that of Sweden or Switzerland and would have to be taken into serious consideration. Obviously, in the case of a major Soviet aggression, Germany would reluctantly be involved and let us hope that she would take her place alongside her former allies.

These same arguments serve also to discredit the concept of disengagement put forward by General Genevey in his article, " Sur les Aspects Militaires du ' Dégagement ' en Europe," [43] which was to some extent a reply to an article, " Esquisse d'un Plan pour une Solution Européenne," [44] by the author of this book.

General Genevey strongly emphasised the dangers of the neutralisation of Germany, overlooking the fact that all the protagonists of disengagement—or, as Sir John Slessor prefers to call it, redeployment—insist that Germany should have strong national forces able to defend her territory. This book has already pointed out that even the Russians have on many occasions suggested that Germany be allowed some 200,000 men. Such apprehensions about the dangers of the neutralisation of Germany seem ill-founded. Furthermore, the arguments on the loss of " depth for manoeuvre " put forward by General Genevey are based on the obsolete doctrines of conventional warfare, outdated in the era of a thermonuclear war. They also ignore the increasing accent placed by Soviet military authorities on " forces-in-being " which would be employed during the first decisive forty-eight hours. *Mutatis mutandis*, this attitude is reminiscent of the situation which prevailed during the German offensive in France in 1940 when the German *Blitzkreig*, employing all the methods of modern warfare, was met by principles deriving directly, and with little modification, from the 1914–1918 war.

General Valluy, Commander-in-Chief of the Central

---

[43] *Politique Etrangère*, No. 2, 1959, p. 348.
[44] *Politique Etrangère*, No. 3, 1959, p. 27.

Front, analysed the weaknesses of the present Western defence system in an article, " L'Otan à l'Ere Atomique," [45] and came to the conclusion that there were two main weaknesses:

(1) only the Anglo-Saxon Powers possessed the proper armoury of tactical atomic weapons,
(2) in the event of war, Western Europe would be the battlefield and, despite all careful efforts to choose only military targets, the bulk of the fighting would take place in that territory and cause grave devastation.

In the light of this the arguments put forward by all those who sponsor plans for a comprehensive disengagement, involving a withdrawal of Soviet troops from Eastern Europe, deserve better attention, from the French particularly; after all, should war break out despite the implementation of such a plan, the battlefield would be not the Elbe but several hundred miles to the east.

Yet in French military circles disengagement is anathema, and is dismissed *a priori* as a solution which could serve only to weaken the West.

Another argument in the series of objections to disengagement and limited forms of regional disarmament is that they would cause " mortal danger." This was put forward in the Report, *Military Implications of the Plans for Regional or Limited Disarmament and the Policy of Disengagement in Central Europe*, submitted to the Assembly of the Western European Union on April 14, 1958, by the Rapporteur, Mr. Goedhardt.

The conclusions of the draft resolution were as follows:

That a policy of disengagement involving a military withdrawal of NATO troops from Western Germany and of Russian troops from Central and Eastern Europe:

(1) would constitute a *mortal danger*[46] for the West, if it were not accompanied by:

---

[45] *Revue de Defense Nationale*, July, 1959, p. 1145.   [46] Author's italics.

the political withdrawal of the Soviet Union from the part of Europe now occupied and controlled by it, and

a thoroughly controlled and inspected general agreement on disarmament between East and West;

(2) would not be acceptable unless a neutralisation of Western Germany was specifically excluded.[47]

Before proceeding further it seems pertinent to add a short comment on these stipulations. All schemes of disengagement aim at the political withdrawal of Russia from the " part of Europe now occupied and controlled by it." A disengagement scheme, with an efficient system of control and inspection, can only be a preliminary step and a useful experiment for the application of more general disarmament projects. As far as " the neutralisation of Germany " is concerned, neutralisation of Germany equivalent to her " complete and absolute " disarmament and demilitarisation, as was suggested by Dean Acheson before the Senate Foreign Relations Committee ten years ago, is certainly not envisaged by all those who advocate disengagement: on the contrary, a fully armed Germany, although without nuclear weapons, is envisaged in all these schemes.

Similar fears reappear from time to time in statements on both sides of the Atlantic. For instance, James B. Conant, former United States High Commissioner in Western Germany, wrote in the " Debate of the Month ":

A neutralised but unarmed Germany protected by international treaty is to me inconceivable in the present state of international tension: nor is it desirable. In short, what does one mean by neutralisation?

There was a time when the German equivalent to the phrase alliance-free was often used by the opponents of Chancellor Adenauer's policy. . . . The military implications of such a proposal were quite clear: NATO would shrink or disappear.[48]

---

[47] Document 81.
[48] *Western World*, July 1958, p. 36.

Again, in the House of Lords' debate on May 4, 1959, Lord Home stated that mutual withdrawal of troops would produce a military " vacuum," and continued:

> . . . disengagement must imply withdrawal of forces and surely it must mean also that there will be a no-man's land between East and West, in which there will be no forces of the Warsaw Pact or of the NATO Alliance.

Even General de Gaulle in a Press Conference on March 25, 1959, expressed the view that the neutralisation or disengagement of Germany would be dangerous for France from the military point of view. Apparently to General de Gaulle the terms " neutralisation " and " disengagement " are identical.

This " mortal danger " is based on a wrong assessment of the Soviet position in Eastern Europe. Those who so passionately object to disengagement and consequently to the withdrawal of Soviet troops from Eastern Europe, simply do not realise that the Soviet political and military leaders are on the horns of a formidable dilemma, and are prepared to go a long way to wrench themselves free.

In spite of the bloody suppression of the Hungarian uprising, and in spite of gradual improvements in Soviet-Polish relations which culminated in Gomulka's trip to Moscow in October-November last year, the Soviet leaders must have come to the conclusion that the policy of integrating Eastern Europe into the Soviet empire has reached, in spite of all efforts, the point of diminishing returns. It is a pity that the Western leaders are so easily impressed by Soviet boasts, which have been part and parcel of Russian policy for centuries: when war broke out with Japan in 1904, the slogan of Russian propaganda was " We shall bury the Japs under our caps." The débâcles at Mukden, Laojan, and the destruction of the Russian fleet at Tsushima, were a bad awakening for the Russian people. Similar boasts were made when in autumn, 1914, Russian troops were marching into the German trap in the Mazurian Lakes.

The grim reality of the position of the Soviet troops in Eastern Europe is an unenviable one, and Soviet military leaders are fully aware of it. This is especially true of the twenty Soviet divisions deployed in Eastern Germany, for so many years a nightmare for Western military planners. These divisions, like all Soviet troops in Eastern Europe, have a double task which unfortunately has escaped the notice of all those who casually compute Soviet numerical superiority in numbers of divisions. First, they have to act as the spearhead in a very hypothetical Soviet overland offensive against the West, and, secondly, by their presence they have to maintain the Communist régimes in power.

The statement by Mr. Khrushchev that if Soviet troops were withdrawn from Eastern Europe the Communist régimes would remain, is no more valid than that made by the Russian generals in 1904.

In view of the double task assigned to Soviet troops in Eastern Europe, including those stationed in Eastern Germany, a proportion of them would have to be assigned on the very first day of hostilities against the possibility of a popular uprising, and to protect the lines of communication through Poland.

If the armoured units of the Bundeswehr were to enter the territory of Eastern Germany in response to the appeals of the population and in support of an uprising, the situation of the Soviet troops would become very precarious indeed. The fact that the Bundeswehr has a large and highly mechanised army would seem to support the hypothesis that it is precisely this kind of operation, aimed to transfer the fighting as far eastward as possible, that is being visualised by the West German planners.

When Khrushchev spontaneously told Polish journalists at the reception on November 18, 1956, in honour of Gomulka, while Soviet guns were firing at Hungarian troops in Budapest, that he was prepared to withdraw his troops from Eastern Germany, Poland and Hungary, there was no trace of deceit in his words: he was an extremely worried man.

There is no doubt that, if the West had at that moment chosen to negotiate the Russians would have jumped at the chance. Unfortunately, the Western political leaders stuck to their defeatist, passive and sterile policy of containment, and the golden opportunity was missed. What is worse, although the West do not even try to test the Soviet proposals, the view is generally accepted in the West that the Russians are not, in fact, interested in disengagement, and that all negotiations on the subject—should matters ever get so far—would be purely for propaganda purposes.

But protagonists of this view must surely realise that the failure of negotiations would be a powerful card in the hands of the West, for all the onus of their failure would be on the shoulders of the Russians.

As Senator Thomas J. Dodd wrote:

> Khrushchev was able to crush the Hungarian Revolution by massing his armoured divisions against the people of Budapest. But the Revolution in defeat exposed the lie of Communism for all peoples to see and overnight converted the Warsaw Pact from a diplomatic asset into a military and diplomatic liability. Thus the most effective deterrent to Communist expansion in Europe at this juncture would be to place our basic diplomatic emphasis on the ultimate freedom of the captive peoples of Eastern Europe. . . . Both our political parties in the 1952 elections committed themselves to the liberation of the subjugated nations. But unfortunately, the word was used more as an electioneering slogan than as a name for a carefully thought out foreign policy that is vital to our own national security. The first step would be to demonstrate the earnestness of our concern by raising the issue of the captive nations at every diplomatic conference and at every UN session. . . . To raise the issue of liberation in this manner would by itself have a great impact on the other side of the Iron Curtain. But the issue must never be permitted to degenerate into a simple propaganda device.[49]

[49] "Our Captive Allies," *New Leader*, July 20–27, 1959, pp. 15–16.

A further argument on military grounds, recently advanced by Dean Acheson, is that disengagement would involve the withdrawal of American troops across the Atlantic. Yet a study of Soviet proposals shows that they speak in terms of withdrawal either from Western Germany or 500 miles in each direction from the Elbe. Russian troops would withdraw to behind the Russian borders, and NATO troops to the broad area along the Atlantic seaboard and in the south of France.

General Genevey, as usual marshalling all the available arguments against disengagement, did not miss the opportunity of claiming that disengagement would result in American withdrawal across the Atlantic: " The policy of disengagement from a zone will, in fact, be an American disengagement. . . ."

It is absolutely absurd to maintain that it would be difficult to accommodate five American combat teams and the American Air Force in that vast area. In point of fact, all American air bases are located west of the Rhine, and SHAPE, probably with the possibility of disengagement in view, has never fully extended its pipeline system into Germany.

Furthermore, should General de Gaulle make too many difficulties in accommodating American troops in France or ask too high a price for agreement, the United States could always transfer her forces to Spain:

> In fact, under a bilateral agreement between the United States and Spain, the 16th Air Force of the United States Strategic Air Command has been established in Spain since the summer of 1957. It is the only one of the various S.A.C. air forces to be stationed outside the United States. It has at its disposal a number of Spanish bases, including large airfields near Madrid, Saragossa and Tarragona with the longest runways in Western Europe, and possibly in the world. A pipeline has been constructed to carry fuel from the Gulf of Cadiz to these bases. . . .
>
> The 16th Air Force has American fighters to protect its bases and maintains close liaison with the Spanish Air Force.

There are a number of prohibited areas in Spain, especially in the Pyrenees region. Little is known about the military installations in these areas but it seems reasonable to suppose that they include long-range missiles.[50]

Spain's admission into NATO appeared only a matter of time. The main opposition to her admission came primarily from British and Scandinavian Socialists on the grounds that Spain was not a democracy in the Western sense of the word. However the same criteria applied to Portugal and Turkey.

Obviously, the cost of redeploying troops would be very high indeed but, after all, the same considerations apply to the Russians. They would have to abandon hundreds of airfields in Eastern Germany built for their interceptor fighters, which constitute the outer ring of the Soviet anti-aircraft defence system, and several launching platforms built in increasing quantities during the preceding years, barracks, depots, etc.

The process of redeploying troops would be an important political factor leading to a political *détente*: as Mr. Selwyn Lloyd said in Washington during his visit with Mr. Macmillan, it would " disengage tension . . ."

According to the *Daily Telegraph* correspondent in Bonn, General Eddleman said on May 8: " Withdrawal of Allied formations behind the Rhine would have little strategic or tactical significance." He qualified this opinion with two stipulations. These were that West German troops should remain in the area between the Rhine and the Iron Curtain, and that the Russians should make a similar withdrawal on their side. The distance from the Iron Curtain to the Rhine was 100–300 miles. With bridges available and modern motorised divisions, this distance had little military significance for American troops. General Eddleman emphasised that he was making a purely military assessment, excluding political or diplomatic considerations.

[50] *Daily Telegraph*, June 11, 1959

The tremendous administrative problems involved in a withdrawal, such as finding new bases, airfields, barracks, schools and married quarters, would be virtually insoluble, but such a withdrawal would have little effect on other NATO arms, such as the Strategic Air Command, the Atlantic Fleet or the Mediterranean forces.

General Eddleman's views raised the inevitable storm in Bonn, and the *Daily Telegraph* correspondent commented:

> A West German Defence Ministry spokesman doubted if it would be possible for NATO to maintain its present strategy if troops withdrew west of the Rhine. "I cannot agree," the spokesman said, "that separating forces by a few hundred miles would not make very much difference. . . . General Eddleman's view was one hundred per cent. in opposition to the concepts of NATO and West German concepts."

General Eddleman was compelled to eat his words. The very next day a statement was dictated by him to Washington, saying that he did not advocate withdrawal of troops. The statement was as follows:

> In answer to the questions . . . as to the tactical and logistical implications of the pull-back of the NATO troops to the Rhine, I did not in any way advocate it, nor did I imply that it was a view acceptable to the United States.
>
> I further pointed out the utter impracticability of making such a move. Naturally such a withdrawal would bear adverse strategic and other implications. . . .

When one recollects how even President Eisenhower, as pointed out in previous chapters, has sometimes had to withdraw opinions which happened not to be in accord with the policy of Bonn, it is all too clear that the policy of the United States is, as Senator J. Kennedy said, "too tightly lashed" to that of Bonn.

Only one of the advocates of disengagement, Sir John Slessor, recommends the withdrawal of American troops from the Continent. In the first of a series of articles, "Test the Soviets on Disengagement," he wrote:

. . . our line should be that we want to negotiate a mutual with-drawal of the Russians from East Germany and other Warsaw Pact countries, and of the British and Americans from the mainland of Europe.[51]

Yet in the second article of the same series he expressed a very strong opinion on the subject of the conditions under which such a withdrawal could take place:

If there is to be any hope of getting NATO agreement to a withdrawal policy it will be a *sine qua non* that the United States—and for that matter, also Great Britain—should assume the most binding undertaking and should engage their honour to stand up to their obligations under a reorganised NATO and under any extended security pact, if their troops leave the main-land of Europe.

Especially interesting is the fact that apparently even some of the American die-hards revised their attitude towards this issue. A booklet, *Democratic Programs for Action : Foreign and Military Policy for Peace and Security*, was published in the summer of 1959 by the Advisory Council of the Democratic National Council, an organisa-tion which counts among its members such prominent personalities as Dean Acheson, Paul Nitze, Senator H. Humphrey, Averill Harriman and others. It stated that

withdrawal of American forces from Europe may well be possible—indeed, we hope it will be—when a settlement of out-standing issues and a more stable power relationship have been achieved in Europe. But to attempt it under present circum-stances would be to destroy the possibility of reaching those settlements, that relationship, and indeed, of preserving a free Western Europe.

Disengagement will not weaken the West provided that it is accompanied by all necessary safeguards as far as con-trol and inspection are concerned; far from lessening the depth of strategic manoeuvre, it will in fact increase it; it need not bring about the withdrawal of American troops from Europe. These are the three propositions which we

[51] *New York Herald Tribune*, January–February, 1958.

have tried to prove, and in the face of them it is difficult to agree with those who say that disengagement will bring about the collapse of NATO.

It is true that in the event of disengagement NATO would have to undergo considerable changes and refashion its strategic concept in accordance with the new military and political situation. But this would be exactly what Field-Marshal Montgomery suggested, only a few months after his resignation as Deputy Supreme Commander: " If NATO is to survive and to become the vigorous and healthy organisation we all desire, there must be changes. The first requirement is a thorough review of the whole organisation." [52] In his lecture, " The present state of the game in the contest between East and West," [53] Field-Marshal Montgomery took an even more drastic view of this problem :

> If we are to progress, the whole NATO organisation must be drastically overhauled : it is complicated, cumbersome and grossly overstaffed. There is an enormous waste of money and effort. . . . The strategical thinking is muddled and confused. The global aspect of defence is totally disregarded. The military structure needs revision.

Captain B. H. Liddell Hart said in his article—" Can NATO Protect Us Today? "—after a very critical analysis of various deficiencies in the NATO defence system : " . . . The whole question needs a thorough investigation by impartial experts." [54] In an article, " Disengagement— Germany and Eastern Europe," Kenneth Younger, M.P., wrote :

> It is time to think about adjusting Western defence require-ments so as to give a higher priority to long-term political strategy in Europe. If this could be done it might even help to create a sense of common purpose among Western govern-ments, the absence of which is today the weakest element in the entire Western position.[55]

[52] *Sunday Times*, April 5, 1959.
[53] Delivered at the Royal United Service Institution, October 24, 1958.
[54] *John Bull*, April 5, 1959.
[55] *The Scotsman*, Survey of NATO, June 17, 1958.

Summing up the military arguments we can conclude that:

1. With all necessary safeguards, disengagement can be considered an acceptable risk and not an unjustifiable gamble, as long as in all stages the balance of power is maintained, so that at no specific point do the Russians have an unfair advantage.

2. In view of the increase in strategic depth, disengagement does not mean a weakening of the Western position.

3. German contingents, although smaller and without nuclear weapons, will still play their role in the defence of German territory if necessary; in the event of war Germany's membership of NATO, terminated by the political settlement resulting from disengagement, would be automatically restored.

4. The national armies of Eastern Europe, no longer satellites of Russia, will become allies of the West in the event of Soviet aggression, and come to their aid in carrying out the relevant undertakings of the European Security Pact.

5. There will be no need for the withdrawal of the American troops, which will in any case be gradually reduced.

6. The redeployment of troops and establishments will not cause the collapse of NATO (after all, when NATO was first conceived, German participation was not even contemplated).

From the point of view of the West, therefore, although admittedly certain calculated risks will have to be taken, the political advantages resulting from disengagement are sufficient to make it seriously worthy of consideration. In the first article in his series in the *New York Herald Tribune*,[56] Sir John Slessor said:

[56] "Test the Soviets on Disengagement," January–February, 1958.

> It would be foolish to pretend there are no risks about this—
> of course there are serious risks: the whole situation is a balance
> of risks. . . . I'd have thought on balance the political advan-
> tages would be overwhelming—including the obvious one that
> to separate in this way the military frontiers of East and West
> would reduce the chances of an accidental stumbling into a war
> nobody wants.

But in any case, there would be no harm in putting
Soviet words to the test. Congressman Henry S. Reuss
said in a speech at Cornell University: "None of this
Communist talk has ever been tested by serious negotiations.
All of it has been contradicted by negative talk at other
times. And all of it is no doubt replete with diplomatic
pitfalls." [57]

As far as Russia is concerned, disengagement will
assuage her deep-rooted fears of German aggression, which,
after all, are not unjustified. This will be especially true if
Germany is not allowed to have nuclear weapons. Official
West German sources would doubtless say that it is absurd
to maintain that twelve German divisions could be a
menace to the powerful Soviet Union. Yet within five years
Western Germany alone will have a potential of some two
million men under arms, not to mention considerable manpower resources in Eastern Germany.

The setting up of a broad belt of neutral countries in
Eastern Europe will provide Russia with the additional
guarantee of security on her western borders, the search
for which is one of the predominant features of the Soviet
policy. Further, the Soviet leaders will have nothing to
fear from those countries, with their national armed forces
limited under an international agreement and subject to
inspection and control.

As far as Germany is concerned, disengagement is the
only way to achieve reunification. Whether the Germans
in the Federal Republic would be glad of an economic
merger is another matter. But the status of military non-

[57] April 14, 1958.

alignment will not in any way prevent Germany from playing the fullest part in the life of Western—or, strictly speaking, reunited—Europe, to which by culture and civilisation she belongs.

Finally, for the countries of Eastern Europe disengagement will be the only way of regaining their freedom and enabling them to take an active part in the economic, cultural and other activities of reunited Europe, where words like " Iron Curtain " and " satellite " will be things of the past.

One thing is certain, and that is that there is no prospect of any satellites of the Titoist sort, as some political or military commentators suggest,[58] because the withdrawal of Soviet troops would mean to the countries of Eastern Europe the end of their satellite status.

In his article, " Sur les Aspects Militaires du ' Degagement ' en Europe," [59] General Genevey expressed the view that the demilitarised zone in the Rhineland gave Europe only a " short respite." When Hitler broke the Versailles Treaty in 1936 by occupying the Rhineland, he claimed there were only two alternatives: either to accept the *fait accompli*—which led to war three years later—or to oppose Hitler, which " would have meant an immediate war." He ignores all the available historical evidence which points to the fact that, had France decided to resist, there would have been no war at all. The commanders of the few German battalions had orders to withdraw immediately in case of the slightest counter-action by the French. Had the French Prime Minister Sarraut and his Commander-in-Chief, General Gamelin, ordered even a partial mobilisation Hitler's wild gamble would have ended in complete failure, leaving the German generals who had plotted against him to put an end to his career. It was this incident, as Monsieur Spaak so truly said, which, even more than Munich, laid the foundations for the last war.[60] It was not

[58] See Lt.-Col. F. Miksche, *The Failure of Atomic Strategy*, p. 77.
[59] *Politique Etrangère*, No. 2, 1959.   [60] *Foreign Affairs*, p. 362.

the failure of the demilitarised zone to fulfil its task, but the lack of courage and will to resist on the part of the French which tempted Hitler. A neutral zone with strong national armed forces, covered by the international guarantees, would not give the Russians any such temptation.

This analysis of the military arguments advanced against disengagement would be far from complete if mention were not made of the arguments put forward by several prominent writers against schemes for arms limitation and control in a European zone.

The arguments put forward by Mr. H. Kissinger in his valuable article, " In Search for Stability," deserve special study:

> If, as seems quite probable, the Soviet Union rejects any reasonable programme for German reunification, there is likely to be mounting pressure for various arms-control schemes along the present political division of Europe, such as a troop freeze or thinning out of forces. The difficulty with most of these proposals is that they do not in themselves come to grips with the real security problem. They do not reduce the likelihood of a political upheaval in Germany—in fact, they may increase it. They do not affect materially the capability of the United States or of the Soviet Union to launch a sudden all-out attack. On the other hand, since present or planned NATO forces are already totally inadequate for offensive ground operations, most schemes for troop withdrawals would merely weaken the capability for local defence of the West without providing an additional reassurance to the Soviet Union. They would improve the offensive, but not the defensive, position of the U.S.S.R. Even a troop freeze has the result of keeping NATO from adapting itself to changed strategic relationship. Unless coupled with a reduction of Soviet forces, it would perpetuate an inequality which will represent a growing invitation to Soviet adventures as Soviet long-range missiles multiply.[61]

More important were his reservations against the setting up of a denuclearised zone in Europe:

> The most frequent suggestion is that a zone free of nuclear weapons be established in the centre of Europe. Given the

[61] *Foreign Affairs*, April, 1959, p. 550.

range of modern weapons, a denuclearised zone in Central Europe would not of itself affect the military situation decisively, assuming that nuclear weapons can be situated in the Low Countries and France. It would create a psychological and political imbalance, for the aggressor would retain his full nuclear arsenal, while the area most menaced would be without the ability to retaliate.

Curiously enough, Mr. Kissinger's arguments overlapped with those of General von Senger und Etterlin [62] that an atom-free zone would not guarantee immunity against atomic destruction. Mr. Khrushchev's words in Warsaw on July 21 are relevant:

> Both the Western countries and the Soviet Union should undertake to treat the territories of the countries covered by this zone as situated beyond the range of rocket and nuclear weapons, and to respect the status of that region. The United Nations could be invited to take part in some form or another in the solution of the problem.

Indeed, in the light of the reservations expressed by several prominent men on the imbalance which would result from the " de-atomisation " of certain areas, Mr. Khrushchev's proposals for the formulation of an international agreement with the participation of UNO deserved great attention. For unless the atom-free zones could be made immune from atomic attack all these schemes would remain not only futile but dangerous.

Furthermore, General Genevey wrote in his article " Sur les Aspects Militaires du ' Degagement ' en Europe ":

> In view of the increasing range of modern means of delivery, aircraft and missiles, the regional limitations would be deprived of any practical purpose in all the zones proposed in Central Europe: it would be possible to intervene from the bases located outside against the targets in the zone and above it. [63]

General Genevey would be surprised to find that his views not only coincided with but were even supported by Mr. Khrushchev's own words in Warsaw on July 21:

[62] *Supra,* p. 337. [63] *Politique Etrangère,* No. 2, 1959, p. 250.

If we consider the range and power of contemporary rocket and nuclear weapons, a mere 100, 200 or 300 kilometres is of no real importance. Thus, rocket- and atom-free zones in a part of Soviet territory will give no guarantees to the Scandinavian countries.

Unless the immunity of atom-free zones from strategic atomic weapons is guaranteed, any such schemes must be treated with great caution.

The setting up of zones of arms limitation *per se* would contribute nothing to the reduction of tension, and would certainly not bring about the settlement of the fundamental causes of the tension. Their value is not as an end in themselves, but as a step forward towards other solutions; they must eventually lead to those supreme goals—German reunification and the liberation of Eastern Europe.

11

Blue-Print

WE have examined the various arguments for and against disarmament and attempted to expose the fallacy inherent in the *status quo*. The time has now come to be more positive.

> . . . The European stalemate is not necessarily permanent. Some day, perhaps, the Europeans will no longer feel the need for the presence of American troops as a symbol of deterrence and the Soviets will no longer insist on politico-ideological conformity from the rulers of Eastern Europe.[1]

But before trying to formulate a plan the basic principles must be established.

Basic Principles

Political and Military Measures

This solution, which for convenience' sake we shall call Disengagement, is an interweaving of military measures for limited disarmament in a limited area and of political settlement. Military measures must precede, not follow, a political settlement, to create an atmosphere of *détente* in which a political settlement can be put into effect.

In an article entitled "Disengagement," *Bulletin* suggested the following definition of the word:

> Disengagement is, strictly speaking, the physical separation of the bulk of the Western and the Soviet forces as a result of setting up a zone between them, which will be either demilitarised or manned by the national armed forces. Further, this expression could also be applied to the elimination of nuclear weapons from such a zone.[2]

The military aspect of this definition is satisfactory. Yet it is only partly correct. Any military measure which does

---

[1] Aron, *op. cit.*, p. 91. [2] April 13, 1959.

not imply the withdrawal of foreign troops (such as the first version of the Rapacki Plan) cannot create the necessary conditions for a political settlement—an integral part of disengagement.

History has seen some very successful examples of neutral or neutralised zones. Philip Noel-Baker describes the Rush-Bagot Agreement of 1817 between the British and United States Governments, which was signed as a result of the perspicacity of Castlereagh and in spite of the opposition of the military advisers. He quotes some prominent British historians. For instance, G. M. Trevelyan:

> Before Castlereagh's career as Foreign Secretary ended, the fortunes of Anglo-American peace had been established on the sound basis of disarmament along the border, enabling future generations to weather many fierce storms and to settle a frontier problem that no other Great Power would have been able to decide without war.

Mr. Noel Baker then adds his own comments:

(1) The disarmament was effected in an area which was regarded as of vital strategic importance.

(2) It was opposed by the military advisers of both Governments and for some years their views prevailed.

(3) It was agreed only after a " sharp struggle " in the British Cabinet.

(4) Those who opposed it said that it left [the weaker] party " defenceless." [3]

How easy it is to find an analogy between the situation which preceded the signature of that momentous agreement and the present situation in Europe.

Two Principles

The Plan combines two principles: first, the gradual disengagement from the area covered by the Plan of

[3] *The Arms Race*, pp. 509–518.

foreign armed forces and their military establishments; and, secondly, the diplomatic engagement by the Great Powers, the signatories of the Plan, to guarantee the political settlement resulting from military disengagement.

Stages

The Plan will have to be realised by stages, each stage drawing upon the experience of the previous one.

The primary condition is that the withdrawal of armed forces and their establishments, and in particular of their airfields and launching sites, must not prejudice the existing balance of power or impair the security of either side. An efficient system of inspection and control must be agreed upon and put into operation before proceeding with military measures of disengagement. The more efficient the system, the more will it contribute to the essential atmosphere of mutual confidence.

Withdrawal from Alliances

The countries covered by the Plan—Germany (to be re-united in the second stage), Poland, Hungary and Czecho-slovakia—will have to withdraw from their military alliances, but they will be free to develop economic and cultural relations with their neighbours and will do so in the second stage.

As these countries will have their national armed forces, their status of military neutrality can be called—in Sir John Slessor's term—one of " military non-alignment."

This form of armed neutrality, based upon national conventional armed forces and the " will to resist," has nothing to do with a similar word, " neutralism," which is associated with Gandhi's philosophy of passive resistance and of that policy of Lord Russell and Sir Stephen King-Hall that Great Britain should adopt a policy of unilateral atomic disarmament.

Defensive Alliances

The countries of the area will be free to form defensive alliances among themselves, but their national armies will be armed with conventional weapons only; in other words, the whole area will be an " atom-free area." The size of the national contingents will be limited under the clauses of the Plan and subject to international control. The same arrangements as for international control will apply to the " de-atomisation " of the area.

Foreign Troops

On no account will foreign troops be allowed to enter the area or be invited by the government of any of the countries concerned. Any such attempt will be considered violation of the neutrality guaranteed by the Great Powers.

We have to disagree with the view Sir John Slessor took in his articles in the *New York Herald Tribune*, in which he suggested applying sanctions against re-entry in Germany's case only. As Mr. Kissinger said in his penetrating article, " Missiles and the Western Alliance " :

> A policy of disengagement which has no answer, political or military, to the problems of upheaval in the Soviet satellite orbit, or to the return of the Soviet forces under another pretext, is likely to bring about the very conditions it seeks to avoid.[6]

Discrimination such as Sir John Slessor suggested would give the Russians a chance to perpetuate their hold over the area from which their troops have been withdrawn. It could serve only to defeat the whole object of the Plan.

Guarantees

Neutrality and territorial integrity will have to be guaranteed by the Great Powers and covered by a European Security Pact, of which the U.S.A. and Russia will be the main signatories. This pact will include non-discriminatory sanctions for all the countries of the area. The problem of

[6] *Foreign Affairs*, April, 1958, p. 396.

whether the sanction to be applied will be in the megaton or the kiloton range—a Big Deterrent or a graduated one—is outside the scope of our deliberations.

Abstention from Propaganda

The West must not encourage violent changes of régime in Eastern Europe, or use the area as an ideological battle-field against Russia. There must be no attempt to present the Soviet withdrawal as a Western victory or distorting facts and intentions. Russia must not attempt any subversion or ideological infiltration into the area.

Polish-German Frontier

The question of the German-Polish frontier must be settled before this Plan comes into operation. The frontier must be guaranteed by the signatories of the Plan.

Elections

Free all-German elections will be organised in the second stage under the supervision of the United Nations. Details will be settled by the two German Governments, which after the elections will merge into that of a reunited Germany.

Outline

It is necessary to work out a plan which not only complies with our moral principles but which facilitates the creation of conditions for joint action in pursuit of the targets desired by all and easily attainable.[7]

The Plan will be put into operation in two stages.

Preliminary Plan

In view of the many complications, both military and political, which could arise during the implementation of

---

[7] Senator E. de la Vallée-Poussin, " Du Plan van Zeeland au Plan Rapacki,' *Revue Generale Belge*, March 1958, p. 17.

the Plan, the preliminary plan will be limited to military measures amounting to limited disarmament. However, there will be a proviso that it must be followed with as short an interval as possible by a political settlement. The agreement will stress that these military measures are not intended to freeze the political *status quo* in the area covered by them.

1. All foreign conventional armed forces—NATO troops in Western Germany and Soviet troops in Eastern Germany—will slowly and by stages, to be agreed by negotiations, move back from the central dividing line: this movement of troops will, in fact, incorporate both Sir Anthony Eden's " thinning out " process and the suggestions put before the United Nations by Mr. Aiken in 1957. The area along the demarcation line vacated by foreign troops must not be filled by the national armies of Western and Eastern Germany: the confrontation of the Bundeswehr and the National People's Army could jeopardise the whole plan at the very start. The present demarcation line, which will become a political frontier and will be the starting-point of a " thinning out " process, must therefore be manned by detachments of an International Police Force. This means that the United Nations will play an increasingly important part in the whole procedure. In view of the fact that the whole mechanism will be put into operation as a result of an agreement with the Russians, there is no likelihood of a Soviet veto in the Security Council or of manoeuvrings at the General Assembly. The foundation of the whole scheme must be one of mutual good will.

2. The gradual withdrawal of foreign troops will probably be accompanied by a reduction in their numbers. This military measure alone will involve a measure of agreement on the limited disarmament of conventional armed forces.

3. The redeployment of armed forces and their numerical reduction will be under international control, probably

under UNO. This measure will be a " pilot scheme for international control " or, as Sir Anthony Eden put it, " a practical experiment in the operative control of armaments."

4. Western and Soviet radar warning stations may remain in this area.

5. The size and the armaments of the national armies of the area must be agreed and subject to international control, but their armaments will be conventional only. In other words, the area will be de-nuclearised, or atom-free.

6. At this stage the national armies of Western Germany and of Eastern Europe will retain their membership of the existing military alliances.

7. The countries of the Warsaw Pact and of NATO may conclude a non-aggression pact. Russia, as a member of the Warsaw Pact, would, by implication, be included in its provisions.

This clause may well meet with resistance from Bonn, for the Pankow régime would be a partner to the signature of the international treaty (no doubt one of the reasons for which Bonn has so strongly resisted the Rapacki Plan).

8. One could safely assume that Russia will have no objections to effective control in the territories of Eastern Europe. As far as the governments of that area are concerned, they are definitely most eager to co-operate. Statements, for example, by Mr. Winiewicz, Polish Deputy Minister of Foreign Affairs, during his talk on the B.B.C. in May, 1959, leave no doubts about this.

Comprehensive Plan

The execution of the Preliminary Plan, an exclusively military measure, will take some months, possibly years. During this period the defence structure of both alliances will have to be refashioned, troops redeployed and operational plans redrafted. At the same time, it will provide an opportunity to acquire experience in the mechanism of disengagement and international control and inspection and will aid the creation of mutual confidence. This will lay the foundations for progress on the Comprehensive Plan, which will contain several important political clauses. The Comprehensive Plan will, as against the purely military character of the Preliminary one, consist of two parts—that is, of largely interdependent military and political measures.

This Comprehensive Plan has as its foundation, on the one hand, the basic principles as outlined above and, on the other, the various plans and proposals put forward during the last few years by such prominent men as M. van Zeeland, Sir Anthony Eden, Mr. Gaitskell and, not least, by the Soviet leaders.

MILITARY MEASURES

1. All foreign armed forces will complete their withdrawal, begun under the Preliminary Plan, from the German Federal Republic, Eastern Germany, Poland, Czechoslovakia and Hungary. The West may try in due course to negotiate with Russia for an extension of the area initially covered by this plan to include Rumania and, possibly, the Baltic States.

As far as the West is concerned, American and British armed forces, although numerically reduced, will remain on the continent of Europe in token of their active participation in a reorganised NATO. NATO will continue to exist as long as the political situation requires it—after all, it came into being primarily as a defensive alliance to counter the threat of armed aggression by Soviet Russia against Western Europe—but it will have to adapt itself to the new military and political situation and, above all, to the withdrawal of Germany from its ranks. If NATO is to survive, it must formulate a new military and political strategy. Mr. D. Healey's words are apposite:

> NATO's new strategy must not only promote confidence between the allies themselves, it must be also compatible with

a political settlement with Russia which opens the way to German unity. . . . The real problem is once more one of confidence within the alliance. Western Europe must be persuaded—as Norway, Greece and Turkey—that NATO will react effectively to a military threat even if American troops are not standing along the threatened line.[8]

As far as the Warsaw Pact is concerned, Russia will have to reorganise what remains of it after the withdrawal of Poland, Czechoslovakia and Hungary. In fact, she will probably disband it altogether.

If the European Security Pact, with its strong and unequivocal sanctions, inspires general confidence and if, as the result of disengagement, international tension gradually relaxes, the existing military alliances may become superfluous. As Fritz Erler put it: " . . . NATO, after all, is not an end in itself . . ."; he quoted President Eisenhower's words: " ' The present arrangements will be maintained as long as the threat exists.' " [9]

2. All countries of the area covered by the Plan will withdraw from their military alliances, adopting a policy of " military non-alignment." The countries of Eastern Europe, on the other hand, may be allowed to form a military defensive alliance between themselves, possibly within the framework of a Federation. Whether reunited Germany would join such a military alliance will depend greatly on the development of the political situation within the area and, above all, on the settlement of the issue of the German-Polish frontier.

3. The size and armaments of a national armed force of the area will be limited as a result of negotiations initiated under the Preliminary Plan. They will be subjected to international control and inspection. The armaments of these troops will be conventional only and the whole area will become " atom-free."

[8] *Observer*, June 7, 1959.
[9] *World Politics*, April, 1958, p. 372.

POLITICAL MEASURES

1. The whole area, freed from foreign armed forces and military alignments, will become a neutral zone covered by a European Security Pact, with the United States and the Soviet Union its main signatories, which will guarantee all frontiers in the area (fixed before the Plan comes into force) and will maintain their territorial integrity. Any attempt to violate the frontiers will be considered a *casus belli* involving sanctions which include, in the last instance, the use of the Big Deterrent.

This clause is, of course, a fundamental and controversial one. But we must bear in mind Senator de la Vallée-Poussin's words that the plan must " comply with our moral principles "; any compromise will lead to the downhill slippery path.

2. German reunification will take place immediately after the completion of the withdrawal of all foreign armed forces from both parts of Germany. The method of German reunification must be agreed upon; but free elections must not be considered as dogma, for they would lead to the complete disappearance of the Pankow régime. This would, of course, be a complete victory for Dr. Adenauer and they remain the focal point of the policy of Bonn. It is for this reason that any suggestion by the West or by Russia that there could be any other method of reunification, including Confederation, meets with an extremely negative reaction from official West German circles. We know the views of one of Dr. Adenauer's closest advisers and confidants, Professor Grewe, formerly Director of the Political Department in the Ministry of Foreign Affairs and at present West German Ambassador in Washington. In a recent article called " Ein Friedensvertrag mit Deutschland," he subjected the concept of Confederation to a bitter attack.[10] He marshalled all the legal arguments at his command and then continued by saying that Confederation

[10] *Europa Archiv.*, May, 1959.

would give the Federal Republic " no chance to assimilate the Soviet zone," [11] and that, on the contrary, Confederation, being a dangerous experiment, could serve only to bring about several irrevocable consequences:

> the legal recognition of the Ulbricht régime, the creation of a second German State, the annulment of the responsibility of the Four Powers to reunite Germany, the virtual destruction of our defence system, the disruption of the political and social structure of the Federal Republic.

In his summing-up he came to the grim conclusion that " the upshot of such a Confederation will be, in point of fact, Communist domination [*Gleichschaltung*] of the Federal Republic."

Despite the great authority which Professor Grewe undoubtedly enjoys, many other authoritative writers had rather different views. Max Beloff adopted a more dispassionate attitude.[12] In contradiction of Professor Grewe, who wrote that " historical experience of Confederation has been not too encouraging," referring to the Confederation of thirteen American States, Mr. Beloff remarked that

> the Germans have known the very loose confederation that was set up as a part of the settlement after the Napoleonic wars and the much tighter North German Confederation that was the direct prelude to the Bismarckian Empire.

He pointed out that it is East Germany, not the Federal Republic, which should be opposed to any concept of Confederation,

> for it is clear that, if there is no guarantee against external interference with the course of events, it is the East German régime that stands to lose in a free competition for the allegiance of the Germans as a whole. . . . It may indeed be a measure of the lack of political self-confidence of the West Germans that there should be so much dismay at the prospect of entering on a period of free competition in which so much would be in their favour.

---

[11] *Ibid.*, p. 310.
[12] " Which Road to German Unity? ", *Daily Telegraph*, February 5, 1959.

Equally, where Professor Grewe deplored the right of veto in a hypothetical confederation, Mr. Beloff wrote that

> it is, for instance, perfectly natural that some element of veto should exist in a confederal structure. Within the fields of the confederation's competence one cannot expect a simple majority to rule: otherwise the whole country might be brought within NATO or be armed with atomic weapons, or pursue revisionist frontier policies—all things that the Russians cannot be expected to accept.

His conclusions were very interesting:

> From the internal German point of view, federation might indeed provide, if not an immediate bridge to unity, at least some mitigation of the evils of the partition as well as machinery through which it might be possible to negotiate dismantling of some of the more oppressive features of the East German régime. . . . The real problems of the proposed confederation are not German but international. There must be a guarantee against external political intervention; the West must also decide what it has to gain—if anything—by accepting the idea of a German confederation outside its inner defensive system.

3. Reunification will take place within frontiers previously agreed and internationally guaranteed by the signatories of the plan and of the Security Pact. One of the most difficult hurdles will be the question of the German-Polish frontier. Although Mr. Gaitskell took a favourable attitude towards the existing frontier, Labour Party policy statements dealing with the issue of disengagement diplomatically avoided going into details. Yet in a recent article in *Foreign Affairs*, Mr. Gaitskell took the view that "as part of a wider agreement, Germany could and would accept the Oder-Neisse Line."[13] Although Monsieur van Zeeland expressed some reservations about this frontier, he too maintained that it must be internationally guaranteed: any modification of it must be agreed through the proper diplomatic channels. In "Debate of the Month" he wrote:

[13] July, 1958, p. 550.

. . . the negotiations would almost certainly involve a treaty determining Germany's Eastern frontier. Although German statesmen are naturally reticent on the subject, there is little doubt that they would be prepared to accept the existing frontier as permanent with perhaps minor adjustments if it was a part of a treaty including German reunification.[14]

Even General de Gaulle, at a Press conference on March 23, 1959, spoke of German reunification " within her present frontiers." And after a short visit to West Berlin, during which he spoke with Herr Brandt, Burgomaster of West Berlin, and Herr Lemmer, the Minister for All-German Affairs, Lord Birdwood, wrote:

I have always felt that the future fate of Europe may be hinged around the Polish-German relationship. If the bitterness of the past could be set aside and negotiations opened between the German Federal Republic and the Poles, the whole European situation would assume a sudden flexibility which could give a new look to any future meetings either between Foreign Ministers or Summit leaders. . . . As regards the Oder-Neisse Line—which is accepted as the heart of the whole problem—the situation can be reduced to one in which both sides have stated their maximum demand, yet both realise that in fact a compromise must be the answer.[15]

Unfortunately it is the attitude of the Bonn Government which jeopardises the chances. Although privately many German politicians will admit that they consider the former German territories in the east to be irrevocably lost, they can never do so in public. Such an action would be political suicide.

In the meantime, the revisionist movements in Federal Germany increase. During the course of 1959 mass meetings took place and resolutions were passed demanding the return not only of the former German territories in the east but of Alsace-Lorraine too, and requiring rectification of the frontier with Belgium and Denmark.

[14] *Western World*, July, 1958, p. 43.
[15] *Yorkshire Post*, February 25, 1959.

Conclusion

This task is, to the author's best ability, now fulfilled.

Part One attempted to expose the fallacy of the belief that the present *status quo* can be maintained in perpetuity. When this book was started at the end of 1958 it required great effort to keep abreast of the sequence of political events and not instead to be overtaken by them. The whole situation is extremely fluid; the failure of the two 1959 Geneva Conferences clearly demonstrates the fragility of the *status quo*, which depends for its strength upon an armaments race, and which has yet become the corner-stone of the policy of the West. As Monsieur van Zeeland said in his address at the Atlantic Congress in June 1959 in London: "One of the most regrettable features of NATO which emerges from these two shortcomings is its disappointing, obstinate and even dangerous immobilism." These blunt words can be applied with equal truth to the official policy of the West.

Senator de la Vallée-Poussin, too, warned the West against

> giving added weight to the impression already existing in the minds of the public following spectacular and repeated Soviet initiatives and Western refusals, that the Atlantic Treaty countries, lacking drive, prefer to maintain an undesirable *status quo*, and that the U.S.S.R. is the champion of evolution towards a more stable peace.[16]

Part Two reviewed the history of negotiations during the last fifteen years or so, from which it emerged on how many occasions the positions of both sides overlapped. The possibility of an agreement was frequently within easy reach. Now, again, the chances of reaching agreement with the Russians have considerably improved. Certainly both sides sincerely want to settle their differences: Denis Healey has said that

[16] *Military Aspects of a Zone of Controlled Armaments in Europe.*

at present, however, Russia seems ready to negotiate the limitation and reduction of armaments in Central Europe on terms which would not only give her no net advantage, but would relieve NATO of some painful strategic dilemmas.[17]

And both the U.S.A. and Great Britain are keen to reach agreement with Russia, but the attitude of other members of the Atlantic Alliance towards this fundamental issue is not identical. In view of the tremendous popularity President Eisenhower enjoyed during his last trip to Europe, it is to be hoped that he will be able to carry with him all the members of the Alliance. The will is certainly there. On his return to Washington he said: " We are prepared to make a real beginning towards solving the problem of a divided Germany."

There is a French proverb: " *Mieux vaut tard que jamais . . .*"

Even a superficial study of the negotiations for the settlement of European problems, and in particular of the position and role of Germany in the defence of Europe, shows that the key to peace is the solution of German problems. The solution of German problems turns on the settlement of the question of her participation in NATO. This is the king-pin of Western policy, a policy which is, at least under present circumstances, incapable of fulfilment. Many people who advocate disengagement have expressed the view that German neutrality must be what Mr. Gaitskell called " the price for her reunification." As Fritz Erler put it: " A unified Germany would remain a partner of the free world even if, in order to exist, it might have to be excluded from membership of the Atlantic Alliance." [18]

But at the same time, the reunification of Germany alone and her " special status " is inconceivable without the simultaneous neutralisation of some countries of Eastern Europe.

---

[17] *The Observer*, September 15, 1959.
[18] " Debate of the Month," *Western World*, May, 1959, p. 18.

Part Three analysed the arguments for and against disengagement in its various forms. The author has put forward his own plan, in which he has tried to profit by the wisdom of those who have advocated disengagement over the preceding years.

An attempt has been made to convince the reader that the policy of the *status quo*, based upon the " delicate balance of terror," is not the best method of securing a stable peace. No less an authority than Mr. Lester Pearson, the former Canadian Minister for External Affairs and Nobel Peace Prize-winner, has stated that

> security cannot be guaranteed, even on a military basis, merely by an overwhelming superiority of arms. . . . In any case, the superiority would be only temporary. . . . The vicious circle of fear and arms, insecurity and more arms would begin, and the ending would not be a happy one either for security or for freedom, even if no shots were ever fired.
>
> Security has not in the past and cannot in the future be guaranteed by arms alone: lasting peace can be gained only through international friendship and understanding.[19]

Both President Eisenhower and Mr. Macmillan put special emphasis on the dangers of a thermonuclear war and on the necessity of securing peace. As President Eisenhower said during his London television broadcast, " . . . peace is an imperative." Mr. Khrushchev, too, has recognised that " in our day there are only two ways: peaceful co-existence or the most destructive war in history. There is no third choice."

Until a solution is found to the present military and political stalemate in Europe, the world will continue its slow but inexorable drift towards war. If the new trend in Soviet strategic thinking really is towards so-called " preemptive strategy," the world is living on a knife-edge.

A solution in the form of a comprehensive disengagement, properly negotiated in an atmosphere of mutual good will and with all necessary safeguards, is the only one

19 " A Measured Defence for the West," *Orbis*, Winter, 1958, pp. 428–429.

which can secure peace in Europe. No pretence can be made that this, like any other course, will not be fraught with risks. One of the greatest virtues of statesmanship is the courage to take calculated risks. The present situation in Europe is the supreme challenge.

APPENDICES

Appendix 1

Soviet Outline of a Peace Treaty with Germany

Note from the Soviet Government to the Three Western Powers, March 10, 1952

THE Governments of the U.S.S.R., U.S.A., Britain and France consider that the drafting of a peace treaty must be done with the participation of Germany, represented by an all-German Government, and that the peace treaty with Germany must be based on the following foundations.

Foundations of Treaty

Participants: Britain, U.S.S.R., U.S.A., France, Poland, Czechoslovakia, Belgium, Holland and other States which with their armed forces took part in the war against Germany.

Political Provisions: (1) Germany to be set up as one State. Thus an end to be put to the division of Germany while a united Germany is to be provided with opportunities for development as an independent, democratic and peace-loving State.

(2) All armed forces of the Occupying Powers to be withdrawn from Germany not later than one year subsequent to the entry into force of the peace treaty. All foreign military bases on the territory of Germany to be liquidated at the same time.

(3) Democratic rights to be secured for the German people so that all persons under German jurisdiction, irrespective of race, sex, language, or religion, may enjoy the rights of man and the fundamental freedoms, including freedom of speech, press, religion, political convictions and assembly.

(4) Free functioning of democratic parties and organisations to be secured in Germany and their right to deal freely with their internal affairs, to hold rallies and meetings and to enjoy the freedom of the Press and of publication.

(5) The existence of organisations hostile to democracy and the cause of maintaining peace not to be allowed on the territory of Germany.

(6) All former members of the German army, including officers and generals, all former Nazis, excluding those who are serving sentences for the commission of crimes, to be granted civil and political rights on a par with all other German citizens to participate in building a peace-loving and democratic Germany.

(7) Germany to pledge herself not to enter into any coalitions or military alliances whatsoever directed against any Power which took part with its armed forces in the war against Germany.

Territory: The territory of Germany to be determined by the frontiers laid down by the decisions of the Potsdam Conference of the major Powers.

Economic Provisions: No restrictions whatsoever to be imposed on Germany regarding the development of a peaceful economy to serve the well-being of the German people. Furthermore, no restrictions to be imposed in respect of trade with other countries, sea navigation and access to world markets.

Military Provisions: (1) Germany to be allowed to have national land, air and sea forces essential to the defence of the country.

(2) Germany to be allowed to produce war materials and equipment in quantities and types not exceeding those necessary to arming the forces as laid down by the peace treaty.

Germany and the UN: States which have concluded a peace treaty with Germany to support Germany's request for membership of UN.

Appendix 2

Meeting of Foreign Ministers,
January 25–February 18, 1954

Speech by Mr. Eden, January 29, 1954

During my opening remarks at our first meeting last Monday, I gave my colleagues a general indication of the views of Her Majesty's Government on the German question.

We believe that the peaceful reunification of Germany and the conclusion of a Peace Treaty would fortify peace and relax tension.

The present unnatural division of the German nation means continuing instability and disunity in Europe, and thus contains the seeds of future conflict and ultimate disaster for us all.

This is the principal problem which has brought us together round this table.

We have a duty to find a just and lasting solution for it.

I informed my colleagues earlier this week that, when the time came for us to discuss German unity, we would have a constructive plan to present.

Accordingly I now wish to lay before you on behalf of the United Kingdom Delegation a Plan for German Reunification.

I know that my colleagues will want to study this plan carefully.

I shall welcome their comments upon it.

I believe that it represents a positive approach to this urgent problem.

If we can have a constructive discussion, and can reach agreement on the principles it sets out, then our work together in Berlin will have been truly fruitful.

We shall at last have made a significant advance on the road to European unity, prosperity and security.

I outlined on Monday the main elements of the plan.

Now that it is before us, it may be useful for me to explain rather more fully the five stages by which we suggest Germany should be reunited.

These stages are set out in the preamble to the plan.

I propose now to take them one by one, and to explain our position on them.

First, free elections throughout Germany.

381

This is, for us, the cardinal element of our plan—or, indeed, of any plan for German reunification.

For any democratic country, free elections are the only way of obtaining a true expression of the people's will.

Before we can deal with representatives of a United Germany we must be certain that those representatives have been freely chosen by the German people for themselves.

Only thus can we be sure that any agreement we reach with Germany is founded on German consent.

This is essential if such agreement is to be durable and a source of future co-operation, rather than of resentment and recrimination.

Free elections throughout Germany are the first essential step.

Our purpose is a Peace Treaty with Germany and the entry of a peaceful and democratic Germany into the United Nations.

We must therefore ensure that the Government which signs the Peace Treaty, and which represents the new Germany in the United Nations, is truly representative of the German people.

If elections are to be really free, there must be certain safeguards established well before and during the elections.

Moreover, under the abnormal conditions prevailing today in Germany, we think it essential that there should be adequate supervision.

This will ensure that the safeguards are observed and the elections properly conducted.

In short, the German people must be enabled freely to choose their own representatives.

It must also be clear to the Germans themselves, and to the rest of the world, that this choice has been free.

The first step must be to prepare an all-German electoral law.

We have carefully studied this problem and have come to the conclusion that the only way of ensuring the due application throughout Germany of an adequate law is for that law to be prepared and promulgated by the Four Powers themselves.

We four must be willing, whenever necessary, to discharge the responsibilities we bear in Germany.

On the other hand, both the West German Bundestag and the Assembly in the Soviet Zone have prepared drafts of all-German electoral laws.

These contain much valuable material.

A Four-Power draft, therefore, should draw very largely upon them.

I have mentioned the need for adequate safeguards for the elections.

Clearly, these must be provided for in the electoral law itself, so that we can be sure that they will be effective throughout Germany.

My colleagues will find what we regard as the main essential safeguards set out in Section I of the plan, under the heading "Guarantees for free elections."

I need not read them to my colleagues.

I think they speak for themselves, and I hope that we shall have no difficulty in agreeing on them, and in ensuring that each of them is effectively covered in the Electoral Law and in its practical application.

Then comes the question of the supervision of the elections.

To suggest that elections in a country like Germany require supervision could perhaps be misrepresented as derogatory or insulting to the German people.

I need hardly say that it is not in this spirit that we have made this proposal, and I am confident that it will not be so regarded by the German voters themselves.

I do not doubt the ability of the German elector, who has learnt many lessons from the past, to choose his representatives with wisdom and discrimination, provided he is truly free to do so.

But conditions are not yet normal in Germany.

Since the end of the war, despite all our efforts, the gulf dividing the country has become increasingly wide.

As a result, bitterness and distrust have also increased.

Two different political systems confront each other across the line dividing the Soviet Zone from the rest of Germany.

The object of the elections which we are proposing is to enable the German people freely to determine the system under which their united country is to be governed.

I believe that the Germans themselves would insist that those elections, which are of such vital importance to their own future, should be under adequate supervision.

Thus they themselves, no less than their friends abroad, can be satisfied that the essential rights and freedoms outlined in our plan are available to every German.

Supervision of the elections, therefore, there must be.

In our plan, we have suggested a method by which this can be carried out.

There should be a Supervisory Commission, on which each of the Four Powers should be represented.

We can discuss whether or not it should include representatives of neutral countries.

The Commission should work on a committee basis.

But, if it is to carry out its tasks effectively, decisions must be taken by majority vote.

I need not attempt at this stage to deal with the functions and powers of the Commission.

As our plan brings out, its main task will be to ensure that the elections take place in genuine freedom and that the electoral law is strictly complied with.

Whatever we finally agree regarding the composition and organisation of the Commission must, I think, be embodied in the electoral law, thus giving the Commission a proper legal basis.

We four Ministers cannot undertake the complicated task of drafting the electoral law ourselves.

But, before we assign such a task to others, we must ourselves agree the principles on which the five stages in our plan are based.

When we have done this, we shall have completed the first essential stage of our work on the German problem.

We can then reasonably claim that we have at last made real progress towards our common goal of a German Peace Treaty.

I therefore suggest that we should first discuss and agree these principles with a view to giving instructions accordingly to a Working Group.

This could most conveniently consist of the four High Commissioners in Germany, or their representatives.

It should work out the necessary details and submit a report to the four Governments.

The plan indicates what we think should be the essential elements of this report, and the general time-table which the working group should adopt.

The next stage in the plan is, of course, the elections themselves.

They should take place as soon as possible after the Four Powers have promulgated the electoral law.

These will result in the first truly representative all-German National Assembly for many years.

This Assembly's first task must be to prepare a Constitution for United Germany.

Meanwhile, and indeed until an all-German Government can assume full control, I am sure that there will be great advantage if we keep in being at least part of the supervisory machinery set up under the electoral law.

Only thus we ensure the continued observance throughout Germany of the conditions of genuine freedom which will have been established.

This is a matter to which the Working Group must give attention.

While the new National Assembly is drafting the Constitution, it may find it convenient to establish some form of provisional all-German Authority.

This would help the Assembly to draft the Constitution.

It could also prepare the nucleus of the future all-German administrative machine to take over, when the time comes, from the existing German machinery in the four zones.

There is another task which it might undertake.

We all wish to conclude a Peace Treaty as quickly as possible.

The National Assembly could, if it wished, request the provisional Authority to open preliminary negotiations with the Four Powers for the Peace Treaty.

All this should be provided for in the Four-Power law.

Next, we come to the adoption of the Constitution and the subsequent, and I hope rapid, formation of an all-German Government.

The Constitution will be the basis on which the all-German Government is formed.

This Government will then at once assume full responsibility for negotiating and concluding the Peace Treaty.

At the same time, other institutions, such as, perhaps, a Supreme Court, can be established, as provided by the Constitution.

Pending the formation of the all-German Government, we must obviously avoid creating a vacuum.

Therefore, the German Federal Republic and the German Administration in the Soviet Zone must continue in being, in order to ensure continuity of administration and the execution of German international obligations.

But when an all-German Government has been formed, there will have to be a transfer of powers to it; and the Federal Republic and the East German Administration must at the right time come to an end.

In our opinion, the decisions about this, especially on timing and procedure, must be left to the National Assembly.

Again, there must not be a complete break in German international relationships with other countries.

The all-German Government, once established, must be free to assume such of the international rights and obligations of the Federal Republic, and of the Soviet Zone of Germany, as it considers necessary.

It must also be free to conclude other international agreements, if it so desire, provided of course that they are consistent with the United Nations Charter.

On the other hand, our four Governments have special rights and responsibilities in Germany until a Peace Treaty comes into force.

The Plan sets out how certain of those rights should be exercised.

So far as Her Majesty's Government are concerned, our rights will be exercised only in the general interests of peace and with special regard to the interests of the German people.

Our present practice in regard to our relations with the German Federal Government is, I hope, sufficient guarantee of this.

The final section of the plan deals with the signature and entry into force of the Peace Treaty.

I think it explains itself.

I hope that what I have said may help my colleagues in their study of the plan.

I look forward to discussing it with them as soon as they feel ready to do so.

May I once again summarise the essential features of the plan and, in particular, the basic thought which runs through it all?

The question of freedom is inseparable from the problem of elections.

We must reach agreement on free elections as the first step.

We must also agree that the all-German Government resulting from those elections must itself be free, especially in the following respects:

    (i) It must be free to assume any international rights and obligations of the Federal Republic or of the East German régime, which are consistent with the United Nations Charter.

    (ii) It must be free to negotiate the Peace Treaty. A dictated Treaty would be unacceptable to Germany and to ourselves.

    (iii) It must be free to associate with other nations for peaceful purposes.

Thus the basic principle of our whole plan is that of genuine freedom.

We believe that that is the only principle upon which to found a new Germany, which will be able to join, as an equal, peaceful and democratic partner, with the other countries of Europe and of the world, in the advance towards peace and prosperity.

Appendix 3

Meeting of Heads of Government, July 18–23, 1955

STATEMENT BY THE RIGHT HONOURABLE SIR ANTHONY EDEN, M.P., JULY 18, 1955

THIS Conference is unique in history because the conditions in which we meet are unmatched in human experience. We all know what unparalleled resources the scientific and technical discoveries of our age have placed within our reach. We have only to stretch out our hand and the human race can enter an age of prosperity such as has never been known. It is equally clear how utterly destructive must be the conditions of any conflict in which the Great Powers are engaged.

There was a time when the aggressor in war might hope to win an advantage and to realise political gain for his country by military action. The more overwhelming the military power the more tempting was the prize and the less might the aggressor expect to have to pay. We can each one of us think of examples of this in history. Nothing of the kind is possible now. No war can bring the victor spoils; it can only bring him and his victim utter annihilation. Neutrals would suffer equally with the combatants.

These are stern facts out of which we can perhaps win enduring peace at last. The deterrent against warlike action holds up a warning hand. But the deterrent cannot of itself solve international problems or remove the differences that exist between us. It is in an attempt to make progress with these problems and differences that we are met here today. And at this Conference we have to deal with them mainly in the context of Europe.

What is the chief among them? There can surely be no doubt of the answer. The unity of Germany. As long as Germany is divided, Europe will be divided. Until the unity of Germany is restored there can be neither confidence nor security in this Continent. Within the limits of our Western Zone we have done all we can to unify Germany. We have broken down the barriers between our zones. We have treated the three Western areas as an economic unit and given them a Federal Government. We have brought the occupation to an end.

Quite apart from the larger issues of German reunification it would mark a real advance if, pending our negotiations for German unity, the Soviet Government felt able to relax the physical restrictions which now aggravate the division of Germany, and prevent contact between Germans in the East and West.

Now I must turn to the wider issues of German unification. What is the reason why the Berlin Conference failed a year ago? We must examine this as dispassionately as we can in order to see what progress we can now make from the apparently fixed positions which the Great Powers on both sides then felt obliged to take. At the Berlin Conference [1] the West proposed the unification of Germany with free elections and the free right of Germany to choose her own foreign policy. Under the so-called Eden Plan Germany could have chosen either association with the West or association with the East or neutrality. But the Soviet Government was unable to accept that plan. Yet we all know in our hearts that Germany must be united and that a great country cannot be permanently prevented from freely deciding its own foreign policy.

The reason why the Berlin Conference failed was because one of the Powers there believed that a united Germany, rearmed and exercising its choice to join the NATO alliance, would constitute an increased threat to its safety and security. I am not now going to argue whether those fears are justified. In these last ten years there have been plenty of occasions for suspicions and alarms. These have found expression in heavy armament programmes. To try to deal with these issues in their wider aspect we have all agreed to work through the Disarmament Commission of the United Nations. We welcome the substantial progress which has recently been made there and the important measure of common thinking which has now emerged between the various proposals of the Western Powers and those recently set before us by the Soviet Government. All these discussions will go on, but, as we know, the immediate need is to make a practical start.

The urgent problem is how to begin the process of reducing tensions and removing suspicion and fear. There is also the practical question of how we can devise and operate together an effective control of armaments and of armed forces.

To reunify Germany will not of itself increase or reduce any threat which may be thought to exist to European security. Everything will depend on the conditions under which reunification takes place. I wish therefore now to suggest that we should consider a number of inter-related proposals which are intended to do two

---

[1] " Miscellaneous No. 15 (1954)," Cmd. 9080.

things. First, they are calculated to meet the apprehension of increased danger which some at Berlin felt might follow the acceptance of our plan. Secondly, they are intended to make a practical experiment in the operative control of armaments. This, if locally successful in Europe, might, as it were, extend outwards from the centre to the periphery. If we can once establish a sense of security over the Continent of Europe—if we can create an effective system to reduce tensions here—can we not hope that this first success will be the preliminary for wider and more far-reaching understanding? We have therefore had in mind certain ideas which we think could be helpful to this end.

As I have said, our purpose is to ensure that the unification of Germany and her freedom to associate with countries of her choice shall not involve any threat to anybody. There are no doubt many ways of doing this. To illustrate what I have in mind let me give some examples. These will consist partly of actions and partly of assurances. Let us take the latter first. We would be prepared to be parties to a security pact of which those round this and a united Germany might be members. By its terms each country could declare itself ready to go to the assistance of the victim of aggression, whoever it might be. There are many forms which such a pact might take. We would be ready to examine them and to set out our views about them. We would propose to inscribe any such agreement under the authority of the United Nations. It would also be our intention that if any member country should break the peace that country would forfeit thereby any rights which it enjoys at present under existing agreements.

Secondly, we would be ready to discuss and try to reach agreement, as to the total of forces and armaments on each side in Germany and the countries neighbouring Germany. To do this it would be necessary to join in a system of reciprocal control to supervise the arrangement effectively. All those represented here would, we hope, be partners in this, together with a united Germany. It would be understood that any proposals in this field would not exclude, or delay, the work of the United Nations Disarmament Commission, to which we attach great importance.

Is there some further reassurance we can give each other? There is one which I certainly think should be considered. We should be ready to examine the possibility of a demilitarised area between East and West.

It is true that these ideas are limited in the first instance to the area of Europe, but I am sure that they could help us here in practice and perhaps as an example. I will sum them up. There is the suggestion of a mutual security pact. There is the prospect of an agreement about the total of forces and armaments of the two groups both in Germany and in the countries neighbouring Germany. This would be subject to reciprocal supervision. There is the concept of a demilitarised area.

If we could start work on these lines we should have a chance of providing a constructive and encouraging plan to ensure peace for Europe. These ideas would give real security: and it is for the lack of that security that Germany is kept divided today. I suggest that they should be further examined. I have given only the summary of them here.

There are other aspects of our work together which I could have mentioned. For instance we would warmly welcome any proposals which would result in a greater freedom of movement and exchange of contacts between our peoples.

But it seems to me that it will be by our success in achieving some practical results about the future of Germany and European security that this Conference will be judged. We want to agree on two things: the urgent need for the unification of Germany and the broad outline of the means by which it can be achieved. I do not pretend that our ideas are anything in the nature of a complete plan but they are the outline sketch which once agreed upon could surely be filled in. If we can draw up something like this before we leave Geneva at the end of this Conference, the peoples of the world will not be disappointed.

Appendix 4

Meeting of Foreign Ministers, October 27–November 16, 1955

Outline of Terms of Treaty of Assurance on the Reunification of Germany by the Governments of France, the United Kingdom and the United States, October 28, 1955

The treaty, which would be concluded concurrently with an agreement on the reunification of Germany under the Eden Plan, would cover the following subjects:

1. *Renunciation of the Use of Force*

Each party would undertake to settle, by peaceful means, any international dispute in which it might be involved, and to refrain from the use of force in any manner inconsistent with the purposes of the United Nations.

2. *Withholding Support from Aggressors*

Each party would agree to withhold assistance, military or economic, to any aggressor, and any party could bring the aggression to the attention of the United Nations, and seek such measures as are necessary to maintain or to restore international peace and security.

3. *Limitation of Forces and Armaments*

In a zone comprising areas of comparable size and depth and importance on both sides of the line of demarcation between a reunified Germany and the Eastern European countries, levels for armed forces would be specified so as to establish a military balance which would contribute to European security and help to relieve the burden of armaments. There would be appropriate provisions for the maintenance of this balance. In parts of the zone which lie closest to the line of demarcation, there might be special measures relating to the disposition of military forces and installations.

4. *Inspection and Control*

The parties would provide information on an agreed progressive basis on their armed forces in the zone. There would be agreement on progressive procedures of mutual inspection to verify such data and to warn against any preparation for surprise attack.

5. *Special Warning System*

In order to provide added depth to the surveillance system on both sides and thus give further protection against surprise attack, provision could be made to establish—

(*a*) in the western part of the zone mentioned in paragraph 3, a radar warning system operated by the Soviet Union and the other eastern members of the treaty, and

(*b*) a like system in the eastern part of that zone operated by the NATO members of the treaty.

6. *Consultation*

There would be suitable provision for consultation among the parties to implement the treaty.

7. *Individual and Collective Self-Defence*

It would be provided that nothing in the treaty would impair or conflict with the right of individual and collective self-defence recognised by the United Nations Charter and Treaties under it. No party would continue to station forces in the territory of any other party without the latter's consent, and upon request of the party concerned any party would withdraw its forces within a stated period, unless these forces are present in the territory concerned under collective defence arrangements.

8. *Obligation to React against Aggression*

Each party would agree that armed attack in Europe by any party, which is also a NATO member, against any party which is not a NATO member, or vice versa, would endanger the peace and security which is the object of this treaty, and that all the parties would then take appropriate action to meet that common danger.

9. *Entry into Force by Stages*

The provisions would come into effect progressively at stages to be agreed.

Appendix 5

Meeting of Foreign Ministers, October 27–November 16, 1955

ANNEX II

GENERAL EUROPEAN TREATY ON COLLECTIVE
SECURITY IN EUROPE (BASIC PRINCIPLES)
PROPOSAL OF THE SOVIET UNION DELEGATION,
OCTOBER 28

1

FOR the purpose of ensuring peace and security and of preventing aggression against any State in Europe,

For the purpose of strengthening international co-operation in conformity with the principles of respect for the independence and sovereignty of States and non-interference in their internal affairs,

Striving to achieve concerted efforts by all European States in ensuring collective security in Europe instead of the formation of groupings of some European States directed against other European States, which gives rise to friction and strained relations among nations and aggravates mutual distrust,

Having in view that the establishment of a system of collective security in Europe would facilitate the earliest possible settlement of the German problem through the unification of Germany on a peaceful and democratic basis,

European States, guided by the purposes and principles of the Charter of the United Nations, conclude a General European Treaty on Collective Security in Europe the basic provisions of which are as follows:

1. All European States, irrespective of their social systems, and the United States of America as well, may become parties to the Treaty provided they recognise the purposes and assume the obligations set forth in the Treaty.

Pending the formation of a united, peace-loving, democratic German State, the German Democratic Republic and the German Federal Republic may be parties to the Treaty, enjoying equal rights with other parties thereto. It is understood that after the unification

393

of Germany, the united German State may be a party to the Treaty under the general provisions hereof.

The conclusion of the Treaty on Collective Security in Europe shall not affect the competence of the Four Powers—the Soviet Union, the United States, the United Kingdom and France—to deal with the German problem, which shall be settled in accordance with decisions previously taken by the Four Powers.

2. The States parties to the Treaty undertake to refrain from aggression against one another and also to refrain from having recourse to the threat or use of force in their international relations, and, in accordance with the Charter of the United Nations, to settle any dispute that may arise among them by peaceful means and in such a way as not to endanger international peace and security in Europe.

3. Whenever, in the view of any State party to the Treaty, there is a threat of an armed attack in Europe against one or more of the States parties to the Treaty, they shall consult one another in order to take effective steps to remove such threat and to maintain security in Europe.

4. An armed attack in Europe against one or several States parties to the Treaty by any State or group of States shall be deemed to be an attack against all the Parties to the Treaty. In the event of such an attack, such of the Parties, exercising the right of individual or collective self-defence, shall assist the State or States so attacked by all means at its disposal, including the use of armed force, for the purpose of re-establishing and maintaining international peace and security in Europe.

5. The States parties to the Treaty undertake jointly to discuss and determine as soon as possible the procedure under which assistance, including military assistance, shall be provided by the States parties to the Treaty in the event of a situation in Europe requiring a collective effort for the re-establishment and maintenance of peace in Europe.

6. The States parties to the Treaty, in conformity with the provisions of the Charter of the United Nations, shall immediately inform the Security Council of the United Nations of any action taken or envisaged for the purpose of exercising the right of self-defence or of maintaining peace and security in Europe.

7. The States parties to the Treaty undertake not to participate in any coalition or alliance and not conclude agreements the objectives of which are contrary to the purposes of the Treaty on Collective Security in Europe.

8. The States parties to the Treaty undertake to promote a broad economic and cultural co-operation among themselves as well as with other States through the development of trade and other economic relations and through the strengthening of cultural ties on a basis excluding any discrimination or restrictions which hamper such co-operation.

9. In order to implement the provisions of the Treaty which refer to consultations among its Parties and to consider questions arising in connection with the task of ensuring security in Europe, the following shall be provided for:

(*a*) Regular or, when required, special conferences at which each State shall be represented by a member of its Government or by some other specially designated representative;

(*b*) The setting up of a permanent consultative political committee, the duty of which shall be the preparation of appropriate recommendations to the governments of the States parties to the Treaty;

(*c*) The setting up of a military consultative organ the terms of reference of which shall be specified in due course.

10. Recognising the special responsibility of the permanent members of the United Nations Security Council for the maintenance of international peace and security, the States parties to the Treaty shall invite the Government of the Chinese People's Republic to designate representatives to the organs set up in accordance with the Treaty in the capacity of observers.

11. The present Treaty shall not impair in any way the obligations of European States under international treaties and agreements to which they are party, provided the principles and purposes of such agreements are in conformity with those of the present Treaty.

2

12. The States parties to the Treaty agree that during the first period (two or three years) of the implementation of measures for the establishment of the system of collective security in Europe under the present Treaty they shall not be relieved of the obligations assumed by them under existing treaties and agreements.

At the same time the States parties to existing treaties and agreements which provide for military commitments shall refrain from the use of armed force and shall settle by peaceful means all the disputes that may arise between them. Consultations shall also take place between the parties to the corresponding treaties and agreements in case any differences or disputes arise among them which might constitute a threat to the maintenance of peace in Europe.

13. Pending the conclusion of agreements on the reduction of armaments and the prohibition of atomic weapons and on the withdrawal of foreign troops from the territories of European countries, the States parties to the Treaty undertake not to take any further steps to increase their armed forces on the territories of other European States under treaties and agreements concluded by them previously.

14. The States parties to the Treaty agree that on the expiration of an agreed time-limit from the entry into force of the present Treaty, the Warsaw Treaty of May 14, 1955, the Paris Agreements of October 23, 1954, and the North Atlantic Treaty of April 4, 1949, shall become ineffective.

15. The duration of the Treaty shall be fifty years.

ANNEX III

DRAFT TREATY ON SECURITY IN EUROPE
PROPOSED BY THE SOVIET DELEGATION, OCTOBER 31

Inspired by the desire to strengthen peace and recognising the necessity to contribute in every possible way to reducing international tension and establishing confidence in relations between States,

Guided by the peaceful purposes and principles of the United Nations,

The Governments ....
....
have agreed to conclude the present Treaty.

The States parties to the Treaty solemnly declare that they assume the following obligations:

ARTICLE 1

The Contracting Parties undertake not to use armed force against one another and also to refrain from having recourse to the threat of force in their relations with each other and to settle any dispute that may arise among them by peaceful means.

ARTICLE 2

In the event that any one or several States parties to the Treaty is subjected to an armed attack in Europe by any State or group of States, the other States parties to the Treaty shall immediately render the State or States so attacked all such assistance, including military assistance, as may be deemed necessary for the purpose of re-establishing and maintaining international peace and security in Europe.

ARTICLE 3

The States parties to the Treaty undertake to refrain from rendering under any pretext any direct or indirect assistance to the attacking State in Europe.

ARTICLE 4

The States parties to the Treaty shall consult one another whenever, in the view of any one of them, there arises a threat of an armed attack in Europe against one or more of the States parties to the Treaty, in order to take effective steps to remove any such threat. They shall immediately conduct the necessary consultations whenever agreed steps may be required for the re-establishment of peace, in the event of an attack on any State party to the Treaty.

ARTICLE 5

The signatory States shall establish, by common consent, a special body (or bodies) for the purpose of holding the above-mentioned consultations and also for taking such other steps to assure security as may be found necessary in connection with the fulfilment by the States of their obligations under the present Treaty.

ARTICLE 6

The States parties to the Treaty agree that obligations under the present Treaty shall not infringe upon the obligations assumed by them under existing treaties and agreements.

ARTICLE 7

The assumption by States of obligations under the present Treaty shall not prejudice the right of the States parties to the Treaty to individual or collective self-defence in the event of an armed attack, as provided for in Article 51 of the United Nations Charter.

ARTICLE 8

The Treaty is of a provisional character and shall remain in effect until replaced by another, more extensive Treaty on European Security which shall replace the existing treaties and agreements.

ANNEX IV

Establishment of an all-German Council
Proposal by the Soviet Government, November 2

Guided by the desire to further the development of full co-operation between the German Democratic Republic and the German Federal Republic and the creation of conditions for the settlement of the German problem and for the reunification of Germany by means of free elections in conformity with the national interests of the German people and the interests of European security, the Foreign Ministers of the Soviet Union, the United States, the United Kingdom and France declare the following:

Under present conditions when the German people are deprived of the possibility of living in a united state, the need to bring about co-operation between the German Democratic Republic and the German Federal Republic which would facilitate the settlement of the problem of Germany's national reunification, is becoming ever more urgent. That purpose would be met by the establishment by agreement between the German Democratic Republic and the German Federal Republic of an all-German body to co-ordinate their efforts in the political, economic and cultural life of the German people and also to co-operate with other States in the consolidation of peace.

Such a representative body of the German people could be an all-German Council to be established on the basis of the following principles:

1. An all-German Council shall be formed, composed of the representatives of the parliaments of the German Democratic Republic and the German Federal Republic, as a consultative body to discuss matters, in the solution of which the German Democratic Republic and the German Federal Republic are interested.

2. Mixed committees shall be set up under the all-German Council, composed of representatives of the Governments of the German Democratic Republic and the German Federal Republic, on matters relating to economic and cultural ties between the two German States, German currency and intra-German financial transactions, customs, post and telegraph, communications, etc.

3. The all-German Council shall bring about accord on the numerical strength, armaments and disposition of units required to ensure the defence of the frontiers and territories of the German Democratic Republic and the German Federal Republic.

Appendix 6

Declaration by the Governments of the United States, United Kingdom, France and the Federal Republic of Germany

THE BERLIN DECLARATION—JULY 29, 1957

TWELVE years have elapsed since the end of the war in Europe. The hopes of the peoples of the world for the establishment of a basis for a just and lasting peace have nevertheless not been fulfilled. One of the basic reasons for the failure to reach a settlement is the continued division of Germany, which is a grave injustice to the German people and the major source of international tension in Europe.

The Governments of France, the United Kingdom and the United States, which share with the Soviet Union responsibility for the reunification of Germany and the conclusion of a peace treaty,

and

the Government of the Federal Republic of Germany, as the only Government qualified to speak for the German people as a whole,

wish to declare their views on these questions, including the question of European security, and the principles which motivate their policies in this regard.

1. A European settlement must be based on freedom and justice. Every nation has the right to determine its own way of life in freedom, to determine for itself its political, economic and social system, and to provide for its security with due regard to the legitimate interests of other nations. Justice requires that the German people be allowed to re-establish their national unity on the basis of this fundamental right.

2. The reunification of Germany remains the joint responsibility of the Four Powers who in 1945 assumed supreme authority in Germany, a responsibility which was reaffirmed in the Directive issued by the four Heads of Government in Geneva in July, 1955. At the same time the achievement of German reunification requires the active co-operation of the German people as a whole under conditions ensuring the free expression of their will.

3. The unnatural division of Germany and of its capital, Berlin, is a continuing source of international tension. So long as Germany remains divided, there can be no German peace treaty and no assurance of stability in Europe. The reunification of Germany in freedom is not only an elementary requirement of justice for the German people, but is the only sound basis of a lasting settlement in Europe.

4. Only a freely elected all-German Government can undertake on behalf of a reunified Germany obligations which will inspire confidence on the part of other countries and which will be considered just and binding in the future by the people of Germany themselves.

5. Such a government can only be established through free elections throughout Germany for an all-German National Assembly.

6. There should be no discrimination against a reunified Germany. Its freedom and security should not be prejudiced by an imposed status of neutralisation or demilitarisation. Its government should be free to determine its foreign policy and to decide on its international associations. It should not be deprived of the right recognised in the Charter of the United Nations for all nations to participate in collective measures of self-defence.

7. Re-establishment of the national unity of Germany in accordance with the freely expressed wishes of the German people would not in itself constitute a threat to Germany's neighbours nor would it prejudice their security. Nevertheless, so as to meet any preoccupation which other governments may have in this respect, appropriate arrangements, linked with German reunification, should be made which would take into account the legitimate security interests of all the countries concerned. It was for this reason that, at the Geneva Foreign Ministers' Conference, the Western Powers made proposals for a Treaty of Assurance on the Reunification of Germany.

8. The Western Powers have never required as a condition of German reunification that a reunified Germany should join the North Atlantic Treaty Organisation. It will be for the people of a reunified Germany themselves to determine through their freely elected government whether they wish to share in the benefits and obligations of the Treaty.

9. If the all-German Government, in the exercise of its free choice, should elect to join NATO, the Western Powers, after consultation with the other members of this Organisation, are prepared to offer, on a basis of reciprocity, to the Government of the Soviet Union and the governments of other countries of Eastern

Europe which would become parties to a European security arrangement, assurances of a significant and far-reaching character. The Western Powers are also prepared, as part of a mutually acceptable European security arrangement, to give an assurance that, in the event of a reunified Germany choosing to join NATO, they would not take military advantage as a result of the withdrawal of Soviet forces.

10. But the Western Powers could not contemplate that the existence of NATO itself should constitute the subject of negotiations.

11. The reunification of Germany accompanied by the conclusion of European security arrangements would facilitate the achievement of a comprehensive disarmament agreement. Conversely, if a beginning could be made toward effective measures of partial disarmament, this would contribute to the settlement of outstanding major political problems such as the reunification of Germany. Initial steps in the field of disarmament should lead to a comprehensive disarmament agreement which presupposes a prior solution of the problem of German reunification. The Western Powers do not intend to enter into any agreement on disarmament which would prejudice the reunification of Germany.

12. Any measures for disarmament applicable to Europe must have the consent of the European nations concerned and take into account the link between European security and German reunification.

The Four Governments continue to hope that the Soviet Government will come to recognise that it is not in its own interest to maintain the present division of Germany. The Western Powers are ready to discuss all these questions with the Soviet Union at any time that there is a reasonable prospect of making progress. At such time there will be many points relating to the procedure for German reunification and the terms of a Treaty of Assurance which will require to be worked out by detailed negotiation. In advance of serious negotiations the Western Powers cannot finally determine their attitude on all points. Nor can they contemplate in advance the making of concessions to which there is no present likelihood of response from the Soviet side. If negotiations are to be fruitful, both sides must approach them in a spirit of accommodation and flexibility. Through this declaration the Western Powers, in full agreement with the Federal Republic, wish again to manifest their sincere desire to enter into negotiations with the Soviet Union in order to reach a European settlement and to give evidence that the paramount objective of their policy is the attainment of a just and lasting peace.

Appendix 7

Memorandum from Polish People's Republic to Great Britain, February 15, 1958

RAPACKI PLAN—FIRST VERSION

. . . I. The proposed zone should include the territory of Poland, Czechoslovakia, German Democratic Republic and German Federal Republic. In this territory nuclear weapons would neither be manufactured nor stockpiled, the equipment and installations designed for their servicing would not be located there, the use of nuclear weapons against the territory of this zone would be prohibited.

II. The contents of the obligations arising from the establishment of the denuclearised zone would be based upon the following premises:

1. The States included in this zone would undertake the obligation not to manufacture, maintain or import for their own use and not to permit the location on their territories of nuclear weapons of any type, as well as not to instal on or to admit to their territories installations and equipment designed for servicing nuclear weapons, including missile launching equipment.

2. The Four Powers (France, United States, Great Britain and U.S.S.R.) would undertake the following obligations:

   (a) Not to maintain nuclear weapons in the armaments of their forces stationed on the territories of States included in this zone, neither to maintain nor to instal on the territories of these States any installations or equipment designed for servicing nuclear weapons, including missile launching equipment.

   (b) Not to transfer in any manner and under any reason whatsoever, nuclear weapons or installations and equipment designed for servicing nuclear weapons, to Governments or other organs in this area.

3. The Powers which have at their disposal nuclear weapons should undertake the obligation not to use these weapons against the territory of the zone or against any targets situated in this zone.

Thus the Powers would undertake the obligation to respect the status of the zone as an area in which there should be no nuclear weapons and against which nuclear weapons should not be used.

4. Other States, whose forces are stationed on the territory of any State included in the zone, would also undertake the obligation not to maintain nuclear weapons in the armaments of these forces and not to transfer such weapons to Governments or to other organs in this area. Neither will they instal equipment or installations designed for the servicing of nuclear weapons, including missile launching equipment, on the territories of States in the zone, nor will they transfer them to Governments or other organs in this area.

The manner and procedure for the implementation of these obligations could be the subject of detailed mutual stipulations.

III. 1. In order to ensure the effectiveness and the implementation of the obligations contained in Part II, paragraphs 1, 2 and 4, the States concerned would undertake to create a system of broad and effective control in the area of the proposed zone and submit themselves to its functioning.

This system could comprise ground as well as aerial control. Adequate control posts, with rights and possibilities of action which would ensure the effectiveness of inspection, could also be established.

The details and forms of the implementation of control can be agreed upon on the basis of the experience acquired up to the present time in this field, as well as on the basis of proposals submitted by various States in the course of the disarmament negotiations, in the form and to the extent in which they can be adapted to the area of the zone.

The system of control established for the denuclearised zone could provide useful experiences for the realisation of broader disarmament agreement.

2. For the purpose of supervising the implementation of the proposed obligations an adequate control machinery should be established. There could participate in it, for example, representatives appointed (not excluding *ad personam* appointments) by organs of the North Atlantic Treaty Organisation and of the Warsaw Treaty. Nationals or representatives of States which do not belong to any military grouping in Europe could also participate in it.

The procedure of the establishment, operation and reporting of the control organs can be the subject of further mutual stipulations.

IV. The most simple form of embodying the obligations of States included in the zone would be the conclusion of an appropriate international convention. To avoid, however, complications which some States might find in such a solution, it can be arranged that:

1. These obligations be embodied in the form of four unilateral declarations, bearing the character of an international obligation, deposited with a mutually agreed upon depository State.

2. The obligations of Great Powers be embodied in the form of a mutual document or unilateral declarations (as mentioned above in paragraph 1).

3. The obligations of other States, whose armed forces are stationed in the area of the zone, be embodied in the form of unilateral declarations (as mentioned above in paragraph 1).

On the basis of the above proposals the Government of the Polish People's Republic suggests initiating negotiations for the purpose of a further detailed elaboration of the plan for the establishment of the denuclearised zone, of the documents and guarantees related to it as well as of the means of implementation of the obligations undertaken.

The Government of the Polish People's Republic has reason to state that acceptance of the proposal concerning the establishment of a denuclearised zone in Central Europe will facilitate the reaching of an agreement relating to an adequate reduction of conventional armaments and of foreign armed forces stationed on the territory of the States included in the zone.

Appendix 8

Statement by Adam Rapacki, Foreign Minister of Poland, November 4, 1958

Rapacki Plan—New Version

" In recent months the Government of the Polish People's Republic has repeatedly stressed that it does not consider the discussion on its proposal for setting up a denuclearised zone in Central Europe to be terminated and that it continues to stand by that proposal.

" This attitude of ours derives from a deep conviction of the need to seek realistic methods of decreasing tension, of disarmament, and of strengthening security in Europe.

" This need has been confirmed, *inter alia*, throughout the discussion on our proposal by the favourable attitude towards that proposal on the part of wide and varied circles of world public opinion, especially in Europe.

" We have given repeated evidence that we are capable of allowing for factual arguments, and even for opinions differing from our own, as well as for the subjective difficulties of the various circles concerned.

" I should here like to recall our Memorandum of February 14, 1958, in which we took into account several such elements.

" In that Memorandum we also set out the principles of a broad system of control over the carrying out of the obligations we proposed.

" We have recently considered other arguments and misgivings voiced in the course of the discussion. We are prepared, in agreement with our allies, to take a new step—in our opinion the most far-reaching step—towards meeting the main comments and reservations put forward regarding our proposal.

" That is, we are prepared to consider the carrying out of our Plan in two stages. In the first stage a ban would be introduced on the production of nuclear weapons on the territories of Poland, Czechoslovakia, the German Democratic Republic and the German Federal Republic. Also, an obligation would be undertaken within the proposed zone to renounce the equipment with nuclear weapons and the relevant installations of armies which do not yet possess them. At the same time, appropriate measures of control would be introduced. This might thus be said to amount to freezing nuclear armaments in the proposed zone.

"The carrying out of the second stage would be preceded by talks on the appropriate reduction of conventional forces. This reduction would be effected simultaneously with the complete denuclearisation of the zone, and again would be accompanied by the introduction of appropriate measures of control.

"This modification of the manner of introducing a denuclearised zone in Central Europe may not satisfy all those who have hitherto opposed our proposal, in particular those who base their political reasoning on the armaments race and the equipment of West Germany with nuclear weapons.

"This modification would, however, meet the suggestions and conclusions resulting from the attitude of many Western politicians who have expressed their opinions on our proposal.

"It should also eliminate major misgivings voiced in the discussion which were primarily intended to justify a negative attitude towards the Polish proposal on the part of certain circles and governments.

"In particular, this relates to the fears—without here considering whether or not they are well-founded—of 'upsetting the existing military equilibrium' between the two groups in Europe, of 'weakening the defences of the West,' or 'withdrawing American forces from Europe,' and so on.

"Attempts have been made to justify all these reservations by one key argument: 'The carrying out of a ban on the production and possession of nuclear weapons in Central Europe would deprive NATO troops of the nuclear shield in face of the superiority of the Warsaw Pact forces in the field of conventional arms.'

"We could never agree with this argument, if only because of our fundamental attitude to weapons of mass destruction.

"We have never been against discussions on the reduction of conventional armaments in Central Europe. On the contrary, we have always favoured such discussions and such reduction.

"If in the last year we have confined ourselves to a proposal narrower in scope, to the proposal for the denuclearisation of Central Europe, it has been simply because the discussion on the limitation of all armaments in this area ran into serious difficulties.

"Moreover, we consider the carrying out of our proposal a first step towards further disarmament measures in that zone.

"Therefore, since many and serious voices have been raised asking for denuclearisation to be linked with reduction of other armaments in Central Europe, we are prepared to consider these voices favourably.

" We put, however, one condition: that the discussions on the two related subjects are not endlessly protracted while nuclear armaments are included in the arsenals of new armies.

" These are the premises of the modifications in the manner of introducing the denuclearised zone which we are prepared to consider."

Appendix 9

Meeting of Foreign Ministers, May 11–June 20, 1959

OUTLINE OF A PHASED PLAN
FOR GERMAN REUNIFICATION, EUROPEAN SECURITY
AND A GERMAN PEACE SETTLEMENT,
PUT FORWARD BY MR. HERTER, MAY 14, 1959

THE Governments of France, the United Kingdom and the United States of America are convinced of the urgent need for a settlement of the German problem. They desire to seek, in such a settlement, progressive solutions which would bring about German reunification and security in Europe. Moreover, they believe that progress on each of the problems of general disarmament, European security and a political settlement in Europe affects the degree of progress possible in the solution of each of the other problems.

They accordingly propose to the Government of the Union of Soviet Socialist Republics an agreement between the Four Governments which would include the measures outlined below relating to a general settlement of the problems at issue. The measures envisaged are closely interrelated and the present proposals are therefore to be regarded as an inseparable whole. They would come into effect progressively at the stages indicated.

Stage I

1. The Four Powers would establish suitable arrangements for consultation among the parties to supervise the implementation of the agreement and to settle any disputes which might arise before the conclusion of a peace settlement with a reunified Germany.

2. With regard to Berlin, the Four Powers would agree that:

(*a*) Berlin is one city and belongs to all of Germany. East and West Berlin should, therefore, be united through free elections held under quadripartite or United Nations supervision. A freely elected Council would be formed for the whole of Berlin until German reunification was achieved and as a first step towards it. Thus Berlin would be retained as the future capital of a reunified Germany.

408

(*b*) Subject to the supreme authority of the Four Powers (with voting procedure as adopted by the Allied authorities in Vienna), the freely elected Berlin Council would be free to administer the city.

(*c*) The freedom and integrity of the united city of Berlin and access thereto would be guaranteed by the Four Powers, who would continue to be entitled as at present to station troops in Berlin.

(*d*) The Four Powers would take the necessary steps to carry out during Stages I and II of the "Phased Plan" the measures described in (*a*) to (*c*) above.

3. In a common declaration, with which other interested States would be invited to associate themselves, they would undertake to:

(*a*) settle, by peaceful means, any international dispute in which they may be involved with any other party;

(*b*) refrain from the use of force in any manner inconsistent with the purposes of the Charter of the United Nations;

(*c*) withhold assistance, military or economic, to an aggressor.

4. In order to facilitate further the solution of political problems and the improvement of international relations, the Four Powers would, in an appropriate forum, initiate discussion of possible staged and controlled comprehensive disarmament measures.

5. The Four Powers would arrange discussions to develop procedures for exchanging information in Stage II on military forces in agreed areas of Europe.

Stage II

Reunification

6. Bearing in mind the complex issues involved in reunification, a transitional period would be agreed. The Four Powers would set up a Mixed German Committee.

7. The Mixed Committee would consist of twenty-five members from the Federal Republic of Germany and ten members from the so-called "German Democratic Republic." These members would be appointed by the Federal Government and the authorities of the so-called German Democratic Republic respectively.

8. The Mixed Committee would take its decisions by a three-quarter majority.

9. The Mixed Committee would be entrusted with the task of formulating proposals:

(*a*) to co-ordinate and expand technical contact between the two parts of Germany;

(*b*) to ensure the free movement of persons, ideas and publications between the two parts of Germany;

(*c*) to ensure and guarantee human rights in both parts of Germany;

(*d*) for a draft law providing for general, free and secret elections under independent supervision.

10. The Mixed Committee would transmit any proposals made by it under sub-paragraphs (*a*) to (*c*) inclusive of paragraph 9 above to the appropriate authorities in both parts of Germany. Such proposals, if no objections are raised with respect of them, should be implemented as appropriate in both parts of Germany.

11. (*a*) Any agreed proposal for an electoral law in accordance with sub-paragraph (*d*) of paragraph 9 above would be submitted to a plebiscite in both parts of Germany.

(*b*) If within one year no such draft law had been formulated by the Committee, the group of members from the Federal Republic on the one hand and the group of members from the so-called German Democratic Republic on the other would each formulate a draft law approved by a majority of its members. These two draft laws would then be submitted to a plebiscite as alternatives. The electoral area for each draft law would consist of both parts of Germany.

(*c*) If any proposal for an electoral law obtained a majority of valid votes in each of the two parts of Germany, it would acquire the force of law and be directly applicable for the entire electoral area.

(*d*) The Four Powers would, at the time of signature of the agreement, expressly authorise the competent German authorities to promulgate any electoral law so approved.

(*e*) The Four Powers would adopt a statute providing for the supervision of the plebiscite.

12. If all-German elections had not been held on or before the termination of a thirty months' period beginning on the date of the signing of the agreement, the Four Powers would determine the disposition to be made of the Committee.

Security.

13. An exchange of information on military forces in the areas referred to in paragraph 5 above would be undertaken.

14. The Four Powers would restrict or reduce their armed forces to agreed maximum limits, for example, United States 2,500,000, Soviet Union 2,500,000. During this same period these States would place in storage depots, within their own territories and under the

supervision of an international control organisation, specific quantities of designated types of armaments to be agreed upon and set forth in lists annexed to the agreement.

15. The Four Powers would be prepared to negotiate on a further limitation of their armed forces and armaments to become effective in Stage III subject to:

(*a*) verification of compliance with the provisions of paragraph 14 above;

(*b*) agreement by other essential States to accept limits on their armed forces and armaments, fixed in relation to the limits of the armed forces and armaments of the Four Powers;

(*c*) installation of an inspection and control system to verify compliance with all agreed security measures.

16. Measures of inspection and observation against surprise attack, helped by such technical devices as overlapping radar systems, could be undertaken in such geographical areas throughout the world as may be agreed by the Four Powers and other States concerned.

17. Since in 1954 the Federal Republic of Germany renounced the production of chemical, biological and nuclear weapons, the Four Powers would make such arrangements as might be appropriate to secure similar measures of renunciation in the remainder of Germany and in other European countries to the East.

18. Inspection systems would be worked out for ensuring compliance with the appropriate security measures envisaged in Stage III.

Stage III

Reunification.

19. Not later than two and a half years after the signature of the agreement elections for an all-German Assembly would be held in both parts of Germany under the terms of the electoral law drafted by the Mixed Committee, approved by the Four Powers and adopted by the German people in a plebiscite (in accordance with the provision in Stage II above).

20. The elections would be supervised by a supervisory commission and supervisory teams throughout all of Germany. The commission and teams would be composed of either (*a*) United Nations personnel and representatives of both parts of Germany, or (*b*) representatives of the Four Powers and representatives of both parts of Germany.

21. The all-German Assembly would have the task of drafting

an all-German constitution. It would exercise such powers as are necessary to establish and secure a liberal, democratic and federative system.

22. As soon as an all-German Government has been formed on the basis of the above-mentioned constitution it would replace the governments of the Federal Republic and the so-called German Democratic Republic and would have:

(a) full freedom of decision in regard to internal and external affairs, subject to the rights retained by the Four Powers as stipulated in paragraph 23 below;

(b) responsibility for negotiating, as soon as possible after its establishment, an all-German Peace Treaty.

23. Pending the signature of a Peace Treaty with an all-German Government formed on the basis of the all-German constitution, the Four Powers would retain only those of their rights and responsibilities which relate to Berlin and Germany as a whole, including reunification and a peace settlement and, as now exercised, to the stationing of armed forces in Germany and the protection of their security.

Security.

24. Implementation of the following security provisions would be dependent upon the establishment of effective control and inspection systems to assure verification and upon the agreement, where appropriate, of the all-German Government to the security measures called for in Stage III.

25. Upon the establishment of an all-German Government, the Four Powers and such other countries as are directly concerned would agree that in a zone comprising areas of comparable size and depth and importance on either side of a line to be mutually determined, agreed ceilings for the indigenous and non-indigenous forces would be put into effect.

26. After conclusion of the Peace Treaty, no party would station forces in any country in this area without the consent of the country involved. Upon the request of the country involved, any party so stationing forces would withdraw them within a stated period and would undertake the obligation not to send forces to that country again without the consent of the government of that country.

27. Should the all-German Government decide to adhere to any security pact:

(a) there might be special measures relating to the disposition of military forces and installations in the area which lies closest to the frontiers between a reunited Germany and countries which are members of another security pact;

(*b*) the Four Powers would be prepared to join with other parties to European security arrangements in additional mutual obligations, covering especially the obligation to react against aggression;

(*c*) the Four Powers would be prepared to join with other parties to European security arrangements herein described in giving an assurance that they would not advance their forces beyond the former line of demarcation between the two parts of Germany.

28. Providing that the limitations and conditions set forth on armed forces and armaments in Stage II are met, the Four Powers would further limit their armed forces together with corresponding reduction on armaments to agreed maximum levels, for example, U.S. 2,100,000; and U.S.S.R. 2,100,000. Reductions in the armed forces and armaments of other essential States to agreed levels would take place at the same time in accordance with paragraph 15 of Stage II.

29. After verified compliance with the above limitations, and subject to the same conditions, negotiations would be undertaken on further limitations (for example, U.S. 1,700,000; and U.S.S.R. 1,700,000) together with corresponding reductions on armaments. The levels of armed forces and armaments of other essential States would be specified at the same time through negotiations with them.

30. The measures provided for above would be harmonised with general disarmament plans so as to be included in a general framework.

31. All of the security measures of the " Phased Plan " would continue in force as long as the control system is operative and effective and the security provisions are being fulfilled and observed.

Stage IV

32. Since a final Peace Settlement can only be concluded with a government representing all Germany, it should be concluded at this stage. The Settlement should be open to signature by all States members of United Nations which were at war with Germany. The Settlement should enter into force when ratified by the Four Powers and by Germany.

Appendix 10

Plans for Disengagement

WESTERN PLANS

Author.	Zone.	Troop withdrawal.	Demilitarisation.	Alliances.	Guarantees and Controls.	Remarks.
F. Byrnes, Secretary of State. Four Foreign Ministers Conference, Paris, April, 1946.	All Germany.	Complete.	Complete.	None.	25-year Four Power Treaty as a guarantee against further German aggression.	On Mr. Molotov's suggestion, agreed to extend the period of Treaty from 25 to 40 years.
G. Marshall, Secretary of State. Four Foreign Ministers Conference, Moscow, March-April, 1947.	All Germany.	Complete.	Complete.	None.	40-years Four Power Treaty.	
G. Marshall, Foreign Ministers Conference, London, Nov.-Dec., 1947.	All Germany.	Complete.	Complete.	None.	40-years Four Power Treaty.	Failure due to Mr. Molotov's opposition.
James Warburg, American banker, former Adviser to U.S. Government on German affairs. Memorandum for Congress, April, 1949.	Territory west of Soviet borders.	All foreign troops to be withdrawn.	Germany to be permanently demilitarised and arms limitations to be imposed in Europe.	Germany to be neutral.	American guarantees against any aggression against any country situated between the Atlantic and Russia's borders.	
Dean Acheson (A-Plan). Four Foreign Ministers Conference, Paris, May-June, 1949.	All Germany.	Phased withdrawal of all foreign troops.	Limitations to be placed on German rearmament.	None.	Four Power control.	This plan was not submitted to the Russians.
Prof. A. Brecht, Prof. Pol. Science. Article, "The Idea of a Safety Belt" in New York, Oct. 1949.	Germany, Austria, Switzerland, Yugoslavia, Greece, Turkey and Eastern	All foreign troops to be withdrawn.	Strong national armed forces, " an armed neutrality" to be formed.	Possibly defensive alliances with the Great Powers.	Agreement between the Great Powers to abstain from re-entry.	

Member of Bundestag, late Ambassador to Yugoslavia. Speech in Wurtemberg, June, 1952.	Eastern Germany and the Federal Republic, containing capital of Germany.	be withdrawn.	NATO troops to remain.			basis for negotiations with Russia about the reunification of Germany.
Prof. Ulrich Noack, "Nauheimer Kreis," Withenausener Proklamation, May 18, 1950.	Reunified Germany; at later stages, a neutral belt to be established stretching from Finland up to Trieste.	All troops of occupation to withdraw after one year of the agreement regarding the setting up of a neutral Germany.	No armed forces, police formations.	No alliances with the Great Powers, and no regional security agreements.	(i) control; (ii) a permanent organ to be set up by the Four Powers to prevent any attempt of German rearmament.	
Walter Lippmann, N.Y. Herald Tribune in 1950 (and 1957).	Reunified Germany and Eastern Europe.	All foreign troops to be withdrawn.		Federal Republic to remain in NATO.	Necessary security guarantees to Russia.	No recognition of the Oder-Neisse Line.
James Warburg (Second Warburg Plan). December, 1952.	Germany.	Not specified, but to be assumed.	Area to be disarmed and demilitarised for 5; perhaps 10, years; if general disarmament not achieved all restrictions to be lifted.	To become neutral for 5 to 10 years.	UNO control.	Frontiers to be fixed.
H. Spaak, then Belgian Foreign Minister, Rapporteur at Cons. Assembly in Strasbourg.	Demilitarised zone on both sides of the Iron Curtain.	All troops to be withdrawn.		Reunited Germany not to remain neutral.	European Security Pact, with U.S.A. and U.S.S.R. as signatories.	
Mons. P. v. Zeeland, Belgian Foreign Minister. Speeches in 1953 (also in a booklet "Les Fondements de la Paix," 1957).	(1) completely demilitarised Eastern Germany. (2) two partly demilitarised zones on both sides of Eastern Germany.	(1) Soviet troops to withdraw from E. Germany. (2) Soviet troops to remain east of Vistula and NATO troops west of the Rhine.	National armed forces to be formed.	Reunited Germany to remain in NATO. Eastern Europe to remain in Warsaw Pact.	European Security Pact, with recognition of Oder-Neisse Line.	Eastern Europe to secure greater freedom.
Secret Western Plan—1953. Disclosed by SDP, March 1959.	Formation by stages of an interim all-German Government with strictly limited powers until the signature of a peace treaty; until then, the existing two German Governments to function.					

Author.	Zone.	Troop withdrawal.	Demilitarisation.	Alliances.	Guarantees and Controls.	Remarks.
Sir Winston Churchill, Prime Minister, May 11, 1953.	A security pact on Locarno lines. Churchill's idea was taken up by Dr. Adenauer who favoured a security pact with Russia - provided it did not perpetuate divisions of Germany.					
V. Tilea, former Rumanian Minister in London, 1939-40. Memorandum to Western Foreign Minister, Dec. 1953, and letter to *The Times*, July, 1957.	Germany and Eastern Europe.	NATO troops to withdraw from Western Germany and Soviet troops from Eastern Europe.	Complete.	To become neutral.	International guarantees, gradual liberation of Eastern Europe.	
Marshal of the R.A.F. Sir John Slessor, "Defence for the West," published in 1954 (and several subsequent lectures).	Reunified Germany.	NATO troops to withdraw from German territory when national troops are strong enough, regardless of whether Soviet troops are withdrawn from Eastern Germany.		Germany to remain in NATO.		
Col. B. v. Bonnin and A. Weinstein, "Keiner kann den Krieg gewinnen."	Federal Republic.	NATO troops to withdraw to west of the Rhine, as a strategic reserve, on the assumption that Russia will do likewise.	A "fortified zone" and strong mobile national forces with anti-tank weapons to be maintained.	Germany to remain in NATO.		
Sir Anthony Eden (Eden Plan, First Version). Conference of Foreign Ministers, Berlin, Jan.-Feb. 1954.	Dealt only with the question of all-German *free elections*: future German Government to be free to associate with the West, the East or to remain neutral. During the course of the Conference an addendum was made to the effect that a future German Government should be free also to reject international obligations of Fed. Republic or of Eastern Germany. (This would apply to the agreement between Eastern Germany and Poland, recognising Oder-Neisse Line as " a frontier of peace.")					
C. Bohy, Socialist, Belgian Delegate to Europ. Consult. Assembly. Speech at Strasbourg, Sept. 1954.	Non-specified zone in Central Europe.	All foreign troops to be withdrawn from a demilitarised zone.	Armaments to be restricted in a pilot scheme for disarmament.	Reunified and neutral Germany a sort of " buffer zone."	Guarantees by Great Powers.	

To set up W.E.U., fixed levels of armed forces, in participation of Germany at 12 divisions, and promoted to Germany atomic weapons and the manufacture of heavy war equipment.

...tern European Union. Resolution at London and Paris Conferences, Oct. 1954.						
H. Ripka, former Minister in Czechoslovak Government in Exile, and in Czechoslovakia, until Communist Coup, 1955.	Germany and Eastern Europe.	NATO troops to withdraw from Western Germany and Soviet troops from Eastern Europe.	Complete.	To become neutral.	International guarantees; gradual liberation of Eastern Europe.	
Herman Rauschning, former Nazi-President of Danzig. Article, June, 1955.	Germany and Eastern Europe.	All foreign troops from Germany and Eastern Europe.	German military potential to be limited.		Guarantees of German territorial integrity; Oder-Neisse to be revised.	
Sir Anthony Eden, Prime Minister (Eden Plan, Second Version). "Summit" Conference, Geneva, July 18 and 22, 1955.	" A demilitarised area between East and West ... limited in first instance to Europe"—on both sides of the eastern frontier of Eastern Germany.	An agreement to be reached as to the total of forces and armaments in countries neighbouring Germany.	Conventional forces and armaments to be reduced.	To remain.	European Collective Security Pact under UN.	
Edgar Faure, French Prime Minister at the same Conference on July 18.	Reunified Germany.	No withdrawal of foreign troops from the Federal Republic.		Reunified Germany to remain in NATO.		
"SUMMIT CONFERENCE" At its conclusion, directives were issued by the Heads of States to their Foreign Ministers, July 23, 1955.	To examine the possibility of: (1) A security pact for Europe or for a part of it; (2) Limitations, control and inspection in regard to armed forces and armaments; (3) Establishment between East and West of a zone in which the disposition of armed forces to be subject to mutual agreement; (4) And to consider other possible proposals.		Armaments to be limited, subject to agreements with the States of the Zone who would be free to take decisions.	Only at the first stage, lasting 2–3 years.	European Collective Security Pact with the participation of the United States for 50 years.	An all-German Council to deal with matters of security and free elections. Point 3 was placed in the British Proposals in 1959.
Resolution of SDP, in anticipation of the Conference of Foreign Ministers, Oct. 26, 1955.	Reunified Germany.	Possibility of withdrawal of troops.	Armaments to be limited.	Present alignments possibly to be changed.	European Security Pact.	

Author.	Zone.	Troop withdrawal.	Demilitarisation.	Alliances.	Guarantees and Controls.	Remarks.
Three Western Ministers (Eden Plan, Third Version). Conference of Foreign Ministers in Geneva, Oct.–Nov. 1955.	"Areas of comparable size, depth and importance on both sides of reunified Germany and Eastern European countries..."	"Level of armed forces [to] be specified to establish a military balance..." Individual nations to have right to request withdrawal of foreign troops.	Restricted armaments to establish a military balance.	To remain.	(i) Ground inspection of forces and armaments. (ii) Mutual obligation to resist aggression.	
Herr von Brentano, Federal Foreign Minister. Interview with *U.S. News and World Report*, Feb. 10, 1956.	" The so often reiterated proposal that Germany's resignation from NATO be offered as a so-called recompense for the agreement of the Soviet Union to reunification, would not, in his opinion, be accepted by the German side."					
Erich Mende, FDP, Member of Bundestag, March and May, 1956.	Reunified Germany, retaining the claim for her territories east of Oder-Neisse Line.	NATO troops to withdraw to west of the Rhine (U.S. troops and Air Force to remain in Palatinate), Soviet troops—from East Germany.	Strong national forces 12–20 divisions.	To remain.	Inclusion of Germany in Five Powers Pact as an alternative condition to an all-European Pact, including Eastern Germany.	
Mr. Harold Stassen, U.S. Delegate to the UN Disarmament Commission, London, March 21, 1956.	" The United States and the Soviet Union each [to] set up an experimental zone covering an area of from 20,000 to 30,000 square miles, including important air and sea ports... in which practical problems arising out of disarmament could be put to test...."					
Fritz Erler, SDP. Member of the Bundestag, and in an article, *Foreign Affairs*, April, 1956.	Reunified Germany.	All foreign troops to withdraw.	Possibly limited national armed forces.	(1) Federal Germany to leave NATO, Eastern Germany the Warsaw Pact. (2) Neutrality.	General Security Pact.	
Prof. F. Friedensburg, CDU Member of Bundestag, 1st April, 1956.	Reunified Germany.	NATO to withdraw troops.		Germany to remain in NATO.	Accent on Germany's peaceable intentions—a mediator between East and West...	

Source	Area	Withdrawal of troops	Armed forces	Membership of alliances	Security pact	Remarks
... Minister. Interview with *U.S. News and World Report*, April 6, 1956.	... in the second stage.	within the framework of a disarmament agreement.	...tions of armed forces in NATO and Warsaw Pact countries.	first stage; after elections, relations to military alliances possibly to be changed.	Pact in a framework of disarmament.	Foreign Ministry issued a comment criticising M. Mollet's views.
G. Kennan. Article, "The Future of Soviet Communism," *Aussenpolitik*, June, 1956.	Reunified Germany, Sweden, Switzerland, Austria and Yugoslavia.	All foreign troops to withdraw.	Germany to be demilitarised.	Germany to be neutral.		
President Eisenhower, Press conference, June 6.	Spoke of the advantages of a neutrality compared with the risks resulting from membership of military alliances.					
Sir Anthony Eden, Prime Minister, Parliament, answering a question by a Labour member, July 23, 1956.	Reunified Germany.	In the case of Germany's withdrawal from NATO foreign troops to be withdrawn.	Limited armaments.	German membership of NATO optional.	Security Pact.	
Mr. A. Ciolkosz, Polish Socialist and Chairman of the Executive Council of Polish National Council, Speech at 37th Plenary Meeting of ACEN at Carnegie Endowment International Centre, New York, Nov. 13, 1956.	Reunified Germany and whole Eastern Europe.	(i) All foreign troops to withdraw; (ii) U.N. troops to remain in rest of Europe.	Restricted national armed forces.	Whole area to remain neutral.	European security pact and guarantees by Great Powers.	
Twelve Democrat Members of Congress. Letter to President Eisenhower, December, 1956.	Neutral area, 1,000 miles wide, from the Rhine to the historic boundaries of Russia.	All foreign troops to withdraw.	Area to be demilitarised.	To remain neutral.	Guarantees by East and West.	
Senator Knowland, Republican Leader, December 14, 1956.	Neutral area consisting of reunified Germany, Austria, Finland, Sweden, Switzerland and satellite countries of Eastern Europe.	All foreign troops to withdraw.		To remain neutral.	Frontier guarantees by Major Powers.	

Author.	Zone.	Troop withdrawal.	Demilitarisation.	Alliances.	Guarantees and Controls.	Remarks.
			AFTER HUNGARIAN UPRISING			
Senator Hubert Humphrey, Democrat Congressman, Chairman of Disarmament Sub-Committee of U.S. Senate, Dec. 15, 1956.	Reunified Germany, a buffer zone.	Foreign troops to make a gradual withdrawal. U.S. troops to remain in rest of Europe.	A balance of military power to be maintained.	To remain temporarily.	Guarantees against aggression.	
Rt. Hon. Hugh Gaitskell, M.P. Leader of Opposition, debate in Parliament, December 16, 1956.	Extensive neutral area in Europe.	All foreign troops to withdraw.		To remain neutral.	Guarantees under security pact.	
Resolution of the European Consultative Assembly, Strasbourg, in January, 1957.	Eastern Germany and Eastern Europe.	Soviet troops to withdraw in the first stage; NATO troops, in case of acceptance of principle of neutrality.	Military balance to be maintained.	Efforts to be made to reach a state of neutrality.	Collective security pact, with all necessary assurances to Russia.	
Rt. Hon. Hugh Gaitskell, (Gaitskell Plan). Lecture in Harvard, Jan. 11, 1957, (repeated in Berlin), and booklet *A Challenge to Co-Existence.*	Germany to be re-united in her present borders (within the Oder-Neisse Line), Poland, Czechoslovakia, Hungary, and possibly Rumania.	Foreign troops to make gradual withdrawal.	Armaments to be restricted.	Alliances to remain in the first stage.	European security pact.	Dr. Adenauer, speaking on April 27, called this plan "unrealistic": "Germany does not want to become a second-rate Power"
Dr. Adenauer, Chancellor, Press conference, Jan. 11, 1957.	In favour of an internationally controlled ban on nuclear weapons; a thinned-out zone in Europe alone will not reduce tension. Doubtful that negotiations on setting up of such a zone would contribute to German reunification.					
Polish Government in Exile. Memorandum to Western Powers, London, Feb. 6, 1957.	Eastern Europe, including Eastern Germany and Baltic States.	Soviet troops to withdraw.	Restricted national armed forces.	Reunified Germany to remain in NATO; Eastern Europe to maintain complete neutrality.	Guarantees of territorial integrity by Great Powers.	

Source						
Socialist Congress, Venice, Feb. 4, and interview with *Combat*, March 18, 1957.	...ing of reunited Germany, Eastern Europe and Middle East.	...tially to withdraw from advanced positions.	forces to be restricted.	from the alliances.	Great Powers.	
"Polish Freedom Movement," Resolution, Britain, March 30, 1957.	Poland, Eastern Europe and Federal German Republic.	All foreign troops to withdraw.	Conventional forces to be restricted; atomic weapons to be prohibited.	To withdraw from respective alliances, neutrality.	European Security Pact with guarantees of external and internal frontiers, as well as against external interference into the internal affairs of the countries of the zone.	
President Eisenhower. Press conference. May 8, 1957.	Spoke sympathetically about Soviet plans to revive Eden's plan for the setting up of a demilitarised zone in Europe.					
Mr. J. Foster Dulles, Secretary of State, Press conference May 14 and 15, 1957.	"The setting up of a demilitarised zone along the Iron Curtain is not the policy of the United States.... I don't think we favour any plan for a neutralised zone. Chancellor Adenauer suggested that with a reunified Germany, he would be willing to agree that NATO forces would not be put into the Eastern Zone ... anything that Chancellor Adenauer wished in that respect would be given very careful and sympathetic consideration by ourselves."					
Dr. Konrad Adenauer, Press conference, Hamburg, May 15, 1957.	Zone of military inspection in Europe, not only in the Federal Republic.	Soviet troops to withdraw from Eastern Germany.	Eastern Germany to be demilitarised, strong national armed forces to remain in Fed. Republic, possibly armed with tactical atomic weapons.	Reunified Germany to remain in NATO.	No NATO or West German troops to be stationed in Eastern Germany after its reunification with Federal Republic.	Dr. Adenauer's views were fully incorporated into the "Berlin Declaration," July 29, 1957.
Erich Ollenhauer, leader of SDP (Ollenhauer Plan), May 25, 1957, and various statements.	Reunified Germany.	All foreign troops.	Armaments to be restricted.	Neutrality, after the signature of a Security Pact.	European Security Pact: guarantees by Great Powers.	
Senator Knowland, referring to Khrushchev's television appearance on June 2, 1957.	Norway to become a member of the Baltic neutral bloc, in exchange for secret free elections in Hungary under UN supervision; alternatively, Soviet troops to withdraw from the Baltic States and agree to free elections.					

Author.	Zone.	Troop withdrawal.	Demilitarisation.	Alliances.	Guarantees and Controls.	Remarks.
Statement in 12 points by Four Foreign Ministers of U.S.A., U.K., France and Federal Republic (Berlin Declaration), July 29, 1957.	Reunified Germany.	Soviet troops to withdraw from Eastern Germany.	Complete demilitarisation of Eastern Germany.	Reunited Germany to remain in NATO but as an assurance to Soviet Union, NATO and West German forces not to be stationed in Eastern Germany.		
Conference of Socialist Union of Central and Eastern Europe, Vienna, July 29–30, 1957.	Germany and Eastern Europe.	Soviet troops.	Partial.	To become neutral.	Guarantees by Great Powers.	
Frank Aiken, Irish Delegate at UNO. Debate on Hungary, Sept. 10, 1957.	Whole Central and Eastern Europe to Soviet borders as established at Yalta and Potsdam.	All non-national armed forces to withdraw gradually.	National armed forces.		Inspection and control by mixed UNO teams.	
Congressman Henry S. Reuss' Statement, Nov. 7, 1957.	" Disengagement in Europe could range from a withdrawal of Great Power troops to a much wider proposal for the reunification of Germany in freedom, peaceful liberation of satellites and the demilitarisation of the whole area with the security guaranteed by East and West.					
G. Kennan. Reith lectures, B.B.C., Nov.-Dec. 1957.	Reunified Germany, Poland, Czechoslovakia and Hungary (details to be negotiated).	NATO troops to withdraw from Federal Republic and Soviet troops from Eastern Europe.	Balance of military power to be maintained by national armed forces and militia.	Restraint of Germany's freedom to associate with NATO or East.	European Security Pact in addition to extended NATO: guarantees by Great Powers.	
Assembly of Captive Nations, Memorandum to NATO Council, Dec. 1957.	Warning against " entering into security pact with the Soviet Union which would cover captive countries or comprise among the signatories any of the Communist puppet régimes."					

Source	Area/Zone	Foreign troops	National forces	Status	Guarantees
Denis Healey, M.P., Labour. Booklet, *A Neutral Belt in Europe*, Jan. 1958.	Reunified Germany, Poland, Hungary and Czechoslovakia, possibly more: Eastern Europe to constitute a psychological and physical barrier between Germany and Russia.	(i) All foreign troops to withdraw from zone. (ii) U.S. troops to remain in other areas in Europe.	Substantial conventional national armed forces.	To become neutral.	European security pact; sanctions against re-entry by limited deterrent.
Congressman Henry S. Reuss, Democrat, Congress, Jan. 27, 1958.	1,000-mile zone between the Rhine and historic borders of Russia.	All foreign troops to withdraw; U.S. troops to remain in rest of Europe.	Restricted national forces.	Reunified Germany to remain in NATO.	Guarantees by Great Powers.
Marshal of the R.A.F. Sir John Slessor: Three articles in the *New York Herald-Tribune*, Jan.-Feb. 1958.	Western Europe and Eastern Europe.	British and U.S. troops to withdraw from the Continent and Soviet troops from Warsaw Pact countries.	Strong conventional armed forces. No tactical atomic weapons: "an atom-free zone, in Germany, Poland and Czechoslovakia."	(i) Germany and E. Europe to withdraw from their present alliances. (ii) To follow status of "military non-alignment."	Guarantees by Britain and U.S.A. under reorganised NATO, with sanctions in case of aggression of Germany only.
Captain B. H. Liddell Hart, *Reynolds News*, February, 1958.	An "international safety belt stretching from Spitzbergen to Himalayas: it might be extended eastward to embrace Burma, Thailand and Indo-China, and to Japan and Korea. In the West, Benelux might join it embracing four Scandinavian countries, six Central European countries, five Balkan countries and Middle East countries: Persia, Afghanistan, India, Pakistan."				
P. Auer, former Hungarian Ambassador to France and member of Hungarian National Council. Article, *Figaro*, Feb. 8, 1958.	Reunited Germany and Eastern Europe.	All foreign troops; U.S. troops remain on the Continent.		To become neutral.	Neutral zone—to be temporarily occupied by U.N. troops, consisting of contingents of Four Great Powers.
Herr Strauss, Federal Defence Minister. Bundestag, February 22, 1958.	Eastern Europe.	Soviet troops.	(i) Strong conventional armed forces—to establish balance between East and West. (ii) Atom-free zone.	Reunified Germany to remain in NATO.	Agreement between Great Powers to eliminate nuclear weapons on the territory of the zone.

Author.	Zone.	Troop withdrawal.	Demilitarisation.	Alliances.	Guarantees and Control.	Remarks.
Marshal Tito. Interview with Mr. Sulzberger for *New York Times*, published in *Borba*, March 6, 1958.	Unspecified zone in Europe.	No withdrawal.	Denuclearised area to be formed.	To remain.		The reason for Tito's interest in such a zone was probably the planned setting up of missile bases in Italy.
A. Bevan. Speech, Copenhagen, April 7, 1958.	Both Germanies, Poland, Czechoslovakia, possibly Hungary.	All foreign troops to withdraw.	Setting up of a denuclearised zone—as a shock absorber.	To be neutral.	Guarantees by the Great Powers.	
Mr. Goedhardt, Rapporteur. Report on the Rapacki Plan and Disengagement, WEU General Assembly, April 14, 1958.	A strongly critical line towards Rapacki Plan and Disengagement—Minority's reservation.					
Labour Party Foreign Policy Statement. Scarborough Conference, April 23, 1958.	Reunified Germany, Poland, Czechoslovakia and Hungary.	Foreign troops to gradually withdraw under effective international control.	National armed forces to be under international control.	To become neutral after withdrawal from existing alliances.	European Security Pact backed by guarantees of Four Powers.	German elections to be settled by the Germans themselves.
French Socialists' Congress. Resolution, May 3-4, 1958.	Zone of tensions in Europe—zone of direct military confrontation.	Troops to be reduced.	Conventional forces to be reduced, atomic weapons to be prohibited.			
Council Conference of Socialist International, Brussels, June 12-14, 1958.	"Central and Eastern Europe."	Details not specified.	Pilot scheme covering both conventional forces and nuclear weapons.	Not specified.	Not specified.	
Anthony Nutting, former Minister of State, *New York Herald Tribune*, Dec. 1, 1958.	The whole issue to be put before the inhabitants of Berlin: "If they decide, we will hand over, all four of us, to an all-Berlin Government, freely elected, by elections supervised by UN and properly guaranteed by UN against aggression, direct or indirect."					

Debate in the House of Commons on December 4, 1958.

	Area	Troops withdrawal	Demilitarisation		Inspection	Opposed / Support
Selwyn Lloyd, Foreign Secretary.	(i) Eastern Germany; (ii) "An area as large as possible."	Soviet troops to withdraw from Eastern Germany.	(i) Eastern Germany to be completely demilitarised; (ii) Ceilings to be placed on numbers and armaments.	To remain.	International system of inspection, starting with the existing armaments.	Opposed to disengagement and to Rapacki Plan.
A. Bevan (Labour).	Both Germanies, Poland, Czechoslovakia, possibly Hungary.	All foreign troops to withdraw.	Arms and troops limitations to be imposed in accordance with the Rapacki Plan.	To remain neutral.	International inspection and control, (details not specified).	Support for Oder-Neisse Line.
A. Henderson (Labour).	Germany.	All foreign troops to withdraw.	Demilitarised zone to be established.	Reunified Germany to follow policy of military non-alignment.	European system of security.	Support for Oder-Neisse Line.
J. Hynd (Labour).	Rapacki Plan recommended as a basis for discussion: German Confederation as an alternative; the problem of Four Powers guarantee for the area, after mutual withdrawal to be examined.					
Viscount Hinchingbrooke (Conservative).	Both Germanies, Poland, Czechoslovakia.	*Half* of the all-foreign troops to withdraw.		"The sensitive fringe area along the Iron Curtain to be overlapped by the security systems West-East."		By leaving half of the foreign troops on the territory of the area, the solution of the political problems is impossible.
J. Biggs-Davidson (Conservative).	Reunification of Germany and liberation of Eastern Europe should be considered interdependent.					
Emrys-Hughes (Labour).	Germany.	All foreign troops to withdraw.				
M. Bonham-Carter (Liberal).	Rapacki Plan should be used as a starting point.					

Author.	Zone.	Troop withdrawal.	Demilitarisation.	Alliances.	Guarantees and Controls.	Remarks.
Denis Healey (Labour).	Both Germanies, Poland, Czechoslovakia, possibly Hungary.	All foreign troops to withdraw.	"Freeze" of the present situation.	To become neutral.	European Security Pact.	Restatement of the principles of the "Labour Party" plan, based upon Gaitskell and Healey-plans.
Congressman Henry S. Reuss, December 7, 1958.	Proposed a "Summit Conference" with the additional participation of all leaders of the opposition parties in the West, and repeated his plan for disengagement:					
	Western and Eastern Germany.	"For some miles" from present positions.	Arms limitations to apply, particularly to nuclear weapons.	Not specified, but free elections to be held in Germany and some "liberalising moves" to be made in satellite States.	Mutual guarantees against aggression, some freedom to choose political, economic and cultural alignments.	
E. Hinterhoff, *The Tablet*, "A solution for Berlin," December 13, 1958.	The whole of Berlin to be constituted a Free City, as a preliminary to negotiations over German reunification and if possible, a European settlement.	NATO and Soviet troops form the respective sectors in Berlin, in the first stage.	Berlin to be completely demilitarised.	To become neutral.	Guarantees by Four Great Powers—internal security to be responsibility of International Police Force.	Free Berlin—capital of reunified Germany.
Debate in the House of Lords, December 18, 1958.						
Lord Henderson (Labour).	Both Germanies, Poland, Czechoslovakia and Hungary.	All foreign troops to withdraw.	First stage: nuclear free zone, and limitations of conventional forces: a semi-demilitarised zone.	To remain; non-aggression pact to be between NATO and Warsaw Pact.	International control.	
Lord Birdwood (Conservative).	Reunited Germany.				To remain free from either NATO or Warsaw Pact.	Support for Oder-Neisse Line.
Lord St. Oswald (Conservative).	A comprehensive disengagement: support for Oder-Neisse Line.					

Lord Hastings (Conservative).	Two alternatives: (i) " disengagement," but what will happen to NATO ? "; (ii) " Reunited Germany—would it be safe left alone ? "				
Three Western Powers: United States, Great Britain and France delivered similar Notes to the Soviet Union on Dec. 31, 1958.	Rejecting Soviet Plan for Berlin, and expressing willingness to negotiate about Germany, as a whole, but not " under menace."				
Gen. C. Spaatz, former Commander of U.S. Strategic Air Force. *Newsweek*, " Free Berlin as UN capital? " Jan. 5, 1959.	Suggested making the whole of Berlin a capital of the United Nations. The suggestion was, as Gen. Spaatz admits, originally made by a former U.S. Ambassador, Mr. John C. Wiley. This plan could be put into effect only in the setting of a mutual withdrawal of NATO and Soviet troops from their sectors of Berlin, and, in view of the standing of personalities involved, shows an interest on the part of the American Administration in the idea of Disengagement.				
Attributed to R. Murphy, Under Secretary of State, but authorship denied by him, *Newsweek*, Jan. 19, 1959.	Replacement of NATO units in Berlin by Bundeswehr. Reunification through " Confederation ": transfer of capital from Bonn to West Berlin.				
Sir Ivone Kirkpatrick, former Permanent Under-Secretary to the Foreign Office, *Sunday Times*, Jan. 19, 1959.	" A demilitarised strip across Europe on both sides of the Iron Curtain."				
Senator Fulbright, Chairman of Senate Foreign Relations Committee, January 30, 1959.	In favour of some sort of disengagement.				
Senator Hubert H. Humphrey, Radio Link over the B.B.C., February 4, 1959.	Germany and Eastern Europe.	Phased withdrawal.	Arms to be limited; a denuclearised zone to be created.	Germany possibly to remain neutral.	Security Pact guarantees by Great Powers.
A. Wolfers, Director of Washington Center for Foreign Policy Research. Testimony before the Senate Disarmament Sub-Committee, Feb. 4, 1959.	"A very narrow zone in Europe" (location not specified).		Troops to be equalised, thinned out and denuclearised.	To remain.	

Author.	Zone.	Troop withdrawal.	Demilitarisation.	Alliances.	Guarantees and Controls.	Remarks.
G. Kennan, testifying before Senate Disarmament Committee and *New Leader*, February 23, 1959.	"The main Soviet aim is to avoid Eastern Zone's being swallowed too drastically by the Federal Republic."		No atomic weapons to be allowed in Western Germany.	"Germany should not be allied nor be an extension of U.S. forces."		
SDP ("Deutschland Plan") March 18, 1959.	Both Germanies, Poland, Czechoslovakia and Hungary to constitute a zone of "reduced tension."	All foreign troops to withdraw gradually.	National armed forces to be limited.	To withdraw from military alliances.	European Security Pact.	Present status of Berlin to be guaranteed until the solution of German question.
FDP (Free Democratic Party), March 20, 1959.	Reunited Germany through free elections.	Withdrawal by stages.	No atomic weapons to be allowed.	To withdraw from alliances.	Security Pact. Settlement of frontiers.	
General de Gaulle, Press Conference, Mar. 25, 1959.	"As near the Urals as to the Atlantic."			Against German neutrality.		
P. Mendes-France, former French Prime Minister, at his Press Conference in Paris, April 2, 1959.	Principle of vertical strips, situated symmetrically along the present demarcation line, with arms restrictions, gradually decreasing: (1) A strip "Zero," say 50 klm. wide, completely demilitarised: responsibility for internal security: local police, or, preferably, UNEF; (2) On both sides of strip "Zero," two strips Nr. 1, only national armed forces, of conventional type, subject to an international control; (3) On both sides of strips Nr. 1, the territory, to be called "Strips Nr. 2," with "the most modern weapons." (4) Germany to remain in NATO: U.S. troops to remain on German soil, only redeployed further west; (5) Countries of Eastern Europe—to remain in the Warsaw Pact, but withdrawal of Soviet troops from the territory of strip Nr. 1, would enable "a new life."			Remain.		

				Remain.		Senator Mansfield dealt primarily with the issue of Berlin.
Jules Moch, former Minister of Interior, and former French Delegate to the UN Disarmament Sub-Committee, in an article in *Le Monde* April 10, 1959.	*Contrary to Mendes-France's vertical strips—symmetrical rings:* (1) All four sectors of Berlin—Zone A—completely demilitarised and under authority and control of UN. (2) The above Zone to be surrounded by Zone B, some 200 klm. deep, which, in the East will run roughly along the German frontier of 1937, and in the West, will cover some 30-40 klm. of the territory of Federal Republik—all foreign troops withdraw from the Zone B. (3) Zone B, to be surrounded by another one—equally in the form of a ring—Zone C—equally some 200 klm. deep, comprising in the West: Oldenburg, Ruhr, Nuremberg and Passau, and in the East: Katowice, Brno, Lodz and Danzig: consequently, and this is important: Zone C, will not overlap with the territory of either Federal Republik nor with that of Poland or Czechoslovakia, and consequently, *all those countries will retain their respective military alliances.*			Remain.		
Senator Mike Mansfield, speech in the Senate in February, reproduced in *Aussenpolitik* in May, 1959.	Germany and Central Europe.	Partial withdrawal—as result of arms limitations.	Limitations of armed forces and denuclearisation of parts of Germany and Central Europe: to take into consideration Eden and Rapacki plans.	Remain.	Not specified.	
Selwyn Lloyd, Foreign Secretary, Interview with Associated Television, May 4, 1959.	"An area" not specified.	Foreign troops not to withdraw, only some thinning out as result of setting "ceilings."	"Ceiling [to be set] upon armed forces and armaments."	To remain.	Inspection and control (details not specified).	
Field-Marshal Lord Montgomery, *Sunday Times*, May 10, 1959.	A small defined zone in the middle of Europe, to be gradually extended as mutual confidence is restored.				Inspection by international teams.	

Author.	Zone.	Troop withdrawal.	Demilitarisation.	Alliances.	Guarantees and Controls.	Remarks.
Mr. Herter, U.S. Secretary of State, Western (Five Stage) Plan, submitted for Four Foreign Ministers, Geneva, May 10, 1959.	Berlin and both parts of Germany.	Reductions in armed forces of Great Powers, taking place in Stage Two.	Zone of arms limitations along a line to be mutually determined in Stage Three.	Reunified Germany to be free to choose alliances.		
Mr. Venizelos, Liberal Leader, and Mr. Markazinis, Progressive Leader—Plan for "*Missile free Balkan area*," announced in Athens, May 29, 1959.	Greece, Roumania, Bulgaria, Albania, without excluding other Balkan States.		Denuclearised zone to be formed.	Alliances to remain.	Security Pact Guarantees by Great Powers.	
Memo of A.C.E.N. on June 4, 1959.	Eastern Europe.	Only Soviet forces.	Non specified.	The Warsaw Pact —to disband: Germany—as one can assume—to remain in NATO.	"Effective mutual security system."	Reunification of Germany, and free and unfettered elections in Eastern Europe.
Resolution of the Political Committee of the Atlantic Congress in London, June 5–10, 1959.	Eastern Europe.	Only Soviet forces.	"Neutralised by an international agreement."	Warsaw Pact to disband—Germany —as one can assume—to remain in NATO.	Not specified.	
David Ben-Gourion. Interview with British United Press, June 8, 1959.	Middle East: Arab States and Israel.		To be neutralised, or completely demilitarised.		International guarantee for territorial integrity.	
Senator de la Vallée-Poussin, Rapporteur of Committee on Defence and Armaments. Draft Preliminary Report "Military aspects of a zone of controlled armaments in Europe" for the Assembly of W.E.U., June 10, 1959.	Germany and Eastern Europe (not specified nearer).	An ultimate aim—complete withdrawal of Soviet troops from Germany and countries of Eastern Europe (not specified); to assume that also NATO troops will withdraw from Germany.	Stage I—a ceiling for forces and armaments in Central Europe; Stage II—reduction by slices of forces brought to the same level; Stage III—ceiling for the forces outside Europe—as a step leading to general disarmament.	Remain in the early stages—ultimate aim: "a special military status previously agreed by international negotiations."	Controls to be based upon budgetary and statistical documents from the governments, accompanied by sample tests and inspections.	Controls would be more acceptable, if not applied to Soviet and American territories.

Plan						
Declaration by the Labour Party and the Trade Unions Congress, June 24, 1959—2-stage plan.	Both parts of Germany, Poland, Czechoslovakia and Hungary.	In the 1st stage—establishment of and effective control of the arms and armed forces in the above area. Stage II—withdrawal of all foreign forces from the area.		In the 2nd stage Poland, Czechoslovakia and Hungary—to withdraw from the Warsaw Pact, and reunified Germany from NATO.	A security pact guaranteeing the frontiers.	
H. Kissinger "In search for stability," *Foreign Affairs*, July, 1959.	Reunified Germany, Poland and Czechoslovakia.	Non-German forces: from Oder to the Weser; Soviet forces: from Oder to the Vistula.	German forces on the one hand, Czech and Polish on the other hand, to be brought in balance both in numbers and in equipment.	To remain.	System of inspection to be established.	
Sixth Congress of Socialist International in Hamburg, July 14-19, 1959.	Confirmed the resolution of the Council Conference in Brussels, June 12-14, 1958, with the following reservations: "Congress emphasises that any disarmament agreement should not alter the balance of military security to the disadvantage of either side."					
Marshal of the R.A.F. Sir John Slessor. "Redeployment in Europe." *Observer*, July 19, 1959.	"Broad belt of States between the frontiers of France and Italy on the one hand, and U.S.S.R. on the other."	To begin in the 2nd stage—gradual—starting from a narrow zone of some 50 miles—aiming at withdrawal of all foreign troops from Continental Europe.	Eastern Germany, after German reunification, to be demilitarised: national armed forces.	(i) Germany to withdraw from NATO, and countries of Eastern Europe from the Warsaw Pact; (ii) "military non-alignment" of the area covered by the above agreement.	(i) UN Force to police the partition line in the early stages of the withdrawal; (ii) Establishment in the first stage of control and inspection arrangements, including "open skies" inspection; (iii) Guarantees under the European Security Pact—on the lines of Brussels Treaty of 1948.	Oder-Neisse to be Eastern frontier of reunited Germany.

Author.	Zone.	Troop withdrawal.	Demilitarisation.	Alliances.	Guarantees and Controls.	Remarks.
Senator Thomas J. Dodd, "Our Captive Allies," *New Leader*, July 20–27, 1959.	Eastern Europe.	Soviet troops.	Partial disarmament.	To remain in the West—to be disbanded in the East.	Not specified.	Liberation of Eastern Europe in exchange for expansion of East-West trade, possibly bigger credits.
Mr. A. Nutting, former Minister of State in his book, *Disarmament* (1959).	Central Europe—not specified nearer.	"A measure of disengagement or thinning out of conventional forces and armaments in Germany and her neighbours East and West."	An atom free zone.	Presumably remain.		
British plan, known as "Macmillan Plan." (Spring, 1959).	Reunified Germany with Eastern Germany completely demilitarised.	No withdrawal of troops in the sense of disengagement, but only in the process of "thinning-out."	(i) Agreed numbers and limits of armaments. (ii) No atom-free zone.	To remain, except Eastern Germany, which will be re-united with Federal Republic.	(i) Guarantees not specified; (ii) System of controls to guard against surprise attack; (iii) System of ground controls and aerial inspection.	Rejection of concept of disengagement. This plan is based on information from British official sources: see footnote 17 on p. 275.
Mr. Selwyn Lloyd's proposals at UNO, Sept. 17, 1959. Plan in 3 phases.	Not specified.	No withdrawal of troops in the sense of disengagement, but only in the process of "thinning-out."	*Phase I*—"Ceilings" for conventional forces; *Phase II*—Reduction of conventional armaments and nuclear weapons; *Phase III*—Final reduction of conventional armaments.	To remain, except Eastern Germany.	*Phase I*—International control over certain armaments. *Phase II*—Inspection against surprise attack. *Phase III*—Re-examination of the possibility of controlling and then eliminating remaining attacks of nuclear weapons and other weapons of mass destruction	Mr. Selwyn Lloyd called his plan "too ambitious."

Hinterhoff outline in two linked phases:						
I. *Preliminary Plan:* military measures.	Both parts of Germany, Poland, Czechoslovakia, Hungary, possibly Roumania.	Gradual withdrawal of foreign troops by stages to be agreed.	(i) Gradual reduction in numbers of foreign troops before their impending withdrawal; (ii) Establishment of a "ceiling" for the national armed forces; (iii) Denuclearisation of the area—subject to (a):	To remain, with the proviso that the countries of the area will withdraw from their respective alliances.	(i) Int. Police Force to man demarcation line from the beginning of redeployment; (ii) Agreement on "ceiling" of national armed forces; (iii) Denuclearisation of the area, subject: (a)	(a) An international agreement, under the auspices of UN providing: (1) denuclearisation of the area; (2) undertaking by Great Powers not to use atomic weapons against any targets or troops in the area.
II. *Comprehensive Plan:* completion of military measures and putting into effect of political measures.	Reunified Germany, (a) Poland, Czechoslovakia and Hungary, possibly Roumania, and other countries of Eastern Europe.	Completion of withdrawal of all foreign troops.	(i) "Ceiling" for the national armed forces; (ii) Denuclearisation of the zone, subject —as (a)—in fact, setting up of a "Zone of controlled armaments."	After the completion of the withdrawal of all foreign troops, countries of the area withdraw from their respective alliances, assuming the status of "military non-alignment."	(i) International Security Pact, guaranteeing territorial integrity of the area, and its frontiers, external and internal—previously agreed with guarantees against any attempt of re-entry in force: agreement on sanctions, and their flexible application. (ii) International control and inspection of the "ceiling," of the troops and of denuclearisation: in fact, creation of a "zone of controlled armaments."	(b) Re-unification of Germany, after completion of withdrawal of all foreign troops, as result either of free elections or of any other method to be agreed upon.

H.D.

EASTERN PLANS

Author.	Zone.	Troop withdrawal.	Demilitarisation.	Alliances.	Guarantees and Controls.	Remarks.
Mr. V. Molotov, Soviet Foreign Minister. Conference of Four Foreign Ministers, Moscow, April, 1947.	Reunified Germany.	All troops of occupation to be withdrawn, after the introduction of measures for the complete demilitarisation of Germany.	To be completely demilitarised.	None.	International control.	(i) Four Power control of the Ruhr; (ii) Land reform liquidation of all cartels; (iii) Setting up of a democratic government in Germany.
Conference of Foreign Ministers of countries of Eastern Europe, Warsaw, June 22–24, 1948.	(i) Earliest withdrawal of all troops of occupation from Germany; (ii) Complete demilitarisation of Germany—in accordance with Potsdam Agreement.					
Conference of Foreign Ministers of countries of Eastern Europe, Prague, Oct. 21, 1950.	Reunified Germany.	Subsequent to the signature of a peace treaty—all occupation troops to withdraw within one year.	To be completely demilitarised.			
Soviet draft peace treaty with Germany, submitted to Three Western Powers on March 10, 1952.	Reunified Germany.	All troops of occupation to withdraw, not later than one year after the signature of a peace treaty.	"[National conventional troops] essential for the defence of the country."			
Mr. Molotov, Soviet Foreign Minister. Conference of Foreign Ministers, Berlin, Jan.–Feb., 1954, and " Soviet proposal of European Security," Feb. 10, 1954.	Reunified Germany.	(1) To be withdrawn within six months of the conclusion of peace treaty, leaving small contingents for security; (2) Right to call back occupation troops in the event of threat to security to be reserved.	Small contingents of occupation troops of agreed size to remain.	(i) Germany to be neutral; (ii) Dissolution of NATO not a prerequisite to Security Pact.	Treaty of Collective Security Pact for 50 years.	Soviet suggestion of German " neutrality " was found unacceptable by Three Western Foreign Ministers.

Source	Reunified Germany	Troops of occupation	Neutrality	European Security Pact / Territorial integrity	Remarks
Soviet Government. Note to Three Western Powers, March 31, 1954.	Repeated proposals made by Mr. Molotov for a European Security Pact with the participation of U.S.A., and suggested the participation of U.S.S.R. in NATO.				
Mr. Molotov. Speech, East Berlin, Oct. 6, 1954.	Reunified Germany.	Troops of occupation to withdraw immediately.		European Security Pact.	Ready to discuss the question of free elections in Germany.
Soviet Government. Note to Three Western Powers on the last day of Paris Conference, Oct. 29, 1954.	Expressed readiness to re-examine Mr. Eden's Plan for free elections in Germany, if decisions of Paris Conference to include Federal Republic in WEU and NATO were not put into effect.				
Conference of Eastern Bloc States. Moscow, Nov. 29, 1954.	(i) Identified itself with Soviet Government draft of European Security Pact. (ii) Confirmed that the remilitarisation of Federal Republic would compel Eastern Bloc to take counter-measures.				
Soviet Government. Statement, Jan. 15, 1955.	Before the ratification by the Bundestag of the Paris Convention, Soviet Government published a statement that its ratification would perpetuate division of Germany: if not, it would be possible to hold all-German free election before the end of 1955.				
International Congress with the participation of a Soviet Delegation, headed by Mr. A. Puzanov, President of Russian Republic and friend of Soviet Prime Minister, Mr. G. Malenkov. Resolutions, Warsaw, Feb. 6, 1955.	Reunified Germany (in accordance with Eden's Plan), and Poland.	All occupation troops to withdraw.	Germany to remain neutral in accordance with Potsdam Conference.	Territorial integrity of Germany, as fixed at Potsdam.	These resolutions passed unnoticed in the West.
Mr. Molotov. Speech before the Supreme Soviet, Feb. 8, 1955.	Criticised Western Powers' rejection of Soviet proposal of a European Security Pact, and announced counter-measures by the Soviet bloc, in the event of Germany's joining NATO and WEU.				
Warsaw Pact, following the ratification of Paris Treaty, May 11–14, 1955.	Concluded in Warsaw, with Soviet Marshal Koniev as Supreme C.-in-C. Eastern Germany not included.				

Author.	Zone.	Troop withdrawal.	Demilitarisation.	Alliances.	Guarantees and Controls.	Remarks.
Mr. Molotov, San Francisco, June 26, 1955.	Again suggested a European Security Pact to be joined by both parts of Germany, in due course reunified.					
Mr. N. Bulganin, Soviet Prime Minister "Summit Conference," Geneva, July 17–23, 1955.	Reunified Germany.	All foreign troops to withdraw from Europe, and the situation pre Second World War to be re-established.	Conventional forces to be reduced and nuclear weapons to be prohibited.	(i) First stage (2–3 years) alliances to remain during the first stage: (ii) Second stage: (a) Neutrality; (b) Optional dissolution of NATO and Warsaw Pacts.	European Collective Security Pact.	No interference in the questions of Eastern Europe.
Soviet Government Statement during Dr. Adenauer's visit to Moscow, Sept. 13, 1955.	(i) German problem can be solved only by way of a European Security Pact to end the existence of military groupings. (ii) Reunification is a matter of a joint effort by both parts of Germany.					
Mr. Molotov, Conference of Foreign Ministers, Geneva, Oct. 27— Nov. 11, 1955.	Expressed a desire to approach Sir Anthony Eden's proposal at Summit Conference by way of "a zone of limitations and inspection of armaments in both parts of Germany and neighbouring states."	Troops to be partly withdrawn, after agreement had been reached on maximum level of foreign troops to be stationed in that zone.	Armaments to be limited subject to agreements with the states of the Zone who would be free to take decisions.	Only at the first stage (2–3 years).	European Collective Security Pact with the participation of the United States—for 50 years.	An all-German Council to deal with matters of security and free elections.
Conference of Eastern Bloc States, Prague, Jan. 27, 1956.	The armed forces of Eastern Germany were integrated into the Warsaw Pact.					
Mr. A. Gromyko, Soviet Delegate at the UN Disarmament Sub-Committee, London, May 27, 1956.	"A zone consisting of both parts of Germany and neighbouring States."	Forces stationed on German territory to be reduced, prior to reaching an agreement.	(i) Armaments to be restricted; (ii) Atomic weapons to be prohibited.	To remain.	Ground inspection of forces and armaments.	

Soviet Government. Statement confirmed by Notes to Three Western Powers, (at the height of Hungarian Uprising) Nov. 17, 1956.	1,000 miles inspection zone in Europe.	Armed forces stationed in Germany to be reduced by 33 per cent.		Non-aggression Pact between NATO and Warsaw Pact.	(i) Effective international control. (ii) An aerial photography; (iii) Control posts against a surprise attack.
Mr. Khrushchev. Reception in the Kremlin for Gomulka, Nov. 18, 1956.	Germany and other countries.	Soviet troops to withdraw from Eastern Germany and Eastern Europe, NATO troops from Western Germany, and bases in foreign countries to be liquidated.	(i) Veto to be placed on atomic armaments; (ii) All foreign bases to be liquidated, within two years; (iii) In due course, armed forces to be completely eliminated.		
Mr. V. Kuznetsov, Soviet Delegate at the Political Committee of UNO, Jan. 14 and Jan. 25, 1957.	NATO and Warsaw Pact countries area.	All foreign bases to be liquidated within in two years.	Armed forces to be considerably reduced in NATO and Warsaw Pact countries.	To remain.	Non-aggression Pact between NATO and Warsaw Pact countries.
Mr. N. Bulganin, Soviet Prime Minister. Letter to Mr. Macmillan, British Prime Minister, April 20, 1957.	Referred to "Sir Anthony Eden's proposals on the establishment in Europe of demilitarised zone and of an area with restricted armaments."	Part of foreign troops to be withdrawn, subsequent to an agreement on reduction of level of forces stationed in Germany.	The nuclear tests to be banned: atomic armaments to be prohibited.	To remain.	General Security Pact, non-aggression Pact between NATO and Warsaw Pact countries.
Soviet Government. Note to German Federal Republic. April 27, 1957.	Atomic armaments of Bundeswehr incompatible with reunification of Germany.				
Mr. J. Zorine, Soviet Delegate to the UNO Disarmament Sub-Committee, London, April 30, 1957.	NATO and Warsaw Pact countries area.	All foreign bases to be liquidated within two years.	Foreign troops to be reduced.	To remain.	Aerial inspection.

Author.	Zone.	Troop withdrawal.	Demilitarisation.	Alliances.	Guarantees and Controls.	Remarks.
Mr. Smirnov, Soviet Ambassador. Letter to Dr. Adenauer, Bonn, May 4, 1957.	Demanded a promise that Federal Republic armed forces would not be armed with atomic weapons and that no foreign troops, armed with them, would be admitted on German territory.					
N. Khrushchev, American TV, Moscow, June 2, 1957.	Both Germanies, Poland, Hungary and Rumania.	All foreign troops to be withdrawn from that area as well as Italy, Turkey and other countries.	Armed forces to be reduced.	Communist régimes to remain, based "upon the will of peoples."		
Mr. N. Bulganin. Letter to Mr. Macmillan, July 20, 1957.	Support for Eden's plan for a demilitarised area between East and West.	Withdrawal to result of reduction of armed forces.		To remain.	Non-aggression Pact between NATO and Warsaw Pact as a first step towards an European Security Pact.	
Herr Grotewohl's Statement two days before the Berlin Declaration, July 27, 1957.	Both parts of Germany.	All foreign troops to withdraw.	Nuclear armaments to be banned.	To be neutral.	Rapprochement between Eastern Germany and Federal Republic, and formation of an all-German Council.	
Chivu Stoica, Rumanian Prime Minister, September, 1957.	Rumania, Bulgaria, Albania-Jugoslavia, Greece and Turkey, a "Balkan zone of peace."		"Atom free zone."	To remain.	Balkan Security Pact.	
Rapacki Plan (First version). UNO on Oct. 2, 1957, and confirmed by Notes sent by Polish Government, Feb., 1958.	Poland, Czechoslovakia, Eastern Germany and Federal Republic.	No withdrawal of troops contemplated.	(a) "Atom free zone"; (b) Use of nuclear weapons against this zone to be prohibited.	To remain.	Four Powers guarantee not to maintain nuclear weapons in the zone, and not to use them against the zone.	Plan rejected by Three Western Powers, May, 1958.

Source					
N. Bulganin. Note to all 82 UNO members, 15 NATO countries, Spain and Switzerland Dec. 10-14, 1957.	Demilitarised zone—both Germanies, Poland and Czechoslovakia.	Troops to withdraw as result of demilitarisation of zone.	(i) Atom free zone; (ii) Atomic tests to be suspended from Jan. 1, 1958.	To remain.	European Security Pact.
N. Khrushchev. Speech at the session of Supreme Soviet, Dec. 21, 1957.	Maintenance of status quo.				
Supreme Soviet. "Peace Plan," (7 points), Dec. 21, 1957.	Both parts of Germany, Poland and Czechoslovakia.	Forces to be reduced by Three Powers.	Atom free zone.	To remain.	Non-aggression Pact between NATO and Warsaw Pact.
N. Bulganin's letter to Mr. Macmillan and President Eisenhower, Jan. 8, 1958.	(i) Endorsed Rapacki Plan. (ii) Suggested "Summit Meeting."		Atom free zone.	To remain.	Non-aggression Pact between NATO and Warsaw Pact.
Soviet Government proposals for easing international tension—Notes sent to all UNO members, NATO countries and Switzerland, on Jan. 8, 1958.	NATO area and Warsaw Pact countries.	All foreign troops and foreign bases to be withdrawn.	(i) Armed forces to be substantially reduced. (ii) Atom free zone.	To remain—to be superseded by a Collective European Security Pact.	
Political Consultative Committee of Warsaw Pact Conference, Moscow, May 24, 1958.	Endorsed Rapacki Plan.				
A. Gromyko, Soviet Foreign Minister, UNO, Sept. 18, 1958.		All foreign bases in other people's territories to be closed.		To remain.	Non-aggression Pact between NATO and Warsaw Pact.

Author.	Zone.	Troop withdrawal.	Demilitarisation.	Alliances.	Guarantees and Controls.	Remarks.
Second version of Rapacki Plan, Nov. 4, 1958.	Both Germanies, Poland and Czechoslovakia.	Troops to withdraw as result of appropriate reduction of conventional forces.	(i) Denuclearisation of the area; (ii) Simultaneous reduction of armed forces.	To remain.	Appropriate measures of control.	
N. Khrushchev. Note to Three Western Powers, Nov. 27, 1958.	West Berlin.	(i) NATO troops to withdraw. (ii) Russia to relinquish all occupation rights in Eastern Germany.	West Berlin to be completely demilitarised.	To become a neutral " Free City."	Guarantees by UNO.	Rejected by the West.
N. Khrushchev. Talk with Philip Noel-Baker, M.P., and his son, Moscow, Dec. 1958.	(i) First stage: Berlin. (ii) Second stage: Germany.	(i) First stage—all occupation troops to withdraw from Berlin. (ii) Second stage—to negotiate.	(i) Military balance to be maintained. (ii) Rapacki Plan.	To remain.	International system of controls.	
Soviet draft of Peace Treaty with Germany. Note to Three Western Powers consisting of 43 articles, Jan. 10, 1959.	(i) Before reunification West Berlin to have status of a Free City; (ii) Germany to be re-unified with frontiers as on Jan. 1, 1959.	(i) All foreign troops to be withdrawn not later than a year after signature of peace treaty. (ii) All foreign bases in Germany to be closed down.	(i) National conventional armed forces to be maintained. (ii) Atom free zone.	To follow policy of military non-alignment.		Treaty to be signed by both Germanies.
A. Mikoyan: Press Conference in Los Angeles on Jan. 11, 1959.	Western and Eastern Germany.	American and Soviet troops.	Not specified.	Not specified.		
A. Mikoyan: Press Conference in Washington, Jan. 16, 1959.	Both sides should withdraw their forces 500 miles in each direction from the river Elbe, thus creating a wide demilitarised zone.					
N. Khrushchev. Speech at the XXI Communist Party Congress, Moscow, Jan. 27, 1959.	Both Germanies, Poland and Czechoslovakia.	Foreign troops and establishments to withdraw.	NATO to dismantle all bases on foreign territories.			

			"Atom free zone."	To remain.	Balkan Security Pact.
Chivu Stoica, Rumanian Prime Minister, Feb.–Mar., 1959.	Rumania, Bulgaria, Albania, Jugoslavia, Greece and Turkey, a "Balkan zone of peace."				
N. Khrushchev—conversation with Prof. Carlo Schmid and Fr. Erler, Moscow, Mar. 16, 1959.	Reunified Germany, Czechoslovakia, Poland, possibly Hungary.	All foreign troops to withdraw.	Atom free zone (support for Rapacki Plan)	To become neutral.	International inspection and control.
N. Khrushchev. Conversation with Field-Marshal Montgomery, Moscow, April 29.		All national forces to return "home."	Atom free zone.	To be disbanded.	Ready to accept a very comprehensive plan for inspection and control.
N. Khrushchev. Speech, Tirana, May 25, 1959.	Balkans and Adriatic area.	No withdrawal.	Atom free zone.	To remain.	
M. N. Khrushchev, Riga, June 11, 1959.	Scandinavian Peninsula and Baltic area.		Zone to be free from atomic weapons and rocket launching platforms	To remain.	
N. Khrushchev. Speech, Warsaw, July 21, 1959.	(i) Central Europe. (ii) Baltic. (iii) Balkans.	No withdrawal.	Atom free zone.	To remain.	(i) Joint Undertaking not to use atomic weapons against the countries of the zone; (ii) UNO to take part in the solution of the problem.
Interparliamentary Union Conference in Warsaw, Aug. 27–Sept. 4, 1959.	Both Germanies, Poland and Czechoslovakia.	No withdrawals except as result of arms limitations.	Limitations of forces, both conventional and nuclear.	Not specified.	Not specified.
Mr. Khrushchev—talk with Mr. Gaitskell on Sept. 4, 1959.	Both parts of Germany, Poland and Hungary.	Soviet troops and NATO troops.	Controlled armaments.	Not specified.	Not specified.

Author.	Zone.	Troop withdrawal.	Demilitarisation.	Alliances.	Guarantees and Controls.	Remarks.
Khrushchev's plan at UNO, Sept. 18, 1959.						
Version 1	The whole world.	All foreign troops in the process of general disarmament.	Complete and universal disarmament within 4 years : (i) Disbandment of all armed forces ; (ii) Destruction of all nuclear weapons ; (iii) Strictly limited contingents of police (and militia), agreed for each country, to remain.	Understood that in the process of general disarmament they will fade away. To remain : a non-aggression pact between NATO and the Warsaw Pact countries.	" International control including all states." An agreement on the prevention of surprise attack.	
Version 2	Europe.	All foreign troops.	All foreign troops. (i) Reduction of foreign troops in countries of Western Europe ; (ii) Closing down of military bases on foreign territories. (iii) An atom-free zone in Central Europe.			

Index of Names

443